영어듣기 모의고사

CooL
LISTENING

2

STRUCTURES & FEATURES
구성과 특징

TEST
실전 모의고사

***CooL* LISTENING** 시리즈는 시·도 교육청 영어듣기평가를 비롯한 다양한 듣기 시험 문제 유형을 분석·반영한 실전 모의고사 20회를 수록했습니다. 다양한 유형의 실전 문제와 실생활에서 사용하는 주제들로 대화 및 담화가 구성되어 있어 실전 감각을 키우고 듣기 실력을 향상시키는 데 도움이 될 것입니다.

DICTATION
받아쓰기

중요 어휘·표현 및 헷갈릴 수 있는 발음을 점검하고 학습할 수 있도록 받아쓰기를 구성했습니다. 모의고사 전 지문의 받아쓰기를 통해서 대화 및 담화 내용을 한 번 더 익히고, 중요 표현을 복습할 수 있습니다.

영어듣기 모의고사

CooL
LISTENING
2

DARAKWON

저자 선생님

조금배
- Hawaii Pacific University TESL 학사 및 석사
- 서강대학교 대학원 영어영문학과 언어학 박사 과정
- 〈Hot Listening〉, 〈Cool Grammar〉 시리즈 등 공저

백영실
- 미국 Liberty University 졸업
- 〈Hot Listening〉, 〈절대어휘 5100〉 시리즈 등 공저

김정인
- 캐나다 Mount Saint Vincent University 영어교육학 석사
- 현 캐나다 온타리오주 공인회계사 (CPA)

영어듣기 모의고사

저자 조금배, 백영실, 김정인
펴낸이 정규도
펴낸곳 (주)다락원

초판 2쇄 발행 2023년 9월 6일

편집 서정아, 정연순, 안혜원
디자인 구수정, 포레스트
삽화 전진희
영문 감수 Michael A. Putlack

다락원 경기도 파주시 문발로 211
내용문의 (02) 736-2031 내선 503, 501, 532
구입문의 (02) 736-2031 내선 250~252
Fax (02) 732-2037
출판등록 1977년 9월 16일 제406-2008-000007호

ISBN 978-89-277-8021-2 54740
        978-89-277-8016-8 54740(set)

http://www.darakwon.co.kr

다락원 홈페이지를 방문하시면 상세한 출판 정보와 함께 MP3 자료 등의 다양한 어학 정보를 얻으실 수 있습니다.

REVIEW TEST
리뷰 테스트

모의고사에서 나온 중요 어휘와 문장을
복습할 수 있는 리뷰 테스트를 수록했습니다.
어휘를 듣고 어휘 및 우리말 뜻 쓰기와, 문장
빈칸 채우기를 통해서 핵심 어휘와 표현을
확실하게 복습할 수 있습니다.

ANSWERS
& SCRIPTS
정답 및 해석

한눈에 들어오는 정답 및 해석으로 편리하게 정답, 대본, 중요 어휘를 확인할 수 있습니다.

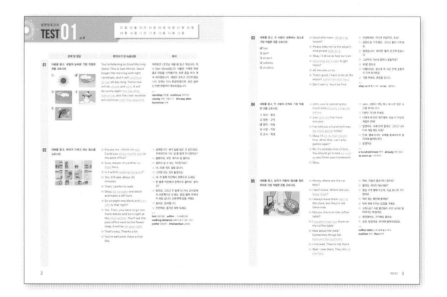

온라인 부가자료 www.darakwon.co.kr
다락원 홈페이지에서 무료로 부가자료를 다운로드하거나 웹에서 이용할 수 있습니다.
• 다양한 MP3 파일 제공: TEST별 (0.8배속 / 1.0배속 / 1.2배속) & 문항별
• 어휘 리스트 & 어휘 테스트

CONTENTS
목차

TEST

실전 모의고사

01 다음을 듣고, 내일의 날씨로 가장 적절한 것을 고르시오.

02 대화를 듣고, 여자가 가려고 하는 장소를 고르시오.

03 대화를 듣고, 두 사람이 대화하는 장소로 가장 적절한 곳을 고르시오.

① taxi
② gym
③ airport
④ subway
⑤ airplane

04 대화를 듣고, 두 사람의 관계로 가장 적절한 것을 고르시오.

① 의사 - 환자   ② 점원 - 고객
③ 엄마 - 아들   ④ 사장 - 직원
⑤ 교사 - 학생

05 대화를 듣고, 남자가 자동차 열쇠를 찾은 위치로 가장 적절한 곳을 고르시오.

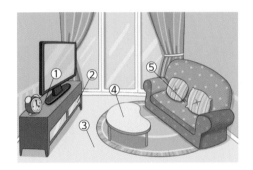

06 대화를 듣고, 여자가 구입할 책의 할인 후 가격으로 가장 적절한 것을 고르시오.

① $6   ② $8
③ $10   ④ $12
⑤ $20

07 대화를 듣고, 여자가 느꼈을 심정의 변화로 가장 적절한 것을 고르시오.

① scared → angry
② bored → excited
③ angry → worried
④ scared → relieved
⑤ happy → embarrassed

08 대화를 듣고, 두 사람의 목적지로 가장 적절한 곳을 고르시오.

	Destination	Gate No.	Time
①	New York	21	12:35 p.m.
②	Seoul	25	1:00 p.m.
③	London	35	1:50 p.m.
④	Tokyo	23	2:30 p.m.
⑤	Paris	45	4:50 p.m.

09 대화를 듣고, 여자의 몸무게가 늘어난 이유로 가장 적절한 것을 고르시오.

① 건강에 이상이 있어서
② 탄산음료를 자주 마셔서
③ 끼니를 간식으로 때워서
④ 운동을 전혀 하지 않아서
⑤ 명절 음식을 많이 먹어서

10 대화를 듣고, 남자가 이용할 교통수단으로 가장 적절한 것을 고르시오.

① 버스
② 택시
③ 지하철
④ 자가용
⑤ 비행기

11 대화를 듣고, 남자가 여자에게 제안한 일로 가장 적절한 것을 고르시오.

① 함께 축구하기
② 매일 운동하기
③ 자신의 팀을 응원하기
④ 집에 가서 옷 갈아입기
⑤ 여자 축구팀에 등록하기

12 다음을 듣고, 남자가 새해 결심으로 언급하지 않은 것을 고르시오.

① 매일 영어 공부하기
② 스마트폰 살 돈 모으기
③ 집안일 돕기
④ 숙제 미루지 않기
⑤ 남동생에게 잘해 주기

13 대화를 듣고, 대화 내용과 일치하지 않는 것을 고르시오.

① 남자는 Peter James를 지지한다.
② 남자는 Peter James가 정직하다고 생각한다.
③ 여자는 Peter James가 무례하다고 생각한다.
④ 남자는 Sandy가 예의 바르다고 생각한다.
⑤ 여자는 Sandy에게 투표할 것이다.

14 대화를 듣고, 남자의 마지막 말에 이어질 여자의 말로 가장 적절한 것을 고르시오.

① I am very proud of you!
② I think will fail this course.
③ I am afraid of making mistakes.
④ Really? Thank you for saying that.
⑤ I have to prepare for my presentation.

15 다음을 듣고, 여자의 마지막 말에 이어질 남자의 말로 가장 적절한 것을 고르시오.

① You look like your mother.
② I don't like my nose either.
③ That's right. Your nose is too big.
④ Yes! Don't worry about your nose.
⑤ I think you should exercise more often.

01 다음을 듣고, 내일의 날씨로 가장 적절한 것을 고르시오.

You're listening to *Good Morning Seoul*. This is Sam Morse. Seoul began the morning with light raindrops, and it will _____ _____ _____ all day long. Tomorrow will be _____ and _____. It will be sunny again _____ _____ _____ _____, and the clear weather will continue _____ _____ _____.

raindrop 빗방울 **continue** 계속되다 **cloudy** 흐린, 구름이 낀 **the day after tomorrow** 모레

02 대화를 듣고, 여자가 가려고 하는 장소를 고르시오.

W Excuse me. I think I'm _____. Could you _____ _____ _____ _____ to the post office?

M Sure, ma'am. It's a little _____ _____ here.

W Is it within _____ _____?

M Yes. It'll take about 20 minutes.

W Then, I prefer to walk.

M Okay. _____ _____ one block and make a left turn.

W Go straight one block and _____ _____. Is that right?

M Yes. Then you have to go two more blocks and turn right at the _____. You'll see the post office _____ _____ the flower shop. It will be _____ _____ _____.

W That's easy. Thanks a lot.

M You're welcome. Have a nice day.

lost 길을 잃은 **within** ~ 이내에[안에] **walking distance** 걸어서 갈 수 있는 거리 **prefer** 선호하다 **intersection** 교차로

03 대화를 듣고, 두 사람이 대화하는 장소로 가장 적절한 곳을 고르시오.

M Good afternoon. _____ _____, ma'am?

W Please take me to the airport. And please _____ _____ _____.

M Okay, I'll drive as fast as I can.

W _____ _____ _____ _____ _____ to get there?

M 40 minutes or so.

W That's good. I have to be at the airport _____ _____ _____.

M Don't worry. You'll be fine.

step on it 빨리 가다 **or so** ~쯤[정도]

04 대화를 듣고, 두 사람의 관계로 가장 적절한 것을 고르시오.

W John, you're spending too much time _____ _____ _____.

M Just _____ _____ five more minutes.

W I've told you a hundred times. _____
_____ _____ today!

M Okay. I'll _____ _____
_____ first. After that, can I play
games again?

W No. It's already nine o'clock. You should
go to bed _____ _____
_____ you finish your homework.

M Okay.

●●
a hundred times 백 번 **already** 이미, 벌써
as soon as ~하자마자

05 대화를 듣고, 남자가 자동차 열쇠를 찾은 위치로 가장
적절한 곳을 고르시오.

M Honey, where are the car keys?

W I don't know. Where did you _____
_____?

M I always leave them _____
_____ the clock but they're not
there now.

W Did you check on the coffee table?

M I _____ _____ _____ them
on the coffee table.

W How about the sofa? Sometimes things
fall _____ _____ _____.

M I checked. They're not there.

W Wait. I see them. They fell _____
_____ _____.

●●
coffee table (소파 앞에 놓는) 탁자 **cushion** 쿠션 **floor** 바닥

06 대화를 듣고, 여자가 구입할 책의 할인 후 가격으로
가장 적절한 것을 고르시오.

W Look, Mark! These books are _____
_____!

M Really? How much are they _____?

W There's a _____% _____ on all
books.

M And the sale is today only.

W Well, I don't _____ _____ books,
but I'll buy this one.

M That's a good idea. How much is the
_____ _____ of this book?

W _____ _____ 10 dollars.

●●
on sale 할인 중인 **reduce** (가격을) 낮추다, 할인하다
discount 할인 **say** ~라고 쓰여 있다

07 대화를 듣고, 여자가 느꼈을 심정의 변화로 가장 적절한
것을 고르시오.

W The _____ _____ happened to
me today.

M What happened?

W I _____ _____ in an elevator
with three other people.

M You _____ _____ _____ so
terrified.

W Yes, I was. But then we started talking.
After a while, we all thought it _____
_____ _____. Then, the elevator
started up again.

M That's an interesting story.

●●
get stuck 갇히다, 꼼짝 못 하다 **terrified** 무서워하는, 겁이 난
after a while 잠시 후에 **relieved** 안도하는

08 대화를 듣고, 두 사람의 목적지로 가장 적절한 곳을 고르시오.

W Hurry up! We have to _____ _____.

M Don't worry. We have _____ _____ _____.

W Please hurry. I don't want to _____ _____ _____.

M Kate, it's only one o'clock.

W Yes, but we have to arrive _____ _____ _____ international flights.

M Oh, then we have to be there _____ _____ _____. By the way, _____ _____ is it? Number 23?

W I don't think so. My ticket says _____.

• •
plenty of 많은 **international flight** 국제선 여객기
gate (공항의) 게이트, 탑승구

09 대화를 듣고, 여자의 몸무게가 늘어난 이유로 가장 적절한 것을 고르시오.

W How was this New Year's holiday, Tom?

M I had a wonderful time with my family. My _____ and _____ were so cute. I _____ _____ _____ for a long time. What about you?

W I had a good time, too.

M Did you _____ _____ _____ during the holiday?

W I sure did. I love _____ _____ _____.

M Did she make a lot of food?

W Too much! I _____ _____ over the holidays.

• •
nephew 남자 조카 **niece** 여자 조카
gain weight 체중이 늘다, 살이 찌다

10 대화를 듣고, 남자가 이용할 교통수단으로 가장 적절한 것을 고르시오.

M What's the best way to _____ _____?

W _____ _____ the bus. But I see you are _____ _____ this city.

M What do you mean?

W Well, the bus is _____ than the subway, but the subway is _____ _____ _____ _____.

M Oh, I see. Then I'll go downtown _____ _____.

W Good idea. It's a few minutes _____.

M That's okay. Thanks for helping me.

• •
recommend 추천하다 **unfamiliar** 익숙하지 않은
figure out 이해하다, 알아내다

11 대화를 듣고, 남자가 여자에게 제안한 일로 가장 적절한 것을 고르시오.

W Hey, what's _____ _____?

M I'm going to _____ _____. Do you want to play?

W Are there _____ _____ on your team?

M No, but you can be _____ _____.

W That _____ _____ _____.

I'll go home and change.

M I'll see you _____ _____

_____.

●●
sound like ~처럼 들리다 **change** (옷을) 갈아입다
field 운동장, 경기장

M Oh, I don't think so. He seems _____

_____ to me.

W Anyway, I've decided to vote for Sandy.

She's the right person _____

_____ _____.

M Okay, we'll see.

●●
vote for ~에 투표하다 **election** 선거 **honest** 정직한
intelligent 지적인, 총명한 **president** 대통령, 회장

12 다음을 듣고, 남자가 새해 결심으로 언급하지 <u>않은</u> 것을
고르시오.

I decide to do something every new year.

My _____ are often about school,

family life, or plans _____ _____

_____. I will tell you my resolutions

for this year: _____ _____

every day, _____ _____ for a

new smartphone, _____ _____

_____ with the housework, and

_____ _____ to my brother. I hope

I can _____ _____ _____.

●●
decide 결심하다 **resolution** 결심 **housework** 가사, 집안일

14 대화를 듣고, 남자의 마지막 말에 이어질 여자의 말로
가장 적절한 것을 고르시오.

M Good job!

W Do you really think so?

M _____! You gave a very good

presentation.

W I've worked on this presentation for the

_____ _____.

M I can tell.

W I _____ _____ _____

though.

M As a matter of fact, I don't think I've

ever seen a presentation _____

_____ _____.

W <u>Really? Thank you for saying that.</u>

●●
absolutely 그렇고 말고 **presentation** 발표 **semester** 학기
as a matter of fact 사실은

13 대화를 듣고, 대화 내용과 일치하지 <u>않는</u> 것을 고르시오.

W Who are you going to _____

_____ in the election?

M Peter James. I think he is _____ and

_____.

W But I think he is a bit rude, too.

15 대화를 듣고, 여자의 마지막 말에 이어질 남자의 말로 가장 적절한 것을 고르시오.

M Mary, why are you so _____?

W When I walk down the street, people always look at my _____.

M You are so _____ about your _____.

W You don't understand how I feel.

M _____ _____ _____ do I have to tell you? You look fine to me.

W But my nose is too big. I want to have _____ _____.

M Listen. You look very _____.

W Do I?

M Yes! Don't worry about your nose.

●●
depressed 의기소침한 **sensitive** 민감한 **appearance** 외모
plastic surgery 성형수술 **attractive** 매력적인

정답 및 해석 p. 7

A 다음을 듣고, 어휘와 우리말 뜻을 쓰시오.

① _____ _____
② _____ _____
③ _____ _____
④ _____ _____
⑤ _____ _____
⑥ _____ _____
⑦ _____ _____
⑧ _____ _____
⑨ _____ _____
⑩ _____ _____
⑪ _____ _____
⑫ _____ _____

B 우리말을 참고하여 빈칸에 알맞은 단어를 쓰시오.

① _____ _____, ma'am?
어디로 모실까요, 손님?

② Is it within _____ _____?
걸어서 갈 수 있는 거리인가요?

③ I _____ _____ over the holidays.
나는 연휴 기간에 살이 쪘다.

④ What's the _____ _____ _____ go downtown?
시내에 가는 가장 좋은 방법이 뭐예요?

⑤ I _____ _____ _____ something every new year.
저는 새해마다 무언가를 하기로 결심합니다.

⑥ Who are you going to _____ _____ in the _____?
선거에서 누구를 뽑을 거니?

⑦ She's the _____ _____ to be _____.
그녀는 회장직에 적합한 인물이야.

⑧ As _____ _____ _____ _____, I don't think I've ever seen a presentation better than that. 사실, 난 이보다 더 좋은 발표를 본 적이 없는 것 같구나.

MY SCORE
········· / 15

01 대화를 듣고, 여자가 강아지를 찾은 위치로 가장 적절한 곳을 고르시오.

02 대화를 듣고, 남자가 가려고 하는 장소를 고르시오.

03 대화를 듣고, 두 사람이 대화하는 장소로 가장 적절한 곳을 고르시오.

① 병원
② 박물관
③ 경기장
④ 백화점
⑤ 놀이공원

04 대화를 듣고, 두 사람의 관계로 가장 적절한 것을 고르시오.

① 점원 - 고객
② 감독 - 선수
③ 면접관 - 구직자
④ 영화감독 - 배우
⑤ 방송 진행자 - 해설자

05 다음을 듣고, 화재 이후 여자가 깨달은 것으로 가장 적절한 것을 고르시오.

① 경험의 중요성
② 가족의 소중함
③ 화재의 위험성
④ 신속한 신고의 필요성
⑤ 최선을 다하는 삶의 중요성

06 대화를 듣고, 남자가 조카보다 얼마나 더 키가 큰지 고르시오.

① 2cm
② 4cm
③ 6cm
④ 8cm
⑤ 10cm

07 대화를 듣고, 남자의 심정으로 가장 적절한 것을 고르시오.

① angry
② jealous
③ energetic
④ exhausted
⑤ disappointed

08 다음을 듣고, 두 사람의 대화가 <u>어색한</u> 것을 고르시오.

①   ②   ③   ④   ⑤

09 대화를 듣고, 여자가 남자에게 병원에 가자고 말한 이유로 가장 적절한 것을 고르시오.

① 다리를 다쳐서
② 남자가 아파서
③ 교통사고가 나서
④ 병문안을 가기 위해서
⑤ 남자가 병원에서 일해서

10 대화를 듣고, 남자가 전화를 건 목적으로 가장 적절한 것을 고르시오.

① 약속 시간을 변경하려고
② 점심 식사에 초대하려고
③ 변경된 일정을 알려주려고
④ 변호사와 만날 약속을 하려고
⑤ 변호사의 전화에 회신을 하려고

11 대화를 듣고, 남자가 여자에게 제안한 일로 가장 적절한 것을 고르시오.

① 버스 타기
② 택시 함께 타기
③ 도보로 이동하기
④ 지도 다시 확인하기
⑤ 자신의 차를 타고 가기

12 대화를 듣고, 오늘 Peter가 한 일이 <u>아닌</u> 것을 고르시오.

① 뒤뜰 청소하기
② 숙제하기
③ 축구 연습 준비하기
④ 합창단 지휘하기
⑤ 피아노 반주하기

13 대화를 듣고, 대화 내용과 일치하지 <u>않는</u> 것을 고르시오.

① 여자는 콘서트 표 4장을 구입할 것이다.
② 여자는 콘서트에 초대 받았다.
③ 여자는 무대와 가까운 좌석을 원한다.
④ 여자는 신용카드로 표를 구입하기를 원한다.
⑤ 여자는 공연 며칠 전에 티켓을 받을 것이다.

14 대화를 듣고, 남자의 마지막 말에 이어질 여자의 말로 가장 적절한 것을 고르시오.

① You can't do it. It's too difficult.
② Put them into the hot pan with oil.
③ Mix them with the sauce. That's all.
④ Vegetables are good for your health.
⑤ You can buy them at the supermarket.

15 대화를 듣고, 여자의 마지막 말에 이어질 남자의 말로 가장 적절한 것을 고르시오.

① I saw it on TV.
② I used to collect coins.
③ Do you need some coins?
④ No, I don't have any coins.
⑤ I think magic is really cool.

DICTATION 02

01 대화를 듣고, 여자가 강아지를 찾은 위치로 가장 적절한 곳을 고르시오.

W I was about to give the puppy a bath, but he _____ _____ and _____.

M Where is he?

W Somewhere in the bedroom. Help me _____ _____.

M Did you check _____ _____ _____?

W Yeah. He's not there.

M Hmm... He's not under the table _____.

W Oh, my gosh. Here he is! He's hiding in the _____ _____!

●●
be about to 막 ~하려는 참이다 **run away** 도망치다
laundry 세탁물

02 대화를 듣고, 남자가 가려고 하는 장소를 고르시오.

M Excuse me. _____ _____ _____ where the H Department Store is?

W Yes. Do you see the tall building _____ _____? That's SBS.

M I see.

W Facing that building is Paris Park. _____ the park and _____ _____ at the corner. Then, _____ _____ the street. You'll see the department store. It's _____ World Apartment and _____ _____ the church.

M I've got it. Thank you.

●●
department store 백화점 **face** 마주보다, 향하다 **pass** 지나가다

03 대화를 듣고, 두 사람이 대화하는 장소로 가장 적절한 곳을 고르시오.

W Excuse me! I have an _____!

M What's the problem?

W My daughter is _____. She's only six years old.

M Oh, dear. What's her name?

W Hannah Kim. She is wearing a yellow _____ and black _____.

M Where _____ _____ _____ her?

W Near the _____ _____. We were watching the _____.

M Okay. _____ _____. We can help you.

●●
emergency 응급 상황 **roller coaster** 롤러코스터
parade 퍼레이드

04 대화를 듣고, 두 사람의 관계로 가장 적절한 것을 고르시오.

W Hello. I'm Mary Dover, the _____ for today's baseball game. _____ _____ is Bob Pierson. He is the _____ for this match. Hello, Mr. Pierson.

M Hello.

W Mr. Pierson, what do you think of _____ _____?.

M Well, let's see. I think it will be a
_____ _____ for the AB Bears
because the Happy Lions have won five
games _____ _____ _____.

W Yes, but the AB Bears don't seem too
_____, maybe because of their
_____ _____.

M Oh, the game is starting.

● ●
sportscaster 스포츠 방송 진행자 **beside** ~의 옆에
commentator 해설자 **tough** 힘든 **in a row** 연속으로, 계속해서
concerned 걱정하는 **excellent** 훌륭한

05 다음을 듣고, 화재 이후 여자가 깨달은 것으로 가장
적절한 것을 고르시오.

One night, my house _____ _____.
Although I lost many things in the fire, the
experience helped me to be _____
_____. Before the fire, I always
_____ _____ my life. Then, the fire
came and _____ _____ we owned.
We were suddenly poor and _____
_____ _____ everything. At first, I
had a hard time, but I slowly began to realize
that I didn't really need my _____
_____. I just needed my _____. It
is true that the fire took many good things
from me, but it _____ _____
_____, too. It taught me to _____
_____ more than things.

● ●
burn down 불에 타다 **mature** 성숙한 **complain** 불평하다
destroy 파괴하다 **own** 소유하다 **realize** 깨닫다
appreciate 고맙게 여기다, 감사하다

06 대화를 듣고, 남자가 조카보다 얼마나 더 키가 큰지
고르시오.

W Look at your nephew. He's almost
_____ _____ _____ you.

M I don't think so, Mom. I am _____
centimeters tall.

W Well, he's _____ centimeters tall and
_____ _____.

M When I was his age, I was almost
_____ centimeters tall, but I haven't
grown much _____ _____.

W Teenagers seem to be _____
_____ these days.

M I think so.

● ●
teenager 십대

07 대화를 듣고, 남자의 심정으로 가장 적절한 것을 고르
시오.

W John, you look great.

M Thanks. I've been _____ a lot
and I feel like _____ _____
_____.

W I should follow your example. It really
_____ _____ _____,
doesn't it?

M It sure does. It has really changed my life.

W That's it! _____ _____, I'm going
to the gym.

M That's a great idea. I'll see you there.

● ●
feel like a million dollars 기분이 매우 좋다 **gym** 체육관

08 다음을 듣고, 두 사람의 대화가 <u>어색한</u> 것을 고르시오.

① M Excuse me, ma'am. You _____ _____ _____.

W Oh, thank you. You're very kind.

② M If I were you, I'd be more careful.

W Wash your hands to _____ _____.

③ M How do you think this suit looks on me?

W It looks _____.

④ M _____ _____ oranges are in the bag?

W There are 12 tasty and fresh oranges in the bag.

⑤ M How do I _____ _____ _____ these troublesome pimples?

W Just keep your face clean.

drop 떨어뜨리다 **prevent** 예방하다 **suit** 정장, 양복
fabulous 아주 멋진 **tasty** 맛있는 **get rid of** 없애다
troublesome 골치 아픈, 성가신 **pimple** 여드름

09 대화를 듣고, 여자가 남자에게 병원에 가자고 말한 이유로 가장 적절한 것을 고르시오.

M Mary, _____ _____ _____ of the body is the appendix?

W It's on the right side. Why do you ask?

M I don't know. I _____ _____ _____ in that area.

W Really?

M In fact, it's getting _____ _____ _____ uncomfortable.

W Well, we'd better take a taxi to the hospital now _____ _____ _____.

appendix 맹장 **discomfort** 불편, 가벼운 통증
uncomfortable 불편한 **just in case** 만일의 경우에 대비해서

10 대화를 듣고, 남자가 전화를 건 목적으로 가장 적절한 것을 고르시오.

W Hello. Elizabeth White's Law Firm.

M Hi. _____ _____ Gabriel Lincoln _____.

W Oh, hello, Mr. Lincoln. How _____ _____ _____ ?

M Just fine. I was hoping I could meet with her _____ _____ _____.

W I don't know, Mr. Lincoln. Her schedule is _____ _____.

M This is really important. I have to meet with her before I _____ _____ _____.

W Well, how about if I ask her and then _____ _____ _____ ?

M Sounds great.

law firm 법률 사무소 **book** 예약하다 **court** 법원, 법정

11 대화를 듣고, 남자가 여자에게 제안한 일로 가장 적절한 것을 고르시오.

W It's _____ _____ _____ _____ for the bus. Can I catch a taxi here?

M Yes, you can. Where are you going?

W I'm going to the Hilton Hotel.

M The Hilton Hotel is too _____

_____ here. You'll pay a _____

_____.

W I know, but it's too late and too cold to

_____ _____ _____.

M The Hilton is near the Manhattan Hotel,

where I'm going. Shall we share a cab and

_____ _____ _____?

W That sounds like a good idea.

● ●

fare 요금 **cab** 택시 **split** 쪼개다, 나누다

W I'd like to _____ _____ for the

Super Concert on September 3.

M All right.

W Are there any seats _____

_____ _____ _____?

M Yes, how many seats do you need?

W Four. Can I _____ _____ a credit

card?

M Of course. We'll send you the tickets

_____ _____ before

the concert.

● ●

reserve 예약하다 **seat** 자리, 좌석 **credit card** 신용카드

12 대화를 듣고, 오늘 Peter가 한 일이 <u>아닌</u> 것을 고르시오.

M _____ _____ _____ Peter?

W Yes, darling. After he _____

_____ the backyard, he did his

homework. Now, he's _____

_____ _____ soccer practice.

M Didn't he play the piano for choir practice

this morning?

W Right. He is always _____ _____

_____ a bee. He has a lot of energy.

M He _____ _____ _____. I'll

tell him to _____ soccer practice

today.

● ●

backyard 뒤뜰 **get ready for** ~을 준비하다 **choir** 합창단
skip 건너뛰다, 생략하다

13 대화를 듣고, 대화 내용과 일치하지 <u>않는</u> 것을 고르시오.

M How may I help you?

14 대화를 듣고, 남자의 마지막 말에 이어질 여자의 말로
가장 적절한 것을 고르시오.

M Can I help you _____ _____?

W Yes, you can. Cook the rice for me,

please.

M I'm not _____ _____ _____,

but I'll try. How much water should I put

into the pot with the rice?

W You should put _____ _____

_____ _____ rice.

M Okay, I think I'm done with that. Can I

help you with _____ _____?

W Yes, could you _____ _____

_____ for me?

M How do I do that?

W <u>Put them into the hot pan with oil.</u>

● ●

pot 냄비, 솥 **fry** (기름에) 볶다, 튀기다

15 대화를 듣고, 여자의 마지막 말에 이어진 남자의 말로 가장 적절한 것을 고르시오.

M _____ _____ _____ _____ something called a magic coin?

W No, I haven't. What is it?

M It's a coin that magicians use when they _____ _____ _____. Do you want to see one? I'll show you.

W Hmm. It looks just like a _____ _____. I can't see _____.

M Look carefully. There is _____ _____ about this coin.

W You're right. There's a _____ _____ in the center of the coin.

M Magicians _____ _____ with this kind of coin and thread.

W How do you know?

M I saw it on TV.

••
magician 마술사 **perform** 하다, 행하다 **magic trick** 마술
normal 보통의 **tiny** 아주 작은 **thread** 실

A 다음을 듣고, 어휘와 우리말 뜻을 쓰시오.

① _____ ⑦ _____

② _____ ⑧ _____

③ _____ ⑨ _____

④ _____ ⑩ _____

⑤ _____ ⑪ _____

⑥ _____ ⑫ _____

B 우리말을 참고하여 빈칸에 알맞은 단어를 쓰시오.

① _____ the park and _____ _____ at the corner.
그 공원을 지나서 길모퉁이에서 왼쪽으로 도세요.

② He's almost _____ _____ _____ you.
그는 거의 너만큼이나 키가 크구나.

③ If I _____ _____, I'd be more careful.
내가 너라면 좀 더 조심할 텐데.

④ How do I _____ _____ _____ these troublesome
pimples? 이 골치 아픈 여드름을 어떻게 없애지?

⑤ Well, we'd better take a taxi to the hospital now _____
_____. 음, 만일의 경우에 대비해서 우리는 지금 택시를 타고 병원에 가는 게 낫겠어.

⑥ Shall we share a cab and _____ _____ _____?
택시를 같이 타고 요금을 나눠 낼까요?

⑦ I'm not _____ _____ _____, but I'll try.
요리는 잘 못하지만 해 볼게.

⑧ You should put _____ _____ _____ as
rice. 쌀의 두 배 정도의 물을 넣어야 해.

MY SCORE

_____ / 15

01 대화를 듣고, 남자가 이번 여름에 한 일로 가장 적절한 것을 고르시오.

①  ②

③  ④

⑤

02 대화를 듣고, 여자가 가려고 하는 장소를 고르시오.

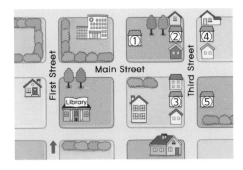

03 대화를 듣고, 두 사람이 대화하는 장소로 가장 적절한 곳을 고르시오.

① 회사
② 식당
③ 경찰서
④ 백화점
⑤ 우체국

04 대화를 듣고, 두 사람의 관계로 가장 적절한 것을 고르시오.

① 버스 기사 - 승객
② 백화점 직원 - 고객
② 자동차 정비사 - 손님
④ 자동차 판매자 - 구매자
⑤ 렌터카 회사 직원 - 손님

05 대화를 듣고, 현재의 계절로 가장 적절한 것을 고르시오.

① 봄
② 여름
③ 가을
④ 초겨울
⑤ 늦겨울

06 대화를 듣고, Christopher Ellis의 현재 몸무게로 가장 적절한 것을 고르시오.

① 60kg
② 70kg
③ 80kg
④ 90kg
⑤ 100kg

07 대화를 듣고, 여자의 심정으로 가장 적절한 것을 고르시오.

① bored
② worried
③ cheerful
④ thankful
⑤ annoyed

정답 및 해석 p. 14

08 대화를 듣고, 두 사람이 관람하고 있는 경기로 가장 적절한 것을 고르시오.

① 골프
② 수영
③ 야구
④ 배구
⑤ 테니스

09 대화를 듣고, 여자가 남자의 제안에 망설인 이유로 가장 적절한 것을 고르시오.

① 다리를 다쳐서
② 다른 약속이 있어서
③ 춤 추는 것을 싫어해서
④ 춤 추는 방법을 몰라서
⑤ 파트너가 마음에 들지 않아서

10 대화를 듣고, 여자가 남자에게 말을 건 목적으로 가장 적절한 것을 고르시오.

① 구입할 물건을 계산하려고
② 작성한 지원서를 제출하려고
③ 직원 채용 여부를 알아보려고
④ 지원서 작성 방법을 확인하려고
⑤ 가까운 편의점 위치를 물어보려고

11 대화를 듣고, 여자가 남자에게 요청한 사항으로 언급하지 <u>않은</u> 것을 고르시오.

① 안전벨트 착용하기
② 등받이 세우기
③ 좌석 밑에 가방 넣기
④ 휴대폰 전원 끄기
⑤ 금연하기

12 대화를 듣고, 여자가 자연에 대해 어떻게 생각하는지 고르시오.

① 아름답다.
② 파괴적일 수도 있다.
③ 영원히 보존되어야 한다.
④ 신비한 힘을 가지고 있다.
⑤ 감사하는 마음을 가져야 한다.

13 대화를 듣고, 여자가 조부모님을 얼마나 자주 방문하는지 고르시오.

① 매일
② 주말마다
③ 1년에 한 번
④ 2년에 한 번
⑤ 방문하지 않음

14 대화를 듣고, 남자의 마지막 말에 이어질 여자의 말로 가장 적절한 것을 고르시오.

① It's seven thirty.
② The clock is broken.
③ It's not a clock. It's a picture.
④ There is no clock on the wall.
⑤ I don't have good eyesight either.

15 대화를 듣고, 여자의 마지막 말에 이어질 남자의 말로 가장 적절한 것을 고르시오.

① I like toast for breakfast.
② Sorry. Diner isn't ready yet.
③ Sure. We'll call you at seven.
④ There's no problem. Just ask the bellboy.
⑤ Breakfast is served between 7 and 10 a.m.

01

대화를 듣고, 남자가 이번 여름에 한 일로 가장 적절한 것을 고르시오.

W _____ _____ _____ car!

M Thanks. I worked really hard this summer to be able to _____ _____.

W Where did you work?

M I worked for a _____ _____.

W Do you mean you planted flowers and stuff?

M No, my _____ was tree trimming.

W Oh, I see. So you cut the _____ _____ off trees.

M That's right.

●●
afford ~을 살[할] 여유가 되다 **landscaping company** 조경 회사
specialty 전공, 전문 **tree trimming** 나뭇가지 자르기
extra 여분의, 필요 이상의 **branch** 나뭇가지

02

대화를 듣고, 여자가 가려고 하는 장소를 고르시오.

W Excuse me. Do you know where the bus terminal is?

M Yes. Walk down First Street, and _____ _____ _____ on Main Street.

W Go straight and turn right...

M Yes. Then, follow Main Street to Third Street and _____ _____ _____. The bus terminal is in the _____ of the block on your right.

W Thank you. You're very kind.

M You're welcome.

03

대화를 듣고, 두 사람이 대화하는 장소로 가장 적절한 곳을 고르시오.

M Excuse me. I _____ _____ _____ this morning.

W Where do you think you lost it?

M On the _____ _____ in the _____ _____.

W Well, you're lucky. A _____ found it about an hour ago.

M Thank goodness! I was really worried.

W Here it is. _____ _____ everything is there.

M Thank you so much.

●●
wallet 지갑 **department** 부서, (백화점의) 매장

04

대화를 듣고, 두 사람의 관계로 가장 적절한 것을 고르시오.

M I'm here to _____ _____ _____.

W _____ _____ _____ do you want?

M Well, actually, I haven't _____ _____ _____ yet.

W Do you want a compact car?

M _____ _____ _____ compact cars do you have?

W We have a Cobbie Morning now.

M Okay. I'll rent it. Can I pay _____ _____?

W I'm afraid not. You can only pay

_____ _____ _____. It's our

policy.

M Okay. Here is my credit card.

●●
make up one's mind 결정하다 **compact car** 소형차
cash 현금

---

05 대화를 듣고, 현재의 계절로 가장 적절한 것을 고르
시오.

W Isn't it wonderful? Soon, the birds will

be _____, and the flowers will be

_____.

M What are you talking about? Are you

_____ _____ _____?

W No, I'm talking about the most beautiful

season.

M Oh, I see. The coming of spring also

_____ _____ _____. Don't

you think so?

W That's true. The snow is still _____

_____ _____, but I can feel the

_____ of the sun.

M Yes, it _____ _____ to our lives.

●●
bloom 개화하다, 꽃이 피다 **recite** 낭송하다 **poem** 시
cheer up 기운을 북돋우다 **warmth** 온기, 따뜻한

---

06 대화를 듣고, Christopher Ellis의 현재 몸무게로 가장
적절한 것을 고르시오.

M Did you _____ _____ the

famous actor Christopher Ellis?

W No, I didn't. _____ _____ him?

M Well, he normally _____ 70

kilograms, but he has gained 20

kilograms to _____ _____

_____ in a movie.

W That's incredible. It _____

_____ _____ _____ for him

to gain all that weight.

M Not really. He said all he did was

_____ _____ for breakfast,

lunch, and supper.

W So if I eat sweets a lot, then can I gain

weight _____ _____?

M Of course!

●●
weigh 무게가 ~이다 **incredible** 놀라운, 믿기 힘든 **sweets** 단 것
supper 저녁 (식사)

---

07 대화를 듣고, 여자의 심정으로 가장 적절한 것을 고르
시오.

M Can I help you with your _____?

W Thank you.

M No problem. I'm walking _____

_____ _____ anyway.

W When I was your age, I had so much

energy, but now...

M You look _____ _____. Is this

your apartment?

W Yes, it is. Can I give you something

_____ _____ _____?

M No, thanks. It was _____ _____.

●●
grocery 식료품 **direction** 방향 **effort** 노력, 수고

08 대화를 듣고, 두 사람이 관람하고 있는 경기로 가장 적절한 것을 고르시오.

W Who's the _____ for the Dodgers?

M Oh, Chris Taylor is the starter.

W Really? I love him. He is a very good _____, isn't he?

M Yes, he is. Look. Oh, that's a _____ _____. The runner was clearly out.

W Well, it _____ _____ _____ that he was safe.

M I don't think so. That is just an example of home-field advantage.

W _____ _____. Why don't you _____ _____ _____ _____ at the replay?

M Okay.

starter (야구의) 선발 투수 **pitcher** 투수 **call** (심판의) 판정
replay 다시 보기

09 대화를 듣고, 여자가 남자의 제안에 망설인 이유로 가장 적절한 것을 고르시오.

M Would you like to _____ _____, Jennifer?

W Well... I would _____ I don't know how.

M It's easy. You just put one foot in front of the other.

W You're joking, right? How can I do that?

M I'll show you _____ _____ _____. Just work with me.

W _____ _____ _____ _____ _____.

M Ready? Let's begin.

except ~만 아니면 **Easier said than done.** 행동보다 말이 쉽다.

10 대화를 듣고, 여자가 남자에게 말을 건 목적으로 가장 적절한 것을 고르시오.

M How can I help you?

W I wonder if you sometimes _____ _____ _____ at your store.

M Yes, sometimes. Do you want to _____ _____ a job?

W Yes, I do.

M Do you have _____ _____ _____?

W Yes, I do. I worked at a convenience store before.

M Just complete this _____. We will contact you when a job is _____.

W Thanks.

hire 고용하다 **staff member** 직원 **apply for** ~에 지원하다, ~을 신청하다 **convenience store** 편의점 **application** 지원서
available 이용할 수 있는

11 대화를 듣고, 여자가 남자에게 요청한 사항으로 언급하지 않은 것을 고르시오.

W The seatbelt sign _____ _____. Please _____ your seatbelt.

M Okay.

W Then, put your seat back _____, please.

M Is this all right?

W Sure. Please put your bag _____ _____ _____.

M Okay, I'll do that. And I have a question. Can I smoke here?

W No. You can't smoke _____

_____ _____ .

fasten 매다, 묶다   **seatbelt** 안전벨트   **seat back** 등받이
upright 똑바로 선, 수직의   **plane** 비행기

12 대화를 듣고, 여자가 자연에 대해 어떻게 생각하는지
고르시오.

W Isn't it so sad to hear about _____

_____ in Southeast Asia?

M Yes. There were so many _____ , and

their lives _____ _____ .

W It's hard to believe that nature can be

_____ _____ .

M We _____ _____ _____ we

don't live in that dangerous area.

W You're right about that. Did you

_____ _____ _____ _____ ?

M Yes, I did that last week.

victim 희생자   **destructive** 파괴적인   **donate** 기부하다

13 대화를 듣고, 여자가 조부모님을 얼마나 자주 방문하
는지 고르시오.

W _____ _____ do you visit your

grandparents?

M I visit them _____ _____

_____ . I wish I could visit them more

often, but I'm too busy.

W You're better than me. I only visit my

grandparents _____ _____

_____ _____ because they live

far away.

M Where do they live?

W They live on Jeju Island.

M That's far away. How often do you

_____ _____ _____ ?

W They live near my apartment, so I visit

them _____ _____ . How about

you?

M My parents live in Japan, so I just talk to

them _____ _____ _____ .

every other year 한 해 걸러, 2년마다

14 대화를 듣고, 남자의 마지막 말에 이어질 여자의 말로
가장 적절한 것을 고르시오.

W It's _____ _____ _____

_____ to the museum.

M Really? What time is it?

W I _____ _____ _____ , but I

think we're late.

M Can you _____ _____

_____ on the wall?

W Where is the clock?

M Over there. It's the big red one. I can't

tell the time because of _____

_____ _____ .

W Let me see. It's _____ _____

_____ .

M Pardon me?

W It's seven thirty.

eyesight 시력   **tell the time** 시계를[시간을] 보다
half past seven 7시 반

15 대화를 듣고, 여자의 마지막 말에 이어질 남자의 말로
가장 적절한 것을 고르시오.

W What time is _____?

M 11 o'clock.

W Can you give me _____ _____

_____ tomorrow morning?

M Yes. What time would you like us to call

you?

W Seven, please. And can I _____

_____ _____ here until

tomorrow night? My flight will leave

tomorrow night.

M Yes, of course. Just leave it here, and

we'll _____ _____ _____ it.

W And can you tell me what time you start

_____ _____?

M Breakfast is served between 7 and 10

a.m.

••
checkout (호텔의) 체크아웃, 퇴숙 절차 **wakeup call** (호텔의) 모닝
콜 **luggage** 짐, 수하물 **take care of** 돌보다, 처리하다
bellboy (호텔의) 벨보이

A 다음을 듣고, 어휘와 우리말 뜻을 쓰시오.

① _____
② _____
③ _____
④ _____
⑤ _____
⑥ _____
⑦ _____
⑧ _____
⑨ _____
⑩ _____
⑪ _____
⑫ _____

B 우리말을 참고하여 빈칸에 알맞은 단어를 쓰시오.

① I haven't _____ _____ my _____ yet.
아직 결정을 못했어요.

② It _____ _____ _____ _____ for him to gain all
that weight. 그가 그렇게 살을 찌우기는 분명 힘들었을 거야.

③ Easier _____ _____ _____.
행동보다 말로는 쉽지.

④ Do you want to _____ _____ a job?
일자리에 지원하고 싶으세요?

⑤ Please _____ your _____.
안전벨트를 착용해 주세요.

⑥ It's hard to believe that _____ can be so _____.
자연이 그렇게 파괴적일 수도 있다는 것이 믿기 힘들어.

⑦ It's _____ _____ seven.
7시 30분이야.

⑧ Can you give me a _____ _____ tomorrow morning?
내일 아침에 전화로 깨워주실 수 있나요?

MY SCORE

········· / 15

01 대화를 듣고, 여자가 구입한 케이크로 가장 적절한 것을 고르시오.

①   ②

③   ④

⑤

02 대화를 듣고, 남자가 가려고 하는 장소를 고르시오.

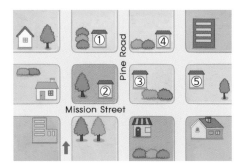

03 대화를 듣고, 두 사람이 대화하는 장소로 가장 적절한 곳을 고르시오.

① 상점
② 극장
③ 공항
④ 기차역
⑤ 버스 터미널

04 대화를 듣고, 두 사람의 관계로 가장 적절한 것을 고르시오.

① 친구 – 친구
② 집주인 – 세입자
③ 호텔 직원 – 투숙객
④ 관광 가이드 – 여행객
⑤ 부동산 중개인 – 고객

05 대화를 듣고, 여자가 요즘 하고 있는 일로 가장 적절한 것을 고르시오.

① 사진 수업을 듣고 있다.
② 그림 수업을 듣고 있다.
③ 전시회 준비를 하고 있다.
④ 흑백 사진을 모으고 있다.
⑤ 자신의 취미를 남에게 가르쳐 주고 있다.

06 대화를 듣고, 남자가 원하는 수면 시간으로 가장 적절한 것을 고르시오.

① 4시간
② 5시간
③ 6시간
④ 8시간
⑤ 10시간

07 다음을 듣고, 어젯밤에 여자가 느꼈을 심정으로 가장 적절한 것을 고르시오.

① bored
② pleased
③ nervous
④ cheerful
⑤ miserable

08 대화를 듣고, 여자가 추측하는 것으로 가장 적절한 것을 고르시오.

① Sandra는 거짓말을 하고 있다.
② Sandra는 아파서 모임에 오지 못했다.
③ Sandra는 모임에 나오는 것을 싫어한다.
④ Sandra가 아르바이트를 여러 개 하고 있다.
⑤ Sandra는 당분간 모임에 나오지 못할 것이다.

09 대화를 듣고, 여자가 모자를 쓰지 않은 이유로 가장 적절한 것을 고르시오.

① 모자가 없어서
② 모자를 잃어버려서
③ 모자를 집에 두고 와서
④ 춥다고 생각하지 않아서
⑤ 모자가 잘 어울리지 않아서

10 대화를 듣고, 여자가 전화를 건 목적으로 가장 적절한 것을 고르시오.

① 제품을 사기 위해서
② 제품을 환불 받기 위해서
③ 제품 고장을 문의하기 위해서
④ 다른 제품으로 교환하기 위해서
⑤ A/S 센터의 위치를 물어보기 위해서

11 다음을 듣고, 남자가 제자들에게 부탁한 일로 가장 적절한 것을 고르시오.

① 질문을 많이 하자.
② 규칙을 준수하자.
③ 유머 감각을 키우자.
④ 서로 연락하고 지내자.
⑤ 긍정적인 태도를 갖자.

12 대화를 듣고, 남자가 대화 직후에 할 일로 가장 적절한 것을 고르시오.

① 주유소에 간다.
② 택시를 부른다.
③ 엔진을 확인한다.
④ 정비사를 부른다.
⑤ 아버지에게 전화한다.

13 대화를 듣고, 대화 내용과 일치하지 <u>않는</u> 것을 고르시오.

① 여자는 약 2년간 영어를 공부했다.
② 여자는 온라인 영어 강좌를 듣는다.
③ 여자는 영자 신문을 잘 읽지 못한다.
④ 여자는 영어회화를 잘 못한다고 생각한다.
⑤ 남자는 여자가 영어회화를 잘한다고 생각한다.

14 대화를 듣고, 남자의 마지막 말에 이어질 여자의 말로 가장 적절한 것을 고르시오.

① That sounds great.
② You'd better see a doctor.
③ Do well on your math test.
④ You'll do fine. Good luck to you.
⑤ To be honest, I'm not interested in English.

15 대화를 듣고, 여자의 마지막 말에 이어질 남자의 말로 가장 적절한 것을 고르시오.

① I'm afraid I can't. I'm busy.
② Let's play the game after school.
③ What kinds of games do you play?
④ My mom doesn't allow me to play computer games.
⑤ Well, I've tried to quit, but I can't stop thinking about it.

01 대화를 듣고, 여자가 구입한 케이크로 가장 적절한 것을 고르시오.

M Do you need any help?

W I am _____ _____ a cake for my father.

M How about this heart-shaped cake? It's not sweet, so _____ _____ like it.

W It's nice, but I want a _____ _____.

M Do you want the cake with a heart-shaped chocolate on it?

W No, I'd like the cake _____ _____ _____ _____.

M Sure.

●●
look for ~을 찾다, 구하다 **adult** 성인

02 대화를 듣고, 남자가 가려고 하는 장소를 고르시오.

M Excuse me. Do you know _____ _____ _____ _____ Village Hotel?

W Hmm... It doesn't _____ _____. Do you know _____ _____ it is on?

M I think it is on Pine Road.

W Ah, yes. If I'm _____ _____, it's the only hotel on that road. Go from here to Mission Street. Then, _____ _____.

M Go to Mission Street and turn right.

W Yes, that's right. Then, _____ _____ _____ _____ Pine Road, turn left. The hotel is _____ _____.

M Okay. Thank you very much.

W No problem.

●●
familiar 익숙한, 친숙한 **mistaken** 잘못 알고 있는, 틀린

03 대화를 듣고, 두 사람이 대화하는 장소로 가장 적절한 곳을 고르시오.

W When is the _____ _____ _____ Chicago?

M There's one at two o'clock.

W How long _____ _____ _____ to get there?

M About three hours and forty minutes.

W How much is a _____ _____?

M 26 dollars.

●●
one-way 편도의

04 대화를 듣고, 두 사람의 관계로 가장 적절한 것을 고르시오.

M Come in. How _____ _____ _____ the house?

W Thank you. It's a great house.

M There are three bedrooms and two bathrooms in this house. _____ _____ _____, it's really clean. The previous owner _____ _____ it. It's like new.

W Yes, I like it. But 1,500 dollars _____ _____ is too expensive.

M I'll _____ _____ the owner to make it 1,250 dollars.

W I would really _____ _____, but is that possible?

M Probably. The house _____ _____ _____ for a couple of months now.

W Super. I'll wait for your call.

●●
previous 이전의 **owner** 주인 **negotiate** 협상하다
empty 비어 있는

05 대화를 듣고, 여자가 요즘 하고 있는 일로 가장 적절한 것을 고르시오.

W _____ _____ _____ if I take your picture?

M Not at all. What is this for?

W I have a _____ _____. I am taking a _____ _____. It's so much fun.

M I've thought about that _____ _____.

W I love _____ _____ _____ pictures. They're so attractive.

M _____ _____ _____ _____.

●●
hobby 취미 **photography** 사진
black and white picture 흑백사진

06 대화를 듣고, 남자가 원하는 수면 시간으로 가장 적절한 것을 고르시오.

W Tom, you _____ _____ _____.

M I only slept for four hours last night.

W Oh, that's too bad. _____ _____ _____ is very important.

M If I don't get _____ _____ of sleep, I'm tired the whole next day.

W What _____ _____ _____ for so long? Exams?

M You got it. I'm so _____ _____ about exams that I usually sleep for _____ _____ _____ _____ these days.

●●
awake 깨어있는

07 다음을 듣고, 어젯밤에 여자가 느꼈을 심정으로 가장 적절한 것을 고르시오.

Last night, I finished my part-time job at 9 p.m. I was tired and hungry and just _____ _____ _____ _____. Then, there was a _____ _____. I waited _____ _____ _____ for the bus to come. Then, when it finally arrived, it didn't even _____! It just drove _____ _____ _____ _____. I didn't get home till 10 p.m., and by that time, I _____ _____.

●●
part-time job 아르바이트, 파트타임직
in a bad mood 기분이 좋지 않은 **sudden** 갑작스러운
thunderstorm 뇌우 **soaked** 흠뻑 젖은

08 대화를 듣고, 여자가 추측하는 것으로 가장 적절한 것을 고르시오.

M Why didn't Sandra _____ _____ for today's meeting?

W I don't know. She told me that she _____ _____ to our meeting today.

M I wonder _____ _____. Is she sick again?

W I don't think so. I think she has been _____ _____.

M Really? How do you know?

W I'm not sure, but she's been _____ _____. I'm only guessing.

•• **show up** 모습을 나타내다, 오다

09 대화를 듣고, 여자가 모자를 쓰지 않은 이유로 가장 적절한 것을 고르시오.

W Can you believe _____ _____ _____ _____ today?

M I know. It's unbelievable. I thought the weather was going to _____ _____.

W Me, too. I think I should move to a _____ _____.

M Why don't you have a _____ _____ for days like today?

W I have one, but I _____ _____ _____.

M I'm sure you _____ _____ the next time.

W You're right about that.

•• **unbelievable** 믿을 수 없는, 믿기 힘든 **tropical** 열대의

10 대화를 듣고, 여자가 전화를 건 목적으로 가장 적절한 것을 고르시오.

M Hello. Samil Electronics. How can I help you?

W Yes, I _____ _____ _____ from one of your stores last week, but it _____ _____.

M Have you _____ _____ _____?

W Yes, I have. The electricity is fine.

M I see. _____ _____ _____ take it to any A/S center near your house? If the blender has a problem, you can get a new one or _____ _____ _____ _____.

W Okay. Thanks.

•• **blender** 믹서기 **work** 작동하다 **electricity** 전기

11 다음을 듣고, 남자가 제자들에게 부탁한 일로 가장 적절한 것을 고르시오.

It was my pleasure to have you guys as my students. I'm _____ _____ _____ you and your work. I want to _____ _____ _____ to all of you. I'll miss your questions, your smiles, and your active and positive attitudes. You _____ _____ _____ my lessons and always agreed with me. All of you obeyed the _____ and did your _____ very well. Let's _____ _____ _____ _____ each other. I hope we meet again soon.

•• **attitude** 태도 **pay attention to** ~에 집중하다, 주의를 기울이다
obey 따르다, 준수하다 **duty** 의무
keep in touch with ~와 연락하고 지내다

12 대화를 듣고, 남자가 대화 직후에 할 일로 가장 적절한 것을 고르시오.

M Oh, no, my car _____ _____.

W What should we do? Did you _____ _____ _____? We don't have enough time to get to the _____ _____.

M I'm really sorry. There's _____ _____ with my old car. This is my fault. I _____ _____ _____ the engine.

W Well, let's _____ _____ _____ first and then _____ _____ _____.

M Okay, but first, I will call my father and tell him that we _____ _____ _____.

W Okay. Then I will call the mechanic.

●●
fault 잘못 **mechanic** 정비사

13 대화를 듣고, 대화 내용과 일치하지 <u>않는</u> 것을 고르시오.

M How long _____ _____ _____ English?

W About two years.

M Are you taking an _____ _____ or something?

W No, I study _____ _____ _____ with books.

M Can you read English newspapers?

W No, I can't read newspapers yet. I know the letters but not _____ _____.

M How about _____?

W I'm not _____ _____ _____ either.

M I thought you were really good at speaking.

W _____ _____. I can only say easy things well.

●●
on one's own 혼자, 혼자 힘으로 **letter** 글자
conversation 대화, 회화 **be good at** ~을 잘하다

14 대화를 듣고, 남자의 마지막 말에 이어질 여자의 말로 가장 적절한 것을 고르시오.

W Where _____ _____ _____ _____ now? You seem to be _____ _____ _____.

M I'm _____ _____ _____ to school. I have an exam in about 30 minutes.

W An exam? What exam? Finals are _____.

M English. I missed the test last week because I was _____ _____ _____.

W So are you taking a _____ _____?

M That's right. I'm _____ _____ the test because I _____ _____ enough.

W <u>You'll do fine. Good luck to you.</u>

●●
head 가다, 향하다 **in a hurry** 바쁜, 서두르는
on one's way to ~에 가는 중인 **make-up test** 재시험

15 대화를 듣고, 여자의 마지막 말에 이어질 남자의 말로
가장 적절한 것을 고르시오.

W You almost _____ _____ in
class. What's wrong with you?

M I'm very _____ these days.

W Why?

M I've been _____ _____
_____ _____ to play an online
computer game.

W What game?

M It's called Great Power. It's a very
_____ _____.

W But staying up all night is very _____
to your health, and you can't _____
on your studies.

M Well, I've tried to quit, but I can't stop
thinking about it.

••
fall asleep 잠들다 **stay up all night** 밤을 새다 **harmful** 해로운
concentrate on ~에 집중하다

A 다음을 듣고, 어휘와 우리말 뜻을 쓰시오.

① _____ ⑦ _____

② _____ ⑧ _____

③ _____ ⑨ _____

④ _____ ⑩ _____

⑤ _____ ⑪ _____

⑥ _____ ⑫ _____

B 우리말을 참고하여 빈칸에 알맞은 단어를 쓰시오.

① I am _____ _____ a cake for my father.
아버지께 드릴 케이크를 찾고 있는데요.

② When is the _____ _____ _____ Chicago?
시카고 행 다음 열차는 언제 있습니까?

③ How long _____ _____ _____ to get there?
그곳까지 가려면 얼마나 걸리나요?

④ _____ kept you _____ for so long?
왜 그렇게 오랫동안 잠을 못 잔 거야?

⑤ Why didn't Sandra _____ _____ for today's meeting?
Sandra가 오늘 모임에 왜 나오지 않았지?

⑥ Let's _____ _____ _____ with each other.
서로 연락하고 지냅시다.

⑦ How long _____ _____ _____ English?
영어 공부를 얼마나 오랫동안 하셨나요?

⑧ I've been _____ _____ all night to play an online computer game.
온라인 컴퓨터 게임을 하느라 밤을 새웠거든.

MY SCORE

········· / 15

01 다음을 듣고, 내일의 날씨로 가장 적절한 것을 고르시오.

①  ②

③  ④

⑤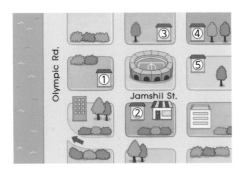

02 대화를 듣고, 남자가 가려고 하는 장소를 고르시오.

03 대화를 듣고, 두 사람이 대화하는 장소로 가장 적절한 곳을 고르시오.

① 공항
② 우체국
③ 경찰서
④ 분실물 센터
⑤ 등산용품 가게

04 대화를 듣고, 두 사람의 관계로 가장 적절한 것을 고르시오.

① boss – secretary
② teacher – student
③ waiter – customer
④ police officer – driver
⑤ flight attendant – passenger

05 대화를 듣고, 여자가 원하는 직업으로 가장 적절한 것을 고르시오.

① 과학자
② 무용가
③ 의사
④ 변호사
⑤ 프로게이머

06 대화를 듣고, 여자가 가지고 있는 만화책이 총 몇 권인지 고르시오.

① 21권
② 22권
③ 23권
④ 24권
⑤ 25권

07 대화를 듣고, 남자의 심정으로 가장 적절한 것을 고르시오.

① upset
② afraid
③ bored
④ pleased
⑤ thankful

08 대화를 듣고, 여자의 마지막 말의 의도로 가장 적절한 것을 고르시오.

① 칭찬
② 거절
③ 부탁
④ 조언
⑤ 후회

09 대화를 듣고, 남자가 일출을 보지 못한 이유로 가장 적절한 것을 고르시오.

① 차가 막혀서
② 날씨가 좋지 않아서
③ 일출 시간을 착각해서
④ 아침에 일찍 일어나지 못해서
⑤ 일출을 볼 수 있는 장소가 없어서

10 대화를 듣고, 무엇에 관한 내용인지 가장 적절한 것을 고르시오.

① 얼음
② 골프공
③ 바깥 날씨
④ 이웃집의 소음
⑤ 지붕 위의 도둑

11 대화를 듣고, 남자가 여자에게 부탁한 일로 가장 적절한 것을 고르시오.

① 숙제 같이 하기
② 노트 빌려 주기
③ 수학 공부 도와주기
④ 영어로 편지 써주기
⑤ 영어 편지 교정 봐주기

12 대화를 듣고, 두 사람이 대화 직후에 할 일로 가장 적절한 것을 고르시오.

① 농구 경기하기
② Bill과 Richard 만나기
③ 티셔츠 주문하기
④ 점심 식사 하기
⑤ 팀 이름 정하기

13 다음을 듣고, 여자가 Jane의 생일 파티에 대해 언급하지 <u>않은</u> 것을 고르시오.

① 파티 요일
② 파티 장소
③ 파티 준비물
④ 초대 인원 수
⑤ 걱정하는 것

14 대화를 듣고, 남자의 마지막 말에 대한 여자의 말로 가장 적절한 것을 고르시오.

① No. Just bring yourself.
② I'm glad you could come.
③ How about some other time?
④ I'd love to, but I have to study.
⑤ You can come later. It finishes at 10 p.m.

15 대화를 듣고, 여자의 마지막 말에 이어질 남자의 말로 가장 적절한 것을 고르시오.

① I'm sure you'll like it.
② Sorry, ma'am. It's not refundable.
③ Yes, there's a one-year guarantee.
④ You can pay with cash or by credit card.
⑤ It's 300 dollars, but you can get a 10% discount.

01 다음을 듣고, 내일의 날씨로 가장 적절한 것을 고르시오.

Good morning. This is Sam Scott with today's weather. I hope all of you _____ _____ _____ the sunshine today, because it's not _____ _____ _____. Tomorrow, the temperature will reach _____ _____ _____ 24℃, and it will be cloudy with _____ _____.

●●
take advantage of ~을 이용하다 **last** 계속되다, 지속하다
temperature 기온 **high** 최고 기온

02 대화를 듣고, 남자가 가려고 하는 장소를 고르시오.

W Hello?

M Sue, this is Jack. Sorry I'm late. I think we're _____.

W Well, where are you now?

M We're calling from the _____ of Olympic Road.

W Okay. _____ _____ down Olympic Road and _____ _____ at Jamshil Street.

M Wait. Let me _____ _____. Go down Olympic Road and make a right at Jamshil Street. Is that right?

W Yes. After that, turn left at the _____ _____. You'll see Olympic Stadium on your left. My apartment is _____ _____ the stadium.

M I got it. Your house is on the _____ _____ of the stadium.

W That's correct. You _____ _____ _____.

M Thanks a lot. See you soon.

●●
entrance 입구 **repeat** 되풀이해서 말하다 **stadium** 경기장
across from ~의 맞은편에 **opposite** 반대편의, 맞은편의
You can't miss it. 쉽게 찾을 거예요.

03 대화를 듣고, 두 사람이 대화하는 장소로 가장 적절한 곳을 고르시오.

W Hello. Can I help you?

M I _____ _____ _____ at the library. Did anyone _____ _____ _____?

W When did you lose it? _____ does it _____ _____ _____?

M I lost it yesterday. It's a brand-new blue backpack.

W _____ _____ _____ first. Is this yours?

M Yes, that's it! Thank you very much.

W You're welcome. You _____ _____ _____ from now on.

●●
backpack 백팩, 배낭 **turn in** ~을 돌려주다
brand-new 완전 새 것의, 신제품의
from now on 앞으로는, 이제부터

04 대화를 듣고, 두 사람의 관계로 가장 적절한 것을 고르시오.

M Linda, could you _____ _____ to Beijing for me?

W Sure. Oh, here are your _____ _____.

M Ms. Graham called again?

W Yes, she wants the _____ _____.

M What did you tell her?

W I told her you'd _____ _____ _____ _____.

M Thanks. I'd better work on that now.

••
financial data 재무자료 **get back to** ~에게 다시 연락하다

05 대화를 듣고, 여자가 원하는 직업으로 가장 적절한 것을 고르시오.

M Jane, what do you _____ _____ _____?

W Well, when I was a child, I wanted to be a scientist.

M Oh, _____ _____ _____.

W But ever since I started high school, I have wanted to be a _____.

M Right! You are _____ _____ _____.

W But my parents _____ _____ to be a doctor.

M That's interesting. My parents have _____ _____ _____ to be a lawyer, but I like to play computer games. So I want to be a _____ _____.

••
ever since ~ 이후로 계속 **expect** 기대하다, 예상하다
lawyer 변호사 **professional gamer** 프로게이머

06 대화를 듣고, 여자가 가지고 있는 만화책이 총 몇 권인지 고르시오.

M What _____ _____ _____ there?

W It's my _____ _____ _____.

M Wow, that's cool.

W I have every book in the *Time Traveler* series _____ _____ the first and third ones.

M _____ _____ _____ _____ in the series?

W There are twenty-five. I've been _____ _____ for two years.

••
collection 수집품

07 대화를 듣고, 남자의 심정으로 가장 적절한 것을 고르시오.

W Brad, are you all right? Your face looks _____.

M My tooth _____ _____ _____ me.

W You'd better _____ _____ _____ about it.

M I've always been _____ _____ dentists. I don't see one unless I _____ _____ _____.

W Really? It's not such a _____ _____. Besides, you'll feel better after he _____ _____ _____ you.

M I know you're right. I'll _____ _____ _____ soon.

••
swollen 부어오른 **bother** 괴롭히다, 신경 쓰이게 하다
dentist 치과 의사, 치과 **fearful** 무서운, 두려운
unless 만약 ~이 아니면 **appointment** 약속, 예약

08 대화를 듣고, 여자의 마지막 말의 의도로 가장 적절한 것을 고르시오.

M Mom, we just _____ _____ _____ milk. Could you get some, please?

W Sure. I will get some _____ _____ _____ _____. What kind of milk do you want?

M I would like to have _____ _____ _____ fat-free milk.

W Sure.

M Wait, Mom. If another kind is _____ _____, I would not mind getting that.

W _____ _____ _____ _____ you are!

•• **run out of** ~이 다 떨어지다 **carton** 곽, 통 **wise** 현명한

09 대화를 듣고, 남자가 일출을 보지 못한 이유로 가장 적절한 것을 고르시오.

W Did you _____ _____ _____ on New Year's morning?

M No, I didn't. I planned to _____ _____, but I was just too tired.

W I thought about _____ _____, but I knew you were celebrating until very late at night.

M Yes, you're right. _____ _____ _____ _____ I could have woken up so early.

W Anyway, you missed an amazing sunrise. It was really nice.

M I'm sorry I missed it. There's always _____ _____ .

•• **sunrise** 일출 **celebrate** 축하하다; 신나게 놀다 **amazing** 놀랄 만한, 굉장한

10 대화를 듣고, 무엇에 관한 내용인지 가장 적절한 것을 고르시오.

M What is that _____ on the roof?

W It sounds like someone is _____ _____ it. It's so loud.

M Look outside! There are huge _____ _____ _____ hitting the ground.

W I've never seen that before. They are _____ _____ _____ golf balls.

M Don't you think this weather is _____?

W You're right. What do you call that?

•• **noise** 소음

11 대화를 듣고, 남자가 여자에게 부탁한 일로 가장 적절한 것을 고르시오.

M What's your _____ _____?

W English. What's _____?

M Math is my favorite. But I'm _____ _____ English. So, I'd like to _____ _____ _____ of you.

W What's that?

M My English teacher _____

_____ _____ _____. I

have to write a letter in English by next

Monday. Will you please _____ my

letter?

W Sure, I'll _____ _____

_____ with you. You help me

_____ _____, and I'll correct

your letter. Deal?

M Okay.

⁕⁕
subject 과목 **be poor at** ~을 잘 못하다
ask a favor of ~에게 부탁하다 **assignment** 과제
proofread 교정보다 **make a deal** 거래하다

12 대화를 듣고, 두 사람이 대화 직후에 할 일로 가장 적절한 것을 고르시오.

W Are you playing in the _____

_____ next week?

M Yes, Bill and Richard _____

_____ _____ me.

W Bill and Richard? Oh, you will make a

tough team.

M _____ _____ _____, we

don't have _____. So we're thinking

of wearing simple black T-shirts. Do you

think that's okay?

W Well, anything with the _____

_____ will be fine. And if it's

possible, put the team name on it.

M Okay. Let's _____ _____ first

and then think about the team name

later.

⁕⁕
tournament 토너먼트, 승자 진출전

13 다음을 듣고, 여자가 Jane의 생일 파티에 대해 언급하지 <u>않은</u> 것을 고르시오.

I'm planning to give Jane a big _____

_____ this Saturday. I prepared

decorations, food, and _____ for

games. I invited thirteen people, and

everyone will _____ _____. I'll ask

everyone _____ _____ _____

Jane about the surprise. But I'm _____

_____ Rachael. Sometimes she can't

_____ _____ _____ _____. I hope

she doesn't tell Jane about the party.

⁕⁕
decoration 장식, 장식품 **prize** 상, 상품
keep a secret 비밀을 지키다

14 대화를 듣고, 남자의 마지막 말에 이어질 여자의 말로 가장 적절한 것을 고르시오.

M Oh, hi, Ruth. How are you?

W Just fine. Listen. I'm having a _____

_____ this Friday night. Would you

like to come?

M Sure. What time?

W Any time _____ _____. Here's

an _____.

M Thank you. Do you want me to _____

_____?

W <u>No. Just bring yourself.</u>

⁕⁕
housewarming party 집들이 **invitation** 초대, 초대장

15 대화를 듣고, 여자의 마지막 말에 이어질 남자의 말로
가장 적절한 것을 고르시오.

M May I help you?

W Yes. I'd like to _____ _____
_____ for my son.

M Do you have _____ _____ in
mind?

W Yes, I'd like to see a smartwatch.

M We have several you _____
_____. How about this one?

W Hmm... Can I see something _____
_____ _____?

M I'm sorry. This is the _____
_____ _____ we have.

W Okay. Does it come with a _____?

M Yes, there's a one-year guarantee.

have ~ in mind ~을 생각하다[염두에 두다] **guarantee** 보증

정답 및 해석 p. 31

A 다음을 듣고, 어휘와 우리말 뜻을 쓰시오.

① _____ _____   ⑦ _____ _____

② _____ _____   ⑧ _____ _____

③ _____ _____   ⑨ _____ _____

④ _____ _____   ⑩ _____ _____

⑤ _____ _____   ⑪ _____ _____

⑥ _____ _____   ⑫ _____ _____

B 우리말을 참고하여 빈칸에 알맞은 단어를 쓰시오.

① My apartment is _____ _____ the stadium.
우리 아파트는 경기장의 맞은편에 있어.

② You can't _____ _____.
쉽게 찾을 거야.

③ My parents have always _____ _____ _____ be a lawyer.
우리 부모님은 항상 내가 변호사가 되기를 바래오셨어.

④ _____ _____ are there in the _____?
그 시리즈가 총 몇 권인데?

⑤ I've been _____ _____ _____ two years.
난 그것들을 2년 동안 모았어.

⑥ I'd like to _____ _____ of you.
너에게 부탁할 게 있어.

⑦ I'm having a _____ _____ this Friday night.
금요일 밤에 집들이를 할 거야.

⑧ Do you _____ anything special _____ _____?
특별히 생각하고 계신 거라도 있습니까?

MY SCORE

.... / 15

01 대화를 듣고, 여자의 손자가 누구인지 고르시오.

①   ②

③   ④

⑤

02 대화를 듣고, 남자가 가려고 하는 장소를 고르시오.

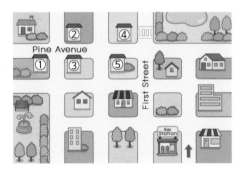

03 대화를 듣고, 두 사람이 고른 점심 메뉴가 아닌 것을 고르시오.

① 스테이크
② 샌드위치
③ 샐러드
④ 아이스크림
⑤ 차

04 대화를 듣고, 두 사람의 관계로 가장 적절한 것을 고르시오.

① 은행원 - 지점장
② 재단사 - 디자이너
③ 세탁소 주인 - 손님
④ 옷가게 직원 - 손님
⑤ 자동차 정비사 - 운전자

05 다음을 듣고, 여자가 오늘 한 일로 언급하지 않은 것을 고르시오.

①  ②

③  ④

⑤

06 대화를 듣고, 남자가 지불해야 할 금액으로 가장 적절한 것을 고르시오.

① $2 ② $3
③ $4 ④ $5
⑤ $6

07 대화를 듣고, 여자의 심정으로 가장 적절한 것을 고르시오.

① sad ② bored
③ pleased ④ nervous
⑤ annoyed

정답 및 해석 p. 32

08 대화를 듣고, 여자가 묻고 있는 것으로 가장 적절한 것을 고르시오.

① 환승역의 위치
② 지하철 환승 방법
③ 목적지까지 소요 시간
④ 목적지까지 가는 방법
⑤ 가장 가까운 지하철역의 위치

09 대화를 듣고, 여자가 화가 난 이유로 가장 적절한 것을 고르시오.

① 미용사가 불친절해서
② 미용실 가격이 너무 비싸서
③ 미용실 예약에 착오가 생겨서
④ 미용실에서 너무 오래 기다려서
⑤ 미용사가 해 준 머리가 마음에 들지 않아서

10 대화를 듣고, 무엇에 관한 내용인지 가장 적절한 것을 고르시오.

① 겨울 축제
② 이상 기후
③ 강릉의 명소
④ 여자의 고향 학교
⑤ 남자의 고향 사람들

11 대화를 듣고, 여자가 남자에게 부탁한 일로 가장 적절한 것을 고르시오.

① 치즈 사 오기
② 사진 찍어 주기
③ 초상화 그려 주기
④ 종탑까지 가는 길 알려 주기
⑤ 자동 사진기 종류 보여 주기

12 대화를 듣고, 남자가 대화 직후에 할 일로 가장 적절한 것을 고르시오.

① 옷을 포장한다.
② 옷을 수선한다.
③ 돈을 거슬러 준다.
④ 여자가 주문한 옷을 보여 준다.
⑤ 여자에게 새로운 옷을 보여 준다.

13 대화를 듣고, 여자가 주말에 한 일과 시간이 일치하지 않는 것을 고르시오.

① 토요일 오전 – 방 청소
② 토요일 오전 – 식물에 물주기
③ 토요일 오후 – 숙제하기
④ 일요일 오전 – 체육관에서 운동하기
⑤ 일요일 오후 – TV 보기

14 대화를 듣고, 남자의 마지막 말에 이어질 여자의 말로 가장 적절한 것을 고르시오.

① I couldn't agree more.
② Okay. We'll see you there.
③ What will you do after graduation?
④ Cheer up. You'll do better the next time.
⑤ Don't worry about it, and thanks for the gift.

15 대화를 듣고, 여자의 마지막 말에 이어질 남자의 말로 가장 적절한 것을 고르시오.

① I wish I had more time.
② Can you wake me up in an hour?
③ I usually go to bed around 10 o'clock.
④ I will try, but it's not going to be easy.
⑤ I just didn't hear the alarm this morning.

01 대화를 듣고, 여자의 손자가 누구인지 고르시오.

W Could you please help me, officer? I
_____ _____ my grandson.

M When did you lose him, ma'am?

W While I was _____ _____
_____ _____ a few minutes ago.

M How old is he, and _____ does he
_____ _____?

W He is five years old, and he has
_____ _____ _____.

M What is he wearing?

W He is wearing _____, a blue shirt,
and yellow _____.

●●
grandson 손자 **curly** 곱슬머리의 **shorts** 반바지

02 대화를 듣고, 남자가 가려고 하는 장소를 고르시오.

M Excuse me. I'm _____ _____ the
West Town Mall on Pine Avenue.

W Let's see… Pine Avenue… Ah, yes, I know.
Take a left at the _____ _____,
and walk up to First Street.

M Up to First Street. Okay. Then, do I turn
left or right?

W Turn right. Go down First Street until
you _____ _____ _____
_____. Just before you come to it,
there's a street _____ _____
_____. That's Pine Avenue.

M That's Pine Avenue. Okay.

W Then, go down Pine Avenue for
two blocks. You'll find it _____
_____ _____.

M Okay. I got it. You're so kind. Thank you.

W No problem.

●●
avenue ~가, 대로 **crosswalk** 횡단보도

03 대화를 듣고, 두 사람이 고른 점심 메뉴가 <u>아닌</u> 것을
고르시오.

W I'm hungry. _____ _____
_____ some steak?

M I want _____ _____ today.
How about going to the Baker's Table? It
serves _____ _____ and salads.

W All right. I'll have an egg sandwich and a
Greek salad then. But the next time, let's
eat what I want to eat.

M Okay. _____ _____. Let's go
to the restaurant. I also _____
_____ _____ some ice cream
and a cup of tea after our meal.

W Well, that _____ _____
_____ me.

●●
fair 공평한 **feel like -ing** ~하고 싶다

04 대화를 듣고, 두 사람의 관계로 가장 적절한 것을 고르
시오.

W Good morning. Can I help you?

M Yes, I bought a _____ here last week, but I don't really like the _____. It looked okay here, but when I got home, it looked _____. I want to _____ _____.

W Yes, sir. Do you have the _____?

M Uh, yeah. Here it is.

W Okay. Uh-oh. Sir, this was _____ _____ when you bought it. I'm sorry, but sale items _____ _____ _____.

M What?

W I'm sorry, but that's the _____ _____.

return 반납하다, 반품하다 **receipt** 영수증

05 다음을 듣고, 여자가 오늘 한 일로 언급하지 <u>않은</u> 것을 고르시오.

What a _____ _____! First, I woke up early and _____ the whole house. Then, I drove to work through a horrible _____ _____. At the office, all I did was type all day because my team's final report is _____ _____. I didn't even take a _____ _____. I was so nervous about not finishing it _____ _____. Finally, after work, I went to the airport to _____ _____ my parents.

vacuum 진공청소기로 청소하다 **horrible** 끔찍한
traffic jam 교통 체증 **due** ~까지 하기로 되어 있는
on time 제시간에 **pick up** (차로) 태우다, 태우러 가다

06 대화를 듣고, 남자가 지불해야 할 금액으로 가장 적절한 것을 고르시오.

M _____ _____? My class is going on a _____ _____.

W Where are you going?

M We're going to the National Museum. Then, we're _____ _____ _____ in the park.

W It sounds like it'll be a lot of fun.

M It really does. And the _____ _____ it will be sunny that day.

W Do you have to _____ _____ that?

M Yes. _____ to the museum is 4 dollars per person, but students can get a _____ % _____.

field trip 견학, 현장 학습   **the National Museum** 국립 박물관
admission 입장료

07 대화를 듣고, 여자의 심정으로 가장 적절한 것을 고르시오.

W Chris, please _____ _____.

M What did you say, Mom?

W _____ _____ the music!

M I just love to turn it up _____.

W There are other people in the house, too. I can't _____ _____ my work because of the music.

M Okay. Then I'll _____ _____ my headphones.

turn down 낮추다, 줄이다 **put on** 입다, 쓰다

TEST 06   51

08 대화를 듣고, 여자가 묻고 있는 것으로 가장 적절한 것을 고르시오.

M Excuse me. Do you need _____ _____?

W Yes, thank you. I'm _____ _____ Yeoksam Station on this map.

M That's easy. Just find the _____ _____. It's line number 2.

W Thank you, sir.

M We're on line number 5 now, which means you must _____ _____ at Yeongdeungpo-gu Office Station.

W You've been _____ _____, sir.

M No problem at all.

09 대화를 듣고, 여자가 화가 난 이유로 가장 적절한 것을 고르시오.

M What's wrong, Linda? You _____ _____.

W I went to the beauty shop, and the person cut my hair _____ _____.

M I don't think it's too short. You look great.

W You're just saying that to _____ _____ _____ _____.

M I'm _____. You look better with short hair. It _____ your face.

W Do you really think so?

M I _____ _____ _____ if I didn't.

highlight 돋보이게 하다

10 대화를 듣고, 무엇에 관한 내용인지 가장 적절한 것을 고르시오.

M Did you hear that Gangneung received 70 centimeters of snow today? It was _____ _____ _____ to the people there.

W 70 centimeters? That's _____. Where I'm from, it's not _____ to get several hundred centimeters of snow _____ _____ _____.

M You _____ _____ _____. I can't imagine that.

W Well, the _____ can be very different in other parts of the world.

M I know, but it's _____ _____ _____ that much snow can fall at one time.

W It's true. Sometimes the schools _____ _____ for several days.

unusual 특이한, 드문 **climate** 기후

11 대화를 듣고, 여자가 남자에게 부탁한 일로 가장 적절한 것을 고르시오.

W _____ _____ _____ taking my picture in front of this tower?

M No, not at all.

W _____ _____ this red button.

M Do I need to _____?

W No, it will focus _____. Please try to get the top of the _____ _____ and also _____ _____ on the left.

M   Okay. I think I can do that. Ready?

_____ _____.

take a picture 사진을 찍다 **focus** 초점을 맞추다
automatically 자동으로

12 대화를 듣고, 남자가 대화 직후에 할 일로 가장 적절한
것을 고르시오.

M   May I help you, madam?

W   I would like to _____ _____ my
suit.

M   Oh, yes. Here you are. Please _____
_____ _____. How do you like
it?

W   It's a bit _____ _____ under the
arms, I think, and around the waist, too.

M   All right. That's easily fixed. How about
the _____?

W   They're fine. _____ _____ is the
total?

M   The total is 300 dollars. Wait here.
I'll _____ _____ _____

_____.

try on (옷·신발 등을) 입어[신어] 보다 **tight** 꼭 끼는
fix 고치다. 수선하다

13 대화를 듣고, 여자가 주말에 한 일과 시간이 일치하지
않는 것을 고르시오.

M   What did you do _____ _____?

W   I did _____ _____ _____

_____ like cleaning my room and
watering the plants in the morning.

M   What did you do in the afternoon?

W   I did my homework.

M   You _____ _____

_____. What about Sunday?

W   I exercised at the gym in the morning and
_____ _____ in the afternoon.
What about you?

M   Well, I _____ _____ the house
and watched TV _____ _____.

W   Do you want to go to the gym together
next week?

M   Yes, I'd love to go there.

water 물을 주다 **sit around** 빈둥거리다

14 대화를 듣고, 남자의 마지막 말에 이어질 여자의 말로
가장 적절한 것을 고르시오.

M   Sandy, I have _____ _____

_____.

W   Really? What is it?

M   It's a gift for your _____.

W   But I graduated from university

_____ _____ _____.

M   I know. It's a _____ graduation
present.

W   You _____ _____ _____ do
this.

M   I'm sorry for _____ your graduation.

W   Don't worry about it, and thanks for the
gift.

graduation 졸업

15 대화를 듣고, 여자의 마지막 말에 이어질 남자의 말로 가장 적절한 것을 고르시오.

W _____ _____ did you go to bed last night?

M I am not sure, but I think it was _____ _____ _____. I had lots of homework to do.

W _____ _____ go to bed early. Do you think you can do your homework _____ _____ _____?

M I am too tired to do it _____ _____ _____.

W I noticed that you _____ _____ these days. Can you _____ _____ _____ take naps anymore?

M I will try, but it's not going to be easy.

● ●
midnight 자정 **take a nap** 낮잠을 자다

A 다음을 듣고, 어휘와 우리말 뜻을 쓰시오.

① _____ _____   ⑦ _____ _____

② _____ _____   ⑧ _____ _____

③ _____ _____   ⑨ _____ _____

④ _____ _____   ⑩ _____ _____

⑤ _____ _____   ⑪ _____ _____

⑥ _____ _____   ⑫ _____ _____

B 우리말을 참고하여 빈칸에 알맞은 단어를 쓰시오.

① He is five years old, and he has _____ _____ _____.
그는 다섯 살이고 짧은 곱슬머리를 하고 있어요.

② I also _____ _____ having some ice cream and a cup of tea after our meal. 그리고 식사 후에는 아이스크림을 먹고 차 한잔을 마시고 싶어.

③ I'm sorry, but sale items can't be _____.
죄송하지만 할인 품목들은 반품이 안 됩니다.

④ At the office, all I did was type all day because my team's final report is
_____ _____.
사무실에서 제가 한 것이라곤 우리 팀 최종 보고서가 내일까지여서 하루 종일 컴퓨터 자판을 두드린 것뿐이었어요.

⑤ I _____ _____ that if I didn't.
그렇지 않으면 너에게 이런 말도 안 하지.

⑥ You must _____ _____.
농담이겠지.

⑦ Well, I _____ _____ the house and _____ TV all day.
음, 난 집에서 빈둥거리며 하루 종일 TV를 봤어.

⑧ You _____ _____ _____ do this.
이렇게 할 필요까진 없는데.

MY SCORE
.... / 15

01 다음을 듣고, 다음 주 화요일의 날씨로 가장 적절한 것을 고르시오.

①

②

③

④

⑤

02 대화를 듣고, 남자가 가려고 하는 장소를 고르시오.

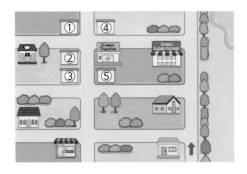

03 대화를 듣고, 두 사람이 대화하는 장소로 가장 적절한 곳을 고르시오.

① 약국
② 경찰서
③ 동물 병원
④ 동물 보호소
⑤ 분실물 센터

04 대화를 듣고, 두 사람의 관계로 가장 적절한 것을 고르시오.

① 경찰관 - 시민
② 연예인 - 매니저
③ 사진 작가 - 모델
④ 매표소 직원 - 손님
⑤ 관광 가이드 - 여행객

05 대화를 듣고, 남자가 가장 좋아하는 배우가 누구인지 고르시오.

06 대화를 듣고, 여자의 운동을 시작하기 전 몸무게로 가장 적절한 것을 고르시오.

① 47kg　　　　② 48kg
③ 51kg　　　　④ 53kg
⑤ 54kg

07 대화를 듣고, 남자의 심정으로 가장 적절한 것을 고르시오.

① 기쁘다　　　　② 피곤하다
③ 재미없다　　　　④ 흥미롭다
⑤ 혼란스럽다

08 대화를 듣고, 여자의 마지막 말의 의도로 가장 적절한 것을 고르시오.

① 불평
② 사과
③ 칭찬
④ 동의
⑤ 감사

09 대화를 듣고, 남자가 화가 난 이유로 가장 적절한 것을 고르시오.

① 여자가 짜증을 내서
② 라디오를 켤 수 없어서
③ 몸을 움직일 수 없어서
④ 교통 체증이 너무 심해서
⑤ 부모님을 만나 뵐 수 없어서

10 대화를 듣고, 남자가 병원을 방문한 목적으로 가장 적절한 것을 고르시오.

① 약을 처방 받기 위해서
② 건강검진을 받기 위해서
③ 입원 환자를 만나기 위해서
④ 엘리베이터를 수리하기 위해서
⑤ 부러진 다리를 치료받기 위해서

11 대화를 듣고, 여자가 영어 숙제에 대해 걱정하는 것으로 가장 적절한 것을 고르시오.

① 조사해야 할 자료가 많다.
② 숙제를 영어로 작성해야 한다.
③ 반 친구들 앞에서 발표해야 한다.
④ 셰익스피어에 관한 지식이 전혀 없다.
⑤ 팀원들의 의견을 하나로 모아야 한다.

12 대화를 듣고, 남자의 충고를 들은 여자가 할 일로 가장 적절한 것을 고르시오.

① 룸메이트에게 편지를 쓴다.
② 룸메이트와 옷을 사러 간다.
③ 룸메이트를 바꿔달라고 말한다.
④ 룸메이트와 문제에 대해 이야기한다.
⑤ 룸메이트 없이 혼자 방을 쓰기로 한다.

13 대화를 듣고, 남자의 이야기에서 친구들이 아픈 소년을 위해 한 일로 가장 적절한 것을 고르시오.

① 헌혈을 해 주었다.
② 수술비를 모금해 주었다.
③ 깜짝 파티를 열어 주었다.
④ 자신들도 머리를 삭발했다.
⑤ 소년의 머리카락을 잘라 주었다.

14 대화를 듣고, 남자의 마지막 말에 이어질 여자의 말로 가장 적절한 것을 고르시오.

① I'm sorry to hear that.
② No, thanks. It tastes terrible.
③ My father is a profess of history.
④ Thanks. I'm glad you think it's nice.
⑤ Thanks. I enjoyed the meal very much.

15 대화를 듣고, 여자의 마지막 말에 이어질 남자의 말로 가장 적절한 것을 고르시오.

① I've worked in a plant for five years.
② Oh, my God. You've killed a lot of plants.
③ If you like, I will tell you my special secret.
④ Well, I'm sure you have a talent for gardening.
⑤ That's great. I envy your ability to raise animals.

01 다음을 듣고, 다음 주 화요일의 날씨로 가장 적절한 것을 고르시오.

Good evening. This is Max Morris from CNB. Here is the _____ _____ for next week. On Monday, it is going to snow _____ _____ _____. Tuesday won't see _____ _____ because of the cloudy skies. On Wednesday, we will have _____ _____, but it will be cold. It'll be sunny and _____ _____ _____ on Thursday and Friday. Thank you.

02 대화를 듣고, 남자가 가려고 하는 장소를 고르시오.

M Excuse me. I think I'm _____.

W What are you looking for?

M I'd like to go to the city library. _____ _____ _____ _____ how to get there, please?

W Well... It is a little far from here, but I think you can go _____ _____.

M I _____ _____ _____ walking there.

W Oh, then go straight two blocks until you get to Green Supermarket. _____ _____ just after the supermarket, and _____ _____ _____.

M After Green Supermarket, make a left and go straight.

W Yes, it's on your right. It is _____ _____ the Green Theater. You _____ _____ _____.

M Thank you, ma'am.

W My pleasure. Have a nice day.

on foot 걸어서, 도보로

03 대화를 듣고, 두 사람이 대화하는 장소로 가장 적절한 곳을 고르시오.

W What _____ _____ _____ the problem with your pet?

M Well, every time I give something to Spot, he only eats a little, and he has _____, too.

W I see. How long has he had these _____?

M I guess for about a week or so.

W You _____ _____ _____ him to my office _____.

M _____ _____ with him? Is he really sick?

W Well... You _____ _____ _____ Spot here for a couple of days.

M Okay. Please _____ _____ _____ him.

diarrhea 설사 **symptom** 증상

04 대화를 듣고, 두 사람의 관계로 가장 적절한 것을 고르시오.

W Now, _____ _____ on our left is John Paul Jones's house.

M Is it open to the _____?

W Yes. You can visit it after we finish this tour _____ _____ _____.

M There's so much _____ in this city.

W If you like historical buildings, you _____ _____ the Banks Museum.

M What's that?

W It's an open-air museum _____ _____ _____.

M It sounds interesting.

public 일반 사람들, 대중 **historical** 역사적인
open-air 옥외의, 야외의

05 대화를 듣고, 남자가 가장 좋아하는 배우가 누구인지 고르시오.

M I can't believe it! That's my _____ _____ over there.

W Where?

M See? He's sitting with his girlfriend at a _____ _____ _____.

W Do you mean the _____ _____ _____?

M No, the one wearing the _____ and _____.

W Oh, I see him. He's eating a steak, right?

M That's him. I'm going to ask him for _____ _____.

W Can you get one for me, too?

autograph 사인

06 대화를 듣고, 여자의 운동을 시작하기 전 몸무게로 가장 적절한 것을 고르시오.

M So I hear you're _____ _____ these days.

W Yeah. I feel great.

M Your skin seems to have _____ _____, too.

W I know. I'm so happy.

M Have you _____ _____?

W No. _____ _____ _____, I recently gained 3 kilograms.

M You're _____.

W No. It's all muscle though. Now I _____ 51 kilograms.

work out 운동하다 **lose weight** 살이 빠지다, 체중이 줄다
believe it or not 믿거나 말거나, 믿기 힘들겠지만 **muscle** 근육

07 대화를 듣고, 남자의 심정으로 가장 적절한 것을 고르시오.

M Do you like football?

W _____ _____. If you mean _____, then the answer is yes. If you mean _____ _____, the answer is no.

M Now I'm _____.

W In England, they _____ _____ "_____."

M To me, the word "football" is strange. _____, do you like soccer?

W Oh, yes. I like soccer very much.

That depends. 상황에 따라 다르다.
confused 혼란스러운, 헷갈리는

08 대화를 듣고, 여자의 마지막 말의 의도로 가장 적절한 것을 고르시오.

M Do you live _____ _____?

W Yes, I live in one of those _____ _____ _____. What about you?

M Oh, I'm staying with a family near the station.

W Are you _____ _____?

M _____ _____. I'm here to study English. I'm from Korea.

W I don't think you need to study English _____. Your English is _____ _____.

on vacation 휴가 중인

09 대화를 듣고, 남자가 화가 난 이유로 가장 적절한 것을 고르시오.

M Oh, no, another traffic jam. I _____ _____ this.

W Take it easy, George. Don't be upset _____ _____ _____.

M It just seems it _____ _____ _____ to get everywhere.

W Let's _____ _____ the radio to see how long it will take.

M There's a traffic jam every year _____ _____ _____.

W Just relax. I'm sure the traffic will move soon. Do you see? It's _____ _____ _____ now.

stand 참다, 견디다 **Take it easy.** 진정해. **it seems** ~인 것 같다
turn on 켜다 **relax** 쉬다, 긴장을 풀다

10 대화를 듣고, 남자가 병원을 방문한 목적으로 가장 적절한 것을 고르시오.

W Hello, sir. What can I _____ _____ _____?

M I'm here to _____ _____ _____.

W What's the name?

M Edward Cane. He came in with a _____ _____.

W Oh, yes. Mr. Cane is _____ _____ _____ _____.

M Thank you.

patient 환자 **broken leg** 골절된 다리 **floor** (건물의) 층

11 대화를 듣고, 여자가 영어 숙제에 대해 걱정하는 것으로 가장 적절한 것을 고르시오.

M That is _____ _____ we have for English class.

W Interesting? It's going to be _____ _____ _____ _____.

M What's so hard about it? We just have to do some research on Shakespeare and _____ _____ _____ in class.

W _____ _____ _____ isn't so hard. But we have to give a speech in class.

M That actually sounds like fun to me.

W That's _____ _____ _____. But it doesn't seem like fun to me.

research 조사 **speech** 연설, 이야기

12 대화를 듣고, 남자의 충고를 들은 여자가 할 일로 가장 적절한 것을 고르시오.

M How are _____ _____ with you and your roommate?

W Not very well. She's the _____ _____ I've ever had.

M It can't be that bad. _____ _____ with your new roommate?

W She always _____ _____ _____ at night and throws her clothes and shoes everywhere.

M I know how you feel. I _____ _____ _____ a roommate like that. Why don't you have a heart-to-heart chat with her?

W I will try. I would like to _____ _____ _____ with her.

M I think that's a good idea. I hope _____ _____ _____.

• •
heart-to-heart 마음을 터놓고 **talk things out** 대화로 풀다

13 대화를 듣고, 남자의 이야기에서 친구들이 아픈 소년을 위해 한 일로 가장 적절한 것을 고르시오.

M I heard a _____ _____ on the radio.

W What was it about?

M A boy who was _____ _____ _____. The harmful effects of the medication caused the boy to _____ _____ _____ _____ and become bald. So the once cheerful boy became very _____.

W What a shame!

M Guess what? All his classmates went to the barber and _____ _____ _____ _____. Since then, the boy has regained his cheerfulness.

W _____ _____ _____ _____ !

• •
heartwarming 마음이 따뜻해지는 **suffer from** ~로 고통 받다
cancer 암 **medication** 약, 약물 치료 **bald** 대머리의
shame 애석한 일, 유감스러운 일 **barber** 이발사, 이발소
shave 깎다, 면도하다 **regain** 회복하다

14 대화를 듣고, 남자의 마지막 말에 이어질 여자의 말로 가장 적절한 것을 고르시오.

M Thank you for inviting me to your _____ _____.

W Thank you for coming.

M When did you _____ _____ ?

W I moved in a month ago.

M Well, I have to say your house looks fabulous. Did you _____ and _____ it yourself?

W Yes, I did. It took me quite a lot of time.

M Well, you have _____ _____ _____ in interior decorating. You're better than a professional designer.

W Thanks. I'm glad you think it's nice.

• •
move in 이사 오다 **furnish** 가구를 놓다[비치하다]
have good taste in ~에 뛰어난 안목이 있다
interior decorating 실내 장식

15 대화를 듣고, 여자의 마지막 말에 이어질 남자의 말로 가장 적절한 것을 고르시오.

M You are good at _____ _____.
    What's your _____?

W If I had one, I'd tell you. Maybe it's just
    luck.

M I don't understand it! I've _____
    _____ with mine, but they are all still
    dying. I _____ _____ _____.

W But I don't do _____ _____.
    I just know when they need to _____
    _____ and where they get the best
    sun in the house.

M <u>Well, I'm sure you have a talent for</u>
    <u>gardening.</u>

••
envy 부러워하다 **raise** 키우다, 기르다

A 다음을 듣고, 어휘와 우리말 뜻을 쓰시오.

① _____ _____

② _____ _____

③ _____ _____

④ _____ _____

⑤ _____ _____

⑥ _____ _____

⑦ _____ _____

⑧ _____ _____

⑨ _____ _____

⑩ _____ _____

⑪ _____ _____

⑫ _____ _____

B 우리말을 참고하여 빈칸에 알맞은 단어를 쓰시오.

① I _____ _____ _____ walking there.
걸어가도 상관 없어요.

② You had better leave Spot here for _____ _____ _____
days. Spot을 이곳에 이틀 정도 두고 가시는 것이 좋겠어요.

③ Please _____ good _____ _____ him.
잘 좀 보살펴 주세요.

④ _____ _____ _____ _____, I recently gained 3
kilograms. 믿거나 말거나, 최근 3킬로그램이 늘었어.

⑤ Are you _____ _____?
휴가 중이신가요?

⑥ Let's _____ _____ the radio to see how long it will take.
얼마나 오래 걸릴지 보기 위해 라디오를 켜보자.

⑦ She's _____ _____ _____ I've ever had.
그녀는 지금까지 내가 겪어본 최악의 룸메이트야.

⑧ Well, you have such _____ _____ in interior decorating.
음, 넌 실내 장식에 뛰어난 안목이 있구나.

MY SCORE

_____ / 15

01 다음을 듣고, 월요일 아침의 날씨로 가장 적절한 것을 고르시오.

①    ②

③    ④

⑤

02 대화를 듣고, 남자가 가려고 하는 장소를 고르시오.

03 대화를 듣고, 두 사람이 대화하는 장소로 가장 적절한 곳을 고르시오.

① home
② office
③ coffee shop
④ computer store
⑤ stationery store

04 대화를 듣고, 두 사람의 관계로 가장 적절한 것을 고르시오.

① friend - friend
② clerk - customer
③ baker - customer
④ bus driver - passenger
⑤ plumber - homeowner

05 대화를 듣고, 여자의 모습 중 최근에 달라진 부분을 고르시오.

06 대화를 듣고, 올해가 몇 년도인지 고르시오.

① 2000년   ② 2010년
③ 2012년   ④ 2022년
⑤ 2025년

07 대화를 듣고, 남자가 한국 문화에 대해 어떻게 생각하는지 고르시오.

① 지루하다   ② 흥미롭다
③ 이상하다   ④ 독특하다
⑤ 관심 없다

08 대화를 듣고, 남자가 하는 일로 가장 적절한 것을 고르시오.

① 도넛 만들기
② 도넛 판매하기
③ 도넛 포장하기
④ 도넛 배달하기
⑤ 도넛 가게 청소하기

12 대화를 듣고, 두 사람이 대화 직후에 할 일로 가장 적절한 것을 고르시오.

① 커피 마시기
② 잔돈 바꾸기
③ 약속 정하기
④ 저녁 식사 하기
⑤ 식당 예약 하기

09 대화를 듣고, 창문이 열리지 않는 이유로 가장 적절한 것을 고르시오.

① 창문이 고장 나서
② 밖이 너무 추워서
③ 창문이 오래 되어서
④ 방 안이 너무 추워서
⑤ 밖에서 창문을 잠가 두어서

13 대화를 듣고, TV 채널과 프로그램이 일치하는 것을 고르시오.

① Channel 4 - *The Animal Kingdom*
② Channel 5 - Talk show
③ Channel 7 - Basketball
④ Channel 8 - *Frozen*
⑤ Channel 11 - *Spiderman*

10 대화를 듣고, 여자의 증상으로 가장 적절한 것을 고르시오.

① 콧물
② 두통
③ 변비
④ 설사
⑤ 구토

14 대화를 듣고, 남자의 마지막 말에 이어질 여자의 말로 가장 적절한 것을 고르시오.

① Oh, yes. Every day.
② I am a night person.
③ I hate getting up early.
④ I usually go to school by bus.
⑤ Yes, I try to exercise every day.

11 대화를 듣고, 여자가 남자에게 해 준 조언으로 가장 적절한 것을 고르시오.

① 운동을 해라.
② 휴식을 취해라.
③ 취미를 가져라.
④ 공부를 열심히 해라.
⑤ 선생님께 도움을 요청해라.

15 대화를 듣고, 여자의 마지막 말에 이어질 남자의 말로 가장 적절한 것을 고르시오.

① What a bad sister you are!
② Your son should be punished.
③ Then everything is all right now.
④ I'm really sorry about your sister.
⑤ I think you should apologize to her.

01 다음을 듣고, 월요일 아침의 날씨로 가장 적절한 것을 고르시오.

This is the weather channel. We're _____ _____ to the weekend. It's going to be a good night heading into tonight. _____ _____ _____ outside. You can see clear skies and feel the _____ _____. This will continue for the next 24 hours. However, _____ _____ Sunday morning, we are going to get _____ _____. It is going to affect your Monday morning _____, so please _____ _____ _____ with you.

look ahead to ~을 앞두다 take a look 한번 보다 rainfall 강우
affect 영향을 미치다 commute 통근, 출퇴근

02 대화를 듣고, 남자가 가려고 하는 장소를 고르시오.

M Wow! You got a _____ _____, didn't you? It looks great.

W I got it as a _____ _____ from my father.

M Where did he buy it?

W At World Store on Main Street.

M Please tell me _____ _____ _____.

W You know where Main Street is. _____ _____ _____ Main Street and turn left.

M Turn left on Main Street?

W Right. Walk down the street, and you'll see a _____ _____ on your right. World Store is _____ it.

stationery store 문구점

03 대화를 듣고, 두 사람이 대화하는 장소로 가장 적절한 곳을 고르시오.

M Have you _____ _____ that new data?

W Almost. What should I do with the _____ when it's _____?

M Make several copies and _____ _____ to the people on this list.

W Okay, but the copier _____ _____ _____ right now. Do I need to print these right away?

M The meeting will be in _____ _____ _____. You can finish them before the meeting.

W Sure. I can do that, sir.

input 입력하다 printout 인쇄된 것, 인쇄물 distribute 나누어주다,
분배하다 copier 복사기 service 점검하다, 수리하다

04 대화를 듣고, 두 사람의 관계로 가장 적절한 것을 고르시오.

M What _____ _____ _____ the problem?

W The sink in the bathroom _____ _____.

M That shouldn't be too difficult. I'll just
_____ _____ the pipe for you.

W Thank you. While you're working on
it, could you _____ _____
_____, too?

M Is the bathtub drain clogged _____
_____?

W Not completely, but it drains _____
_____.

M I see. Well, I'll take a look at it.

○○
be clogged 막히다 **tub** 욕조 **drain** 배수구: 물이 빠지다
awfully 몹시, 대단히

05 대화를 듣고, 여자의 모습 중 최근에 달라진 부분을
고르시오.

W Don't you notice _____ _____
about me?

M Uh, I don't know. Did you get a _____
_____?

W No, guess again.

M Aha! I know. It's your dress. That's a new
dress, _____ _____?

W I've had this dress _____ _____.
Don't tell me you don't _____ it.

M Oh, of course. I knew that. Ah... how
about a _____?

W Look deep into my eyes.

M Your glasses are _____! When did
you get _____ _____?

○○
notice 알아채다 **haircut** 이발, 머리 모양 **for ages** 오랫동안
recognize 알아보다 **contact lenses** 콘택트렌즈

06 대화를 듣고, 올해가 몇 년도인지 고르시오.

M Carrie, is that you?

W James? _____ _____ has it
been?

M It's been too long. _____ _____
_____ _____?

W Very well. Thanks. When was the
_____ _____ we saw each
other?

M At our high school _____, I think. We
were the class of _____.

W It has already been 10 years since then.
_____ _____, doesn't it?

○○
the class of 2012 2012년 졸업반

07 대화를 듣고, 남자가 한국 문화에 대해 어떻게 생각하
는지 고르시오.

W Have you watched the video that I
_____?

M I never knew Korean _____
_____ was so beautiful.

W There is a lot you don't know about
Korea.

M You're right. Where can I learn more
about _____ _____?

W We could go to the _____.

M Let's go now. I want to learn more.

W _____ _____. It's 10:00 p.m. It's
already closed. You'll have to _____
_____ _____ to go there.

M Okay. Maybe I can find some information
_____ _____ _____.

○○
folk dancing 민속춤 **information** 정보

08 대화를 듣고, 남자가 하는 일로 가장 적절한 것을 고르시오.

W So what do you do _____ _____ _____?

M I make donuts at a donut shop.

W _____ _____! Do you ever eat on the job?

M I _____ _____ in the beginning, but now I'm kind of _____ _____ donuts.

W I understand. You _____ _____ _____ _____ what you do.

M I'm not bad. _____ _____ _____ this job for several years now.

•• **for a living** 생계를 위해 **on the job** 근무 중에
be tired of ~에 질리다

---

09 대화를 듣고, 창문이 열리지 <u>않는</u> 이유로 가장 적절한 것을 고르시오.

W Please open the window. It's _____ _____ _____.

M All right. It's... uh... stuck. It must be very _____ _____ today.

W Let me _____ _____ _____ _____. You're right. It's stuck. It must be _____.

M We may have to wait until the weather _____ _____ to open it.

W I can't _____ _____ _____. I'm going to the library where the _____ _____ _____.

M Wait for me. I'll go with you.

•• **give it a try** 한번 해 보다 **frozen** 얼어붙은

---

10 대화를 듣고, 여자의 증상으로 가장 적절한 것을 고르시오.

W I've been running to the bathroom _____ _____.

M What's wrong? Are you sick?

W I ate potato salad for lunch, and it really _____ _____ _____.

M You mean...

W That's right. _____.

M Try to relax. It will _____ _____.

•• **upset one's stomach** 배탈이 나게 하다 **eventually** 결국

---

11 대화를 듣고, 여자가 남자에게 해 준 조언으로 가장 적절한 것을 고르시오.

M Aw, I'm so upset!

W What are you _____ _____?

M I _____ _____ _____ on the midterm exam. Now I am very worried and upset.

W Listen. You _____ _____ _____ big things _____ _____ little things.

M No, it's not a little thing. It's _____ to me.

W _____ _____ _____ . You will get a good grade because you always study hard.

M But I _____ _____ _____ if I don't get a good grade.

W You _____ _____ _____ for the midterm and it's over. You should stop thinking about it and _____ _____ _____ .

●●
tend to ~하는 경향이 있다 **grade** 성적 **serious** 심각한, 진지한

12 대화를 듣고, 두 사람이 대화 직후에 할 일로 가장 적절한 것을 고르시오.

M That was a _____ _____ .

W I thought you would like that _____ .

M We should go there again.

W Of course. Whenever you want to go, _____ _____ _____ .

M Would you like _____ _____ _____ _____ ?

W Yes, but I don't have _____ _____ .

M Don't worry. I have enough.

W Thank you. The next time I'll _____ _____ .

●●
change 잔돈 **treat** 한턱 내다

13 대화를 듣고, TV 채널과 프로그램이 일치하는 것을 고르시오.

W What's _____ _____ ? Is there anything interesting?

M I don't know. I'm _____ _____ on channel 5.

W I hate sports. _____ _____ _____ a talk show on channel 7?

M That's too _____ .

W _____ _____ _____ the TV programs. Oh! *Frozen* is showing on channel 4, *Spiderman* is on channel 11, and *The Animal Kingdom* is on channel 8.

M Then let's watch *Frozen*. I _____ _____ _____ .

W Okay.

14 대화를 듣고, 남자의 마지막 말에 이어질 여자의 말로 가장 적절한 것을 고르시오.

M _____ _____ do you get up?

W I get up around six.

M What _____ _____ _____ ? Does your mother wake you up?

M No. My alarm clock wakes me up.

M Do you get up _____ ?

W No, I _____ _____ _____ for a few minutes because it takes me a while to _____ _____ .

M Is this your _____ _____ ?

W Oh, yes. Every day.

●●
immediately 곧, 즉시 **lie in bed** 침대에 누워 있다
get motivated 의욕이 생기다 **routine** 일상

15 대화를 듣고, 여자의 마지막 말에 이어질 남자의 말로
가장 적절한 것을 고르시오.

W I've been _____ _____

_____.

M What happened?

W I _____ _____ my sister. I felt

terrible about it later.

M Why did you _____?

W My son Sam did _____ _____,

and I _____ him. My sister defended

Sam. I told her _____ _____

_____.

M What did your sister say?

W She _____. Then, of course, I

apologized, too.

M <u>Then everything is all right now.</u>

●●
quarrel 말다툼하다 **argue** 논쟁하다 **punish** 벌 주다
defend 방어하다 **apologize** 사과하다

A 다음을 듣고, 어휘와 우리말 뜻을 쓰시오.

① _____ ⑦ _____
② _____ ⑧ _____
③ _____ ⑨ _____
④ _____ ⑩ _____
⑤ _____ ⑪ _____
⑥ _____ ⑫ _____

B 우리말을 참고하여 빈칸에 알맞은 단어를 쓰시오.

① The meeting will be in _____ _____ _____.
회의는 30분 후에 있어요.

② When was _____ _____ _____ we saw each other?
우리가 서로 마지막으로 본 것이 언제였지?

③ _____ _____, doesn't it?
시간 정말 빠르다, 그렇지 않니?

④ What do you do _____ _____ _____?
어떤 일을 하시나요?

⑤ Let me _____ _____ a _____.
내가 한번 해 볼게.

⑥ I didn't _____ _____ on the midterm exam.
중간고사를 잘 못 봤어.

⑦ You _____ _____ make big things _____ _____
little things. 너는 작은 일을 크게 만드는 경향이 있어.

⑧ The next time, I'll _____ _____.
다음엔 제가 살게요.

MY SCORE

.... / 15

01 대화를 듣고, 남자가 구입할 의상으로 가장 적절한 것을 고르시오.

①

②

③

④

⑤

02 대화를 듣고, 남자가 가려고 하는 장소를 고르시오.

03 대화를 듣고, 두 사람이 대화하는 장소로 가장 적절한 곳을 고르시오.

① shoe store
② beauty salon
③ jewelry store
④ grocery store
⑤ movie theater

04 대화를 듣고, 두 사람의 관계로 가장 적절한 것을 고르시오.

① mother - son
② husband - wife
③ teacher - student
④ boyfriend - girlfriend
⑤ travel agent - customer

05 대화를 듣고, 여자가 여가 시간에 하는 일로 가장 적절한 것을 고르시오.

① 식물 기르기
② 자원봉사하기
③ 과학 만화 읽기
④ 공원에서 쓰레기 줍기
⑤ 환경 다큐멘터리 시청하기

06 다음을 듣고, 내일의 최고 기온으로 가장 적절한 것을 고르시오.

① 10℃
② 12℃
③ 15℃
④ 20℃
⑤ 25℃

07 대화를 듣고, 남자의 심정으로 가장 적절한 것을 고르시오.

① bored
② nervous
③ unhappy
④ confident
⑤ disappointed

08 대화를 듣고, 남자의 마지막 말의 의도로 가장 적절한 것을 고르시오.

① 사과
② 동의
③ 조언
④ 감사
⑤ 거절

09 대화를 듣고, 남자가 난처해하는 이유로 가장 적절한 것을 고르시오.

① 집에 일찍 가야 해서
② 여자의 질문을 이해하지 못해서
③ 저녁 식사 초대에 응하고 싶지 않아서
④ 요리 방법을 몰라 대답해 줄 수 없어서
⑤ 음식에 대해 솔직하게 말하기 어려워서

10 대화를 듣고, 여자가 이용한 교통수단으로 가장 적절한 것을 고르시오.

① bus
② train
③ ferry
④ plane
⑤ subway

11 대화를 듣고, 남자가 여자에게 해 준 조언으로 가장 적절한 것을 고르시오.

① 다이어트 하기
② 성형 수술 하기
③ 미용 기술 배우기
④ 머리 모양 바꾸기
⑤ 건강에 좋은 음식 먹기

12 대화를 듣고, 대화에서 credits가 의미하는 것으로 가장 적절한 것을 고르시오.

① 영화 제공 회사
② 영화의 관람 등급
③ 영화의 평가 점수
④ 영화에 투자한 사람들의 명단
⑤ 영화 제작에 도움을 준 사람들의 명단

13 대화를 듣고, 두 사람이 이번 주말에 가려고 하는 곳을 고르시오.

① 시장
② 백화점
③ 이마트
④ 월마트
⑤ 볼링장

14 대화를 듣고, 남자의 마지막 말에 이어질 여자의 말로 가장 적절한 것을 고르시오.

① Of course not! I promise.
② I forget things all the time.
③ It was nice to see you again.
④ Let's talk about something else.
⑤ I've always wanted to study abroad.

15 대화를 듣고, 여자의 마지막 말에 이어질 남자의 말로 가장 적절한 것을 고르시오.

① I have something in my eye.
② Really? I have double vision.
③ My sister had good eyesight.
④ The glasses look good on you.
⑤ Then you'd better see a doctor.

01 대화를 듣고, 남자가 구입할 의상으로 가장 적절한 것을 고르시오.

M Mom, can I _____ a Halloween _____ online?

W Which one?

M I want _____ a Spiderman _____ skeleton costume.

W Let me see. I like _____, but I don't think they have _____ _____ _____ for you. These are all for small kids.

M I can _____ _____. How about this ghost?

W It looks _____ _____.

M I like it, but I think I have a _____ _____ at home. I want to try a _____ _____ this year.

W I think a pirate one _____ _____ _____.

order 주문하다 costume 의상 either A or B A나 B 중 하나
skeleton 해골 ghost 유령 pirate 해적

02 대화를 듣고, 남자가 가려고 하는 장소를 고르시오.

M Hello. May I speak to Ana?

W _____ _____ _____. Who am I speaking to?

M It's Tom. Ana, do you remember that strawberry pie you gave me _____ _____ _____? Where did you buy it?

W At Jimmy's Bakery. Why?

M Oh, it was very delicious. So I want to buy one for my mother. Where is it _____?

W It's just _____ _____ _____ from our school. It's near the CLJ English Institute.

M I know where that is. If I am _____ _____ _____, should I go left or right?

W Go left. You can't miss it. Just _____ _____ _____.

M Thanks, Ana.

the other day 지난번에 institute 학회, 연구소; 학원

03 대화를 듣고, 두 사람이 대화하는 장소로 가장 적절한 곳을 고르시오.

W Good evening. Can I help you, sir?

M Yes. May I take a look at the _____ _____ _____ over there?

W Do you mean the one _____ _____ _____?

M No, the second one on the right.

W That's a very good bracelet, sir. It's really _____ _____ _____.

M How much is it?

W The _____ is 125 dollars. It's _____ _____. You can get 20% _____.

M Good. I'd like to have it.

bracelet 팔찌 on display 전시된, 진열된

04 대화를 듣고, 두 사람의 관계로 가장 적절한 고르시오.

W Honey, it's our _____ _____

_____ .

M Yes, we should take a _____

_____ .

W Really? Where do you _____

_____ _____ ? Can we go to

Hawaii?

M Hawaii… That's very expensive and

_____ _____ .

W I know, but I really want to go there.

Maybe someday…

M Well… _____ _____ going to

Phuket? It'll be _____ _____

and _____ _____ Hawaii.

W Really? That's _____ _____ that

I want to go to. You're so wonderful.

M I'm happy you like it.

●●
wedding anniversary 결혼기념일

05 대화를 듣고, 여자가 여가 시간에 하는 일로 가장 적절한 것을 고르시오.

M What do you do in your _____

_____ ?

W I volunteer by teaching children about

_____ _____ .

M That's incredible! Is it _____ ?

W Oh, yes. They love to learn about the

_____ , _____ , and _____ .

M Well, the children are the future.

W That is _____ _____ .

●●
spare time 여가 시간 **volunteer** 자원봉사하다 **environmental**
환경의 **rewarding** 보람 있는 **certainly** 확실히. 틀림없이

06 다음을 듣고, 내일의 최고 기온으로 가장 적절한 것을 고르시오.

Good morning. This is Ann Smith here with

your _____ _____ _____ .

Right now, it is 25℃ and clear. But toward

the end of the day, it will start to _____

_____ , and we can expect _____

_____ _____ 12℃ tonight.

Tomorrow, the temperature will only reach

_____ _____ _____ 20℃,

and we will see some rain in the afternoon.

Next week, we can _____ _____

_____ , and the temperatures will be in

the high 20s to low 10s.

●●
cool off 서늘해지다 **low** 최저 기온

07 대화를 듣고, 남자의 심정으로 가장 적절한 것을 고르시오.

W Don, could you _____

_____ _____ ?

M Why don't you look at the clock

_____ ?

W Why are you in _____ _____

_____ _____ ?

M I guess I'm just tired. I'm sorry.

W You'd better _____ _____

_____ . That'll make you feel better.

M I wish _____ _____ . But I

have so many _____ _____

_____ .

08 대화를 듣고, 남자의 마지막 말의 의도로 가장 적절한 것을 고르시오.

W Don't you have a _____ _____ tomorrow?

M Yes, I do.

W Then you should study now.

M Just wait. I've _____ _____ this level.

W When are you _____ _____ _____ that computer game?

M After this level, there is only one more level.

W Tony, you can play the game _____ you want to do after the test is _____. Please, study first.

M Okay, Mom. I _____ _____ start studying before it's _____ _____.

09 대화를 듣고, 남자가 난처해하는 이유로 가장 적절한 것을 고르시오.

W I want to thank you all for _____ _____ _____. Did you like the soup, Dick?

M Uh... it was... uh... good.

W Are you sure? You _____ _____.

M I can see you put _____ _____ _____ _____ into it. Thank you, but...

W But what?

M It needed just a little more _____. Then it _____ _____ _____ _____.

W Were you disappointed?

M No. Please _____ _____ _____. I really enjoyed the food.

uncertain 불확실한 **put time into** ~에 시간을 투자하다
offend 기분 상하게 하다

10 대화를 듣고, 여자가 이용한 교통수단으로 가장 적절한 것을 고르시오.

M I heard you went to Japan for the _____.

W That's right. I went to Tokyo _____ _____ _____.

M What was it like?

W It was great. _____ _____ are always interesting.

M How did you get there, _____ _____ or _____ _____?

W You know, I prefer _____ _____.

for a change 기분 전환으로 **foreign country** 외국
ferry 페리, 여객선

11 대화를 듣고, 남자가 여자에게 해 준 조언으로 가장 적절한 것을 고르시오.

W I'm thinking about having _____ _____.

M Are you sure? I don't understand. You look great just _____ _____ _____.

W Well, I'm pleased with my eyes and nose, but I'm not _____ _____ my lips. They're too thin.

M That's _____. You've got a nice face that makes people _____ _____. Having plastic surgery is not a good idea.

W Do you really _____ _____?

M Yes. But if you want to _____ _____ about yourself, why don't you change your _____?

W Maybe I should. Thanks for _____ _____.

●●
be pleased with ~에 기뻐하다, ~에 만족하다
be satisfied with ~에 만족하다 **ridiculous** 웃기는, 말도 안 되는
advice 충고, 조언

12 대화를 듣고, 대화에서 credits가 의미하는 것으로 가장 적절한 것을 고르시오.

M Come on. Let's go, the movie's over.

W No, wait. I want to see the credits right _____ _____ _____ _____.

M The credits?

W The credits are the _____ _____ _____ who help make a film, record, or television program.

M Oh, I know _____ _____ _____. But do you really want to see them?

W My sister's in the _____ _____, and she worked on this movie.

M Really? What does she do?

W She's a costume designer. Look. _____ _____ _____. That's her name just coming up now.

13 대화를 듣고, 두 사람이 이번 주말에 가려고 하는 곳을 고르시오.

M Where did you buy that dress?

W Do you like it? I got it at the _____ _____ _____.

M Where is it?

W It's just _____ _____ _____ from that E-Mart where we went shopping last month. Do you remember?

M Yes, I remember that. Hmm... it may be _____ _____ the post office.

W No, that's Wal-Mart. The department store is on Main Street.

M Oh, I see. You mean the bowling alley that was _____ _____ _____ _____ before it closed down.

W That's right. They _____ _____ the bowling alley and _____ _____ a brand-new building for the department store. We _____ _____ _____ this weekend.

●●
bowling alley 볼링장 **tear down** 허물다 **put up** 세우다

14 대화를 듣고, 남자의 마지막 말에 이어질 여자의 말로 가장 적절한 것을 고르시오.

W Thanks for having this _____ _____ for me, Mark. I really _____ it.

M Oh, no problem. I just wanted you to know how much I'm going to _____ _____. Are you excited about moving?

W I am a little nervous, but I'm _____ _____ _____ it, too. The school there _____ _____ _____ _____ good, and I'm sure I'll make some _____ _____.

M Don't forget your old friends!

W <u>Of course not! I promise.</u>

● ●
farewell party 송별회 **look forward to** ~을 몹시 기다리다
be supposed to ~하기로 되어 있다

15 대화를 듣고, 여자의 마지막 말에 이어질 남자의 말로 가장 적절한 것을 고르시오.

M Your eyes are _____. They look _____. Are you okay?

W My eyes _____, and they _____.

M Do you wear contact lenses?

W Yes, how did you know?

M My sister wears them, so I've _____ _____ _____ before.

W My eyesight seems to be _____ _____.

M <u>Then you'd better see a doctor.</u>

● ●
painful 고통스러운 **water** 눈물이 나다 **gradually** 점점, 서서히
worsen 나빠지다

정답 및 해석 p. 56

A 다음을 듣고, 어휘와 우리말 뜻을 쓰시오.

① _____   ⑦ _____

② _____   ⑧ _____

③ _____   ⑨ _____

④ _____   ⑩ _____

⑤ _____   ⑪ _____

⑥ _____   ⑫ _____

B 우리말을 참고하여 빈칸에 알맞은 단어를 쓰시오.

① Who am I _____ _____?
(전화에서) 누구세요?

② If I am _____ the institute, should I go _____ or _____?
학원을 바라 봤을 때 왼쪽으로 가야 해 오른쪽으로 가 야 해?

③ Why are you in such a _____ _____?
너 왜 그렇게 기분이 안 좋아?

④ Please don't be _____.
기분 나쁘게 생각하지 마.

⑤ I went to Tokyo _____ _____ _____.
기분 전환하러 도쿄에 갔었어.

⑥ I'm thinking about _____ _____ _____.
나 성형수술을 할까 해.

⑦ You look great just _____ _____ _____.
너는 지금 있는 그대로가 보기 좋아.

⑧ I am a little nervous, but I'm _____ _____ _____ it, too.
좀 긴장이 되긴 하지만 몹시 기다려지기도 해.

MY SCORE

········· / 15

01 다음을 듣고, 여자의 직업으로 가장 적절한 것을 고르시오.

①    ②

③   ④

⑤

02 대화를 듣고, 여자가 가려고 하는 장소를 고르시오.

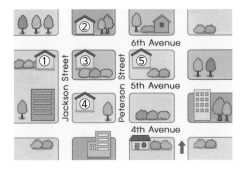

03 대화를 듣고, 두 사람이 대화하는 장소로 가장 적절한 곳을 고르시오.

① 버스
② 식당
③ 공원
④ 지하철
⑤ 엘리베이터

04 대화를 듣고, 두 사람의 관계로 가장 적절한 것을 고르시오.

① 의사 - 환자
② 구급대원 - 시민
③ 승무원 - 탑승객
④ 자동차 정비사 - 손님
⑤ 렌터카 회사 직원 - 손님

05 대화를 듣고, 여자가 취해야 할 동작으로 가장 적절한 것을 고르시오.

①    ②

③    ④

⑤

06 대화를 듣고, 지난 달과 이번 달에 낸 가스 요금의 차액을 고르시오.

① $15   ② $20
③ $35   ④ $45
⑤ $50

07 대화를 듣고, 여자의 심정으로 가장 적절한 것을 고르시오.

① sad   ② tired
③ proud   ④ nervous
⑤ cheerful

08 다음을 듣고, 두 사람의 대화가 <u>어색한</u> 것을 고르시오.

① ② ③ ④ ⑤

09 대화를 듣고, 여자가 박물관에 가고 싶어하는 이유로 가장 적절한 것을 고르시오.

① 흥미로운 그림들이 있어서
② 한 번도 가 본 적이 없어서
③ 무료 전시회가 열리고 있어서
④ 에어컨 시설이 잘 되어 있어서
⑤ 유명 화가의 전시가 열리고 있어서

10 대화를 듣고, 남자가 전화를 건 목적으로 가장 적절한 것을 고르시오.

① 장난감을 사기 위해서
② 장난감을 환불받기 위해서
③ 장난감을 수리하기 위해서
④ 건전지를 교환하기 위해서
⑤ 다른 장난감으로 교환하기 위해서

11 대화를 듣고, 남자가 여자에게 해 준 조언으로 가장 적절한 것을 고르시오.

① 이사하기
② 새 옷 사기
③ 옷 입어 보기
④ 오래된 옷 버리기
⑤ 안 입는 옷 기부하기

12 대화를 듣고, 여자가 대화 직후에 할 일로 가장 적절한 것을 고르시오.

① 안내 방송 하기
② 기내 영화 보기
③ 화장실 다녀오기
④ 안전벨트 착용하기
⑤ 오렌지주스 가져다 주기

13 대화를 듣고, 대화 내용과 일치하지 <u>않는</u> 것을 고르시오.

① 여자는 초조할 때면 손톱을 물어 뜯는다.
② 여자는 요리를 잘하지는 못한다.
③ 여자의 직장 동료들이 여자의 집을 방문할 것이다.
④ 여자는 중국 음식점에서 요리를 주문할 것이다.
⑤ 여자는 직장 동료들을 위해 직접 요리를 할 것이다.

14 대화를 듣고, 남자의 마지막 이어질 여자의 말로 가장 적절한 것을 고르시오.

① You are such a wonderful pianist.
② I'm afraid I can't go to your concert.
③ When did you start playing the cello?
④ Can you tell me where I can buy a guitar?
⑤ I can't believe you can play two instruments.

15 대화를 듣고, 여자의 마지막 말에 이어질 남자의 말로 가장 적절한 것을 고르시오.

① That's 23 dollars, please.
② Sorry. I don't know that place.
③ I'll put your luggage in the trunk.
④ Thanks. Don't forget your things.
⑤ It will take about one hour to get there.

01 다음을 듣고, 여자의 직업으로 가장 적절한 것을 고르시오.

Well, it's a tough job. _____ _____ _____ in the military is never easy, but I enjoy the challenge. I've always liked _____ _____, and with practice, I've become _____ _____ _____ weapons, too. But most of all, I like the feeling of knowing I'm _____ _____ _____.

●●
military 군대 **challenge** 도전 **physical** 육체적인
be good with ~을 잘 쓰다[다루다] **weapon** 무기

02 대화를 듣고, 여자가 가려고 하는 장소를 고르시오.

W Excuse me. How do I _____ _____ ABC Mart _____ _____?

M ABC Mart? Yes, that's on 6th Avenue. Go two blocks and then turn left. _____ _____ _____ _____ Peterson Street... Oh, no. I mean Jackson Street. It's _____ _____ _____.

W Let me see if I've got that. _____ _____ two blocks and turn left. Then, go to Jackson Street. It's on my right.

M That's correct. You _____ _____ _____.

W Thank you.

03 대화를 듣고, 두 사람이 대화하는 장소로 가장 적절한 곳을 고르시오.

W Ow! Hey!

M Oh, I'm sorry. Did I _____ _____?

W Watch _____ _____ _____.

M I'm really sorry. It was an _____. The bus suddenly _____ _____ _____. Are you okay?

W Never mind.

M I was _____, and I didn't see you there. Really sorry.

W That's okay. Just _____ _____ in the future.

●●
accident 사고, 우발적인 일 **suddenly** 갑자기
make a stop 멈추다 **careless** 부주의한

04 대화를 듣고, 두 사람의 관계로 가장 적절한 것을 고르시오.

W My car sounds a bit strange. What _____ _____ _____ is wrong with it?

M Well, your brakes are old.

W How long _____ _____ _____ to repair it?

M I'll be able to get it done by _____ _____ _____ _____.

W _____ _____ it will take so long?

M We don't have the parts, so we _____ _____ _____ them. That will take _____ _____ _____ days.

W Okay. How much _____ _____

_____ ?

M 200 dollars.

••
brake 브레이크, 제동장치 **how come** 왜, 어째서 **repair** 수리하다
part 부품

05 대화를 듣고, 여자가 취해야 할 동작으로 가장 적절한
것을 고르시오.

W Do you know any good exercises for the
_____ _____ ?

M Sure. Start by _____ _____ on
your left side.

W Can I _____ _____ my elbow
like this?

M Yeah, okay. Now lift your right leg up at
about a 35-degree _____ .

W Is this right?

M Uh-huh. Keep your _____ _____
though.

W This is hard. Can I put my leg down now?

M Of course. Just keep slowly _____
_____ _____ it.

••
thigh 허벅지 **lie down on one's side** 옆으로 눕다
lean on ~에 기대다 **elbow** 팔꿈치 **angle** 각도 **knee** 무릎
raise 올리다 **lower** 내리다

06 대화를 듣고, 지난 달과 이번 달에 낸 가스 요금의
차액을 고르시오.

W Wow, our _____ _____ this
month is _____ dollars. That's
_____ _____ last month.

M Really? How much was the bill last
month?

W Last month, it was only _____
dollars.

M _____ _____ that it's January
and that it's winter.

W I know. I know. I just didn't expect
_____ _____ _____ .

M All prices are going up these days.
They're _____ _____
_____ .

W _____ _____ _____
_____ . I think I may have to get a
second job.

••
gas bill 가스 요금 **increase** 증가 **out of control** 통제 불가능한,
어쩔 수 없는 **Tell me about it.** 그러게 말이야., 내 말이.

07 대화를 듣고, 여자의 심정으로 가장 적절한 것을 고르
시오.

M Jane, I am so sorry _____ _____
_____ . My condolences.

W Thank you.

M Were you very _____ _____
your grandmother?

W Yes, I was. She taught me a lot of
_____ _____ . I will miss her very
much.

M Please _____ _____ _____
if you need any help from me. I am
_____ _____ _____ .

W Thank you so much for your kindness.

••
loss 상실, 죽음 **condolences** 애도, 조의 **close** 가까운, 친밀한

08 다음을 듣고, 두 사람의 대화가 <u>어색한</u> 것을 고르시오.

① W These new shoes are _____ _____ _____.

M Then why don't you buy a new pair of shoes?

② M The weather is _____ _____, isn't it?

W I prefer science-fiction novels.

③ W Can I use this telephone?

M Sure, you _____ _____ _____ 9 to get an outside line.

④ M Can you name five Korean presidents?

W Yes, that's _____ _____ _____ _____.

⑤ W What would you _____ _____ _____?

M I'll have a tuna sandwich, please.

●●
science-fiction novel 공상 과학 소설   **outside line** 외선, 외부 전화   **name** 이름을 대다   **a piece of cake** 식은 죽 먹기, 아주 쉬운 일

09 대화를 듣고, 여자가 박물관에 가고 싶어하는 이유로 가장 적절한 것을 고르시오.

W Let's sit on this bench _____ _____ _____. It's very hot today.

M All right. Let's _____ _____ _____. What should we do next?

W We could _____ _____ _____ _____. I heard it has some interesting paintings.

M That sounds good. I've _____ _____ _____ a museum before.

W Great. Let's go!

M _____ _____ for just a few minutes longer. Okay?

●●
take a break 잠시 휴식을 취하다   **rest** 쉬다

10 대화를 듣고, 남자가 전화를 건 목적으로 가장 적절한 것을 고르시오.

W Hello. Toys For You. May I help you?

M Yes. I bought a robot toy for my son at your store, but it _____ _____.

W Have you _____ _____ _____?

M Yes, I am sure the batteries _____ _____. I put new ones in yesterday. Can I _____ _____ _____ _____, please?

W Certainly. If you bring us your toy and _____, we'll give you your money back.

M Thank you very much. I'll _____ _____ _____.

●●
battery 건전지   **get a refund** 환불받다

11 대화를 듣고, 남자가 여자에게 해 준 조언으로 가장 적절한 것을 고르시오.

M What can I do for you?

W Would you _____ _____ _____ _____ with this box? I want to move it.

M Sure. It's so heavy! No wonder you couldn't _____ _____ _____ _____ . What's in it?

W Oh, just some old clothes. I don't know _____ _____ _____ with them.

M You know, you really should _____ _____ some of these things. You _____ _____ them.

W You're right. I think I'll _____ _____ this old blouse.

••
no wonder 당연히 ~하다 **lift** 들어올리다 **(all) by oneself** 혼자, 도움을 받지 않고 **throw away** 버리다 **blouse** 블라우스

W When I am nervous, I always bite my nails.

M What's _____ _____ _____ ?

W My co-workers are visiting my house this Saturday.

M _____ _____ with that?

W That means I have to cook. I know _____ _____ _____ , but I can't cook very well.

M I have an idea. _____ _____ _____ order food from a Chinese restaurant?

W That's a good idea! Thanks.

••
bite 물다 **fingernail** 손톱 **co-worker** 동료

12 대화를 듣고, 여자가 대화 직후에 할 일로 가장 적절한 것을 고르시오.

M Excuse me. Why is the plane _____ ?

W Don't worry. It happens a lot. Just keep _____ _____ on.

M This is my _____ _____ _____ , so I'm a little _____ .

W I understand. Can I get you _____ _____ _____ ?

M Orange juice, please.

W I'll be right back. Just _____ _____ and enjoy the in-flight movie.

••
shake 흔들리다 **sit back** 편안히 앉다 **in-flight movie** 기내 영화

13 대화를 듣고, 대화 내용과 일치하지 <u>않는</u> 것을 고르시오.

M Why are you _____ _____ ?

14 대화를 듣고, 남자의 마지막 말에 이어질 여자의 말로 가장 적절한 것을 고르시오

W Can you come to my _____ _____ this Saturday?

M _____ _____ _____ ?

W Six.

M I'm sorry. I _____ _____ .

W Why? You should come.

M I play in the school orchestra, and we _____ _____ every Saturday.

W You play in the orchestra? _____ _____ do you play?

M I play the violin, and I also play the clarinet.

W <u>I can't believe you can play two instruments.</u>

••
make it (모임 등에) 가다 **orchestra** 오케스트라, 관현악단 **instrument** 악기 **violin** 바이올린 **clarinet** 클라리넷

15 대화를 듣고, 여자의 마지막 말에 이어질 남자의 말로
가장 적절한 것을 고르시오.

M Where can I take you, ma'am?

W Please _____ _____ _____
the King Bookstore.

M _____ _____ do you want, the
one in Gwanghwamun or Gangnam?

W _____ _____ two King
Bookstores? I didn't know that.

M Yes, the Gangnam branch is a _____
_____.

W Please go to the Gangnam branch.

M Sure. Would you please _____
_____ _____? It's for your
safety.

W Of course. How long _____
_____ _____ to get there?

M It will take about one hour to get there.

••
branch 지점 **safety** 안전

A 다음을 듣고, 어휘와 우리말 뜻을 쓰시오.

① _____ ⑦ _____

② _____ ⑧ _____

③ _____ ⑨ _____

④ _____ ⑩ _____

⑤ _____ ⑪ _____

⑥ _____ ⑫ _____

B 우리말을 참고하여 빈칸에 알맞은 단어를 쓰시오.

① _____ _____ it will take so long?

왜 그렇게 오래 걸리는 건가요?

② Start by _____ _____ on your left _____ .

왼쪽 옆으로 눕는 것으로 시작 해.

③ _____ your knee _____ though.

무릎을 일직선으로 유지해야 해.

④ Please _____ if you need any help from

me. 제 도움이 필요하시면 알려주세요.

⑤ Yes, that's a _____ _____ _____ .

그럼, 식은 죽 먹기지.

⑥ Can I _____ , please?

환불받을 수 있을까요?

⑦ _____ _____ you couldn't lift it by yourself.

네가 그걸 혼자 들 수 없었던 게 당연하네.

⑧ This is my _____ _____ _____ , so I'm a little nervous.

비행기 타는 것이 처음이라 조금 떨려요.

MY SCORE

.... / 15

01 대화를 듣고, 남자가 그린 그림으로 가장 적절한 것을 고르시오.

①   ②

③  ④

⑤

02 대화를 듣고, 여자가 가려고 하는 장소를 고르시오.

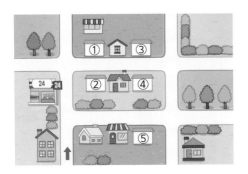

03 대화를 듣고, 두 사람이 대화하는 장소로 가장 적절한 곳을 고르시오.

① 집
② 극장
③ 학교
④ 상점
⑤ 도서관

04 대화를 듣고, 두 사람의 관계로 가장 적절한 것을 고르시오.

① boss – staff
② doctor – patient
③ foreigner – passerby
④ professor – instructor
⑤ receptionist – student

05 대화를 듣고, 남자의 형이 누구인지 고르시오.

06 대화를 듣고, 남자가 지불해야 할 금액으로 가장 적절한 것을 고르시오.

① $3　　　　② $6
③ $12　　　④ $30
⑤ $36

07 대화를 듣고, 두 사람의 심정으로 가장 적절한 것을 고르시오.

① upset　　　② bored
③ scared　　　④ relieved
⑤ confident

08 대화를 듣고, 남자의 마지막 말의 의도로 가장 적절한 것을 고르시오.

① 실망
② 사과
③ 비난
④ 후회
⑤ 기대

09 대화를 듣고, Kevin의 다리가 부러진 이유로 가장 적절한 것을 고르시오.

① 학교 친구와 싸워서
② 축구 경기 중에 다쳐서
③ 학교 운동장에서 넘어져서
④ 자전거를 타다가 넘어져서
⑤ 발이 걸려 계단에서 넘어져서

10 대화를 듣고, 여자의 증상으로 가장 적절한 것을 고르시오.

① 감기
② 일사병
③ 뾰루지
④ 알레르기
⑤ 소화불량

11 대화를 듣고, 남자가 여자에게 해 준 조언으로 가장 적절한 것을 고르시오.

① 동물 병원에 데려가기
② 고양이 사료 바꿔주기
③ 너무 많이 먹이지 않기
④ 고양이의 털 자주 빗어주기
⑤ 고양이가 마시는 물 바꿔주기

12 대화를 듣고, 두 사람이 조깅하기 전에 해야 할 일로 가장 적절한 것을 고르시오.

① 물 마시기
② 근육 풀어 주기
③ 화장실 다녀오기
④ 숨을 깊이 들이쉬기
⑤ 알맞은 조깅복 입기

13 대화를 듣고, 대화 내용과 일치하지 <u>않는</u> 것을 고르시오.

① 여자는 서울에서 태어났다.
② 여자는 서울에서 고등학교를 마칠 때까지 살았다.
③ 여자는 부산에서 몇 년 동안 살았다.
④ 여자는 1년 전에 서울로 돌아왔다.
⑤ 여자의 자매들은 모두 서울에 살고 있다.

14 대화를 듣고, 남자의 마지막 말에 이어질 여자의 말로 가장 적절한 것을 고르시오.

① Okay, I'll see you them.
② I hope he gets well soon.
③ You seem very happy today.
④ Do you want some more soup?
⑤ Oh, now I know why you're in a bad mood.

15 대화를 듣고, 여자의 마지막 말에 이어질 남자의 말로 가장 적절한 것을 고르시오.

① You have to finish this tonight.
② Well, I don't know what to do first.
③ You must be very proud of yourself.
④ Then I'll help you with one of your projects.
⑤ Tell me whatever you want to say. I'll listen.

01 대화를 듣고, 남자가 그린 그림으로 가장 적절한 것을 고르시오.

M Mom, _____ _____ _____!
I made this card at school today.

W Great! It's really cute. What does this letter S mean?

M It is the _____ _____ of dad's name, Steve, and his _____ _____ is the dog.

W Oh, so you put the S right _____ _____ the dog.

M Yes. I put a J next to the cat here because your favorite animal is a cat.

W I didn't know this card was _____ _____.

M Tomorrow is _____ _____.

02 대화를 듣고, 여자가 가려고 하는 장소를 고르시오.

W Excuse me. I'm looking for the new _____ _____ near here. Could you help me find it?

M Sure, it's easy. Just _____ _____ this street and _____ the convenience store. Then, turn right.

W So go down the street until I see the convenience store, and then _____ _____ I pass the convenience store, turn right?

M Yes. _____ _____ _____ _____ on your right is the hospital.

W Thank you very much. You've been a great help.

M _____ _____ _____.

03 대화를 듣고, 두 사람이 대화하는 장소로 가장 적절한 곳을 고르시오.

W Mike... Mike! You'd better _____ _____ the TV now.

M Oh, no. This is one of my _____ _____ _____!

W I know. But you've watched too much TV today. You should _____ _____ _____ before you go to bed.

M Can I finish watching this first?

W No. And now _____ _____ _____ _____. They're all over the living room floor.

M Okay. I'll turn it off. _____ _____ _____.

W Good boy. I can help you.

M Thank you, Mom.

●●
turn off 끄다 **pick up** (어질러진 물건들을) 치우다, 정리하다
Just a minute. 잠깐만요.

04 대화를 듣고, 두 사람의 관계로 가장 적절한 것을 고르시오.

M Hello. How can I help you?

W I want to _____ _____.

M _____ _____ do you want to learn?

W I want to learn _____ _____ _____ English well.

M _____ _____ _____ any English conversation classes before?

W Yes, but I can speak _____ _____ _____ English and make simple sentences.

M OK, I see. Then you have to take a _____ _____.

W Where should I do that?

M Go to room number 505 on the _____ _____.

placement test 반 편성 시험

05 대화를 듣고, 남자의 형이 누구인지 고르시오.

M Here's a _____ of my brother's old heavy metal band.

W _____ _____ is your brother?

M I'll _____ _____ _____ _____. He has long hair.

W _____ _____ two of them have long hair.

M He's also tall, like me.

W Is this him? The one _____ _____?

M Yeah, that's my brother.

heavy metal (음악 장르) 헤비메탈 **all but** ~외에 모두

06 대화를 듣고, 남자가 지불해야 할 금액으로 가장 적절한 것을 고르시오.

W Welcome to my flower shop. How can I help you?

M I'd like to _____ _____ _____ for my wife. It is our wedding anniversary.

W _____ _____ _____ flowers are you thinking of?

M I don't know. Maybe some roses?

W That's a _____ _____. They are _____ _____ _____.

M Great. I'll take a _____.

W I'm sure your wife will love these.

M I _____ _____. Thanks.

dozen 12개

07 대화를 듣고, 두 사람의 심정으로 가장 적절한 것을 고르시오.

W It is dark now. I think we _____ _____.

M I am not sure _____ _____ _____ now.

W We're in an _____ _____ of town.

M Do you hear the sounds of _____ _____ _____?

W Let's walk down this street.

W Sure. I hope we can see people or town _____ _____ _____.

roar 으르렁거리다

08 대화를 듣고, 남자의 마지막 말의 의도로 가장 적절한 것을 고르시오.

M When will it _____ _____?

W The weather forecast said _____ _____ _____ is expected over the weekend.

M Do you think we can still _____ this weekend?

W I think it will be very dangerous to _____ _____ _____.

M Well, we planned this trip almost _____ _____ _____.

W I know, but I think we should _____ _____.

M That's too bad. I was really _____ _____ _____ it.

postpone 연기하다

09 대화를 듣고, Kevin의 다리가 부러진 이유로 가장 적절한 것을 고르시오.

W Did you see Kevin?

M Yes, I did. He _____ _____ _____.

W Do you know _____ _____ _____ him?

M I heard that he _____ and _____ _____ the school steps last Thursday.

W _____ _____ he broke his leg?

M That's what happened.

W I _____ _____ for him.

trip (발이) 걸리다 **fall down** 넘어지다 **step** 계단

10 대화를 듣고, 여자의 증상으로 가장 적절한 것을 고르시오.

W Do you know what? I feel _____ _____ _____.

M Sick? How long have you been out _____ _____ _____?

W Oh, a few hours. Maybe four.

M But it's over 30 degrees. You probably have been in the sun for too long. You need to _____ _____ _____ right away and _____ _____ _____ the sun.

W Yes. It _____ to be out in the sun for so long.

M Well, you have to be _____ _____ these days.

get out of ~에서 나오다

11 대화를 듣고, 남자가 여자에게 해 준 조언으로 가장 적절한 것을 고르시오.

W My cat _____ _____ _____ these days. What should I do?

M _____ _____ _____ changing its cat food?

W No, I haven't.

M My aunt's cat had the same problem, and _____ _____ _____ was change the food.

W I'll _____ _____ _____.

M You know, cats can be _____ _____.

••
picky 까다로운

12 대화를 듣고, 두 사람이 조깅하기 전에 해야 할 일로 가장 적절한 것을 고르시오.

M Are you ready for our _____ _____?

W Yes, I am. What are you doing there?

M We should do some _____ _____ before we start. Our muscles are still too cold for jogging.

W I see. I'm sure I can _____ _____ _____ from you.

M After our warm-up, we should then _____ _____ _____.

W I got it. Then we jog, right?

M That's right.

••
jog 조깅, 조깅하다 **warm-up exercise** 준비 운동
stretch 펴다, 늘이다

13 대화를 듣고, 대화 내용과 일치하지 <u>않는</u> 것을 고르시오.

M So tell me a little about yourself.

W I _____ _____ right here in Seoul and lived here until I _____ _____ _____. I lived in Busan for several years, and then I _____ _____ _____ two years ago.

M Do you have any _____ _____ _____?

W Yes. I have two sisters. They both live in Seoul.

14 대화를 듣고, 남자의 마지막 말에 이어질 여자의 말로 가장 적절한 것을 고르시오.

M This soup is _____! What did you do to it?

W _____ _____.

M And the tea is cold. Why didn't you _____ _____ _____?

W John, I know you are in a bad mood this morning, but don't _____ _____ _____.

M I'm sorry. I didn't _____ _____ _____ last night, so I'm pretty moody now.

W <u>Oh, now I know why you're in a bad mood.</u>

••
yell 소리치다 **moody** 기분이 좋지 않은, 침울한

15 대화를 듣고, 여자의 마지막 말에 이어질 남자의 말로 가장 적절한 것을 고르시오.

M Jessica, you _____ _____. What happened?

W I didn't _____ _____ _____ last night.

M Did you have something _____ _____ _____? You look worried.

W Well, I'm under _____ _____ _____ _____. My boss assigned me three projects. Now the deadlines are near, and I still _____ _____ any of my projects.

M _____ _____ _____ I can do to help you?

W Well, I guess no one can help me _____ _____. For the moment, I just need _____ _____ _____ _____ so that I can _____ _____ _____.

M <u>Tell me whatever you want to say. I'll listen.</u>

pale 창백한 **sleep a wink** 한잠 자다 **assign** 맡기다, 할당하다
deadline 마감일 **relieve** 경감하다, 덜다

○ 정답 및 해석 p. 68

A 다음을 듣고, 어휘와 우리말 뜻을 쓰시오.

① _____   ⑦ _____

② _____   ⑧ _____

③ _____   ⑨ _____

④ _____   ⑩ _____

⑤ _____   ⑪ _____

⑥ _____   ⑫ _____

B 우리말을 참고하여 빈칸에 알맞은 단어를 쓰시오.

① Don't _____ _____.
별말씀을요.

② _____ _____ _____ any English conversation classes
before? 전에 영어 회화 수업을 수강한 적이 있나요?

③ I'll take a _____.
열 두 개 주세요.

④ I think it will be very _____ _____ _____ in snow.
눈이 오는데 운전하는 건 아주 위험할거야.

⑤ Do you know _____ _____ _____ him?
그에게 무슨 일이 있었는지 알고 있니?

⑥ _____ _____ have you been out in the sun?
밖에서 햇볕에 얼마나 오래 있었니?

⑦ Do you have any _____ _____ _____?
형제나 자매는 있나요?

⑧ Well, I'm _____ a lot of _____.
글쎄, 난 너무 부담스러워.

01 대화를 듣고, 남자가 가장 귀엽게 생각하는 원숭이를 고르시오.

02 대화를 듣고, 여자가 가려고 하는 장소를 고르시오.

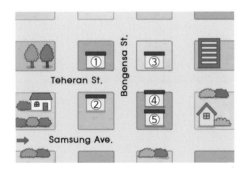

03 대화를 듣고, 두 사람이 대화하는 장소로 가장 적절한 곳을 고르시오.

① 공항
② 경찰서
③ 여행사
④ 학교 기숙사
⑤ 분실물 센터

04 대화를 듣고, 두 사람의 관계로 가장 적절한 것을 고르시오.

① 감독 – 선수
② 교사 – 학생
③ 점원 – 고객
④ 경찰관 – 행인
⑤ 버스 기사 – 승객

05 대화를 듣고, 여자가 좋아하는 운동으로 가장 적절한 것을 고르시오.

① 축구
② 배구
③ 탁구
④ 테니스
⑤ 배드민턴

06 대화를 듣고, 남자의 학급 학생 수로 가장 적절한 것을 고르시오.

① 5명
② 6명
③ 20명
④ 30명
⑤ 40명

07 대화를 듣고, 남자의 성격으로 가장 적절한 것을 고르시오.

① shy
② lazy
③ polite
④ energetic
⑤ responsible

08 대화를 듣고, 오늘 저녁과 내일 점심 메뉴로 가장 적절한 것을 고르시오.

	오늘 저녁	내일 점심
①	fish	pizza
②	pizza	spaghetti
③	hamburger	pizza
④	spaghetti	pizza
⑤	spaghetti	fish

09 대화를 듣고, 남자가 집중할 수 없는 이유로 가장 적절한 것을 고르시오.

① 잠을 자지 못해서
② 음식을 먹지 못해서
③ 할 일이 너무 많아서
④ 커피를 너무 많이 마셔서
⑤ 좋아하는 여자가 도서관에 있어서

10 대화를 듣고, 여자가 생각하는 남자의 증상으로 가장 적절한 것을 고르시오.

① 독감
② 빈혈
③ 식중독
④ 불면증
⑤ 우울증

11 대화를 듣고, 여자가 남자에게 부탁한 일로 가장 적절한 것을 고르시오.

① 동생 돌봐주기
② 동생과 같이 놀아주기
③ 동생의 숙제 도와주기
④ 동생에게 게임기 양보하기
⑤ 동생에게 게임하는 법 알려주기

12 대화를 듣고, 여자가 대화 직후에 할 일로 가장 적절한 것을 고르시오.

① 시험공부하기
② 시험 보러 가기
③ Helen에게 전화하기
④ 남자와 함께 산책하기
⑤ 창문 열어 환기 시키기

13 대화를 듣고, 대화 내용과 일치하지 <u>않는</u> 것을 고르시오.

① 남자는 예약을 하지 않았다.
② 남자는 2인실에 묵을 예정이다.
③ 남자는 80달러를 지불해야 한다.
④ 남자는 작은 서류 가방만 가지고 있다.
⑤ 호텔 직원이 방까지 안내해 줄 것이다.

14 대화를 듣고, 남자의 마지막 말에 이어질 여자의 말로 가장 적절한 것을 고르시오.

① I had a great time in Seoul.
② I don't like traveling by plane.
③ I hope you visit there sometime.
④ Wow! It must have been beautiful!
⑤ How long will you stay on Jeju Island?

15 대화를 듣고, 여자의 마지막 말에 이어질 남자의 말로 가장 적절한 것을 고르시오.

① I'm sorry. Maybe next time.
② I really hate mathematics class.
③ Well, I know I am good at writing.
④ No, I can't. I handed in my essay yesterday.
⑤ Okay, I will do that. Thanks for your advice.

01 대화를 듣고, 남자가 가장 귀엽게 생각하는 원숭이를 고르시오.

W Which monkey _____ _____ _____ is the cutest?

M I like the one over there _____ _____ _____.

W That one? You think he's cute?

M Yeah. See how he's _____ _____ _____ on his head.

W I think his friend is about to _____ _____ from him.

M Monkeys are so much _____ _____ _____.

W I'm glad you're having a good time.

•• **balance** 균형을 잡다 **steal** 훔치다

02 대화를 듣고, 여자가 가려고 하는 장소를 고르시오.

W Excuse me. Can you tell me _____ _____ _____ the COEX Mall?

M Sure. Walk along Samsung Avenue _____ _____ _____ Bongeunsa Street.

W So I should go to Bongeunsa Street, right?

M Yes, that's right. _____ _____ there. Then, go one block and turn right onto Teheran Street. It's _____ _____.

W Turn left on Bongeunsa Street and go one block. Then, turn right onto Teheran Street, and it's on my right?

M _____ _____. You can't miss it.

03 대화를 듣고, 두 사람이 대화하는 장소로 가장 적절한 곳을 고르시오.

M Where are you from?

W I'm from Korea.

M _____, please. What's the _____ of your visit?

W I'm here to _____ _____ at the University of Chicago for one year.

M What is your _____ while you're here?

W I'm going to stay in the _____ _____.

M All right. Here is your passport. _____ _____ with your studies.

W Thank you. Goodbye.

•• **passport** 여권 **purpose** 목적 **address** 주소
dormitory 기숙사

04 대화를 듣고, 두 사람의 관계로 가장 적절한 것을 고르시오.

M Excuse me. Do you know _____ _____ _____ _____?

W No, I'm sorry. I don't.

M You are supposed to _____

_____ _____. That's why they

are there.

W I still _____ _____ _____.

M You crossed the street in the middle

of the road. You could _____

_____ or cause a _____

_____.

W I'm sorry. I just wasn't thinking. I'm

_____ _____ work.

M I won't _____ _____ _____

_____ this time, but I will if I catch

you again.

follow 이해하다. (설명 등을) 따라가다 **injure** 부상을 입히다
ticket (위반) 딱지

---

05 대화를 듣고, 여자가 좋아하는 운동으로 가장 적절한 것을 고르시오.

M What time is that soccer game

_____? I thought it started at two.

W We must have gotten the _____

_____. Oh, well. Soccer is not my

favorite sport anyway. I _____

_____ badminton.

M Really? I thought your favorite sport

was tennis. I'm _____ _____

_____ _____ badminton, too.

W How about _____ _____

_____ sometime?

M Sure. Why don't we play now since the

soccer game _____ _____?

W That's great! Let's go.

on 진행 중인, 시작된

---

06 대화를 듣고, 남자의 학급 학생 수로 가장 적절한 것을 고르시오.

W Do you like your class?

M _____ _____. There are too

many students in my class.

W Really? How many are there?

M Hmmm... There are _____ _____,

with _____ _____ in each row...

W You're right. There really are a lot of

students in your class.

M There's also too much _____. It's

_____ _____ _____ _____.

W My class is the same.

row 줄, 열

---

07 대화를 듣고, 남자의 성격으로 가장 적절한 것을 고르시오.

W Let's _____ _____ before our

parents get home.

M Why don't you start first, and I'll

_____ _____ _____?

W No way! We both made this mess, so

_____ _____ _____ will

clean it up.

M I don't want to. _____ _____

watch TV.

W Don't be a _____ _____. Come

on. We don't have much time.

M I said I don't want to. Stop _____

_____.

make a mess 어지럽히다
couch potato 소파에 앉아 TV만 보며 많은 시간을 보내는 사람

08 대화를 듣고, 오늘 저녁과 내일 점심 메뉴로 가장 적절한 것을 고르시오.

M Mom, Paul is coming to _____ _____ _____ for two days before school starts.

W Oh, really? Do you want _____ _____ _____?

M Oh, no, Mom. Don't cook fish.

W _____ _____? You like fish.

M But Paul doesn't. He hates fish.

W Well, what _____ _____ _____?

M He likes spaghetti, and he loves pizza.

W Okay, _____ _____ spaghetti for dinner tonight.

M And _____ _____ _____ tomorrow.

W All right, Mike. All right.

●●
spaghetti 스파게티

09 대화를 듣고, 남자가 집중할 수 없는 이유로 가장 적절한 것을 고르시오.

W Are you going to the library to study tonight?

M I'm sorry. I can't. I _____ _____ for several days, so I need to go _____ _____ _____.

W Oh, that's too bad. How do you feel?

M I can't _____, and I feel kind of _____.

W Some people _____ _____ without sleep while others can't _____ _____ _____. What type of person are you?

M I'm definitely in the _____ _____. Sleep is _____ to me.

●●
directly 곧장 **function** 기능하다, 활동하다
definitely 분명히, 확실히 **essential** 필수적인

10 대화를 듣고, 여자가 생각하는 남자의 증상으로 가장 적절한 것을 고르시오.

W What _____ _____ _____ here today?

M I have some _____ _____ in my stomach.

W I see. What _____ _____ _____ today?

M Well, I only ate a sandwich I bought at a _____ _____.

W That might be the problem. Please be careful of _____ _____ _____.

●●
sharp pain 찌릿듯한 통증

11 대화를 듣고, 여자가 남자에게 부탁한 일로 가장 적절한 것을 고르시오.

M Mom! Tell her to _____ _____ _____ my game player.

W Why don't you let your sister play it _____ _____ _____?

M I didn't say she could play with it.

W Well, if she asks you, will you _____ _____ _____ _____ ?

M If she asks me... well... Okay.

W That's a good boy. It's important to _____ _____ _____ , isn't it?

M You're right, Mom.

12 대화를 듣고, 여자가 대화 직후에 할 일로 가장 적절한 것을 고르시오.

W Do you know what Helen did?

M No. Did she do _____ _____ ?

W Yeah, she did. She borrowed my biology notes, and then she _____ _____ .

M She lost your biology notes?

W Yes, we have a test tomorrow. I feel like telling her _____ _____ _____ _____ .

M Calm down. You'd better _____ _____ before you do anything.

W I'll be all right _____ _____ _____ , but I'm so mad right now.

M Why don't you _____ _____ _____ _____ with me before you call her?

W That's a good idea. I need some _____ _____ .

••
borrow 빌리다 **biology** 생물학 **count** 세다
after a while 잠시 후에 **go for a walk** 산책하러 가다

13 대화를 듣고, 대화 내용과 일치하지 <u>않는</u> 것을 고르시오.

W Good afternoon. May I help you?

M Do you have a _____ _____ _____ ? I don't have a _____ .

W Yes, we do. A single room or a _____ _____ ?

M A single room with a _____ _____ , please. And what is the _____ _____ ?

W 80 dollars _____ _____ .

M That's good. I'll take it.

W Please _____ _____ this card. Do you need help _____ _____ ?

M No, I just have a small _____ .

W Okay. Our bellman will take you up to your room.

••
have a reservation 예약되어 있다 **single room** 1인실
double room 2인실 **rate** 요금 **fill out** 작성하다
briefcase 서류 가방 **bellman** (호텔에서 객실까지 안내해주는) 벨맨

14 대화를 듣고, 남자의 마지막 말에 이어질 여자의 말로 가장 적절한 것을 고르시오.

W Have you ever traveled _____ _____?

M Yes, I went to Jeju Island _____ _____ last summer.

W How long _____ _____ _____ from Seoul to Jeju Island?

M Only an hour.

W Did you get a _____ _____ of Jeju Island?

M I did. The sky was very clear, so we could see for _____ _____ _____.

W Wow! It must have been beautiful!

●●
by air[plane] 비행기로 **miles and miles** 아주 멀리

M Okay, I will do that. Thanks for your advice.

●●
hand[turn] in 제출하다

15 대화를 듣고, 여자의 마지막 말에 이어질 남자의 말로 가장 적절한 것을 고르시오.

W Are you _____ _____ your essay for English class?

M I finished it this morning, and I'm about to _____ _____ _____.

W Do you mind if I _____ _____ _____ at it?

M Sure. I need _____ _____ _____ it. How is it?

W Honestly? I don't think you should _____ _____ _____ now.

M Why?

W I think you should add _____ _____ in the body of the paper.

A 다음을 듣고, 어휘와 우리말 뜻을 쓰시오.

① _____ _____
② _____ _____
③ _____ _____
④ _____ _____
⑤ _____ _____
⑥ _____ _____
⑦ _____ _____
⑧ _____ _____
⑨ _____ _____
⑩ _____ _____
⑪ _____ _____
⑫ _____ _____

B 우리말을 참고하여 빈칸에 알맞은 단어를 쓰시오.

① Can you tell me _____ _____ to the COEX Mall?
코엑스몰 가는 길 좀 가르쳐 주시겠어요?

② What's the _____ of _____ _____?
방문 목적이 뭔가요?

③ We _____ _____ gotten the time _____.
우리가 시간을 잘못 안게 틀림없어.

④ I'm a _____ _____ of badminton, too.
나도 배드민턴의 열렬한 팬이야.

⑤ I have some _____ _____ in my stomach.
위가 찌르는 것처럼 아파요.

⑥ I don't have a _____.
예약은 하지 않았는데요.

⑦ Please _____ _____ this card.
이 카드를 작성해 주세요.

⑧ Do you mind if I _____ _____ _____ at it?
한번 봐도 되겠니?

MY SCORE

.... / 15

01 대화를 듣고, 두 사람이 구입할 스웨터로 가장 적절한 것을 고르시오.

①   ②

③   ④

⑤

02 다음을 듣고, 남자가 하는 말의 내용으로 가장 적절한 것을 고르시오.

① 매장 위치 안내
② 매장 운영 시간
③ 할인 행사 안내
④ 할인 쿠폰 사용
⑤ 신규 회원 모집

03 다음을 듣고, 여자가 설명하는 운동으로 가장 적절한 것을 고르시오.

① soccer
② fishing
③ skating
④ swimming
⑤ water-skiing

04 대화를 듣고, 두 사람의 관계로 가장 적절한 것을 고르시오.

① 교사 – 학생
② 승무원 – 탑승객
③ 은행 직원 – 고객
④ 매표소 직원 – 손님
⑤ 컴퓨터 수리 기사 – 고객

05 대화를 듣고, 여자가 방문한 나라로 언급하지 않은 곳을 고르시오.

① 영국
② 프랑스
③ 스페인
④ 독일
⑤ 이탈리아

06 대화를 듣고, 사진 속에 있는 사람들이 모두 몇 명인지 고르시오.

① 4명
② 5명
③ 6명
④ 7명
⑤ 8명

07 대화를 듣고, 여자의 심정으로 가장 적절한 것을 고르시오.

① angry
② proud
③ thankful
④ disappointed
⑤ embarrassed

08 대화를 듣고, 남자의 마지막 말의 의도로 가장 적절한 것을 고르시오.

① 격려
② 조언
③ 부탁
④ 동의
⑤ 불평

09 대화를 듣고, 쓰레기를 저녁 6시 이후에 버려야 하는 이유로 가장 적절한 것을 고르시오.

① 행인들의 안전을 위해서
② 낮 동안 악취가 날 수 있어서
③ 차량 통행을 원활하게 하기 위해서
④ 청소 업체가 밤 사이에 운영을 해서
⑤ 도시가 지저분해 보이지 않게 하기 위해서

10 대화를 듣고, 여자가 전화를 건 목적으로 가장 적절한 것을 고르시오.

① 길을 물어보기 위해서
② 택시를 부르기 위해서
③ 화재를 신고하기 위해서
④ 구급차를 부르기 위해서
⑤ 납치 사건을 신고하기 위해서

11 대화를 듣고, 남자가 여자에게 부탁한 일로 가장 적절한 것을 고르시오.

① 편지 쓰기
② 편지 보내기
③ 우편물 찾기
④ 숙제 도와주기
⑤ 우체국까지 태워주기

12 대화를 듣고, 두 사람이 대화 직후에 할 일로 가장 적절한 것을 고르시오.

① 상점에 가기
② 병원 예약하기
③ 따뜻한 차 마시기
④ 상점 폐점 시간 문의하기
⑤ 인터넷으로 가습기 주문하기

13 대화를 듣고, 대화 내용과 일치하지 않는 것을 고르시오.

① 남자는 여가 시간에 개를 산책시킨다.
② 남자는 여가 시간에 TV를 본다.
③ 남자는 쇼핑하는 것을 싫어한다.
④ 남자는 현재 이혼한 상태이다.
⑤ 남자는 현재의 삶에 만족한다.

14 대화를 듣고, 남자의 마지막 말에 이어질 여자의 말로 가장 적절한 것을 고르시오.

① I'm glad you had a good time.
② You should know how to swim.
③ I hope you have a nice vacation.
④ It must be dangerous to go surfing.
⑤ Don't worry about it. You will be fine.

15 대화를 듣고, 여자의 마지막 말에 이어질 남자의 말로 가장 적절한 것을 고르시오.

① I'm sorry to hear that.
② I want to be a professor.
③ We're going to miss you so much.
④ That's great news. Congratulations!
⑤ Long time, no see. How have you been?

01 대화를 듣고, 두 사람이 구입할 스웨터로 가장 적절한 것을 고르시오.

M Let's get one of the sweaters here for Peter's _____ _____.

W Great idea! How about this one? It has the _____ _____ on it.

M It is nice, but it looks _____ _____ without any pictures.

W Peter likes monkeys. He _____ _____ _____ because it has a monkey picture.

M It is cute, but he likes dogs, too.

W That's right. _____ _____ looks good, so you pick one.

M Let's buy the sweater with the _____ picture and the letter _____.

W Sounds good.

02 다음을 듣고, 남자가 하는 말의 내용으로 가장 적절한 것을 고르시오.

Hello, and _____ _____ S-Mart. We have good news for _____ today. We are having a big sale now. A _____ _____ are only $1.00, _____ are only $2.50 a pound, and ramen is only $5.50 a box. _____ _____ this chance. Thank you for shopping at S-Mart.

● ●
pound (무게 단위) 파운드

03 다음을 듣고, 여자가 설명하는 운동으로 가장 적절한 것을 고르시오.

My father helped me by holding my hands as I _____ _____ _____. Sometimes he would _____ _____ _____ me. Then, I would get scared and _____ _____ _____ him, but he just kept saying that I could _____ if I'd kick my feet and move my arms. One day, I just did it. I was moving around the pool _____ _____ _____, and my father was very _____ of me.

● ●
kick (발로) 차다 **let go of** ~을 놓다 **grab** 붙잡다 **float** 뜨다

04 대화를 듣고, 두 사람의 관계로 가장 적절한 것을 고르시오.

W Excuse me. Could you please tell me _____ _____ _____ this machine?

M Well, first put your card _____ _____ _____. Then, enter your _____ _____. Okay?

W Okay. First I put my card in the slot. Next I enter my secret number. Then what?

M Next, push "_____" and the amount of _____ _____ _____. Take your card out. Then, _____ _____.

W I see. That _____ _____ very

hard. I think _____ _____

_____.

> slot (가느다란) 구멍, 투입구 withdrawal 인출

05 대화를 듣고, 여자가 방문한 나라로 언급하지 <u>않은</u> 곳을
고르시오.

M So you're _____ _____

_____. How was it?

W It was a lot of fun. I'd _____

_____ _____ Europe before. It

was my first time there.

M I've been there _____ _____

_____. I never _____ _____

_____ going there. Where did you

go _____ _____?

W I went to France, Spain, and Germany. I

had a really great time.

M You didn't go to Italy?

W Oh, yes, I did. I took _____ _____

_____ _____ there, too.

> abroad 해외; 해외로 in particular 특히, 특별히

06 대화를 듣고, 사진 속에 있는 사람들이 모두 몇 명인지
고르시오.

M Hey, is this a picture of your family?

W Yes, it is. These are all my _____

_____.

M It looks like you have a _____

_____.

W Yes. Here are my mom, my dad, my two

sisters, and one brother.

M It's a very nice picture. But _____

_____ _____? You are not

_____ _____ _____.

W I was in Tokyo studying Japanese when

they _____ _____.

M Did you feel sorry that you _____

_____ _____?

W Yes, but it's okay. We are going to take

_____ _____ _____ this

year.

> moment 순간

07 대화를 듣고, 여자의 심정으로 가장 적절한 것을 고르
시오.

M Susan, please answer question four.

W I'm sorry, but I _____ _____

question four.

M Did you do any of the questions?

W I'm _____ _____ _____

that I did not. I was so _____ last

night that I just _____ _____

_____.

M That's not a very _____ _____.

W I'm sorry. I won't _____ _____

_____.

> ashamed 부끄러운 excuse 변명

08 대화를 듣고, 남자의 마지막 말의 의도로 가장 적절한 것을 고르시오.

M You _____ _____. May I help you?

W Yes, I've been _____ _____ _____ the Grace Hotel for an hour.

M Well, you're going the _____ _____. I think that the hotel is on Lenox Avenue.

W _____ _____ is it from here?

M Let me see. It's about four blocks _____ _____ _____.

W How can I get there?

M Why don't you go there _____ _____?

09 대화를 듣고, 쓰레기를 저녁 6시 이후에 버려야 하는 이유로 가장 적절한 것을 고르시오.

W Don't forget that the _____ _____ _____ after six o'clock in the evening.

M Sure, thanks. _____ _____ _____, why do we have to wait?

W That law was made to ensure the city _____ _____ _____ during the day.

M Oh, that _____ _____. I never thought about that before.

W There are reasons for rules, you know.

M I _____ _____ now.

garbage 쓰레기 **ensure** 확실히 하다 **make sense** 이해가 되다

10 대화를 듣고, 여자가 전화를 건 목적으로 가장 적절한 것을 고르시오.

M 911. Do you need the fire department, the police, or an ambulance?

W The police, I'm calling to _____ _____ _____. Please! Hurry! There's a _____ _____ in the street.

M Where are you? Give me the _____.

W 135 Maple Avenue. I'm in front of KNG Bank.

M Can you see her?

W Yes. A man is pushing her into a car. She's trying to _____ _____ _____ him.

M An officer will be there soon. _____ _____ _____ _____. Number 2, Number 2, go to 135 Maple Avenue _____. Very _____.

fire department 소방서 **ambulance** 구급차
report 알리다, 신고하다 **kidnapping** 납치 **urgent** 긴급한

11 대화를 듣고, 남자가 여자에게 부탁한 일로 가장 적절한 것을 고르시오.

M Karen, are you _____ _____ _____ to work?

W Yes, I am. Why?

M Would you _____ _____ _____ to the post office on your way to work?

W Sure.

M It's just that I'm _____ _____ _____, and the letter _____ _____ _____ right away.

W It's no problem at all. Just _____ _____ _____ when I need one.

••
return the favor 보답을 하다

12 대화를 듣고, 두 사람이 대화 직후에 할 일로 가장 적절한 것을 고르시오.

M Why are you _____ _____ _____?

W It's the winter weather. It's very dry here.

M Why don't we buy a _____? That would _____ _____ _____.

W I know. I've just been _____ _____ _____ _____ to the store.

M Well, let's go now. We still _____ _____ _____ before it closes.

W OK, that _____ _____ a good idea.

••
cough 기침하다 **humidifier** 가습기

13 대화를 듣고, 대화 내용과 일치하지 <u>않는</u> 것을 고르시오.

W Can I ask you some questions about your life?

M Sure. _____ _____.

W What do you _____ _____ _____ in your free time?

M Well, I usually _____ _____ _____, watch TV, and read magazines.

W Okay. Now, what do you _____ _____ _____ the most?

M That's difficult. Hmm, I hate to _____ _____ with my wife. It's too _____.

W Are you _____? Oh, I thought you were _____. Then is there anything that you want to _____ in your life?

M I'm _____ _____ my life. I love my life.

••
married 결혼을 한, 기혼의 **single** 독신인, 혼자인

14 대화를 듣고, 남자의 마지막 말에 이어질 여자의 말로 가장 적절한 것을 고르시오.

W Did you make plans for this _____?

M Yes, I'm going to Hawaii with my family. I'm going to _____ _____ and scuba diving there.

W Have you ever _____ _____ Hawaii?

M No, this will be my first time, so I'm _____ _____ _____ it.

M <u>I hope you have a nice vacation.</u>

••
surfing 서핑, 파도타기 **scuba diving** 스쿠버 다이빙

15 대화를 듣고, 여자의 마지막 말에 이어질 남자의 말로 가장 적절한 것을 고르시오.

W It's nice of you to _____ _____ _____.

M Not at all. I certainly hope you had a nice time _____ _____ _____ in Seoul.

W I did _____. You and your family were so kind to me. I _____ _____ very much.

M We hope you'll be able to come back to Seoul for a _____ _____.

W Of course I will.

M Are you going to _____ _____ again when you come back?

W Yes, I _____ _____ an English teaching position at a university.

M <u>That's great news. Congratulations!</u>

●●
see off 배웅하다 **indeed** 정말로, 실제로 **offer** 제안하다

A 다음을 듣고, 어휘와 우리말 뜻을 쓰시오.

① _____   ⑦ _____

② _____   ⑧ _____

③ _____   ⑨ _____

④ _____   ⑩ _____

⑤ _____   ⑪ _____

⑥ _____   ⑫ _____

B 우리말을 참고하여 빈칸에 알맞은 단어를 쓰시오.

① Could you please tell me _____ _____ _____ this
machine? 이 기계를 어떻게 사용하는 지 말씀해 주실 수 있나요?

② I've been there about _____ _____.
난 세 번쯤 다녀왔어.

③ I never _____ _____ _____ going there.
난 그곳에 가는 것이 절대 질리지 않아.

④ Where did you go _____ _____?
넌 특별히 어디를 갔었니?

⑤ Well, you're going the _____ _____.
음, 길을 잘못 드신 것 같군요.

⑥ Oh, that _____ _____.
오, 이해가 되네.

⑦ Would you take this letter to the post office _____ _____
_____ to work? 출근하는 길에 이 편지를 우체국에 가서 부쳐 줄 수 있니?

⑧ Just _____ _____ _____ when I need one.
내가 필요할 때 보답해 주면 돼.

TEST 14

MY SCORE

-------- / 15

01 대화를 듣고, 여자가 설명하는 동작으로 가장 적절한 것을 고르시오.

①   ②

③   ④

⑤

02 대화를 듣고, Jane이 누구인지 고르시오.

03 대화를 듣고, 두 사람이 대화하는 장소로 가장 적절한 곳을 고르시오.

① 학교
② 마트
③ 문구점
④ 체육관
⑤ 콘서트홀

04 대화를 듣고, 두 사람의 관계로 가장 적절한 것을 고르시오.

① 웨이터 – 손님
② 경찰관 – 시민
③ 승무원 – 탑승객
④ 매표소 직원 – 손님
⑤ 관광 가이드 – 여행객

05 다음을 듣고, 남자가 소개하는 물건으로 가장 적절한 것을 고르시오.

①   ②

③   ④

⑤

06 대화를 듣고, 여자가 받을 한달 용돈으로 가장 적절한 것을 고르시오.

① $40   ② $44
③ $48   ④ $60
⑤ $80

07 대화를 듣고, 여자의 심정으로 가장 적절한 것을 고르시오.

① angry   ② happy
③ proud   ④ nervous
⑤ surprised

08 다음을 듣고, 두 사람의 대화가 <u>어색한</u> 것을 고르시오.

① ② ③ ④ ⑤

09 대화를 듣고, 여자가 집에 있고 싶은 이유로 가장 적절한 것을 고르시오.

① 감기에 걸려서
② 휴식이 필요해서
③ 집에서 해야 할 일이 있어서
④ 가족과 시간을 보내기 위해서
⑤ 보고 싶은 TV 프로그램이 있어서

10 대화를 듣고, 남자가 전화를 건 목적으로 가장 적절한 것을 고르시오.

① 안부를 묻기 위해서
② 병문안을 가기 위해서
③ 숙제를 물어보기 위해서
④ 데이트를 신청하기 위해서
⑤ 약속 시간을 변경하기 위해서

11 대화를 듣고, 남자가 출근하는 방법으로 가장 적절한 것을 고르시오.

① 택시
② 버스
③ 도보
④ 지하철
⑤ 자전거

12 대화를 듣고, 두 사람이 대화 직후에 할 일로 가장 적절한 것을 고르시오.

① 차 수리하기
② 차 열쇠 복사하기
③ 운전면허 시험 보기
④ 시내에서 시험 운전하기
⑤ 고속도로에서 시험 운전하기

13 대화를 듣고, 대화 내용과 일치하지 <u>않는</u> 것을 고르시오.

① 남자는 계단에서 넘어졌다.
② 남자는 발목을 삐었다고 생각한다.
③ 남자는 혼자 걸을 수 없다.
④ 남자는 구급차를 기다리고 있다.
⑤ 남자는 응급실에 가려고 한다.

14 대화를 듣고, 남자의 마지막 말에 이어질 여자의 말로 가장 적절한 것을 고르시오.

① Just be patient. You'll pass.
② Fencing is my favorite sport, too.
③ I'm sorry. I didn't mean to upset you.
④ Good for you! I knew you could do it.
⑤ Don't give up. We can do this together.

15 대화를 듣고, 여자의 마지막 말에 이어질 남자의 말로 가장 적절한 것을 고르시오.

① That sounds perfect!
② That's very disappointing.
③ Then I will be back tomorrow.
④ I won't be able to make your party.
⑤ Thanks for inviting me to your party.

01 대화를 듣고, 여자가 설명하는 동작으로 가장 적절한 것을 고르시오.

M I'm so _____ and _____.

W Why don't you try exercising and stretching?

M Okay. Can you show me _____ _____ _____ it?

W Sure. First, _____ _____ _____ _____. And put your hands on the back of your head. Now, _____ _____ _____ from side to side.

M That sounds easy. I can do that.

●●
put one's feet apart 양발을 벌리다 **twist** 비틀다
from side to side 좌우로

02 대화를 듣고, Jane이 누구인지 고르시오.

W It's a great day to be out _____ _____ _____.

M Yeah, but I don't know if we can find a _____ _____ _____ out here. Look at all these people.

W Well, look at that girl _____ _____. Is that Jane?

M There are so many. _____ _____?

W The girl _____ _____ who's sitting under the parasol.

M There are _____ _____ _____.

W She is wearing a _____ _____ and drinking juice.

M Oh, I see her. Let's go and _____ _____.

●●
parasol 파라솔 **floral** 꽃무늬의 **swimsuit** 수영복

03 대화를 듣고, 두 사람이 대화하는 장소로 가장 적절한 곳을 고르시오.

M Excuse me. Where can I get _____?

W Did you say _____? They are _____ _____ _____.

M No, I said, pans. Frying pans.

W Oh, pans! _____ _____ _____, you should go to aisle 7.

M Thank you.

W You're welcome. I'm happy to help you, sir. _____ _____ _____.

●●
aisle 통로

04 대화를 듣고, 두 사람의 관계로 가장 적절한 것을 고르시오.

M _____ _____. Can you show me your _____ _____, please?

W Here it is. Where is _____ _____?

M 12G is on the _____ _____.

W Thank you. Oh, I would like an _____ _____.

M Certainly, ma'am. I'll be right back. Just _____ _____ and relax.

••
aboard 탑승한, 승선한 **boarding pass** 탑승권 **blanket** 담요 **be seated** 앉다

M Good for you! How much did you receive before?

W I was receiving _____ dollars _____ _____. Now I got a _____% _____.

M Congratulations! I guess that means you're _____ _____ _____.

W I guess so.

••
in a good mood 기분이 좋은 **allowance** 용돈 **receive** 받다

05 다음을 듣고, 남자가 소개하는 물건으로 가장 적절한 것을 고르시오.

Today, I'm going to _____ _____ _____ our new product. It is _____ _____ _____ the one you've been using. It can _____ _____, even in those hard-to-reach corners. And it has a cord _____ _____ _____ _____ the old models. During this _____ _____, we will give everyone who purchases this item a belt set _____ _____ _____ _____ our appreciation.

••
promotional 홍보의, 판촉의 **period** 기간 **purchase** 구입하다 **as a token of one's appreciation** 감사의 표시로

06 대화를 듣고, 여자가 받을 한달 용돈으로 가장 적절한 것을 고르시오.

M You seem to be _____ _____ _____ _____ today.

W Well, you would be too if your parents _____ _____ _____.

07 대화를 듣고, 여자의 심정으로 가장 적절한 것을 고르시오.

W Mark, can I _____ _____ _____ for a minute, please?

M Yes, Mom. What is it?

W I asked you to _____ _____ the living room, and you _____ _____ it. Why?

M I forgot. I'll do it now.

W Cleaning up from time to time is not a _____ _____ _____ _____.

M I know, Mom.

••
from time to time 가끔

08 다음을 듣고, 두 사람의 대화가 <u>어색한</u> 것을 고르시오.

① M Can you _____ _____
  _____ _____?

  W Maybe. What is it?

② W What are you _____ _____
  _____ at university?

  M I don't know yet. There are so many choices.

③ M I'll have some ice cream, please.

  W Okay. I want _____ _____
  _____ spaghetti with cheese.

④ W It's really _____ _____
  _____ to help me.

  M Oh, it's my pleasure.

⑤ M _____ _____ _____ are there in the USA?

  W Well, let's see. There are fifty.

plate 접시 **state** (미국) 주(州)

10 대화를 듣고, 남자가 전화를 건 목적으로 가장 적절한 것을 고르시오.

M Hello. May I _____ _____ Kelly?

W This is Kelly _____.

M Oh, hi! This is Kobe. How are you doing?
  I _____ _____ _____
  _____ in a long time.

W Kobe! I'm great. Thank you. How are you
  _____ _____?

M I'm the same _____ _____. How is your sister Jane doing?

W She's doing fine, too. She _____
  _____ _____ now.

M Say hello to her for me.

W Okay, I will.

get along 지내다

09 대화를 듣고, 여자가 집에 있고 싶은 이유로 가장 적절한 것을 고르시오.

W I want to _____ _____ tonight. I don't know what to do.

M Do you want to _____ _____?

W No. I just want to stay home.

M _____ _____ watching Netflix?

W Yeah, that sounds all right. I don't want to _____ tonight. I just want to _____.

M I know. You've been _____
  _____ _____ lately. You need a _____.

lately 최근에, 요즈음

11 대화를 듣고, 남자가 출근하는 방법으로 가장 적절한 것을 고르시오.

W Sam said you come to work _____
  _____. Is that true?

M Yes, it is. It takes about _____
  _____ to get to work on foot.

W Why do you choose _____
  _____ _____ _____ to get to work?

M It's a perfect time _____ _____.
  Walking is very healthy.

W That takes a lot of _____. What about on rainy days?

M Even on rainy days.

W You _____ _____ _____ to do it every day.

12 대화를 듣고, 두 사람이 대화 직후에 할 일로 가장 적절한 것을 고르시오.

W That was a _____ _____. When did you get your new car?

M Last week. Would you like to take it _____ _____?

W Really? Are you sure?

M Yes. You're a _____ _____ _____. Go ahead. Take the keys.

W Thanks. Can we go right now?

M Yes, let's drive _____ _____ _____.

W I think there's _____ _____ at this hour so I'd rather drive _____ _____ _____.

M Okay, let's drive on the highway then.

13 대화를 듣고, 대화 내용과 일치하지 <u>않는</u> 것을 고르시오.

W Is something wrong?

M I _____ _____ the stairs.

W Are you okay?

M No. I hurt my foot, and I can't walk by myself. I think I _____ _____ _____.

W Do you want me to _____ _____ _____?

M If you could get a taxi, I think I can go to the _____ _____.

W Okay. I'll _____ _____ _____.

M Thank you. Please hurry up.

14 대화를 듣고, 남자의 마지막 말에 이어질 여자의 말로 가장 적절한 것을 고르시오.

W Hi, Paul! How have you been?

M Great! It's been _____ _____ _____ since I last saw you.

W I know. I've been busy. How are your _____ _____ going?

M I tried to get into the second level, but I _____ already.

W _____ _____ have you taken lessons for?

M Almost three months now. The students _____ _____ _____ are in the third level now. I don't know _____ _____.

W <u>Just be patient. You'll pass.</u>

15 대화를 듣고, 여자의 마지막 말에 이어질 남자의 말로
가장 적절한 것을 고르시오.

W Hello. Momo Restaurant.

M I'd like to _____ _____
_____ for this Saturday afternoon.

W All right. _____ _____ would
you like to come?

M Can I come at five thirty?

W Five thirty. How many people are there
_____ _____ _____ ?

M There are fifteen of us.

W Fifteen! I'm sorry, but we can't take

_____ _____ _____

_____ .

M That's very disappointing.

●●
party 일행 **disappointing** 실망스러운

정답 및 해석 p. 85

A 다음을 듣고, 어휘와 우리말 뜻을 쓰시오.

① _____ _____ ⑦ _____ _____

② _____ _____ ⑧ _____ _____

③ _____ _____ ⑨ _____ _____

④ _____ _____ ⑩ _____ _____

⑤ _____ _____ ⑪ _____ _____

⑥ _____ _____ ⑫ _____ _____

B 우리말을 참고하여 빈칸에 알맞은 단어를 쓰시오.

① First, _____ your feet _____.
먼저 양발을 벌려.

② Can you show me your _____ _____, please?
탑승권 좀 보여 주시겠습니까?

③ We will give everyone who purchases this item a belt set as a _____ of our _____. 이 제품을 구입하시는 모든 분께는 감사의 표시로 벨트 세트를 드리도록 하겠습니다.

④ I want to do something tonight. I don't know _____ _____ _____. 오늘 밤에 뭔가를 하고 싶긴 한데. 뭘 해야 할지 모르겠어.

⑤ You _____ _____ _____ to do it every day.
매일 그렇게 하다니 넌 정말 단호하구나.

⑥ It's been _____ _____ _____ since I last saw you.
지난 번에 본 이후로 오래간만이네.

⑦ I'd like to _____ _____ _____ for this Saturday afternoon. 이번 주 토요일 오후로 예약하고 싶습니다.

⑧ _____ _____ people are there in your _____?
일행이 몇 분이시죠?

MY SCORE

········· / 15

01 대화를 듣고, 오늘의 날씨로 가장 적절한 것을 고르시오.

①    ②

③    ④

⑤

02 대화를 듣고, 여자가 가려고 하는 장소를 고르시오.

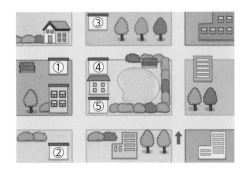

03 대화를 듣고, 두 사람이 대화하는 장소로 가장 적절한 곳을 고르시오.

① 병원
② 학교
③ 체육관
④ 수영장
⑤ 스키장

04 대화를 듣고, 남자의 직업으로 가장 적절한 것을 고르시오.

① waiter   ② engineer
③ car dealer   ④ hairdresser
⑤ car repairman

05 대화를 듣고, 여자가 설명하는 범인이 누구인지 고르시오.

①   ②

③   ④

⑤

06 대화를 듣고, 여자가 지불해야 할 금액으로 가장 적절한 것을 고르시오.

① 2,000원   ② 4,000원
③ 14,000원   ④ 16,000원
⑤ 18,000원

07 대화를 듣고, 남자의 심정으로 가장 적절한 것을 고르시오.

① proud   ② lonely
③ envious   ④ regretful
⑤ ashamed

08 대화를 듣고, 여자의 마지막 말의 의도로 가장 적절한 것을 고르시오.

① 걱정
② 비난
③ 후회
④ 조언
⑤ 격려

09 대화를 듣고, 남자가 채소를 재배하는 이유로 가장 적절한 것을 고르시오.

① 취미가 필요해서
② 귀농을 결심하고 있어서
③ 이웃에게 자랑하기 위해서
④ 친환경적인 채소를 먹기 위해서
⑤ 필요한 채소를 자급자족하기 위해서

10 대화를 듣고, 남자가 전화를 건 목적으로 가장 적절한 것을 고르시오.

① 카메라를 빌리기 위해서
② 숙제를 물어보기 위해서
③ 약속 일정을 정하기 위해서
④ 함께 찍은 사진을 주기 위해서
⑤ 휴대폰을 두고 왔는지 묻기 위해서

11 대화를 듣고, 남자가 모임에 온 방법으로 가장 적절한 것을 고르시오.

① by car
② by bus
③ by taxi
④ on foot
⑤ by subway

12 대화를 듣고, 여자가 내일 저녁에 할 일로 가장 적절한 것을 고르시오.

① 수영하러 가기
② 친구에게 편지 쓰기
③ 파티에 가기
④ 병원에 가기
⑤ 집에서 쉬기

13 대화를 듣고, 대화 내용과 일치하지 않는 것을 고르시오.

① 집 주인은 일본에서 유학 중이다.
② 남자는 집 열쇠를 가지고 있다.
③ 집은 1999년에 지어졌다.
④ 남자는 시공 회사를 기억하지 못한다.
⑤ 지붕은 2년 전에 새로 얹었다.

14 대화를 듣고, 남자의 마지막 말에 이어질 여자의 말로 가장 적절한 것을 고르시오.

① If you like, I'll lend it to you.
② Well, the story was too boring.
③ It's a traditional American story.
④ I like this kind of story very much.
⑤ You must read it if you get the chance.

15 대화를 듣고, 여자의 마지막 말에 이어질 남자의 말로 가장 적절한 것을 고르시오.

① It's not sour.
② Here is the receipt.
③ I'll get you a fresh one.
④ Yes. These watermelons are fresh.
⑤ We take both Visa and MasterCard.

01

대화를 듣고, 오늘의 날씨로 가장 적절한 것을 고르시오.

M I'm so _____ _____ going on the camping trip tomorrow.

W You should _____ _____ _____.

M Why? It's a beautiful sunny day.

W I know. But the _____ _____ said it's going to rain tomorrow morning.

M That's terrible. I've been _____ _____ _____ this camping trip.

W Don't _____ _____. Fortunately, it will stop raining in the afternoon.

M That's a _____.

●●
relief 안도, 안심

02

대화를 듣고, 여자가 가려고 하는 장소를 고르시오.

W Excuse me. _____ _____ _____ this school?

M Yes, I do.

W I'm _____ _____. I'm looking for the student center.

M I'll show you _____ _____ _____. Look at this campus map here.

W Okay.

M We're here. Go straight one block and turn left _____ _____ _____.

W And then?

M _____ _____ one block and turn right. _____ _____ _____ _____ the block, you'll see the student center on your right.

W Thank you very much. I think I can easily find it now.

M Welcome to the school. _____ _____ _____.

03

대화를 듣고, 두 사람이 대화하는 장소로 가장 적절한 곳을 고르시오.

M Maria, are you doing okay?

W I'm _____ _____. Do you know what just happened?

M What? Did you _____ _____?

W I made it all the way down the slope _____ _____ _____ even once.

M Really? That's pretty good for a _____. However, you need to be _____ _____ your form.

W All right. Would you please check my form while I am _____?

M Okay. I'll check your form this time.

●●
slope 경사지, (스키장) 슬로프   **novice** 초보자
be concerned about ~에 대해 걱정하다[신경쓰다]

04 대화를 듣고, 남자의 직업으로 가장 적절한 것을 고르시오.

M How can I help you?

W Well, I'm looking for something _____ and _____.

M Perhaps I can interest you in our _____ _____ _____.

W Hmm… It looks compact, but it doesn't look very affordable.

M Don't worry. We have a special promotion right now. If you _____ _____ _____ with us today, all the options are _____ _____ _____.

W All the options? That sounds like a pretty _____ _____.

M How about going for a _____ _____?

W Sure.

●●
affordable 가격이 적당한 **latest** 최근의, 최신의
free of charge 무료로

05 대화를 듣고, 여자가 설명하는 범인이 누구인지 고르시오.

M _____ _____ those five men, which one do you think is the _____?

W Well… I think it's the man with the _____ in the middle.

M Are you sure?

W Not really. Umm… It's him! The one with the _____ and the beard.

M Do you mean the man _____ _____?

W No, the one on the other side. He's got his hair _____ _____ _____.

●●
robber 강도 **beard** 턱수염 **mustache** 콧수염
ponytail 포니테일, 말총머리

06 대화를 듣고, 여자가 지불해야 할 금액으로 가장 적절한 것을 고르시오.

W I would like to _____ _____ _____ to the U.S., please.

M Are you sending them by _____ or _____ _____?

W _____ _____. How much is each?

M If you send them by airmail, they will cost _____ won each. Express mail will cost _____ won each.

W I have two letters here, and the _____ are different. I need this one to _____ _____, so I'll send it express.

M What about _____ _____ _____?

W Just airmail will be fine.

●●
airmail 항공 우편 **express mail** 빠른 우편 **recipient** 수신인

07 대화를 듣고, 남자의 심정으로 가장 적절한 것을 고르시오.

M I've finally _____ _____ _____.

W Wow, congratulations! How do you feel?

M I feel a strong _____ _____ _____.

W Good for you. You _____ _____. After all, you worked hard.

M I did, didn't I?

W A chapter of your life _____ _____, and a new one will _____.

●●
graduate 졸업하다 **accomplishment** 성취
deserve ~할 가치가[자격이] 있다 **after all** 결국에는, 어쨌든
chapter 장, (인생의) 한 시기

08 대화를 듣고, 여자의 마지막 말의 의도로 가장 적절한 것을 고르시오.

W Did you read today's _____ _____?

M No, what happened?

W A doctor who was performing an operation _____ _____ inside a patient.

M That's _____. What did he _____ _____?

W He left some gauze inside.

M I can't believe it. The doctor _____ _____ _____ _____ _____.

W I hope the patient is all right now.

article (신문) 글, 기사 **operation** 수술 **gauze** 거즈

09 대화를 듣고, 남자가 채소를 재배하는 이유로 가장 적절한 것을 고르시오.

M This year, I'm going to _____ _____ in my garden. They are so _____.

W That's a good idea. _____ _____ will you grow?

M I'll grow potatoes, onions, and cucumbers.

W Oh, you _____ _____ _____ any food at the grocery store, will you?

M My goal is to grow all the vegetables I eat _____ _____.

W How does it feel to grow _____ _____ _____?

M It feels really good.

cucumber 오이 **for oneself** 혼자, 스스로

10 대화를 듣고, 남자가 전화를 건 목적으로 가장 적절한 것을 고르시오.

M Hi, Linda. This is Bob.

W Hi, Bob. What's _____ _____?

M Did you _____ _____ _____ my cellphone? I think I _____ _____ at your house.

W No, I didn't. But I'll _____ _____ _____ around the houses and then I'll ask my mom if _____ _____ _____.

M Thanks, Linda. I hope that you can find it there.

W Don't worry too much. It should be here because we _____ _____ _____ with your phone in my room. I can _____ _____ _____ later.

M Thanks a lot. I'll _____ _____ your phone call.

11 대화를 듣고, 남자가 모임에 온 방법으로 가장 적절한 것을 고르시오.

M I'm sorry I'm late for the meeting. My car _____ _____.

W You're _____ so much. Please go to the washroom and clean up.

M I had _____ _____. It's 35 degrees outside, and I had no money to take the subway because I _____ _____ _____ at home.

W It really is a bad day today, isn't it?

M I _____ _____ _____ _____ two kilometers just to get here. I'm bushed.

W Please _____ _____ _____ and drink some water.

●●
break down 고장나다 **sweat** 땀을 흘리다 **washroom** (공공건물의) 세면장, 화장실 **bushed** 몹시 지친 **have a seat** 앉다

12 대화를 듣고, 여자가 내일 저녁에 할 일로 가장 적절한 것을 고르시오.

M Do you have _____ _____ for this weekend?

W Yes, I'm going to _____ and _____ _____ to my friends back in Korea.

M What about tomorrow evening?

W I don't have _____ _____ _____.

M I was _____ _____ _____ _____ tomorrow evening. Would you like to go with me?

W Who is _____ _____ _____ _____?

M Mike is going to have a dance party.

W Well, I'd like to go, but I'm _____ _____ _____ these days. I need some time to relax at home by myself.

M I see. _____ _____ _____ _____, you should just relax.

13 대화를 듣고, 대화 내용과 일치하지 <u>않는</u> 것을 고르시오.

W Well, is this the house that _____ _____?

M Right. The owner went to Japan _____ _____, but I have the keys.

W It looks _____ _____. When was it built?

M It was built _____ _____.

W What company built this house?

M _____ _____ I forgot. Is it important?

W No, not really. Is that a new roof?

M Yes. It _____ _____ _____ two years ago.

●●
on business 사업상, 업무로

14 대화를 듣고, 남자의 마지막 말에 이어질 여자의 말로 가장 적절한 것을 고르시오.

M Do you have any novels _____ _____ _____?

W Yes, I have one.

M Where did you get it? I'm _____ _____ _____ one.

W I didn't buy it. My professor _____ _____ _____ _____.

M Have you read the _____ _____?

W Yes, I have. The book is so interesting that I've read it _____ _____ _____ _____.

M What kind of story is it?

W <u>It's a traditional American story.</u>

●●
novel 소설 **over and over** 계속 반복해서

15 대화를 듣고, 여자의 마지막 말에 이어질 남자의 말로
가장 적절한 것을 고르시오.

W Are these apples _____?

M Sure. They are very sweet and fresh.

W Give me _____ _____. Those
bananas don't look ripe.

M You're right. But these ones here are ripe
and very sweet.

W How much is it _____ _____
_____?

M Five dollars.

W Well, this one seems to be _____.

M I'll get you a fresh one.

••
ripe 익은 **bunch** 다발, 송이 **bruised** 멍든

A 다음을 듣고, 어휘와 우리말 뜻을 쓰시오.

① _____ _____

② _____ _____

③ _____ _____

④ _____ _____

⑤ _____ _____

⑥ _____ _____

⑦ _____ _____

⑧ _____ _____

⑨ _____ _____

⑩ _____ _____

⑪ _____ _____

⑫ _____ _____

B 우리말을 참고하여 빈칸에 알맞은 단어를 쓰시오.

① If you make a deal with us today, all the options are _____ _____
_____. 오늘 저희와 거래하시게 되면 모든 선택 사항들이 무료입니다.

② He's got his hair _____ _____ _____.
그는 머리를 하나로 묶고 있어요.

③ Are you sending them _____ _____ or express mail?
항공 우편과 특급 우편 중 어느 것으로 보내실 건가요?

④ I feel a strong _____ _____ _____.
강한 성취감이 들어.

⑤ Good for you. You _____ _____.
잘됐다. 너는 그럴만한 자격이 있어.

⑥ The doctor _____ _____ _____ more careful.
그 의사는 더 조심했어야 했어.

⑦ Did you _____ _____ _____ my cellphone?
혹시 내 휴대폰 봤어?

⑧ Do you have any novels _____ _____ _____?
영어로 쓰여진 소설책이 있니?

01 다음을 듣고, 금요일의 날씨로 가장 적절한 것을 고르시오.

①
②
③
④
⑤

02 다음을 듣고, 남자가 하는 말의 내용으로 가장 적절한 것을 고르시오.

① 할인 판매
② 화재 신고
③ 선거 유세
④ 소방 훈련 공지
⑤ 체험 활동 안내

03 대화를 듣고, 두 사람이 대화하는 장소로 가장 적절한 곳을 고르시오.

① 은행
② 호텔
③ 환전소
④ 경찰서
⑤ 백화점

04 대화를 듣고, 두 사람의 관계로 가장 적절한 것을 고르시오.

① 교사 - 학생
② 감독 - 선수
③ 영화감독 - 배우
④ 연예인 - 매니저
⑤ 디자이너 - 모델

05 다음 그림의 상황에 가장 적절한 대화를 고르시오.

① ② ③ ④ ⑤

06 대화를 듣고, 남자가 지불할 총 금액으로 가장 적절한 것을 고르시오.

① $27 　② $30
③ $35 　④ $40
⑤ $45

07 대화를 듣고, 여자의 심정으로 가장 적절한 것을 고르시오.

① upset 　② bored
③ excited 　④ nervous
⑤ thankful

정답 및 해석 p. 92

08 대화를 듣고, 남자가 구입할 물건으로 가장 적절한 것을 고르시오.

① 설탕, 자몽
② 설탕, 포도
③ 후추, 포도
④ 소금, 자몽
⑤ 소금, 포도

12 대화를 듣고, 여자가 내일 할 일로 가장 적절한 것을 고르시오.

① 쇼핑하기
② 전시회 가기
③ 도서관 가기
④ 집에서 책 읽기
⑤ 가족과 시간 보내기

09 대화를 듣고, 남자가 집에서 7시 정각에 나가는 이유로 가장 적절한 것을 고르시오.

① 출근 전 운동을 하려고
② 버스에서 앉아서 가려고
③ 지하철의 혼잡을 피하려고
④ 회사 동료와 함께 출근하려고
⑤ 회사에 지각하면 벌금이 있어서

13 대화를 듣고, 대화 내용과 일치하지 않는 것을 고르시오.

① 여자는 빨간색 지갑을 잃어버렸다.
② 여자의 이름은 김영미이다.
③ 여자의 지갑에는 현금이 들어 있다.
④ 여자의 지갑은 커피숍에 있다.
⑤ 여자는 1시간 30분 후에 남자를 만날 것이다.

10 대화를 듣고, 남자가 전화를 건 목적으로 가장 적절한 것을 고르시오.

① 요금제를 변경하기 위해서
② 수리 기사를 요청하기 위해서
③ 회원 정보를 변경하기 위해서
④ 전화 요금을 납부하기 위해서
⑤ 전화 요금을 확인하기 위해서

14 대화를 듣고, 남자의 마지막 말에 이어질 여자의 말로 가장 적절한 것을 고르시오.

① Oh, here is a larger pair.
② Would you like a gift bag?
③ What kind of shoes do you need?
④ Here are your receipt and change.
⑤ Sure. The fitting rooms are over there.

11 대화를 듣고, 여자가 남자에게 부탁한 일로 가장 적절한 것을 고르시오.

① 커피 사오기
② 도넛 사오기
③ 요리 도와주기
④ 병원 데려다 주기
⑤ 알레르기 치료법 알아보기

15 대화를 듣고, 여자의 마지막 말에 이어질 남자의 말로 가장 적절한 것을 고르시오.

① I just rejected her proposal.
② It's a nice place for a vacation.
③ Have you ever been to Sokcho?
④ Okay. It's kind of you to say that.
⑤ I often took trips with her family.

01 다음을 듣고, 금요일의 날씨로 가장 적절한 것을 고르시오.

I'm Mina Kim with the weather for Friday, tomorrow. It's been hot for several days _____ _____ _____. Tonight, the temperature will begin to _____ _____ as clouds are expected to _____ _____. There'll be a _____ _____ of rain tomorrow morning. The temperature will _____ _____ 15 degrees Celsius. The clouds will _____ by this weekends, and you will see _____ _____.

● ●
cool down 서늘해지다 **possibility** 가능성

02 다음을 듣고, 남자가 하는 말의 내용으로 가장 적절한 것을 고르시오.

_____, students! This is your _____ _____. Tomorrow at 11 o'clock there will be a _____ _____. At that time, the fire alarm will ring, and you are to _____ _____ your teacher out of the school. You must _____ _____ until the alarm rings again. This is important, so let's _____ _____ _____.

● ●
attention (안내 방송에서) 알려드립니다, 주목하세요 **principal** 교장
fire drill 소방 훈련

03 대화를 듣고, 두 사람이 대화하는 장소로 가장 적절한 곳을 고르시오.

W Hi. I'd like to _____ 500 dollars.
M Certainly. Please _____ _____ _____ _____. Do you want it in cash or a check?
W Cash, please. Is that all right?
M Yes. Would you please _____ your PIN number here?
W Okay.
M _____ _____ that your PIN number isn't right.
W Oh, sorry. I forgot it. Can I _____ my PIN number?
M Yes. May I have your ID?
W _____ _____ _____.

● ●
withdraw 인출하다 **check** 수표 **PIN number** 비밀번호
reset 다시 맞추다, 재설정하다

04 대화를 듣고, 두 사람의 관계로 가장 적절한 것을 고르시오.

M Lights and camera ready? Standby. Action! Cut!
W Can we _____ _____ _____ _____?
M Let's just finish _____ _____ _____ _____ and then take a break. Just a few more scenes...
W But I'm _____ _____.
M Really? Then let's _____ _____ _____.

W   Thank you.

M   This scene is _____ _____ than I expected.

W   _____ _____ _____ _____. The weather's so hot.

M   We have to hurry if we want to finish before _____.

●●
while we are at it 하는 김에   **scene** 장면   **thirsty** 목마른

---

05   다음 그림의 상황에 가장 적절한 대화를 고르시오.

①   M   Can you _____ _____ _____ _____?

W   Here you go.

②   W   What would you like to order?

M   I'd like to order _____ _____ _____.

③   M   I'm looking for some shorts for my brother.

W   How about these ones _____ _____?

④   W   Is there anything you want to _____ _____ _____ _____?

M   Could you write my mom's name on it?

⑤   M   What are you doing?

W   I'm _____ _____ _____ on the web.

●●
pass 건네주다   **post** 올리다, 게시하다

---

06   대화를 듣고, 남자가 지불할 총 금액으로 가장 적절한 것을 고르시오.

M   I can't _____ _____ this tipping system.

W   What's the problem?

M   Well, our bill _____ _____ 30 dollars. So how much _____ _____ _____ the waiter?

W   They say we should tip _____ 10% _____ 15%.

M   So will 5 dollars be okay?

W   _____ _____ _____ _____.

●●
tipping system 팁 제도   **bill** 계산서, 청구서
come to (총계가) ~이 되다

---

07   대화를 듣고, 여자의 심정으로 가장 적절한 것을 고르시오.

W   Hey, you! You're so _____.

M   Who? Me? Are you talking to me?

W   Yes, you. What _____ _____ _____ you're doing?

M   Huh? I'm just _____ _____ a taxi. Did I do _____ _____ _____?

W   Can't you see there's a line?

M   Oh, there is? I'm sorry. I didn't mean to _____ _____. I didn't _____ there was a line.

W   That's all right, but you should _____ _____ _____.

M   Of course, I will.

●●
selfish 이기적인   **cut in** 끼어들다, 새치기하다

08 대화를 듣고, 남자가 구입할 물건으로 가장 적절한 것을 고르시오.

W Could you _____ _____ _____ _____, please?

M Certainly. What is it?

W Could you _____ _____ _____ the store? We need a few things.

M Sure. What do you _____ _____ _____ _____?

W Well, could you pick up _____ _____?

M Okay. How much?

W A small bag. I guess we also need _____ _____.

M Is that everything?

W I think so.

●●
run over to ~에 잠깐 들르다

09 대화를 듣고, 남자가 집에서 7시 정각에 나가는 이유로 가장 적절한 것을 고르시오.

W You _____ _____ at exactly 7:00 a.m. every day, don't you?

M _____, aren't you?

W Very much so. Please _____ _____ _____.

M If I leave home at exactly this time, I can get on the subway _____ _____ _____.

W Oh, I see.

M If I am ever five minutes late leaving home, I'm caught in a tide of people _____ _____ _____ _____ to get on the subway.

●●
curious 궁금한 **crowd** 군중 **be caught in** ~에 갇히다
tide of people 인파 **push and shove** 밀치락달치락하다

10 대화를 듣고, 남자가 전화를 건 목적으로 가장 적절한 것을 고르시오.

W LS Telecom Company. May I help you?

M Yes. I think there's a _____ on my bill. I believe I was _____.

W I see. _____ _____ _____, I have to ask you some questions. What's your name?

M My name is Peter Kim.

W What is your phone number?

M My phone number is _____-_____-_____.

W All right. Please hold on, and I'll _____ _____ _____.

M Thank you.

●●
overcharge 너무 많이 청구하다 **security** 보안
hold on (전화상으로) 잠시 기다리다 **record** 기록

11 대화를 듣고, 여자가 남자에게 부탁한 일로 가장 적절한 것을 고르시오.

M I'm going to the donut shop. What can I _____ _____?

11

W Anything. _____ _____

_____ there are no peanuts in it.

M Why? You don't like peanuts?

W Actually, I love them, but they don't love

me. I'm _____ _____ peanuts.

M _____ _____ if you eat one?

W I have to go _____ _____

_____ _____ .

••
peanut 땅콩 **be allergic to** ~에 알레르기가 있다

12 대화를 듣고, 여자가 내일 할 일로 가장 적절한 것을 고르시오.

M I'm going to go to the Korean Museum

with my family tomorrow.

W That's great! Does it still have that

special _____ _____ there?

M Yes, that's actually _____ _____

_____ _____ .

W I went there last week. You really have to

go and see it.

M Was it _____ _____ _____ ?

W Oh, yes. It was a really _____

_____ for me.

M Thank you for telling me. What are

_____ _____ for tomorrow?

W I was going to _____ _____ , but

I've decided to go to the _____ .

••
exhibit 전시 **worth** ~의 가치가 있는 **educational** 교육적인

13 대화를 듣고, 대화 내용과 일치하지 <u>않는</u> 것을 고르시오.

W Hello? I _____ _____ _____

_____ in your coffee shop yesterday.

M Could you tell me your name?

W My name is Young-mi Kim.

M May I ask _____ _____

_____ in your wallet?

W I had credit cards, my _____

_____ and about 30,000 won.

M Oh, yes. We have your wallet.

W I'll be there _____ _____

_____ .

M We'll be waiting for you.

••
driver's license 운전면허증

14 대화를 듣고, 남자의 마지막 말에 이어질 여자의 말로 가장 적절한 것을 고르시오.

M I want to buy _____ _____

_____ black shoes.

W Do you want a pair we have _____

_____ or one specially made?

M I'll buy a pair in stock, please.

W Okay. We have plenty of shoes.

_____ _____ _____ .

M I'll try these on. Can you give me a

_____ ?

W Sure. These are the _____

_____ shoes we have. How do you

like them?

M I like them, but they are _____

_____ _____ .

W Oh, here is a larger pair.

••
shoehorn 구둣주걱

15 대화를 듣고, 여자의 마지막 말에 이어질 남자의 말로
가장 적절한 것을 고르시오.

W Do you have _____ _____ for
the break?

M I'm not sure but I _____ _____
_____ at the beach in Sokcho.

W Lucky you! How did that _____
_____?

M My girlfriend rented a _____
_____ in Sokcho for a week and
invited me to _____ _____ with
her and her family.

W That sounds great. But why aren't you
going _____ _____?

M Well, I'm very _____. I have to spend
time with her family, but I _____
_____ _____ them before.

W Come on. You will be fine. Don't be afraid
of _____ _____.

M Okay. It's kind of you to say that.

••
come about 생기다, 일어나다 **seaside villa** 해변의 별장
for sure 확실히 **proposal** 제안

A 다음을 듣고, 어휘와 우리말 뜻을 쓰시오.

① _____ ⑦ _____

② _____ ⑧ _____

③ _____ ⑨ _____

④ _____ ⑩ _____

⑤ _____ ⑪ _____

⑥ _____ ⑫ _____

B 우리말을 참고하여 빈칸에 알맞은 단어를 쓰시오.

① I'd _____ _____ _____ 500 dollars.
500달러를 인출하고 싶은데요.

② I'm _____ a photo _____ _____ _____ .
나는 웹에 사진을 올리고 있어.

③ I didn't _____ _____ cut in.
새치기하려던 것은 아니었어요.

④ For _____ _____ , I have to ask you some questions.
보안상의 이유로 몇 가지 질문을 하겠습니다.

⑤ Please _____ _____ , and I'll check our records.
잠시만 기다려 주시면 기록을 확인해 보겠습니다.

⑥ I'm _____ _____ _____ .
나는 땅콩 알레르기가 있거든.

⑦ Was it _____ your _____ ?
시간을 낼 만큼 가치가 있었니?

⑧ Do you want a pair we have _____ _____ or one specially made?
기성화로 드릴까요, 아니면 주문 제품으로 드릴까요?

MY SCORE
.... / 15

01 대화를 듣고, 남자가 구입할 벽지로 가장 적절한 것을 고르시오.

①  ②

③  ④

⑤

02 다음을 듣고, 남자가 하는 말의 내용으로 가장 적절한 것을 고르시오.

① 도로 공사 안내
② 화재 대피 훈련
③ 가스 안전 수칙
④ 수사 협조 요청
⑤ 겨울철 화재 예방 방법

03 대화를 듣고, 두 사람이 대화하는 장소로 가장 적절한 곳을 고르시오.

① 병원
② 공항
③ 우체국
④ 경찰서
⑤ 분실물 센터

04 대화를 듣고, 두 사람의 관계로 가장 적절한 것을 고르시오.

① wife - husband
② teacher - student
③ salesclerk - customer
④ movie director - staff
⑤ hotel manager - guest

05 다음 그림의 상황에 가장 적절한 대화를 고르시오.

① ② ③ ④ ⑤

06 대화를 듣고, 두 사람이 만나기로 한 시각을 고르시오.

① 3:55 p.m.　② 4:55 p.m.
③ 5:00 p.m.　④ 5:05 p.m.
⑤ 5:10 p.m.

07 대화를 듣고, 남자가 추천하는 공부 방법으로 가장 적절한 것을 고르시오.

① 쓰면서 공부하기
② 참고 도서 활용하기
③ 배운 내용 복습하기
④ 소리 내어 읽어 보기
⑤ 매일 꾸준히 공부하기

08 대화를 듣고, 여자의 마지막 말의 의도로 가장 적절한 것을 고르시오.

① 칭찬
② 사과
③ 비난
④ 후회
⑤ 걱정

09 대화를 듣고, 여자의 친구가 새 아파트로 이사한 이유로 가장 적절한 것을 고르시오.

① 집에서 쥐가 나와서
② 아파트 임대료가 비싸서
③ 이웃과 사이가 안 좋아서
④ 이웃의 시끄러운 소리 때문에
⑤ 학교까지 거리가 너무 멀어서

10 대화를 듣고, 무엇에 관한 내용인지 가장 적절한 것을 고르시오.

① 청주로 여행가기
② 어린 시절의 추억
③ 나무로 집 만드는 법
④ 자연환경의 아름다움
⑤ 주말을 즐겁게 보내는 법

11 다음을 듣고, 남자가 안내 방송에서 언급하지 <u>않은</u> 것을 고르시오.

① 비행기 편명
② 출발지
③ 목적지
④ 이륙 전 유의 사항
⑤ 도착 시간

12 대화를 듣고, 여자가 일요일에 할 일로 가장 적절한 것을 고르시오.

① 남자와 함께 점심 식사 하기
② 남자와 함께 저녁 식사 하기
③ 노트북을 고치러 수리점에 가기
④ 노트북을 구입하러 상점에 가기
⑤ 노트북을 빌리러 남자의 집에 가기

13 대화를 듣고, 대화 내용과 일치하지 <u>않는</u> 것을 고르시오.

① 여자는 남자에게 전화를 했었다.
② 남자는 약속 시간보다 30분 늦게 도착했다.
③ 고속도로에서 교통사고가 났다.
④ 남자는 교통사고를 당했다.
⑤ 남자는 다치지 않았다.

14 대화를 듣고, 남자의 마지막 말에 이어질 여자의 말로 가장 적절한 것을 고르시오.

① I need a perm today.
② I hate this color on me.
③ I like this style. Thank you.
④ Do you have a hairstyle book?
⑤ Where did you get your hair done?

15 대화를 듣고, 여자의 마지막 말에 이어질 남자의 말로 가장 적절한 것을 고르시오.

① I'd rather stay home today.
② I'll help you with the dishes.
③ Thank you for cleaning the room.
④ Okay, I will clean up my room, too.
⑤ I don't want to play with my puppy today.

01 대화를 듣고, 남자가 구입할 벽지로 가장 적절한 것을 고르시오.

W Hello. What can I do for you?

M I'm looking for some _____ for my daughter's room.

W _____ _____ is your daughter?

M She's seven years old. Can you _____ _____ for my little girl?

W I'm pretty sure that she would like prints of _____ or _____.

M Hmm... I don't think so. Do you have any patterns of _____?

W How about prints of _____ or _____?

M I think she would prefer the one _____ _____.

W Okay. I hope she likes it.

●●
wallpaper 벽지 **pattern** 무늬

02 다음을 듣고, 남자가 하는 말의 내용으로 가장 적절한 것을 고르시오.

Ladies and gentlemen, your attention, please. You have to _____ _____ _____ this yellow police line right away. Someone _____ _____ to this place. Your cooperation will help us _____ and _____ the person who set the fire. Please _____ _____ _____ anything you find in this area. If you see _____ _____, please inform a police officer _____. Thank you for _____ _____.

●●
step away from ~로 부터 떨어지다 **set fire** 불을 지르다
cooperation 협조 **investigate** 수사하다, 조사하다
suspicious 의심스러운 **inform** 알리다

03 대화를 듣고, 두 사람이 대화하는 장소로 가장 적절한 곳을 고르시오.

M Do you have _____ _____ _____?

W No, nothing. All these are my _____ _____.

M Have you read the _____ _____, ma'am?

W Yes, I have.

M OK, then could you open up your _____ for me, please? You're one of the travelers _____ _____ _____.

W Certainly. No problem.

●●
declare (세관에서) 신고하다 **belongings** 소지품 **customs** 세관
suitcase 여행 가방 **examination** 검사, 심사

04 대화를 듣고, 두 사람의 관계로 가장 적절한 것을 고르시오.

M May I help you, ma'am?

W Yes, please. I'm looking for _____ _____ _____ _____.

M How about _____ _____

_____ ?

W Jeans for my husband? That's a great idea.

M These jeans are _____ _____

for _____ % _____ .

W I think they'll _____ _____

_____ my husband. I'll take them.

M You've made a _____ _____ .

look good on ~에게 어울리다

05 다음 그림의 상황에 가장 적절한 대화를 고르시오.

① W _____ _____ _____

_____ your steak?

M I'll have mine medium.

② M I'd like to _____ _____

_____ _____ .

W Sure. May I see your library card, please?

③ M I'd like to _____ _____

_____ for one in a bigger size.

W What size do you need?

④ M Do you have *The Mixed-Up Chameleon* by Erick Carle?

W I'm sorry. That book is _____

_____ _____ now.

⑤ M Hello. I'd like to _____ _____ .

W Sure. Do you have a reservation?

check out (책을) 대출하다   exchange 교환하다
out of stock 품절인   check in 체크인하다. 투숙[탑승] 수속을 하다

06 대화를 듣고, 두 사람이 만나기로 한 시각을 고르시오.

W Hey, John. What's _____ _____ ?

M Not much. I just called to see if you

_____ _____ _____

_____ .

W That would be great.

M What time do you _____ _____

_____ ?

W I'm off at five, but why don't you come

here _____ _____ _____ ?

M Sure, but why?

W The people in my office want to meet you.

get off work 퇴근하다

07 대화를 듣고, 남자가 추천하는 공부 방법으로 가장 적절한 것을 고르시오.

M We will _____ _____ _____

in our next class.

W Will the English exam be difficult?

M No, it won't be difficult.

W I've _____ _____ _____

several times, but I can't understand all of it.

M _____ _____ too much. This exam is a spelling and grammar test.

W Then, how _____ _____

_____ ?

M All you have to do is _____

_____ _____ _____ you've

learned.

material 자료   spelling 철자   grammar 문법
go over 검토하다. 복습하다

08 대화를 듣고, 여자의 마지막 말의 의도로 가장 적절한 것을 고르시오.

W I can't believe _____ _____ you ate the meal.

M I'm sorry if I ate _____ _____ _____. I was so hungry.

W You were finished in five minutes.

M I _____ _____ all day, and your food was so delicious. Do you have more?

W Sure. _____ _____.

M Thank you. I think you're the _____ _____ in the world.

W It's _____ _____ _____ that. There's plenty of food, so _____ _____ _____. I'm afraid you'll get a _____.

•• eat like a pig 게걸스럽게 먹다 Help yourself. 마음껏 드세요.
stomachache 복통, 배탈

09 대화를 듣고, 여자의 친구가 새 아파트로 이사한 이유로 가장 적절한 것을 고르시오.

W You know Joyce, right? She _____ _____ a new apartment.

M Why is that?

W Well, one morning, she got up to get a glass of water in the kitchen, and she saw _____ _____ _____ _____ _____.

M How did she react? Was she afraid?

W The neighbors _____ _____ from two blocks away.

M Oh, that's too bad. Is her new place clean and _____ _____ _____?

W Oh, yes. It's a brand-new building.

M It _____ _____ _____ though.

W It is, but she feels better in the new place.

•• stare 빤히 쳐다보다. 응시하다 react 반응하다
neighbor 이웃 scream 소리를 지르다 free of ~이 없는

10 대화를 듣고, 무엇에 관한 내용인지 가장 적절한 것을 고르시오.

M Look at that boy, Jane. I _____ _____ _____ _____ when I was a kid.

W Oh, really?

M Yeah, there was a _____ _____ behind the house, and my brother and I used to _____ _____ _____ and hide there.

W But you don't climb trees now, do you?

M _____ _____ _____. I quit doing that when I was about 14, but I still love the woods. I'd like to _____ _____ _____ _____ someday.

W When I was very little, my family _____ _____ _____ in Chung-ju.

M That sounds nice.

W Oh, it was. It was a _____ _____ in my life. Every Sunday, I would go into the forest and _____ _____ _____.

•• woods[forest] 숲

11 다음을 듣고, 남자가 안내 방송에서 언급하지 <u>않은</u> 것을 고르시오.

M Good evening, ladies and gentlemen. This is your _____ _____. I'd like to _____ _____ _____ Korean Airlines flight 051 from Incheon International Airport to Honolulu, Hawaii. Please put your seats in the _____ _____, fasten your _____, and turn your cellular phones off until we _____ _____. And no smoking _____ _____ in all areas of the plane. Thank you. _____ _____ _____.

••
captain 기장 **take off** 이륙하다 **be allowed** 허용되다

12 대화를 듣고, 여자가 일요일에 할 일로 가장 적절한 것을 고르시오.

W Could you _____ _____ _____ _____?

M Yes, if it's something I can do.

W Would you _____ _____ _____ your laptop this Sunday? _____ _____ _____ _____.

M Certainly. You _____ _____ _____ any time you want.

W Would you mind if I _____ _____ your house on Sunday morning to _____ _____ _____ _____?

M Not at all. I'll be _____ _____.

W Thank you. Let me take you _____ _____ tonight.

M Oh, you _____ _____ _____ _____ do that.

••
come by 잠깐 들르다 **expect** 기대하다, 기다리다

13 대화를 듣고, 대화 내용과 일치하지 <u>않는</u> 것을 고르시오.

W Why didn't you _____ _____ _____, Jason? You are 30 minutes late, and I'm _____ _____ _____.

M I'm sorry. There was a _____ _____ _____ _____ on the highway and...

W What? Are you hurt?

M What are you talking about? Hurt? I'm not hurt.

W You said you were _____ _____ _____ _____!

M You _____. It wasn't my car. It was _____ _____.

W What? Then why were you so late?

M I _____ _____ the accident.

••
misunderstand 오해하다

14 대화를 듣고, 남자의 마지막 말에 이어질 여자의 말로 가장 적절한 것을 고르시오.

W I'd like to _____ _____
_____, please.

M How do you want your hair cut?

W Just a _____, please. Don't make it
_____ _____.

M How do you want _____ _____?

W Please layer the back.

M _____ _____ _____
_____ it? If you don't want this style,
please tell me now.

W <u>I like this style. Thank you.</u>

●●
trim 다듬기, 손질 **layer** 층이 지게 하다

15 대화를 듣고, 여자의 마지막 말에 이어질 남자의 말로 가장 적절한 것을 고르시오.

W It's _____ _____ in here. Who
did this?

M Don't _____ _____. It was me. I
did it.

W You did this to the entire room?

M Yes, it's _____ _____
_____.

W Why did you make _____ _____
_____?

M I didn't _____ _____. I was
playing with the puppy.

W If you want to play with your puppy,
please _____ _____ and play.

M <u>Okay, I will clean up my room, too.</u>

●●
messy 지저분한, 엉망인

정답 및 해석 p. 103

A 다음을 듣고, 어휘와 우리말 뜻을 쓰시오.

① _____   ⑦ _____

② _____   ⑧ _____

③ _____   ⑨ _____

④ _____   ⑩ _____

⑤ _____   ⑪ _____

⑥ _____   ⑫ _____

B 우리말을 참고하여 빈칸에 알맞은 단어를 쓰시오.

① If you see anyone _____, please inform a police officer _____.
만약 의심스러운 사람을 보시면 즉시 경찰관에게 알려주십시오.

② These jeans are _____ _____ for 35% off.
이 청바지는 35% 할인 중입니다.

③ _____ _____ _____ _____ your steak?
스테이크 굽기를 어떻게 해드릴까요?

④ I'd like to _____ _____ these books.
이 책들을 대출하고 싶어요

⑤ That book is _____ _____ _____ now.
그 책은 지금 품절입니다.

⑥ Is her new place clean and _____ _____ mice?
새로 이사한 곳은 깨끗하고 쥐가 없니?

⑦ You are 30 minutes late, and I'm _____ _____ _____.
네가 30분이나 늦어서 막 가려던 참이야.

⑧ I'd like to _____ a _____, please.
머리를 자르려고 하는데요.

MY SCORE

.... / 15

01 다음을 듣고, 금요일의 날씨로 가장 적절한 것을 고르시오.

①  ②

③  ④

⑤

02 다음을 듣고, 남자가 하는 말의 내용으로 가장 적절한 것을 고르시오.

① 대학 면접
② 구직 면접
③ 직장 사직
④ 취업 성공 비결
⑤ 추천서 작성 요청

03 대화를 듣고, 두 사람이 대화하는 장소로 가장 적절한 곳을 고르시오.

① hotel
② restaurant
③ dental clinic
④ car repair shop
⑤ department store

04 대화를 듣고, 두 사람의 관계로 가장 적절한 것을 고르시오.

① 의사 - 환자 ② 교사 - 학생
③ 교사 - 학부모 ④ 상담원 - 고객
⑤ 은행원 - 고객

05 대화를 듣고, 여자가 설명하는 동작으로 가장 적절한 것을 고르시오.

06 대화를 듣고, 현재 시각을 고르시오.

① 2:30 p.m. ② 3:30 p.m.
③ 4:00 p.m. ④ 4:30 p.m.
⑤ 5:00 p.m.

07 대화를 듣고, 남자의 심정으로 가장 적절한 것을 고르시오.

① angry ② fearful
③ hopeful ④ surprised
⑤ indifferent

08 대화를 듣고, 남자가 살았던 장소가 <u>아닌</u> 곳을 고르시오.

① Miami

② Chicago

③ Boston

④ Los Angeles

⑤ Hawaii

09 대화를 듣고, 여자가 속상해하는 이유로 가장 적절한 것을 고르시오.

① 기다리는 메시지가 오지 않아서

② 자신의 유튜브 채널이 갑자기 사라져서

③ 남자의 유튜브 채널의 구독자가 더 많아서

④ 자신의 유튜브 채널이 큰 주목을 받지 못해서

⑤ 자신의 유튜브 채널에 안 좋은 댓글이 달려서

10 대화를 듣고, 무엇에 관한 내용인지 가장 적절한 것을 고르시오.

① 한국의 즐길 거리

② 외국의 공중목욕탕

③ 피부를 부드럽게 하는 방법

④ 한국인들의 해외 여행 실태

⑤ 외국인들의 한국 공중목욕탕 이용

11 대화를 듣고, 남자가 여자에게 추천한 교통수단으로 가장 적절한 것을 고르시오.

① 버스

② 지하철

③ 택시

④ 승용차

⑤ 자전거

12 대화를 듣고, 두 사람이 대화 직후에 할 일로 가장 적절한 것을 고르시오.

① 도서관 가기

② TV 시청하기

③ 숙제 끝마치기

④ 점심 요리하기

⑤ 먹을 것 사오기

13 대화를 듣고, 대화 내용과 일치하지 <u>않는</u> 것을 고르시오.

① 두 사람은 주유소에 있다.

② 여자는 방향 지시등을 켜지 않았다.

③ 남자의 트럭이 여자의 차를 칠 뻔했다.

④ 여자는 초보 운전자이다.

⑤ 남자의 트럭에는 가스 탱크가 있다.

14 대화를 듣고, 남자의 마지막 말에 이어질 여자의 말로 가장 적절한 것을 고르시오.

① Thank you for saying so.

② I'm planning to buy a new computer.

③ Let's play a computer game together!

④ I prefer using a laptop over a desktop.

⑤ I'm sorry. I'll be more careful from now on.

15 대화를 듣고, 여자의 마지막 말에 이어질 남자의 말로 가장 적절한 것을 고르시오.

① I've never driven a car before.

② I usually go to work by subway.

③ If you want, I can give you a ride.

④ Make sure you are on time for the bus.

⑤ That's why you moved to a place closer to work.

01
다음을 듣고, 금요일의 날씨로 가장 적절한 것을 고르시오.

Hello. This is Jonathan with the Toronto weather report. Let's _____ _____ _____ at the weather for this week. We've had been _____ _____ since last weekend. I'm afraid the _____ will continue until Tuesday. We're expecting _____ _____ starting on Wednesday. As the weather continues to be clear, the atmosphere will _____ _____. On Thursday, there's a high _____ _____ _____. So don't forget your _____ when you go out. The rain will continue _____ _____.

●●
freezing 몹시 추운 **atmosphere** 대기

02
다음을 듣고, 남자가 하는 말의 내용으로 가장 적절한 것을 고르시오.

Actually, I like my _____ _____ very much, and I get along very well with my _____. The basic reason why I want to _____ _____ _____ is that there is no room for _____. So the only chance for me to _____ _____ _____ is to find a new job. I read your _____, and I know that your company is the _____ _____ for me. If you hire me, I will _____ _____ _____.

●●
present 현재의 **get along with** ~와 잘 지내다 **room** 여지
growth 성장 **improve** 향상시키다 **career** 경력
advertisement 광고 **do one's best** 최선을 다하다

03
대화를 듣고, 두 사람이 대화하는 장소로 가장 적절한 곳을 고르시오.

W May I help you?
M Yes, I'd like to _____ _____ _____. My name is Steven Harper.
W Is it just for a _____, or are you having trouble _____ _____ _____?
M I think I want a checkup.
W Well, can you _____ _____ tomorrow morning?
M That's fine. I'll come again.

●●
checkup 검사, 건강 검진

04
대화를 듣고, 두 사람의 관계로 가장 적절한 것을 고르시오.

W I'm Tony's mother Nancy. Nice to meet you, Mr. Pearson.
M Nice to meet you, too. Tony _____ _____ _____ I wanted to meet you today.
W Is there a _____ _____ _____?
M No, it's not really a problem. It's just that he seems a bit _____, and he's _____ _____.
W The truth is, his father and I _____ _____ _____.
M Oh, I see. That's why Tony can't _____ _____ in class.

W I'm so sorry. I _____ _____

_____ you earlier...

M No, it's a _____ to know now. I'll be

sure to pay special attention to Tony

_____ _____ _____ .

●●
divorce 이혼하다

05 대화를 듣고, 여자가 설명하는 동작으로 가장 적절한 것을 고르시오.

W Do you want to _____ _____

_____ with me?

M What do you _____ _____

_____ ?

W Stand up and put _____ _____

together. Raise your arms out to

_____ _____ at shoulder level,

parallel to the _____. Bend your

_____ _____ .

M It's not _____ _____ _____

you.

W Now, stand up straight again. Let's do

this about _____ _____ .

M I've got the idea, but can we do

_____ _____ ?

W You should do this every day. Then, you'd

_____ _____ _____ it.

●●
side 옆, 옆구리 **parallel** 평행한 **bend** 구부리다
halfway 중간에, 절반만 **get used to** ~에 익숙해지다

06 대화를 듣고, 현재 시각을 고르시오.

W Thanks for _____ _____

_____ at the train station.

M You're welcome. Please have a _____

_____ . When do you _____ ?

W My train leaves _____ _____

_____ .

M Oh, so your train leaves at 3:30 p.m.?

W Yes, so we have more _____

_____ _____ .

●●
depart 떠나다, 출발하다

07 대화를 듣고, 남자의 심정으로 가장 적절한 것을 고르시오.

W _____ _____ _____ on

your face?

M I have some _____ on my face.

W You should go to _____ _____

_____ .

M For some pimples? I don't really think

that is _____ .

W You'd better _____ _____

_____ your skin.

M Don't worry. They will _____

_____ .

W I just hope you don't get pimples on your

face _____ .

M Okay. I will go to see a doctor soon.

●●
necessary 필요한 **go away** 없어지다, 사라지다
indifferent 무관심한

08 대화를 듣고, 남자가 살았던 장소가 <u>아닌</u> 곳을 고르시오.

M Where _____ _____ _____?

W I was born in Miami.

M Really? Me, too!

W Wow, _____ _____ _____!
What made you come from Miami to
Hawaii?

M Well, first, I _____ _____
Chicago, and then I _____ Chicago
and went to Boston for a little while.
Finally, I came to Hawaii _____
_____.

W _____ _____ in a lot of places.

M Yeah, but I like Hawaii the best. I plan
on staying here _____ _____
_____.

•• coincidence 우연의 일치   plan on ~할 예정이다

09 대화를 듣고, 여자가 속상해하는 이유로 가장 적절한
것을 고르시오.

W Can you _____ _____
_____ I uploaded on my YouTube
channel? _____ _____
_____ is checking it.

M Of course. I'll leave a _____ after I
watch it.

W Thank you. My channel has only
_____ subscribers.

M Don't be too sad. I have _____
_____ subscribers on my channel.

W I thought I would get a lot of attention
_____ _____ _____ I made
my channel.

M I thought so, too. _____ _____
_____ too sad.

•• comment 논평, 댓글   subscriber 구독자

10 대화를 듣고, 무엇에 관한 내용인지 가장 적절한 것을
고르시오.

M Did you know that some tourists come
to Korea just to enjoy the _____
_____?

W Yes, I did. But can't they go to any in their
own countries?

M It is _____ _____ _____.
You see, Koreans make a special effort
to _____ _____ _____,
making it feel smooth and clean. But
they don't.

W Oh, I see. I _____ _____
_____.

•• public bath 공중목욕탕   scrub the skin 때를 밀다
smooth 매끄러운

11 대화를 듣고, 남자가 여자에게 추천한 교통수단으로
가장 적절한 것을 고르시오.

W How am I _____ _____
_____ in this city?

M Well, the bus system is terrible. Sometimes you have to wait _____ _____ _____ for a bus. And there aren't _____ _____ _____ to go anywhere you want.

W Can I _____ _____ _____ here then?

M Sure, but it's _____ to take a taxi.

W Then what should I do?

M I think if you have a driver's license, you'd better _____ _____ _____ _____.

W Isn't that expensive?

M If you rent an _____ _____, it's not too expensive.

12 대화를 듣고, 두 사람이 대화 직후에 할 일로 가장 적절한 것을 고르시오.

M How about going out for _____ _____ _____? It's two o'clock.

W I think we should _____ _____ _____ first.

M I don't think so. I'm so hungry, and it's so hot. We should look for a restaurant where the air conditioner _____ _____. We can study tonight.

W Remember? There's a _____ _____ _____ on tonight.

M That's right. I want to see *Wheel of Fortune* tonight.

W _____ _____ _____ get something to eat first and finish our homework before the program?

M Okay, let's go.

● ●
air conditioner 에어컨

13 대화를 듣고, 대화 내용과 일치하지 <u>않는</u> 것을 고르시오.

M Hey, lady! You _____ _____ _____ your turn signal when you changed lanes. My truck _____ _____ your car.

W Oh! I'm sorry. I'm an _____ _____. I forgot.

M Can't you see that I have a full tank of gas on my truck?

W You were once a _____ yourself, weren't you? Please _____ _____ _____ my mistake.

M Why don't you _____ _____ busy streets like this until you _____ _____ _____?

W Okay, maybe I will. Sorry.

● ●
turn signal 방향 지시등 **lane** 차선
inexperienced 경험이 부족한, 미숙한 **stay off** 피하다, 멀리하다

14 대화를 듣고, 남자의 마지막 말에 이어질 여자의 말로 가장 적절한 것을 고르시오.

M _____ _____ _____ with the computer? It doesn't _____ _____ _____ _____.

W Really? There was no problem when I used it.

M I think the computer _____ _____ _____ a virus. Did you open a strange link or install a program you don't know?

W Well, I _____ _____ _____ while on the Internet.

M That could be the _____ of the problem. I need to call a _____ _____.

W I'm sorry. I'll be more careful from now on.

●●
be infected with ~에 감염되다 **install** 설치하다
repairman 수리공, 수리 기사

W The problem was that there were only a few buses _____ _____ _____.

M Well, why didn't you _____ then?

W No way. It's _____ _____ than taking the subway. The _____ _____ _____ was terrible.

M That's why you moved to a place closer to work.

●●
public transportation 대중 교통 **neighborhood** 이웃, 동네
rush hour 러시아워, 혼잡 시간대

15 대화를 듣고, 여자의 마지막 말에 이어질 남자의 말로 가장 적절한 것을 고르시오.

M I heard you moved last month.

W Yeah, I did. I had a hard time _____ _____ _____.

M Really? I thought you were using _____ _____?

W Yeah, but it used to take me more than two hours _____ _____.

M Are you serious? Why didn't you _____ _____ _____?

A 다음을 듣고, 어휘와 우리말 뜻을 쓰시오.

① _____   ⑦ _____

② _____   ⑧ _____

③ _____   ⑨ _____

④ _____   ⑩ _____

⑤ _____   ⑪ _____

⑥ _____   ⑫ _____

B 우리말을 참고하여 빈칸에 알맞은 단어를 쓰시오.

① I _____ _____ very well _____ my co-workers.

저는 제 동료들과도 매우 잘 지냅니다.

② If you _____ me, I will _____ _____ _____.

저를 고용하신다면 최선을 다 하겠습니다.

③ Is it just for a _____, or are you having trouble with your _____?

검사만 하실 건가요, 아니면 치아에 문제가 있습니까?

④ Raise your arms out to your sides at shoulder level _____ _____

the ground. 팔은 어깨 높이에서 땅과 평행이 되도록 옆으로 벌려.

⑤ Wow, what a _____!

와, 우연의 일치네요!

⑥ I thought I would get a lot of attention _____ _____

_____ I made my channel. 난 내 채널을 만들자마자 큰 주목을 받을 줄 알았어.

⑦ Oh! I'm sorry. I'm an _____ _____.

오! 죄송해요. 제가 초보 운전자라서요.

⑧ I think the computer is _____ _____ a virus.

내 생각엔 컴퓨터가 바이러스에 감염된 것 같아.

01 다음을 듣고, 시애틀의 현재 날씨로 가장 적절한 것을 고르시오.

①
②
③
④
⑤

02 다음을 듣고, 남자가 하는 말의 내용으로 가장 적절한 것을 고르시오.

① 임시 휴교 안내
② 독감 예방 방법
③ 축제 일정 소개
④ 축제 취소 공지
⑤ 학교 예산 안내

03 대화를 듣고, 두 사람이 대화하는 장소로 가장 적절한 곳을 고르시오.

① 식당
② 문구점
③ 미술관
④ 체육관
⑤ 백화점

04 대화를 듣고, 두 사람의 관계로 가장 적절한 것을 고르시오.

① 의사 - 환자
② 교사 - 학생
③ 약사 - 손님
④ 수의사 - 손님
⑤ 승무원 - 탑승객

05 다음을 듣고, 여자가 시험 중 유의 사항으로 언급하지 않은 것을 고르시오.

① 책 덮기
② 책상 위에 펜, 지우개, 시험지만 두기
③ 시험 중 잡담하지 않기
④ 시험 중 커닝하지 않기
⑤ 시험이 끝나면 시험지 제출하기

06 대화를 듣고, 여자가 잘못 누른 전화번호로 가장 적절한 것을 고르시오.

① 356-5511
② 366-1331
③ 366-5115
④ 366-5511
⑤ 336-5115

07 대화를 듣고, 두 사람의 심정으로 가장 적절한 것을 고르시오.

① upset
② scared
③ hopeful
④ touched
⑤ disappointed

08 다음을 듣고, 두 사람의 대화가 <u>어색한</u> 것을 고르시오.

① ② ③ ④ ⑤

09 대화를 듣고, 남자가 여자에게 고마워하는 이유로 가장 적절한 것을 고르시오.

① 여자가 파티를 열어줘서
② 여자가 깜짝 선물을 줘서
③ 여자가 추천서를 잘 써줘서
④ 여자가 수학 공부를 도와줘서
⑤ 여자가 좋은 선생님을 소개해줘서

10 대화를 듣고, 무엇에 관한 내용인지 가장 적절한 것을 고르시오.

① 세금을 내는 이유
② 수요와 공급의 법칙
③ 세금의 종류와 쓰임새
④ 가격에 영향을 주는 요인
⑤ 상품과 서비스에 부과되는 세금

11 대화를 듣고, 여자가 남자에게 부탁한 일로 가장 적절한 것을 고르시오.

① 다시 전화하기
② 버스로 갈아타기
③ 휴대폰 수리하기
④ 약속 시간 변경하기
⑤ 지하철역으로 마중 나오기

12 대화를 듣고, 여자가 대화 직후에 할 일로 가장 적절한 것을 고르시오.

① 다른 디자인 보여주기
② 더 저렴한 제품 보여주기
③ 남자에게 맞는 사이즈 찾아오기
④ 인라인스케이트 착용법 설명해주기
⑤ 인라인스케이트 잘 타는 법 알려주기

13 대화를 듣고, 대화 내용과 일치하지 <u>않는</u> 것을 고르시오.

① 여자는 운동을 좋아한다.
② 여자가 가장 좋아하는 운동은 수영이다.
③ 여자는 물속에서 약 5분간 숨을 참을 수 있다.
④ 여자는 물속에서 남자보다 더 오랫동안 숨을 참을 수 있다.
⑤ 물속에서 숨 참기 기네스 세계 기록은 약 24분이다.

14 대화를 듣고, 남자의 마지막 말에 이어질 여자의 말로 가장 적절한 것을 고르시오.

① I'm glad to hear that.
② Yes, that would be great!
③ Here you go. Thanks for your help.
④ Sorry, but I don't have any right now.
⑤ The garbage truck left just a minute ago.

15 대화를 듣고, 여자의 마지막 말에 이어질 남자의 말로 가장 적절한 것을 고르시오.

① I've had enough. Thank you.
② Yes, I did. It was very interesting.
③ Okay. I will not forget that next time.
④ Do you think I can borrow that book?
⑤ Well, I guess I will have to read it later.

01 다음을 듣고, 시애틀의 현재 날씨로 가장 적절한 것을 고르시오.

Good morning. This is Anna Kennedy with the Seattle _____ _____. Right now, it's very _____, and the sky is covered with _____ _____. There is a chance of some rain starting tonight. It will rain _____ _____ _____, and the temperature will drop _____ _____ _____ 5 degrees Celsius. The rain will _____ _____ _____ at night, and it will snow on Wednesday. Please be careful on the _____ _____.

●●
humid 습한 **thick** 두꺼운, 짙은 **turn into** ～로 바뀌다
icy road 빙판길

02 다음을 듣고, 남자가 하는 말의 내용으로 가장 적절한 것을 고르시오.

Good morning, students. I am sorry to _____ that the faculty has _____ _____ _____ this year's festival. It is due to the flu virus that _____ _____ _____ throughout the country. I know you've been _____ _____ _____ having the festival, but we have no choice. We will have more _____ for next year's festival and will make it a good one. I hope you _____ _____ _____. Thank you.

●●
faculty 교수진 **cancel** 취소하다 **due to** ～때문에 **flu** 독감
funds 자금

03 대화를 듣고, 두 사람이 대화하는 장소로 가장 적절한 곳을 고르시오.

M Look at this _____ _____. It looks so cute!

W It's not just cute and pretty. With all these pockets and everything, it sure will _____ _____ _____.

M Oh, I see.

W See this button here? If you want to _____ the carriage, all you have to do is _____ _____ _____.

M Wow, amazing!

W Well, _____ _____ _____ buy it?

●●
baby carriage 유모차 **come in handy** 쓸모가 있다, 유용하다
fold 접다

04 대화를 듣고, 두 사람의 관계로 가장 적절한 것을 고르시오.

W Hello. How may I help you?

M I have a _____.

W Do you have a _____, too?

M No, just a headache. Do I need a _____?

W No, you don't need one. I'll give you _____ for two days.

M _____ _____ should I take this?

W Take it _____ _____ _____ _____.

M Okay. And do you have some band-aids?

W _____ _____ _____,
   please. Here you are. It _____
   _____ 15 dollars _____.

M Okay. Here is my credit card.

●●
headache 두통 **fever** 열 **prescription** 처방전 **medicine** 약

W Hello. My name is Claire. May I speak to
   Mr. Smith, please?

M Sorry. There's no one here _____
   _____ _____. I think you have
   _____ _____ _____.

W Isn't this 366-5115?

M No, this is 366-5511.

W Oh, I'm sorry to _____ _____.

M That's okay.

05 다음을 듣고, 여자가 시험 중 유의 사항으로 언급하지
않은 것을 고르시오.

All right, everyone. Please close your books
and _____ _____ _____
the test. Now clear your desk. Everybody
_____ _____ _____ to have
a pen or pencil, the test, and an eraser on
your desk. There's _____ _____
during the test. The test _____
_____ _____. When you're finished
with the test, please _____ _____
to the front. _____ _____
_____ your test.

●●
timed 시간이 정해진

06 대화를 듣고, 여자가 잘못 누른 전화번호로 가장 적절한
것을 고르시오.

M Hello. This is Tom speaking. May I help
   you?

07 대화를 듣고, 두 사람의 심정으로 가장 적절한 것을
고르시오.

W This scene always _____ _____
   _____.

M I agree. It's the best part of the movie.

W This is the scene where the main
   character _____ _____
   _____ for the woman just before he
   dies.

M I usually don't like sad movies, but this is
   an _____.

W How could you _____ _____
   this movie? It breaks my heart, but it's
   beautiful.

M I _____ _____ _____
   _____.

●●
main character 주인공 **confess** 고백하다 **exception** 예외
totally 완전히, 전적으로

08 다음을 듣고, 두 사람의 대화가 <u>어색한</u> 것을 고르시오.

① M May I help you?

W I'm just _____ _____. Thank you.

② W Do you _____ _____ _____ in your house?

M Yes, I have a dog.

③ M Do you ever _____ _____ _____ _____ in summer?

W I go every summer, but I couldn't go this year.

④ W Will you _____ _____ _____? It's too heavy.

M I think I've left my bag in the car.

⑤ M This is my grandmother. She is _____ _____ _____.

W Nice to meet you.

●●
look around 둘러보다, 구경하다 **pet** 애완동물 **carry** 들다

09 대화를 듣고, 남자가 여자에게 고마워하는 이유로 가장 적절한 것을 고르시오.

M Happy birthday!

W A surprise birthday party! I can't believe it.

M You _____ _____. You've helped me all throughout the school year.

W Oh, it was _____ _____.

M _____ your help, I _____ _____ _____ math this year.

W You did all the work _____. I just helped a little.

M You're too modest. _____ _____ your candles.

●●
modest 겸손한 **blow out** 끄다

10 대화를 듣고, 무엇에 관한 내용인지 가장 적절한 것을 고르시오.

M Do you know that the government is putting a 10% tax _____ _____ _____?

W Oh, I didn't know. So if I buy a hundred-dollar item, then the tax will be 10 dollars?

M That's right. Taxes will be applied to the prices of services _____ _____ _____ goods.

W I see. I think it's putting a _____ on consumers.

M Let's think _____ _____. Taxes are used to help the people when the economy _____ _____ _____.

W I think you're right.

●●
government 정부 **tax** 세금 **apply** 적용하다 **A as well as B** A뿐만 아니라 B도 **goods** 상품, 제품 **burden** 부담 **economy** 경제

11 대화를 듣고, 여자가 남자에게 부탁한 일로 가장 적절한 것을 고르시오.

M Hello. Is Janet there?

W _____. Tony, where are you?

M I'm _____ _____ _____ to school.

W Hello. I can hardly hear you. You're _____ _____.

M Really? I think the reason is that I'm _____ _____ _____ now.

W Why don't you call me _____ _____ _____ _____ the subway?

M Okay. I'm getting off _____ _____ _____ anyway.

●● **break up** (전화가) 끊겨서 들리다 **get off** 내리다, 하차하다

12 대화를 듣고, 여자가 대화 직후에 할 일로 가장 적절한 것을 고르시오.

W May I help you, sir?

M Well, I'd like to buy some in-line skates, but I don't know _____ _____ _____ _____.

W Are you a _____ _____?

M I've only tried it five times.

W Okay. How much do you _____ _____ _____?

M Well, I don't have much money.

W Then I have just the pair for you. They are _____ _____ _____, and they're _____ _____ now. They are made especially for _____.

M Oh, I like the design and the price. Can I _____ _____ _____? I need a size 7.

W Sure. Please wait. I will be right back _____ _____ _____ _____.

●● **of good quality** 질이 좋은 **especially** 특히, 특별히

13 대화를 듣고, 대화 내용과 일치하지 <u>않는</u> 것을 고르시오.

M _____ _____ _____ you like sports very much.

W You're right. I love sports.

M What's your favorite sport?

W I like _____.

M Me, too. Can you _____ _____ for a long time?

W I can _____ _____ _____ for about 5 minutes.

M I can do that for about 10 minutes.

W You're _____! I heard the Guinness World Record is about _____ minutes.

●● **underwater** 물속에서 **hold one's breath** 숨을 참다

14 대화를 듣고, 남자의 마지막 말에 이어질 여자의 말로 가장 적절한 것을 고르시오.

W Sam, can you _____ _____ _____ _____ for me?

M I'm sorry, Mom. I can't help you because I'm _____ _____ _____.

W Please. The garbage truck will be here _____ _____ _____ _____, and I'm busy now.

M Okay, where is it?

W It's by the front door.

M Oh, the garbage _____ _____ out of the bag.

W Do you want _____ _____ _____?

M Yes. Could you give me another one, please?

W Here you go. Thanks for your help.

●●
take out the garbage 쓰레기를 내놓다 **front door** 현관
spill 엎지르다, 흐르다, 새다 **trash bag** 쓰레기 봉투

M It's about a robot that can read _____ and deliver _____ _____ through human expressions. You should read it _____ _____.

W Well, I guess I will have to read it later.

●●
front-page (신문) 1면의 **headline** 표제, 머리기사 **emotion** 감정
comforting 위로가 되는 **expression** 표현, 표정

15 대화를 듣고, 여자의 마지막 말에 이어질 남자의 말로 가장 적절한 것을 고르시오.

M Good morning, James. Did you read _____ _____?

W No, I haven't seen it yet. Is there any _____ _____?

M Yes. The from-page headline was really interesting.

W _____ was it _____?

A 다음을 듣고, 어휘와 우리말 뜻을 쓰시오.

① _____
② _____
③ _____
④ _____
⑤ _____
⑥ _____
⑦ _____
⑧ _____
⑨ _____
⑩ _____
⑪ _____
⑫ _____

B 우리말을 참고하여 빈칸에 알맞은 단어를 쓰시오.

① There's no one here _____ _____ _____.
여기 그런 이름을 가진 사람은 없는데요.

② I'm just _____ _____. Thank you.
그냥 둘러보는 거예요. 고마워요.

③ _____ your help, I _____ _____ _____ math this
year. 네 도움이 없었다면 나는 올해 수학에서 낙제를 했을 거야.

④ I can _____ hear you. You're _____ _____.
네 말이 거의 안 들려. 전화가 끊겨서 들리네.

⑤ I'm _____ _____ at this station anyway.
어쨌든 이번 역에서 내릴 거야.

⑥ They are _____ _____ _____, and they're on sale now.
품질이 좋고 지금 할인 중입니다.

⑦ I can _____ _____ _____ for about 5 minutes.
전 5분 정도 숨을 참을 수 있어요.

⑧ Can you _____ _____ _____ for me?
쓰레기 좀 버리고 와 주겠니?

MY SCORE
.... / 15

01 대화를 듣고, 여자가 파티에서 입을 드레스로 가장 적절한 것을 고르시오.

02 대화를 듣고, 여자의 선생님이 누구인지 고르시오.

03 대화를 듣고, 두 사람이 대화하는 장소로 가장 적절한 곳을 고르시오.

① 은행
② 매표소
③ 여행사
④ 우체국
⑤ 대사관

04 대화를 듣고, 남자의 직업으로 가장 적절한 것을 고르시오.

① pilot
② clerk
③ waiter
④ secretary
⑤ flight attendant

05 다음 그림의 상황에 가장 적절한 대화를 고르시오.

① ② ③ ④ ⑤

06 대화를 듣고, 여자가 안경에 지불한 금액으로 가장 적절한 것을 고르시오.

① $20
② $40
③ $60
④ $80
⑤ $100

07 대화를 듣고, 여자의 심정으로 가장 적절한 것을 고르시오.

① tired
② angry
③ envious
④ thankful
⑤ impressed

정답 및 해석 p. 116

08 대화를 듣고, 남자가 서점에서 살 물건으로 가장 적절한 것을 고르시오.

① 영어 참고서
② 수학 참고서
③ 공책
④ 펜
⑤ 자

09 대화를 듣고, 남자가 전화를 받지 않은 이유로 가장 적절한 것을 고르시오.

① 수업 중이어서
② 잠이 깊이 들어서
③ 점심을 먹고 있어서
④ 전화기가 고장이 나서
⑤ 전화기를 찾을 수가 없어서

10 대화를 듣고, 여자의 증상이 <u>아닌</u> 것을 고르시오.

① 콧물
② 기침
③ 인후통
④ 열
⑤ 두통

11 대화를 듣고, 남자가 여자에게 해 준 조언으로 가장 적절한 것을 고르시오.

① 낮잠 자지 않기
② 커피 마시지 않기
③ 휴식 취하기
④ 약 처방 받기
⑤ 시험공부 계획 세우기

12 대화를 듣고, 남자가 대화 직후에 할 일로 가장 적절한 것을 고르시오.

① 목걸이 환불해주기
② 목걸이 교환해주기
③ 영수증 재발급하기
④ 목걸이 수리 맡기기
⑤ 매니저에게 전화하기

13 대화를 듣고, 대화 내용과 일치하지 <u>않는</u> 것을 고르시오.

① 날씨에 대해 이야기 하고 있다.
② 오늘은 날씨가 매우 덥고 습하다.
③ 두 사람 모두 덥고 습한 날씨를 싫어한다.
④ 여자는 사막보다 정글 여행을 선호한다.
⑤ 두 사람은 선풍기를 틀 것이다.

14 대화를 듣고, 남자의 마지막 말에 이어질 여자의 말로 가장 적절한 것을 고르시오.

① I can't find the remote control.
② You're sitting too close to the TV.
③ Can you turn up the volume a little?
④ How about a talk show on channel 5?
⑤ Turn off the TV if you're not watching it.

15 대화를 듣고, 여자의 마지막 말에 이어질 남자의 말로 가장 적절한 것을 고르시오.

① No one can tell the future.
② My brother has a talent for music.
③ I guess you should quit your present job.
④ You could handle this situation by yourself.
⑤ I think you're good at writing and making stories.

01 대화를 듣고, 여자가 파티에서 입을 드레스로 가장 적절한 것을 고르시오.

M Mina, have you decided _____ _____ _____ for the dinner party?

W I just found the best dress.

M Oh, that's great. What does the dress _____ _____?

W It's a short dress with _____ _____.

M What color is it?

W It's orange, and there's a piece of _____ _____ around the waist that ties in the front. It's the perfect dress for me.

M I want to _____ _____ _____ that dress.

•• **stripe** 줄무늬 **fabric** 천 **tie** 묶다

02 대화를 듣고, 여자의 선생님이 누구인지 고르시오.

W Thank you for _____ _____ _____ _____, Dad.

M You're welcome. You're not late, are you?

W No, we're early. Oh, _____ _____ the window! There's my teacher at the bus stop!

M Who? Do you mean the man _____ _____ _____ in his left hand?

W No. I mean the man _____ _____ the bus stop sign.

M Oh, I see. Do you mean the man _____ _____ _____ _____?

W That's right. He's my teacher.

03 대화를 듣고, 두 사람이 대화하는 장소로 가장 적절한 곳을 고르시오.

M Can I help you?

W Yes, I'd like to _____ _____ _____ _____. Could you tell me when I can do that?

M Certainly. You can apply _____ _____ _____ between nine and five.

W Thank you, Oh, and do I need anything?

M You'll need your _____.

W Okay, I'll _____ _____ _____ soon.

•• **weekday** 평일

04 대화를 듣고, 남자의 직업으로 가장 적절한 것을 고르시오.

W Excuse me. Could I have _____ _____ _____, please?

M Sure. What would you like?

W I'd like some _____ _____.

M Will that be all for you?

W　Oh, and could I have some _____

　　_____ ?

M　Sure. Here you go.

W　And by the way, what time _____

　　_____ _____ in Toronto?

M　Our expected arrival time is 5:30 p.m.

　　_____ _____ .

expected arrival time 도착 예정 시간　**local time** 현지 시간

05 다음 그림의 상황에 가장 적절한 대화를 고르시오.

① M　How do you go to school every day?

　　W　I usually go to school _____

　　　_____ .

② M　I heard you had a car accident. Are

　　　you okay?

　　W　Yes. The cars were _____

　　　_____ , but no one was _____ .

③ W　I _____ _____ _____ .

　　M　Hold your breath for a minute.

④ M　What's the matter?

　　W　I _____ _____ _____

　　　while I was cooking.

⑤ W　Could you hand me the remote control

　　　for the TV?

　　M　Sure. _____ _____

　　　_____ _____ I can do for

　　　you?

damaged 손상된　**hiccup** 딸꾹질　**hand** 건네주다

06 대화를 듣고, 여자가 안경에 지불한 금액으로 가장 적절한 것을 고르시오.

M　Wow, you _____ _____ today.

　　What did you do?

W　I'm wearing contact lenses.

M　That's it. You look good _____

　　_____ _____ .

W　Thanks. The glasses cost _____

　　_____ _____ _____ the

　　lenses.

M　I think they were a good _____ .

W　I do, too. The lenses only cost me

　　_____ dollars.

investment 투자

07 대화를 듣고, 여자의 심정으로 가장 적절한 것을 고르시오.

W　Do you know what?

M　What?

W　I lent Jim my book two months ago, but

　　he still _____ _____ _____ .

M　Really? That's very _____ . Why don't

　　you call him?

W　I think I will. But I don't understand why

　　I have to call him. He should have just

　　returned it _____ _____ . Is he

　　hoping to keep it?

M　I don't think so. People just forget. Just

　　_____ _____ politely.

W　I'm _____ _____ _____

　　_____ politeness. This is the second

　　time he's done this.

inconsiderate 남을 배려할 줄 모르는, 사려깊지 못한
remind 상기시키다　**in no mood for** ~할 기분이 아닌
politeness 예의, 공손

08 대화를 듣고, 남자가 서점에서 살 물건으로 가장 적절한 것을 고르시오.

W These books are so _____! I can't believe it.

M I know. This English reference book _____ _____ _____. I have to buy it now.

W Do you have to buy a math reference book?

M No, my brother's friend will _____ _____ _____.

W That's great! Is there _____ _____ you need?

M I need some notebooks, pens, and _____, too.

W But it's a lot cheaper to buy that stuff from the _____ _____.

M Good idea. We'll just get the _____ _____ here.

●●
reference book 참고 도서 **ruler** 자 **stuff** 것, 물건

09 대화를 듣고, 남자가 전화를 받지 않은 이유로 가장 적절한 것을 고르시오.

M Hi, Olga.

W It's great to see you here. _____ _____ _____ during lunch today?

M Were you looking for me?

W Yes. I tried to _____ _____ _____ _____ on your cellphone, but you didn't answer.

M Oh, I _____ _____ _____.

W Why?

M Because I was _____ _____ _____ class. I couldn't answer the phone.

●●
get hold of ~에게 연락하다 **in the middle of** ~의 도중에

10 대화를 듣고, 여자의 증상이 <u>아닌</u> 것을 고르시오.

W Hello. What can I do for you?

M Good morning, Doctor. I have a _____ _____ and a _____. I think I've _____ _____ _____.

W Okay. And what else?

M I have a _____ _____, too.

W Let me check your temperature. Well, your temperature is _____. Did you take _____ _____?

M Yes, I took a _____ this morning because I had a _____.

W Okay. I'm going to give you a _____. Make sure to get _____ _____ _____.

M Okay. Thank you, Doctor.

●●
runny nose 콧물 **sore throat** 인후통, 목아픔 **painkiller** 진통제

11 대화를 듣고, 남자가 여자에게 해 준 조언으로 가장 적절한 것을 고르시오.

W I'm having trouble _____ _____ _____ these days.

M Are you under _____ _____

_____ _____ at school?

W Yes, I am taking _____ _____

next week, and I'm really worried about

them.

M Do you _____ _____?

W Yes, but I usually have coffee in the

morning.

M Hmm... I think you need to relax more

and try _____ _____ _____

so much about your exams.

W Okay. I'll _____ _____

_____.

12 대화를 듣고, 남자가 대화 직후에 할 일로 가장 적절한 것을 고르시오.

W I bought this necklace here yesterday,

but this part is _____.

M Oh, is it? May I take a look at it more

closely?

W Sure. _____ _____ _____

it?

M Yes, of course. Do you have the

_____?

W No, can I exchange it without the receipt?

I lost it.

M I don't think you can. But I'll _____

_____ _____ and ask.

W Thank you.

13 대화를 듣고, 대화 내용과 일치하지 <u>않는</u> 것을 고르시오.

W It's really hot today.

M You can _____ _____

_____.

W I can't stand it when it's _____ and

_____.

M _____ _____. The humidity

makes my skin very _____.

W I like it better hot and dry.

M So if you had to travel to the desert

or the jungle, would you _____

_____ _____?

W Of course.

M Let's _____ _____ the fan and

_____ _____.

• •

You can say that again. 정말 그래., 동감이야.
former 전자, 앞의 것 **fan** 선풍기

14 대화를 듣고, 남자의 마지막 말에 이어질 여자의 말로 가장 적절한 것을 고르시오.

M Hey, Susan. _____ _____ the

TV, please.

W Where is the _____ _____?

M It's on the table.

W What would you like to watch?

M I don't know. Let's see _____

_____.

W Oh, there's a cooking show _____

_____ _____.

M Is there anything else on?

W How about a talk show on channel 5?

15 대화를 듣고, 여자의 마지막 말에 이어질 남자의 말로 가장 적절한 것을 고르시오.

M Do you know what the _____

_____ _____ of a successful

person is?

W I'm not sure, but I think _____ is the

key to success.

M Do you know _____ _____

_____ nowadays?

W I don't know. What?

M _____ is the key to success.

W I guess you're right. I'm afraid I'm not a

very _____ _____.

M You _____ _____ _____

your hidden talents.

W What do you think my hidden talents

are?

M <u>I think you're good at writing and making</u>

<u>stories.</u>

● ●

quality 질, 자질 **creativity** 창의성 **hidden** 숨겨진 **talent** 재능

정답 및 해석 p. 121

A 다음을 듣고, 어휘와 우리말 뜻을 쓰시오.

① _____   ⑦ _____

② _____   ⑧ _____

③ _____   ⑨ _____

④ _____   ⑩ _____

⑤ _____   ⑪ _____

⑥ _____   ⑫ _____

B 우리말을 참고하여 빈칸에 알맞은 단어를 쓰시오.

① Have you decided _____ _____ _____ for the dinner
party? 디너파티에 뭘 입을지 결정했어?

② I want to _____ _____ _____ that dress.
네가 그 드레스를 입고 있는 것을 보고 싶어.

③ I'd like to _____ _____ a _____.
비자를 신청하고 싶은데요.

④ Our expected _____ is 5:30 p.m. _____
_____. 도착 예정 시간은 현지 시간으로 오후 5시 30분입니다.

⑤ You look good _____ your _____.
안경을 벗으니까 좋아 보인다.

⑥ I have a _____ and a _____.
콧물이 나고 기침이 나요.

⑦ I'm _____ _____ _____ at night these days.
난 요즘 밤에 잠을 자는 게 힘들어.

⑧ Creativity is the _____ _____ _____.
창의성이 성공의 열쇠다.

영어듣기 모의고사
CooL
LISTENING
정답 및 해석

2

문제 및 정답	받아쓰기 및 녹음내용	해석

01

다음을 듣고, 내일의 날씨로 가장 적절한 것을 고르시오.

① ②

③ ④

⑤

You're listening to *Good Morning Seoul*. This is Sam Morse. Seoul began the morning with light raindrops, and it will <u>continue to rain</u> all day long. Tomorrow will be <u>cloudy</u> and <u>cool</u>. It will be sunny again <u>the day after tomorrow</u>, and the clear weather will continue <u>until this weekend</u>.

여러분은 〈굿모닝 서울〉을 듣고 계십니다. 저는 Sam Morse입니다. 서울은 가벼운 빗방울로 아침을 시작했으며, 하루 종일 비가 계속 내리겠습니다. 내일은 흐리고 선선하겠습니다. 모레는 다시 화창하겠으며, 맑은 날씨는 이번 주말까지 계속되겠습니다.

●●
raindrop 빗방울 **continue** 계속되다
cloudy 흐린, 구름이 낀 **the day after tomorrow** 모레

02

대화를 듣고, 여자가 가려고 하는 장소를 고르시오.

W Excuse me. I think I'm <u>lost</u>. Could you <u>show me the way</u> to the post office?

M Sure, ma'am. It's a little <u>far from</u> here.

W Is it within <u>walking distance</u>?

M Yes. It'll take about 20 minutes.

W Then, I prefer to walk.

M Okay. <u>Go straight</u> one block and make a left turn.

W Go straight one block and <u>turn left</u>. Is that right?

M Yes. Then, you have to go two more blocks and turn right at the <u>intersection</u>. You'll see the post office <u>next to</u> the flower shop. It will be <u>on your right</u>.

W That's easy. Thanks a lot.

M You're welcome. Have a nice day.

여 실례합니다. 제가 길을 잃은 것 같은데요. 우체국으로 가는 길 좀 알려 주시겠어요?

남 물론이죠, 부인. 여기서 좀 멀어요.

여 걸어서 갈 수 있는 거리인가요?

남 네. 20분 정도 걸릴 겁니다.

여 그러면 걷는 것이 좋겠어요.

남 네. 한 블록 직진해서 왼쪽으로 도세요.

여 한 블록 직진해서 왼쪽으로 돌아요. 맞지요?

남 맞아요. 그리고 두 블록 더 가서 교차로에서 오른쪽으로 도세요. 꽃집 옆에 우체국이 보일 겁니다. 오른편에 있을 거예요.

여 쉽네요. 감사합니다.

남 천만에요. 즐거운 하루 되세요.

●●
lost 길을 잃은 **within** ~ 이내에[안에]
walking distance 걸어서 갈 수 있는 거리
prefer 선호하다 **intersection** 교차로

03 대화를 듣고, 두 사람이 대화하는 장소로 가장 적절한 곳을 고르시오.

① taxi
② gym
③ airport
④ subway
⑤ airplane

M Good afternoon. <u>Where to</u>, ma'am?

W Please take me to the airport. And please <u>step on it</u>.

M Okay, I'll drive as fast as I can.

W <u>How long will it take</u> to get there?

M 40 minutes or so.

W That's good. I have to be at the airport <u>within the next hour</u>.

M Don't worry. You'll be fine.

남 안녕하세요. 어디로 모실까요, 손님?

여 공항으로 가주세요. 그리고 빨리 가주세요.

남 알겠습니다. 최대한 빨리 운전하겠습니다.

여 그곳까지 가는 데 얼마나 걸릴까요?

남 40분 정도요.

여 다행이네요. 앞으로 한 시간 안에 공항까지 가야 하거든요.

남 걱정 마세요. 괜찮을 겁니다.

●●
step on it 빨리 가다 **or so** ~쯤[정도]

---

04 대화를 듣고, 두 사람의 관계로 가장 적절한 것을 고르시오.

① 의사 - 환자
② 점원 - 고객
③ 엄마 - 아들
④ 사장 - 직원
⑤ 교사 - 학생

W John, you're spending too much time <u>playing computer games</u>.

M Just <u>give me</u> five more minutes.

W I've told you a hundred times. <u>No more games</u> today!

M Okay. I'll <u>do my homework</u> first. After that, can I play games again?

W No. It's already nine o'clock. You should go to bed <u>as soon as</u> you finish your homework.

M Okay.

여 John, 컴퓨터 게임 하는 데 너무 많은 시간을 보내는구나.

남 5분만 기다려 주세요.

여 너에게 백 번은 얘기했어. 오늘 더 이상의 게임은 안돼!

남 알겠어요. 숙제 먼저 할게요. 그리고 나서 다시 게임 해도 되죠?

여 안돼. 벌써 9시야. 숙제를 끝내자마자 잠자리에 들어야 한다.

남 알겠어요.

●●
a hundred times 백 번 **already** 이미, 벌써
as soon as ~하자마자

---

05 대화를 듣고, 남자가 자동차 열쇠를 찾은 위치로 가장 적절한 곳을 고르시오.

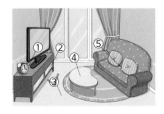

M Honey, where are the car keys?

W I don't know. Where did you <u>leave them</u>?

M I always leave them <u>next to</u> the clock, but they're not there now.

W Did you check on the coffee table?

M I <u>wouldn't have put</u> them on the coffee table.

W How about the sofa? Sometimes things fall <u>between the cushions</u>.

M I checked. They're not there.

W Wait. I see them. They fell <u>on the floor</u>.

남 여보, 자동차 열쇠 어디 있어요?

여 몰라요. 어디다 뒀는데요?

남 항상 시계 옆에 두는데, 지금 보니까 거기 없네요.

여 탁자 위는 확인해 봤어요?

남 탁자 위에 두지는 않았을 거예요.

여 소파는요? 가끔 물건들이 쿠션 사이로 떨어지기도 하잖아요.

남 확인했어요. 거기에도 없어요.

여 잠깐. 찾았어요. 바닥에 떨어져있네요.

●●
coffee table (소파 앞에 놓는) 탁자
cushion 쿠션 **floor** 바닥

06

대화를 듣고, 여자가 구입할 책의 할인 후 가격으로 가장 적절한 것을 고르시오.

① $6
② $8
③ $10
④ $12
⑤ $20

W Look, Mark! These books are on sale!

M Really? How much are they reduced?

W There's a 20% discount on all books.

M And the sale is today only.

W Well, I don't usually buy books, but I'll buy this one.

M That's a good idea. How much is the original price of this book?

W It says 10 dollars.

여 이것 봐, Mark! 이 책들은 할인 중이야!

남 정말? 얼마나 할인되는데?

여 모든 책이 20% 할인이야.

남 그리고 오늘만 할인하는구나.

여 음, 난 보통 책을 사지는 않지만 이것은 사야겠어.

남 좋은 생각이야. 이 책의 원래 가격이 얼마지?

여 10달러라고 써 있어.

•• **on sale** 할인 중인 **reduce** (가격을) 낮추다, 할인하다 **discount** 할인 **say** ~라고 쓰여 있다

07

대화를 듣고, 여자가 느꼈을 심정의 변화로 가장 적절한 것을 고르시오.

① scared → angry
② bored → excited
③ angry → worried
④ scared → relieved
⑤ happy → embarrassed

W The strangest thing happened to me today.

M What happened?

W I got stuck in an elevator with three other people.

M You must have been so terrified.

W Yes, I was. But then we started talking. After a while, we all thought it made us relieved. Then, the elevator started up again.

M That's an interesting story.

여 나한테 오늘 진짜 이상한 일이 생겼었어.

남 무슨 일인데?

여 나랑 다른 세 사람이 엘리베이터 안에 갇히고 말았어.

남 정말 무서웠겠다.

여 응, 그랬어. 그런데 우리끼리 대화를 나누기 시작했어. 잠시 후에 우리 모두 그것이 우리를 안도하게 만들었다고 생각했지. 그러자 엘리베이터가 다시 올라가기 시작했어.

남 그거 흥미로운 이야기구나.

•• **get stuck** 갇히다, 꼼짝 못 하다 **terrified** 무서워하는, 겁이 난 **after a while** 잠시 후에 **relieved** 안도하는 **embarrassed** 당황스러운, 난처한

08

대화를 듣고, 두 사람의 목적지로 가장 적절한 곳을 고르시오.

	Destination	Gate No.	Time
①	New York	21	12:35 p.m.
②	Seoul	25	1:00 p.m.
③	London	35	1:50 p.m.
④	Tokyo	23	2:30 p.m.
⑤	Paris	45	4:50 p.m.

W Hurry up! We have to leave now.

M Don't worry. We have plenty of time.

W Please hurry. I don't want to miss the plane.

M Kate, it's only one o'clock.

W Yes, but we have to arrive three hours before international flights.

M Oh, then we have to be there by one fifty. By the way, what gate is it? Number 23?

W I don't think so. My ticket says 45.

여 서둘러! 우리는 지금 출발해야 해.

남 걱정 마. 시간은 많으니까.

여 제발 서둘러. 비행기를 놓치고 싶지 않아.

남 Kate, 겨우 한 시야.

여 알아, 하지만 국제선을 타려면 3시간 전에 도착해야 해.

남 아, 그럼 우린 1시 50분까지 도착해야 하는구나. 그런데 몇 번 탑승구지? 23번?

여 그렇지 않을 걸. 내 티켓에는 45라고 써 있어.

•• **plenty of** 많은 **international flight** 국제선 여객기 **gate** (공항의) 게이트, 탑승구

09 대화를 듣고, 여자의 몸무게가 늘어난 이유로 가장 적절한 것을 고르시오.

① 건강에 이상이 있어서
② 탄산음료를 자주 마셔서
③ 끼니를 간식으로 때워서
④ 운동을 전혀 하지 않아서
⑤ 명절 음식을 많이 먹어서

W How was this New Year's holiday, Tom?
M I had a wonderful time with my family. My <u>nephews</u> and <u>nieces</u> were so cute. I <u>haven't seen them</u> for a long time. What about you?
W I had a good time, too.
M Did you <u>visit your parents</u> during the holiday?
W I sure did. I love <u>my mother's cooking</u>.
M Did she make a lot of food?
W Too much! I <u>gained weight</u> over the holidays.

여 Tom, 이번 설 연휴 어땠어?
남 가족들이랑 좋은 시간을 보냈어. 내 조카들이 너무 귀엽더라. 난 그들을 오랫동안 보지 못했거든. 너는 어때?
여 나도 좋은 시간을 보냈어.
남 이번 연휴에 부모님을 뵈러 갔었어?
여 물론 그랬지. 난 우리 엄마의 요리를 정말 좋아하거든.
남 어머님이 음식을 많이 해 주셨니?
여 너무 많이 하셨어! 내가 연휴 기간에 살이 쪘잖아.

●●
nephew 남자 조카 niece 여자 조카
gain weight 체중이 늘다, 살이 찌다

---

10 대화를 듣고, 남자가 이용할 교통수단으로 가장 적절한 것을 고르시오.

① 버스
② 택시
③ 지하철
④ 자가용
⑤ 비행기

M What's the best way to <u>go downtown</u>?
W <u>I recommend</u> the bus. But I see you are <u>unfamiliar with</u> this city.
M What do you mean?
W Well, the bus is <u>faster</u> than the subway, but the subway is <u>easier</u> to <u>figure out</u>.
M Oh, I see. Then I'll go downtown <u>by subway</u>.
W Good idea. It's a few minutes <u>longer</u>.
M That's okay. Thanks for helping me.

남 시내에 가는 가장 좋은 방법이 뭐예요?
여 버스를 추천해요. 그런데 당신은 이 도시에 익숙하지 않군요.
남 무슨 뜻이죠?
여 음, 버스가 지하철보다 더 빠르긴 하지만 지하철이 이해하기 더 쉬워요.
남 아, 그렇군요. 그렇다면 저는 지하철로 시내에 가야겠어요.
여 좋은 생각이에요. 몇 분 더 걸리긴 해요.
남 괜찮아요. 도와줘서 고마워요.

●●
recommend 추천하다 unfamiliar 익숙하지 않은 figure out 이해하다, 알아내다

---

11 대화를 듣고, 남자가 여자에게 제안한 일로 가장 적절한 것을 고르시오.

① 함께 축구 하기
② 매일 운동 하기
③ 자신의 팀을 응원하기
④ 집에 가서 옷 갈아입기
⑤ 여자 축구팀에 등록하기

W Hey, what's <u>going on</u>?
M I'm going to <u>play soccer</u>. Do you want to play?
W Are there <u>any girls</u> on your team?
M No, but you can be <u>the first</u>.
W That <u>sounds like fun</u>. I'll go home and change.
M I'll see you <u>on the field</u>.

여 야, 무슨 일이야?
남 축구 하려고. 너도 할래?
여 너희 팀에 여자도 있어?
남 아니, 하지만 네가 처음이 될 수도 있지.
여 재미있겠다. 집에 가서 옷 갈아입고 올게.
남 경기장에서 보자.

●●
sound like ~처럼 들리다 change (옷을) 갈아입다 field 운동장, 경기장

12 다음을 듣고, 남자가 새해 결심으로 언급하지 않은 것을 고르시오.

① 매일 영어 공부하기
② 스마트폰 살 돈 모으기
③ 집안일 돕기
④ 숙제 미루지 않기
⑤ 남동생에게 잘해 주기

I decide to do something every new year. My resolutions are often about school, family life, or plans for the future. I will tell you my resolutions for this year: studying English every day, saving money for a new smartphone, helping my parents with the housework, and being nice to my brother. I hope I can keep them all.

저는 새해마다 무언가를 하기로 결심합니다. 제 결심들은 주로 학교나 가정 생활, 또는 미래에 대한 계획들입니다. 제 결심들을 여러분께 말씀드리겠습니다. 매일 영어 공부하기, 새 스마트폰 살 돈 모으기, 부모님을 도와 집안일 하기, 그리고 남동생에게 잘해 주는 것입니다. 저는 제가 이것들을 모두 지킬 수 있기를 바랍니다.

decide 결심하다 resolution 결심
housework 가사, 집안일

---

13 대화를 듣고, 대화 내용과 일치하지 않는 것을 고르시오.

① 남자는 Peter James를 지지한다.
② 남자는 Peter James가 정직하다고 생각한다.
③ 여자는 Peter James가 무례하다고 생각한다.
④ 남자는 Sandy가 예의 바르다고 생각한다.
⑤ 여자는 Sandy에게 투표할 것이다.

W Who are you going to vote for in the election?
M Peter James. I think he is honest and intelligent.
W But I think he is a bit rude, too.
M Oh, I don't think so. He seems pretty polite to me.
W Anyway, I've decided to vote for Sandy. She's the right person to be president.
M Okay, we'll see.

여 선거에서 누구를 뽑을 거니?
남 Peter James. 나는 그가 정직하고 지적이라고 생각해.
여 하지만 그는 좀 무례하기도 해.
남 아, 난 그렇게 생각하지 않아. 그는 내게는 매우 예의 바른 것처럼 보였어.
여 어쨌든, 나는 Sandy에게 투표하기로 결정했어. 그녀는 회장직에 적합한 인물이야.
남 좋아, 지켜보자.

vote for ~에 투표하다 election 선거
honest 정직한 intelligent 지적인, 총명한
president 대통령, 회장

---

14 대화를 듣고, 남자의 마지막 말에 이어질 여자의 말로 가장 적절한 것을 고르시오.

① I am very proud of you!
② I think I will fail this course.
③ I am afraid of making mistakes.
④ Really? Thank you for saying that.
⑤ I have to prepare for my presentation.

M Good job!
W Do you really think so?
M Absolutely! You gave a very good presentation.
W I've worked on this presentation for the whole semester.
M I can tell.
W I made several mistakes though.
M As a matter of fact, I don't think I've ever seen a presentation better than that.
W Really? Thank you for saying that.

남 잘했어!
여 정말 그렇게 생각하세요?
남 그렇고 말고! 넌 발표를 아주 잘 했어.
여 학기 내내 이번 발표를 준비했어요.
남 알지.
여 몇 가지 실수를 하기는 했지만요.
남 사실, 난 이보다 더 좋은 발표를 본 적이 없는 것 같구나.
여 정말이요? 그렇게 말씀해 주시니 감사합니다.

① 당신이 매우 자랑스러워요!
② 저는 이 과목에서 낙제할 것 같아요.
③ 저는 실수를 하는 게 두려워요.
⑤ 저는 발표 준비를 해야 해요.

absolutely 그렇고 말고 presentation 발표
semester 학기 as a matter of fact 사실은
proud 자랑스러운 fail 실패하다, 낙제하다
prepare 준비하다

15 대화를 듣고, 여자의 마지막 말에 이어질 남자의 말로 가장 적절한 것을 고르시오.

① You look like your mother.

② I don't like my nose either.

③ That's right. Your nose is too big.

④ Yes! Don't worry about your nose.

⑤ I think you should exercise more often.

M Mary, why are you so depressed?

W When I walk down the street, people always look at my nose.

M You are so sensitive about your appearance.

W You don't understand how I feel.

M How many times do I have to tell you? You look fine to me.

W But my nose is too big. I want to have plastic surgery.

M Listen. You look very attractive.

W Do I?

M Yes! Don't worry about your nose.

남 Mary, 왜 그렇게 의기소침한 거야?

여 내가 길을 걸을 때면 사람들이 내 코만 보는 것 같아.

남 넌 네 외모에 정말 민감하구나.

여 넌 내 기분이 어떤지 이해하지 못해.

남 내가 얼마나 여러 번 말해야겠니? 내가 볼 때 넌 예뻐.

여 하지만 내 코는 너무 커.

남 내 말 들어. 넌 정말 매력적이야.

여 내가?

남 그래! 네 코에 대해서는 걱정하지 마.

① 너는 어머니를 닮았구나.

② 나도 내 코가 마음에 안 들어.

③ 맞아. 네 코는 너무 커.

⑤ 너는 더 자주 운동을 해야 할 것 같아.

depressed 의기소침한 sensitive 민감한
appearance 외모 plastic surgery
성형수술 attractive 매력적인

REVIEW TEST p. 15

A
① cloudy, 흐린, 구름이 낀 ② intersection, 교차로 ③ floor, 바닥 ④ nephew, 남자 조카
⑤ recommend, 추천하다 ⑥ resolution, 결심 ⑦ absolutely, 그렇고 말고 ⑧ semester, 학기
⑨ depressed, 의기소침한 ⑩ figure out, 이해하다, 알아내다 ⑪ get stuck, 갇히다, 꼼짝 못 하다
⑫ the day after tomorrow, 모레

B
① Where to ② walking distance ③ gained weight
④ best way to ⑤ decide to do ⑥ vote for, election
⑦ right person, president ⑧ a matter of fact

문제 및 정답	받아쓰기 및 녹음내용	해석

01

대화를 듣고, 여자가 강아지를 찾은 위치로 가장 적절한 곳을 고르시오.

W I was about to give the puppy a bath, but he <u>ran</u> <u>away</u> and <u>hid</u>.

M Where is he?

W Somewhere in the bedroom. Help me <u>find</u> <u>him</u>.

M Did you check <u>under</u> <u>the</u> <u>bed</u>?

W Yeah. He's not there.

M Hmm… He's not under the table <u>either</u>.

W Oh, my gosh. Here he is! He's hiding in the <u>laundry</u> <u>basket</u>!

여 나는 지금 막 강아지를 목욕시키려는데, 그 녀석이 도망쳐서 숨어버렸어.

남 강아지가 어디 있는데?

여 침실 어딘가에 있어. 강아지 찾는 것 좀 도와줘.

남 침대 밑은 확인해 봤니?

여 응. 거기 없어.

남 음… 탁자 아래에도 없네.

여 오, 이런. 여기 있어! 이 녀석이 세탁물 바구니 안에 숨어 있네!

●●
be about to 막 ~하려는 참이다 **run away** 도망치다 **laundry** 세탁물

02

대화를 듣고, 남자가 가려고 하는 장소를 고르시오.

M Excuse me. <u>Do</u> <u>you</u> <u>know</u> where the H Department Store is?

W Yes. Do you see the tall building <u>over</u> <u>there</u>? That's SBS.

M I see.

W Facing that building is Paris Park. <u>Pass</u> the park and <u>turn</u> <u>left</u> at the corner. Then, <u>go</u> <u>down</u> the street. You'll see the department store. It's <u>behind</u> World Apartment and <u>next</u> <u>to</u> the church.

M I've got it. Thank you.

남 실례합니다. H백화점이 어디 있는지 아세요?

여 네. 저기 높은 빌딩 보이세요? 저 빌딩이 SBS방송국이에요.

남 그렇군요.

여 그 건물을 마주보고 있는 것이 파리 공원이에요. 그 공원을 지나서 길모퉁이에서 왼쪽으로 도세요. 그리고 나서 길을 따라 가세요. 백화점을 볼 수 있을 거예요. 그것은 월드아파트 뒤쪽 교회 옆에 있어요.

남 알겠어요. 감사합니다.

●●
department store 백화점 **face** 마주보다, 향하다 **pass** 지나가다

03

대화를 듣고, 두 사람이 대화하는 장소로 가장 적절한 곳을 고르시오.

① 병원
② 박물관
③ 경기장
④ 백화점
⑤ 놀이공원

W Excuse me! I have an <u>emergency</u>!

M What's the problem?

W My daughter is <u>lost</u>. She's only six years old.

M Oh, dear. What's her name?

W Hannah Kim. She is wearing a yellow <u>sweater</u> and black <u>jeans</u>.

M Where <u>did</u> <u>you</u> <u>lose</u> her?

W Near the <u>roller</u> <u>coaster</u>. We were watching the <u>parade</u>.

M Okay. <u>Don't</u> <u>worry</u>. We can help you.

여 실례합니다! 응급 상황이에요!

남 뭐가 문제죠?

여 딸을 잃어버렸어요. 그 애는 겨우 여섯 살이에요.

남 오, 이런. 그 애 이름이 뭐죠?

여 Hannah Kim이에요. 그 애는 노란색 스웨터와 검은색 청바지를 입고 있어요.

남 따님을 어디서 잃어버리셨나요?

여 롤러코스터 근처에서요. 우리는 퍼레이드를 구경하고 있었어요.

남 알겠습니다. 걱정 마세요. 저희가 도와드릴게요.

●●
emergency 응급 상황 **roller coaster** 롤러코스터 **parade** 퍼레이드

04 대화를 듣고, 두 사람의 관계로 가장 적절한 것을 고르시오.

① 점원 - 고객
② 감독 - 선수
③ 면접관 - 구직자
④ 영화감독 - 배우
⑤ 방송 진행자 - 해설자

W Hello. I'm Mary Dover, the <u>sportscaster</u> for today's baseball game. <u>Beside</u> <u>me</u> is Bob Pierson. He is the <u>commentator</u> for this match. Hello, Mr. Pierson.

M Hello.

W Mr. Pierson, what do you think of <u>today's game</u>?

M Well, let's see. I think it will be a <u>tough game</u> for the AB Bears because the Happy Lions have won five games <u>in a row</u>.

W Yes, but the AB Bears don't seem too <u>concerned</u>, maybe because of their <u>excellent teamwork</u>.

M Oh, the game is starting.

여 안녕하세요. 오늘 야구 경기를 중계할 Mary Dover입니다. 제 옆에는 Bob Pierson 씨가 와 계십니다. 이 경기의 해설을 맡아 주시겠습니다. 안녕하세요, Pierson 씨.

남 안녕하세요.

여 Pierson 씨, 오늘 경기를 어떻게 보십니까?

남 음, 글쎄요. 오늘 경기는 Happy Lions 팀이 다섯 경기에서 연속으로 승리했기 때문에 AB Bears 팀에게 힘든 경기가 될 것 같습니다.

여 네, 하지만 AB Bears 팀은 훌륭한 팀워크를 가지고 있기 때문에 그렇게 걱정은 안 하는 것 같습니다.

남 아, 경기가 시작됐네요.

● ●

sportscaster 스포츠 방송 진행자 **beside** ~의 옆에 **commentator** 해설자 **tough** 힘든 **in a row** 연속으로, 계속해서 **concerned** 걱정하는 **excellent** 훌륭한

---

05 다음을 듣고, 화재 이후 여자가 깨달은 것으로 가장 적절한 것을 고르시오.

① 경험의 중요성
② 가족의 소중함
③ 화재의 위험성
④ 신속한 신고의 필요성
⑤ 최선을 다하는 삶의 중요성

One night, my house <u>burned down</u>. Although I lost many things in the fire, the experience helped me to be <u>more mature</u>. Before the fire, I always <u>complained about</u> my life. Then, the fire came and <u>destroyed everything</u> we owned. We were suddenly poor and <u>had to borrow</u> everything. At first, I had a hard time, but I slowly began to realize that I didn't really need my <u>old things</u>. I just needed my <u>family</u>. It is true that the fire took many good things from me, but it <u>gave me something</u>, too. It taught me to <u>appreciate people</u> more than things.

어느 날 밤, 우리 집이 불타 버렸다. 비록 그 화재로 나는 많은 것들을 잃었지만 그 경험은 나를 더욱 성숙하게 해 주었다. 화재가 나기 전, 나는 항상 내 삶에 대해 불평했다. 그런데 화재가 나서 우리가 가진 모든 것을 파괴해버렸다. 우리는 갑자기 가난해졌고 모든 것을 빌려야만 했다. 처음에는 힘든 시간을 보냈지만, 점차 나는 내 옛 물건들이 꼭 필요하지는 않다는 것을 깨닫기 시작했다. 나는 단지 나의 가족이 필요할 뿐이었다. 화재가 나에게서 많은 좋은 것들을 가져간 것은 사실이지만 나에게 중요한 것도 주었다. 그것은 나에게 물건들보다 사람들에게 감사해야 한다는 것을 가르쳐 주었다.

● ●

burn down 불에 타다 **mature** 성숙한 **complain** 불평하다 **destroy** 파괴하다 **own** 소유하다 **realize** 깨닫다 **appreciate** 고맙게 여기다, 감사하다

06 대화를 듣고, 남자가 조카보다 얼마나 더 키가 큰지 고르시오.

① 2cm
② 4cm
③ 6cm
④ 8cm
⑤ 10cm

W Look at your nephew. He's almost <u>as tall as</u> you.
M I don't think so, Mom. I am <u>180</u> centimeters tall.
W Well, he's <u>176</u> centimeters tall and <u>still growing</u>.
M When I was his age, I was almost <u>178</u> centimeters tall, but I haven't grown much <u>since then</u>.
W Teenagers seem to be <u>growing taller</u> these days.
M I think so.

여 네 조카 좀 보렴. 거의 너만큼이나 키가 크구나.
남 그렇지 않아요, 엄마. 제 키는 180센티미터예요.
여 글쎄, 그는 176센티미터지만 계속 자라고 있잖니.
남 저도 그 나이였을 때는 키가 거의 178센티미터였는데, 그 이후로는 별로 안 자랐어요.
여 요즘 십대들은 키가 더 많이 크는 것 같구나.
남 그런 것 같네요.

●●
teenager 십대

---

07 대화를 듣고, 남자의 심정으로 가장 적절한 것을 고르시오.

① angry
② jealous
③ energetic
④ exhausted
⑤ disappointed

W John, you look great.
M Thanks. I've been <u>exercising</u> a lot, and I feel like <u>a million dollars</u>.
W I should follow your example. It really <u>gives you energy</u>, doesn't it?
M It sure does. It has really changed my life.
W That's it! <u>Starting tomorrow</u>, I'm going to the gym.
M That's a great idea. I'll see you there.

여 John, 너 정말 좋아 보인다.
남 고마워. 운동을 많이 해왔더니 기분이 매우 좋아.
여 너를 본보기로 삼아야겠어. 운동하면 정말 에너지가 넘치지?
남 물론이지. 정말로 내 인생을 바꿔 놓았어.
여 그거야! 내일부터 나는 체육관에 갈 거야.
남 좋은 생각이다. 그럼 거기에서 보자.

●●
feel like a million dollars 기분이 매우 좋다
gym 체육관 **jealous** 부러운 **exhausted** 지친 **disappointed** 실망한

---

08 다음을 듣고, 두 사람의 대화가 <u>어색한</u> 것을 고르시오.

① ② ③ ④ ⑤

① M Excuse me, ma'am. You <u>dropped your purse</u>.
  W Oh, thank you. You're very kind.
② W If I were you, I'd be more careful.
  M Wash your hands to <u>prevent colds</u>.
③ M How do you think this suit looks on me?
  W It looks <u>fabulous</u>.
④ W <u>How many</u> oranges are in the bag?
  M There are 12 tasty and fresh oranges in the bag.
⑤ M How do I <u>get rid of</u> these troublesome pimples?
  W Just keep your face clean.

① 남 실례합니다, 부인. 지갑을 떨어뜨리셨어요.
  여 아, 고마워요. 정말 친절하시군요.
② 여 내가 너라면 좀 더 조심할 텐데.
  남 감기를 예방하려면 손을 깨끗이 씻어.
③ 남 이 양복 나한테 어떤 것 같니?
  여 아주 멋져 보여.
④ 여 가방에 오렌지가 몇 개나 있니?
  남 가방에 맛있고 신선한 오렌지가 12개 들어 있어.
⑤ 남 이 골치 아픈 여드름을 어떻게 없애지?
  여 그냥 얼굴을 깨끗이 해.

●●
drop 떨어뜨리다 **prevent** 예방하다 **suit** 정장, 양복 **fabulous** 아주 멋진 **tasty** 맛있는 **get rid of** 없애다 **troublesome** 골치 아픈, 성가신 **pimple** 여드름

09 대화를 듣고, 여자가 남자에게 병원에 가자고 말한 이유로 가장 적절한 것을 고르시오.

① 다리를 다쳐서
② 남자가 아파서
③ 교통사고가 나서
④ 병문안을 가기 위해서
⑤ 남자가 병원에서 일해서

M Mary, <u>on which side</u> of the body is the appendix?

W It's on the right side. Why do you ask?

M I don't know. I <u>have some discomfort</u> in that area.

W Really?

M In fact, it's getting <u>more and more</u> uncomfortable.

W Well, we'd better take a taxi to the hospital now <u>just in case</u>.

남 Mary, 우리 몸 어느 쪽에 맹장이 있지?

여 오른쪽에 있어. 왜 물어보는데?

남 몰라. 그 쪽이 조금 불편해서.

여 정말?

남 사실은 점점 더 불편해지고 있어.

여 음, 만일의 경우에 대비해서 우리는 지금 택시를 타고 병원에 가는 게 낫겠어.

appendix 맹장 **discomfort** 불편, 가벼운 통증 **uncomfortable** 불편한 **just in case** 만일의 경우에 대비해서

---

10 대화를 듣고, 남자가 전화를 건 목적으로 가장 적절한 것을 고르시오.

① 약속 시간을 변경하려고
② 점심 식사에 초대하려고
③ 변경된 일정을 알려주려고
④ 변호사와 만날 약속을 하려고
⑤ 변호사의 전화에 회신을 하려고

W Hello. Elizabeth White's Law Firm.

M Hi. <u>This is</u> Gabriel Lincoln <u>calling</u>.

W Oh, hello, Mr. Lincoln. How <u>have you been</u>?

M Just fine. I was hoping I could meet with her <u>sometime this afternoon</u>.

W I don't know, Mr. Lincoln. Her schedule is <u>completely booked</u>.

M This is really important. I have to meet with her before I <u>go to court</u>.

W Well, how about if I ask her and then <u>call you back</u>?

M Sounds great.

여 여보세요. Elizabeth White 법률 사무소입니다.

남 안녕하세요. 저는 Gabriel Lincoln입니다.

여 오, 안녕하세요, Lincoln 씨. 어떻게 지내셨나요?

남 잘 지내요. 오늘 오후에 그녀를 만날 수 있길 바라고 있었습니다.

여 모르겠습니다, Lincoln 씨, 그녀의 일정은 예약이 꽉 차있어요.

남 이것은 정말 중요합니다. 법원에 가기 전에 그녀를 만나야 해요.

여 음, 제가 그녀에게 물어보고 다시 전화 드리면 어떨까요?

남 그게 좋겠군요.

law firm 법률 사무소 **book** 예약하다 **court** 법원, 법정

---

11 대화를 듣고, 남자가 여자에게 제안한 일로 가장 적절한 것을 고르시오.

① 버스 타기
② 택시 함께 타기
③ 도보로 이동하기
④ 지도 다시 확인하기
⑤ 자신의 차를 타고 가기

W It's <u>too cold to wait</u> for the bus. Can I catch a taxi here?

M Yes, you can. Where are you going?

W I'm going to the Hilton Hotel.

M The Hilton Hotel is too <u>far from</u> here. You'll pay a <u>huge fare</u>.

W I know, but it's too late and too cold to <u>take the bus</u>.

M The Hilton is near the Manhattan Hotel, where I'm going. Shall we share a cab and <u>split the fare</u>?

W That sounds like a good idea.

여 버스를 기다리기에는 너무 춥군요. 여기서 택시를 잡을 수 있나요?

남 네, 잡을 수 있어요. 어디 가시는데요?

여 힐튼 호텔에 가는 길이예요.

남 힐튼 호텔은 여기서 꽤 멀어요. 요금이 많이 나올 거예요.

여 알아요, 하지만 버스를 타기에는 너무 늦은데다 추워서요.

남 힐튼 호텔은 제가 가려는 맨해튼 호텔 근처에 있어요. 택시를 같이 타고 요금을 나눠 낼까요?

여 좋은 생각이에요.

fare 요금 **cab** 택시 **split** 쪼개다, 나누다

12 대화를 듣고, 오늘 Peter가 한 일이 <u>아닌</u> 것을 고르시오.

① 뒤뜰 청소하기
② 숙제하기
③ 축구 연습 준비하기
④ 합창단 지휘하기
⑤ 피아노 반주하기

M Have you seen Peter?
W Yes, darling. After he finished cleaning the backyard, he did his homework. Now, he's getting ready for soccer practice.
M Didn't he play the piano for choir practice this morning?
W Right. He is always as busy as a bee. He has a lot of energy.
M He must be tired. I'll tell him to skip soccer practice today.

남 Peter 봤어요?
여 네, 여보. 그 애는 뒤뜰 청소를 하고 나서 숙제를 했어요. 지금은 축구 연습을 준비하고 있고요.
남 그 애는 오늘 아침 합창 연습에서 피아노 반주를 하지 않았어요?
여 맞아요. 그 애는 항상 벌처럼 바빠요. 그 애는 힘이 넘쳐요.
남 틀림없이 피곤하겠군요. 오늘은 축구 연습을 빠지라고 말해야겠어요.

●●
backyard 뒤뜰 **get ready for** ~을 준비하다
choir 합창단 **skip** 건너뛰다, 생략하다

---

13 대화를 듣고, 대화 내용과 일치하지 <u>않는</u> 것을 고르시오.

① 여자는 콘서트 표 4장을 구입할 것이다.
② 여자는 콘서트에 초대 받았다.
③ 여자는 무대와 가까운 좌석을 원한다.
④ 여자는 신용카드로 표를 구입하기를 원한다.
⑤ 여자는 공연 며칠 전에 티켓을 받을 것이다.

M How may I help you?
W I'd like to reserve tickets for the Super Concert on September 3.
M All right.
W Are there any seats close to the stage?
M Yes, how many seats do you need?
W Four. Can I pay with a credit card?
M Of course. We'll send you the tickets a few days before the concert.

남 무엇을 도와드릴까요?
여 9월 3일에 있을 슈퍼 콘서트를 예약하고 싶은데요.
남 좋습니다.
여 무대에서 가까운 좌석이 있나요?
남 네, 몇 좌석이나 필요하신가요?
여 네 개요. 신용카드로 지불할 수 있나요?
남 물론이죠. 콘서트 몇 일전에 티켓을 발송해 드리겠습니다.

●●
reserve 예약하다 **seat** 자리, 좌석
credit card 신용카드

---

14 대화를 듣고, 남자의 마지막 말에 이어질 여자의 말로 가장 적절한 것을 고르시오.

① You can't do it. It's too difficult.
② Put them into the hot pan with oil.
③ Mix them with the sauce. That's all.
④ Vegetables are good for your health.
⑤ You can buy them at the supermarket.

M Can I help you prepare dinner?
W Yes, you can. Cook the rice for me, please.
M I'm not good at cooking, but I'll try. How much water should I put into the pot with the rice?
W You should put twice as much water as rice.
M Okay, I think I'm done with that. Can I help you with anything else?
W Yes, could you fry the vegetables for me?
M How do I do that?
W Put them into the hot pan with oil.

남 저녁 준비하는 거 도와줄까?
여 그래, 좀 도와줘. 나 대신 밥 좀 해줘.
남 요리는 잘 못하지만 해 볼게. 쌀이 들어있는 솥에 물을 얼마나 넣어야 하지?
여 쌀의 두 배 정도의 물을 넣어야 해.
남 알았어, 내 생각으론 다한 것 같은데. 다른 거 도와줄까?
여 응, 채소 좀 볶아 주겠니?
남 그건 어떻게 하는데?
여 <u>뜨거운 프라이팬에 기름과 함께 그걸 넣으면 돼.</u>

① 너는 그걸 할 수 없어. 그건 너무 어려워.
③ 그걸 소스와 섞어. 그게 다야.
④ 채소는 네 건강에 좋아.
⑤ 너는 그걸 슈퍼마켓에서 살 수 있어.

●●
pot 냄비, 솥 **fry** (기름에) 볶다, 튀기다
sauce 소스

15 대화를 듣고, 여자의 마지막 말에 이어질 남자의 말로 가장 적절한 것을 고르시오.

① I saw it on TV.
② I used to collect coins.
③ Do you need some coins?
④ No, I don't have any coins.
⑤ I think magic is really cool.

M <u>Have you heard of</u> something called a magic coin?

W No, I haven't. What is it?

M It's a coin that magicians use when they <u>perform</u> <u>magic tricks</u>. Do you want to see one? I'll show you.

W Hmm. It looks just like a <u>normal coin</u>. I can't see <u>any difference</u>.

M Look carefully. There is <u>something different</u> about this coin.

W You're right. There's a <u>tiny hole</u> in the center of the coin.

M Magicians <u>do tricks</u> with this kind of coin and thread.

W How do you know?

M <u>I saw it on TV.</u>

남 마술 동전에 대해 들어 봤니?

여 아니, 못 들어 봤어. 그게 뭔데?

남 그건 마술사들이 마술을 할 때 사용하는 동전이야. 보고 싶니? 보여 줄게.

여 흠. 그냥 보통 동전처럼 보이는데. 차이점이 전혀 안 보여.

남 자세히 봐. 이 동전에는 다른 점이 있어.

여 맞아. 동전 가운데 아주 작은 구멍이 있네.

남 마술사들은 이런 동전과 실을 가지고 속임수를 쓰지.

여 너는 어떻게 알아?

남 TV에서 봤거든.

② 나는 동전을 모으곤 했어.
③ 동전 좀 필요해?
④ 아니, 동전이 하나도 없어.
⑤ 마술은 정말 멋진 것 같아.

● ●
magician 마술사 **perform** 하다, 행하다
magic trick 마술 **normal** 보통의
tiny 아주 작은 **thread** 실

◗ REVIEW TEST p. 23

A ① laundry, 세탁물 ② tough, 힘든 ③ tiny, 아주 작은 ④ mature, 성숙한 ⑤ emergency, 응급 상황
⑥ reserve, 예약하다 ⑦ tasty, 맛있는 ⑧ prevent, 예방하다 ⑨ choir, 합창단
⑩ appreciate, 고맙게 여기다, 감사하다 ⑪ run away, 도망치다 ⑫ in a row, 연속으로, 계속해서

B ① Pass, turn left ② as tall as ③ were you
④ get rid of ⑤ just in case ⑥ split the fare
⑦ good at cooking ⑧ twice as much water

문제 및 정답	받아쓰기 및 녹음내용	해석

01

대화를 듣고, 남자가 이번 여름에 한 일로 가장 적절한 것을 고르시오.

①  ②

③   ④

⑤

W What a nice car!

M Thanks. I worked really hard this summer to be able to afford it.

W Where did you work?

M I worked for a landscaping company.

W Do you mean you planted flowers and stuff?

M No, my specialty was tree trimming.

W Oh, I see. So you cut the extra branches off trees.

M That's right.

여 정말 멋진 차야!

남 고마워. 내가 그걸 마련하려고 이번 여름에 진짜 열심히 일했거든.

여 어디에서 일했는데?

남 조경 회사에서 일했어.

여 꽃과 같은 것들을 심었다는 거야?

남 아니, 내 전공은 나무 다듬기였어.

여 오, 알겠다. 그렇다면, 나무에서 필요 없는 가지들을 잘랐구나.

남 맞아.

●● **afford** ~을 살[할] 여유가 되다 **landscaping company** 조경 회사 **specialty** 전공, 전문 **tree trimming** 나뭇가지 자르기 **extra** 여분의, 필요 이상의 **branch** 나뭇가지

02

대화를 듣고, 여자가 가려고 하는 장소를 고르시오.

W Excuse me. Do you know where the bus terminal is?

M Yes. Walk down First Street, and make a right on Main Street.

W Go straight and turn right...

M Yes. Then, follow Main Street to Third Street and make a left. The bus terminal is in the middle of the block on your right.

W Thank you. You're very kind.

M You're welcome.

여 실례합니다. 버스 터미널이 어디에 있는지 아세요?

남 네. 1번가를 따라 걷다가 메인가에서 오른쪽으로 도세요.

여 직진해서 오른쪽으로 돌고…

남 맞아요. 그리고 나서 메인가를 따라 3번가까지 가셔서 왼쪽으로 도세요. 버스 터미널은 그 블록의 오른쪽 중간에 있어요.

여 고맙습니다. 정말 친절하시군요.

남 천만에요.

03

대화를 듣고, 두 사람이 대화하는 장소로 가장 적절한 곳을 고르시오.

① 회사
② 식당
③ 경찰서
④ 백화점
⑤ 우체국

M Excuse me. I lost my wallet this morning.

W Where do you think you lost it?

M On the fifth floor in the furniture department.

W Well, you're lucky. A salesman found it about an hour ago.

M Thank goodness! I was really worried.

W Here it is. Make sure everything is there.

M Okay. Thank you so much.

남 실례합니다. 오늘 아침에 제 지갑을 잃어 버렸습니다.

여 어디서 잃어버린 것 같습니까?

남 5층, 가구 매장에서요.

여 음, 운이 좋으시네요. 매장 직원이 한 시간 전에 발견했습니다.

남 감사합니다! 걱정을 많이 했거든요.

여 여기 있습니다. 모두 제대로 있는지 확인해 보세요.

남 네. 정말 감사합니다.

●● **wallet** 지갑 **department** 부서, (백화점의) 매장

04

대화를 듣고, 두 사람의 관계로 가장 적절한 것을 고르시오.

① 버스 기사 - 승객
② 백화점 직원 - 고객
② 자동차 정비사 - 손님
④ 자동차 판매자 - 구매자
⑤ 렌터카 회사 직원 - 손님

M I'm here to <u>rent</u> <u>a car</u>.

W <u>What</u> <u>size</u> <u>car</u> do you want?

M Well, actually, I haven't <u>made</u> <u>up</u> <u>my</u> <u>mind</u> yet.

W Do you want a compact car?

M <u>What</u> <u>kinds</u> <u>of</u> compact cars do you have?

W We have a Cobbie Morning now.

M Okay. I'll rent it. Can I pay <u>with</u> <u>cash</u>?

W I'm afraid not. You can only pay <u>by</u> <u>credit</u> <u>card</u>. It's our policy.

M Okay. Here is my credit card.

남 차를 빌리려고 왔어요.

여 어떤 크기의 차를 원하시죠?

남 글쎄요, 사실은 아직 결정을 못했어요.

여 소형차를 원하세요?

남 어떤 종류의 소형차가 있나요?

여 지금은 Cobbie 회사의 Morning이 있어요.

남 좋아요. 그것으로 빌릴게요. 현금으로 내도 되나요?

여 죄송하지만 안됩니다. 신용카드로만 지불하실 수 있어요. 저희 회사 방침이라서요.

남 알겠습니다. 여기 제 신용카드 있어요.

●●
make up one's mind 결정하다 **compact car** 소형차 **cash** 현금

05

대화를 듣고, 현재의 계절로 가장 적절한 것을 고르시오.

① 봄
② 여름
③ 가을
④ 초겨울
⑤ 늦겨울

W Isn't it wonderful? Soon, the birds will be <u>singing</u>, and the flowers will be <u>blooming</u>.

M What are you talking about? Are you <u>reciting</u> <u>a poem</u>?

W No, I'm talking about the most beautiful season.

M Oh, I see. The coming of spring also <u>cheers</u> <u>people</u> <u>up</u>. Don't you think so?

W That's true. The snow is still <u>on</u> <u>the</u> <u>ground</u>, but I can feel the <u>warmth</u> of the sun.

M Yes, it <u>brings</u> <u>hope</u> to our lives.

여 정말 멋지지 않니? 곧 새들이 노래하고 꽃들이 피어날 거야.

남 무슨 소리야? 시 낭송하고 있는 거야?

여 아니, 가장 아름다운 계절에 대해 말하고 있는 거야.

남 아, 그렇구나. 봄이 오고 있다는 사실은 사람들의 기운을 북돋게 해. 그렇지 않니?

여 맞아. 아직 땅 위에 눈이 쌓여 있지만 태양의 따사로움이 느껴져.

남 응, 봄은 우리 삶에 희망을 가져다 주지.

●●
bloom 개화하다, 꽃이 피다 **recite** 낭송하다 **poem** 시 **cheer up** 기운을 북돋우다 **warmth** 온기, 따뜻함

06

대화를 듣고, Christopher Ellis의 현재 몸무게로 가장 적절한 것을 고르시오.

① 60kg
② 70kg
③ 80kg
④ 90kg
⑤ 100kg

M Did you <u>hear</u> <u>about</u> the famous actor Christopher Ellis?

W No, I didn't. <u>What</u> <u>about</u> him?

M Well, he normally <u>weighs</u> 70 kilograms, but he has gained 20 kilograms to <u>play</u> <u>a role</u> in a movie.

W That's incredible. It <u>must</u> <u>have</u> <u>been</u> <u>difficult</u> for him to gain all that weight.

M Not really. He said all he did was <u>eat</u> <u>sweets</u> for breakfast, lunch, and supper.

W So if I eat sweets a lot, then can I gain weight <u>as</u> <u>well</u>?

M Of course!

남 유명 배우 Christopher Ellis에 대한 얘기 들었어?

여 아니. 그가 왜?

남 글쎄, 그는 보통 70킬로그램 정도 나가는데, 영화에서 배역을 맡기 위해 20킬로그램이나 몸무게를 늘렸어.

여 대단하다. 그가 그렇게 살을 찌우기는 분명 힘들었을 거야.

남 그렇지도 않은가 봐. 그가 말하기를 자기가 한 것은 아침, 점심, 저녁으로 단 것을 먹은 것 뿐이래.

여 그럼 나도 단 것을 많이 먹으면 살이 찔 수 있을까?

남 물론이지!

●●
weigh 무게가 ~이다 **incredible** 놀라운, 믿기 힘든 **sweets** 단 것 **supper** 저녁 (식사)

07 대화를 듣고, 여자의 심정으로 가장 적절한 것을 고르시오.

① bored
② worried
③ cheerful
④ thankful
⑤ annoyed

M Can I help you with your <u>groceries</u>?
W Thank you.
M No problem. I'm walking <u>in your direction</u> anyway.
W When I was your age, I had so much energy, but now...
M You <u>look healthy</u> yet. Is this your apartment?
W Yes, it is. Can I give you something <u>for your effort</u>?
M No, thanks. It was <u>my pleasure</u>.

남 식료품 좀 들어 드릴까요?
여 고마워요.
남 아닙니다. 저도 어차피 그 방향으로 가고 있어요.
여 저도 그 나이 때는 힘이 넘쳤는데, 지금은…
남 아직 건강해 보이세요. 여기가 부인의 아파트 인가요?
여 네, 맞아요. 수고하셨는데 제가 뭐라도 드려도 될까요?
남 괜찮습니다. 제가 좋아서 한 일인데요.

●●
grocery 식료품 **direction** 방향 **effort** 노력, 수고 **annoyed** 짜증이 난

---

08 대화를 듣고, 두 사람이 관람하고 있는 경기로 가장 적절한 것을 고르시오.

① 골프
② 수영
③ 야구
④ 배구
⑤ 테니스

W Who's the <u>starter</u> for the Dodgers?
M Oh, Chris Taylor is the starter.
W Really? I love him. He is a very good <u>pitcher</u>, isn't he?
M Yes, he is. Look. Oh, that's a <u>terrible call</u>. The runner was clearly out.
W Well, it <u>seems to me</u> that he was safe.
M I don't think so. This is just an example of home-field advantage.
W <u>Calm down</u>. Why don't you <u>take a closer look</u> at the replay?
M Okay.

여 다저스의 선발이 누구니?
남 아, Chris Taylor가 선발이네.
여 정말? 나는 그가 너무 좋아. 그는 훌륭한 투수잖아, 그렇지 않니?
남 그래, 맞아. 봐. 아, 저건 형편없는 판정이다. 주자는 분명히 아웃이야.
여 글쎄, 내가 보기에는 세이프 같은데.
남 난 그렇게 생각 안 해. 이건 단지 홈그라운드 이점의 한 예일 뿐이야.
여 진정해. 다시 보기할 때 자세히 보는 것이 어때?
남 좋아.

●●
starter (야구의) 선발 투수 **pitcher** 투수 **call** (심판의) 판정 **replay** 다시 보기

---

09 대화를 듣고, 여자가 남자의 제안에 망설인 이유로 가장 적절한 것을 고르시오.

① 다리를 다쳐서
② 다른 약속이 있어서
③ 춤 추는 것을 싫어해서
④ 춤 추는 방법을 몰라서
⑤ 파트너가 마음에 들지 않아서

M Would you like to <u>go dancing</u>, Jennifer?
W Well... I would <u>except</u> I don't know how.
M It's easy. You just put one foot in front of the other.
W You're joking, right? How can I do that?
M I'll show you <u>how to dance</u>. Just work with me.
W <u>Easier said than done</u>.
M Ready? Let's begin.

남 Jennifer, 춤 추러 가지 않을래?
여 글쎄… 춤 추는 법을 모르지만 않으면 갈 텐데.
남 쉬워. 너는 그냥 한쪽 발을 다른 쪽 발 앞에 두기만 하면 돼.
여 농담이지? 내가 그걸 어떻게 하겠어?
남 내가 어떻게 추는지 보여 줄게. 그냥 나를 따라 해.
여 행동보다 말로는 쉽지.
남 준비됐어? 시작해 보자.

●●
except ~만 아니면 **Easier said than done.** 행동보다 말이 쉽다.

10

대화를 듣고, 여자가 남자에게 말을 건 목적으로 가장 적절한 것을 고르시오.

① 구입할 물건을 계산하려고
② 작성한 지원서를 제출하려고
③ 직원 채용 여부를 알아보려고
④ 지원서 작성 방법을 확인하려고
⑤ 가까운 편의점 위치를 물어보려고

M How can I help you?
W I wonder if you sometimes <u>hire</u> <u>staff</u> <u>members</u> at your store.
M Yes, sometimes. Do you want to <u>apply</u> <u>for</u> a job?
W Yes, I do.
M Do you have <u>any</u> <u>work</u> <u>experience</u>?
W Yes, I do. I worked at a convenience store before.
M Just complete this <u>application</u>. We will contact you when a job is <u>available</u>.
W Thanks.

남 무엇을 도와드릴까요?
여 이 가게에서 가끔 직원을 채용하는지 궁금합니다.
남 네, 가끔이요. 지원하고 싶으세요?
여 네, 하고 싶어요.
남 일해 본 경험이 있으신가요?
여 네, 있어요. 전에 편의점에서 일했어요.
남 일단 이 양식을 작성하세요. 일자리가 생기면 연락 드릴게요.
여 고맙습니다.

●●
hire 고용하다   staff member 직원
apply for ~에 지원하다, ~을 신청하다
convenience store 편의점   application
지원서   available 이용할 수 있는

11

대화를 듣고, 여자가 남자에게 요청한 사항으로 언급하지 <u>않은</u> 것을 고르시오.

① 안전벨트 착용하기
② 등받이 세우기
③ 좌석 밑에 가방 넣기
④ 휴대폰 전원 끄기
⑤ 금연하기

W The seatbelt sign <u>is</u> <u>on</u>. Please <u>fasten</u> your seatbelt.
M Okay.
W Then, put your seat back <u>upright</u>, please.
M Is this all right?
W Sure. Please put your bag <u>under</u> <u>the</u> <u>seat</u>.
M Okay, I'll do that. And I have a question. Can I smoke here?
W No. You can't smoke <u>on</u> <u>the</u> <u>plane</u>.

여 안전벨트 신호가 켜졌습니다. 안전벨트를 착용해 주세요.
남 알겠습니다.
여 그런 다음 등받이를 세워 주세요.
남 이렇게요?
여 네. 가방은 좌석 아래 놓아 주세요.
남 네, 그렇게 할게요. 그리고 질문이 하나 있는데요. 여기서 담배를 피워도 되나요?
여 안됩니다. 비행기 안에서는 담배를 피우실 수 없습니다.

●●
fasten 매다, 묶다   seatbelt 안전벨트
seat back 등받이   upright 똑바로 선, 수직의
plane 비행기

12

대화를 듣고, 여자가 자연에 대해 어떻게 생각하는지 고르시오.

① 아름답다.
② 파괴적일 수도 있다.
③ 영원히 보존되어야 한다.
④ 신비한 힘을 가지고 있다.
⑤ 감사하는 마음을 가져야 한다.

W Isn't it so sad to hear about <u>what</u> <u>happened</u> in Southeast Asia?
M Yes. There were so many <u>victims</u>, and their lives <u>changed</u> <u>forever</u>.
W It's hard to believe that nature can be <u>so</u> <u>destructive</u>.
M We <u>should</u> <u>be</u> <u>thankful</u> we don't live in that dangerous area.
W You're right about that. Did you <u>donate</u> <u>some</u> <u>money</u>?
M Yes, I did that last week.

여 동남아시아에서 일어났던 일을 들으니 정말 슬프지 않니?
남 그래. 정말 많은 희생자가 생겨났고, 그들의 삶은 영원히 바뀌었어.
여 자연이 그렇게 파괴적일 수도 있다는 것이 믿기 힘들어.
남 우리가 그런 위험 지역에 살지 않는 것에 감사해야 해.
여 네 말이 맞아. 기부금은 좀 냈니?
남 응, 지난 주에 냈어.

●●
victim 희생자   destructive 파괴적인
donate 기부하다

13 대화를 듣고, 여자가 조부모님을 얼마나 자주 방문하는지 고르시오.

① 매일
② 주말마다
③ 1년에 한 번
④ 2년에 한 번
⑤ 방문하지 않음

W How often do you visit your grandparents?
M I visit them once a year. I wish I could visit them more often, but I'm too busy.
W You're better than me. I only visit my grandparents once every other year because they live far away.
M Where do they live?
W They live on Jeju Island.
M That's far away. How often do you see your parents?
W They live near my apartment, so I visit them every weekend. How about you?
M My parents live in Japan, so I just talk to them on the phone.

여 조부모님을 얼마나 자주 찾아 뵙니?
남 1년에 한 번. 더 자주 찾아 뵙고 싶지만 너무 바빠서.
여 나보다는 낫구나. 나는 조부모님이 너무 멀리 사셔서 2년에 한 번씩만 찾아 뵙고 있어.
남 어디 사시는데?
여 제주도에 사셔.
남 멀구나. 부모님은 얼마나 자주 뵙니?
여 부모님은 내 아파트 근처에 사셔서 주말마다 찾아 뵙고 있어. 너는?
남 우리 부모님은 일본에 사셔서 전화 통화만 해.

●● **every other year** 한 해 걸러, 2년마다

14 대화를 듣고, 남자의 마지막 말에 이어질 여자의 말로 가장 적절한 것을 고르시오.

① It's seven thirty.
② The clock is broken.
③ It's not a clock. It's a picture.
④ There is no clock on the wall.
⑤ I don't have good eyesight either.

W It's too late to go to the museum.
M Really? What time is it?
W I don't know exactly, but I think we're late.
M Can you see the clock on the wall?
W Where is the clock?
M Over there. It's the big red one. I can't tell the time because of my bad eyesight.
W Let me see. It's half past seven.
M Pardon me?
W It's seven thirty.

여 박물관에 가기에는 너무 늦었어.
남 정말? 몇 시인데?
여 정확히는 모르겠지만 늦은 것 같아.
남 벽에 시계 보이니?
여 시계가 어디 있어?
남 저기. 크고 빨간 시계 말이야. 난 시력이 나빠서 시계를 볼 수가 없어.
여 어디 보자. 7시 30분이야.
남 뭐라고?
여 7시 30분이라고.

② 저 시계는 고장 났어.
③ 그건 시계가 아니야. 그건 그림이야.
④ 벽에는 시계가 없어.
⑤ 나도 시력이 안 좋아.

●● **eyesight** 시력 **tell the time** 시계를[시간을] 보다 **half past seven** 7시 반

18

15 대화를 듣고, 여자의 마지막 말에 이어질 남자의 말로 가장 적절한 것을 고르시오.

① I like toast for breakfast.
② Sorry. Diner isn't ready yet.
③ Sure. We'll call you at seven.
④ There's no problem. Just ask the bellboy.
⑤ Breakfast is served between 7 and 10 a.m.

W What time is checkout?
M 11 o'clock.
W Can you give me a wakeup call tomorrow morning?
M Yes. What time would you like us to call you?
W Seven, please. And can I leave my luggage here until tomorrow night? My flight will leave tomorrow night.
M Yes, of course. Just leave it here, and we'll take care of it.
W And can you tell me what time you start serving breakfast?
M Breakfast is served between 7 and 10 a.m.

여 체크아웃은 몇 시입니까?
남 11시입니다.
여 내일 아침에 전화로 깨워주실 수 있나요?
남 네. 저희가 몇 시에 전화를 드릴까요?
여 7시요. 그리고 내일 밤까지 짐을 여기에 두어도 될까요? 제 비행기가 내일 밤에 떠나거든요.
남 네, 물론이죠. 여기 두시면 저희가 맡아드리겠습니다.
여 그리고 아침 식사는 몇 시부터 제공되나요?
남 아침 식사는 오전 7시에서 10시 사이에 제공됩니다.

① 저는 아침 식사로 토스트를 좋아합니다.
② 죄송합니다. 저녁 식사는 아직 준비되지 않았습니다.
③ 물론이죠. 7시에 전화 드리겠습니다.
④ 문제 없어요. 벨보이에게 요청하시면 됩니다.

checkout (호텔의) 체크아웃, 퇴숙 절차 **wakeup call** (호텔의) 모닝콜 **luggage** 짐, 수하물 **take care of** 돌보다, 처리하다 **bellboy** (호텔의) 벨보이

REVIEW TEST p. 31

A
① department, 부서, (백화점의) 매장 ② cash, 현금 ③ bloom, 개화하다, 꽃이 피다
④ poem, 시 ⑤ grocery, 식료품 ⑥ victim, 희생자 ⑦ luggage, 짐, 수하물
⑧ incredible, 놀라운, 믿기 힘든 ⑨ available, 이용할 수 있는 ⑩ eyesight, 시력
⑪ compact car, 소형차 ⑫ every other year, 한 해 걸러, 2년마다

B
① made up, mind ② must have been difficult ③ said than done
④ apply for ⑤ fasten, seatbelt ⑥ nature, destructive
⑦ half past ⑧ wakeup call

문제 및 정답	받아쓰기 및 녹음내용	해석

01

대화를 듣고, 여자가 구입할 케이크로 가장 적절한 것을 고르시오.

① 　②

③ 　④

⑤

M Do you need any help?

W I am <u>looking for</u> a cake for my father.

M How about this heart-shaped cake? It's not sweet, so <u>most adults</u> like it.

W It's nice, but I want a <u>round one</u>.

M Do you want the cake with the heart-shaped chocolate on it?

W No, I'd like the cake <u>with strawberries</u> <u>on it</u>.

M Sure.

남 도움이 필요하신가요?

여 아버지께 드릴 케이크를 찾고 있는데요.

남 이 하트 모양 케이크는 어떠세요? 달지 않아서다 성인들 대부분이 좋아해요.

여 좋긴 한데, 전 동그란 것이 맘에 드네요.

남 그 위에 하트 모양의 초콜릿이 있는 것으로 드릴까요?

여 아니요, 딸기가 있는 것으로 주세요.

남 알겠습니다.

●●
look for ~을 찾다, 구하다 **adult** 성인

02

대화를 듣고, 남자가 가려고 하는 장소를 고르시오.

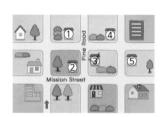

M Excuse me. Do you know <u>where I</u> can <u>find</u> the Village Hotel?

W Hmm... It doesn't <u>sound familiar</u>. Do you know <u>what street</u> it is on?

M I think it is on Pine Road.

W Ah, yes. If I'm <u>not mistaken</u>, it's the only hotel on that road. Go from here to Mission Street. Then, <u>turn right</u>.

M Go to Mission Street and turn right?

W Yes, that's right. Then, <u>once you get to</u> Pine Road, turn left. The hotel is <u>on your right</u>.

M Okay. Thank you very much.

W No problem.

남 실례합니다. Village Hotel이 어디 있는지 아세요?

여 음… 낯설게 들리네요. 어느 도로에 있는 건지 아세요?

남 아마 파인가에 있는 것 같은데요.

여 아, 네. 제가 틀리지 않다면, 그 호텔이 그 도로에 있는 유일한 호텔이거든요. 여기서 미션가까지 가세요. 그런 다음 오른쪽으로 도세요.

남 미션가까지 가서 오른쪽으로 돌라고요?

여 네, 맞아요. 그런 다음 파인가에 도착하면 왼쪽으로 도세요. 그 호텔은 오른쪽에 있어요.

남 알겠습니다. 정말 고맙습니다.

여 별말씀을요.

●●
familiar 익숙한, 친숙한 **mistaken** 잘못 알고 있는, 틀린

03

대화를 듣고, 두 사람이 대화하는 장소로 가장 적절한 곳을 고르시오.

① 상점
② 극장
③ 공항
④ 기차역
⑤ 버스 터미널

W When is the <u>next train to</u> Chicago?

M There's one at two o'clock.

W How long <u>does it take</u> to get there?

M About three hours and forty minutes.

W How much is a <u>one-way</u> ticket?

M 26 dollars.

여 시카고 행 다음 열차는 언제 있습니까?

남 2시에 하나 있어요.

여 그곳까지 가려면 얼마나 걸리나요?

남 3시간 40분 정도요.

여 편도 승차권은 한 장에 얼마입니까?

남 26달러입니다.

●●
one-way 편도의

04 대화를 듣고, 두 사람의 관계로 가장 적절한 것을 고르시오.

① 친구 – 친구
② 집주인 – 세입자
③ 호텔 직원 – 투숙객
④ 관광 가이드 – 여행객
⑤ 부동산 중개인 – 고객

M Come in. How <u>do you like</u> the house?
W Thank you. It's a great house.
M There are three bedrooms and two bathrooms in this house. <u>As you can see</u>, it's really clean. The previous owners <u>hardly used</u> it. It's like new.
W Yes, I like it. But 1,500 dollars <u>per month</u> is too expensive.
M I'll <u>negotiate with</u> the owner to make it 1,250 dollars.
W I would really <u>appreciate that</u>, but is that possible?
M Probably. The house <u>has been empty</u> for a couple of months now.
W Super. I'll wait for your call.

남 들어오세요. 집이 마음에 드세요?
여 고맙습니다. 정말 좋은 집인 것 같아요.
남 이 집에는 침실 3개와 화장실 2개가 있습니다. 보시다시피 무척 깨끗합니다. 전 주인 분들이 거의 사용하지 않았어요. 새 집이나 다름없지요.
여 네, 좋네요. 그런데 한 달에 1,500달러는 너무 비싸요.
남 제가 집주인과 협상해서 1,250달러로 해보겠습니다.
여 그럼 정말 감사하지만, 그게 가능할까요?
남 아마도요. 이 집은 지금 두 달째 비워져 있거든요.
여 좋아요. 연락 기다릴게요.

●●
previous 이전의 **owner** 주인 **negotiate** 협상하다 **empty** 비어 있는

---

05 대화를 듣고, 여자가 요즘 하고 있는 일로 가장 적절한 것을 고르시오.

① 사진 수업을 듣고 있다.
② 그림 수업을 듣고 있다.
③ 전시회 준비를 하고 있다.
④ 흑백 사진을 모으고 있다.
⑤ 자신의 취미를 남에게 가르쳐 주고 있다.

W <u>Do you mind</u> if I take your picture?
M Not at all. What is this for?
W I have a <u>new hobby</u>. I am taking a <u>photography</u> class. It's so much fun.
M I've thought about that <u>as well</u>.
W I love <u>black and white</u> pictures. They're so attractive.
M <u>So do I</u>.

여 네 사진 좀 찍어도 괜찮겠어?
남 괜찮지. 근데 왜 찍으려는 건데?
여 나에게 새로운 취미가 생겼어. 사진 수업을 듣고 있거든. 너무 재미있어.
남 나도 들을까 생각했는데.
여 난 흑백 사진이 정말 좋아. 너무 멋져.
남 나도 그래.

●●
hobby 취미 **photography** 사진
black and white picture 흑백사진

---

06 대화를 듣고, 남자가 원하는 수면 시간으로 가장 적절한 것을 고르시오.

① 4시간
② 5시간
③ 6시간
④ 8시간
⑤ 10시간

W Tom, you <u>look so tired</u>.
M I only slept for four hours last night.
W Oh, that's too bad. <u>Getting enough sleep</u> is very important.
M If I don't get <u>eight hours</u> of sleep, I'm tired the whole next day.
W What <u>kept you awake</u> for so long? Exams?
M You got it. I'm so <u>stressed out</u> about exams that I usually sleep for <u>five hours a night</u> these days.

여 Tom, 너 피곤해 보인다.
남 어젯밤에 4시간 밖에 못 잤거든.
여 이런, 너무 안됐다. 충분히 자는 건 매우 중요해.
남 나는 하루에 8시간을 자지 않으면 다음 날 하루 종일 피곤해.
여 왜 그렇게 오랫동안 잠을 못 잔 거야? 시험 때문에?
남 맞아. 요즘 시험 때문에 너무 스트레스 받아서 보통 5시간 밖에 잘 수가 없어.

●●
awake 깨어 있는

07

다음을 듣고, 어젯밤에 여자가 느꼈을 심정으로 가장 적절한 것을 고르시오.

① bored
② pleased
③ nervous
④ cheerful
⑤ miserable

Last night, I finished my part-time job at 9 p.m. I was tired and hungry and just <u>in a bad mood</u>. Then, there was a <u>sudden thunderstorm</u>. I waited <u>half an hour</u> for the bus to come. Then, when it finally arrived, it didn't even <u>stop</u>! It just drove <u>right by me</u>. I didn't get home till 10 p.m., and by that time, I <u>was soaked</u>.

어젯밤에 나는 밤 9시에 아르바이트가 끝났다. 나는 피곤하고 배고팠으며 그냥 기분도 좋지 않았다. 그런데 갑자기 뇌우가 쏟아졌다. 나는 버스가 올 때까지 30분을 기다렸다. 그러다 드디어 도착했는데 버스는 멈추지 않았다! 버스는 바로 내 옆을 지나쳐갔다. 나는 밤 10시가 되어서야 집에 도착했고, 그때쯤 나는 흠뻑 젖어 있었다.

●●
part-time job 아르바이트, 파트타임직 **in a bad mood** 기분이 좋지 않은 **sudden** 갑작스러운 **thunderstorm** 뇌우 **soaked** 흠뻑 젖은 **pleased** 기쁜 **miserable** 비참한, 슬픈

08

대화를 듣고, 여자가 추측하는 것으로 가장 적절한 것을 고르시오.

① Sandra는 거짓말을 하고 있다.
② Sandra는 아파서 모임에 오지 못했다.
③ Sandra는 모임에 나오는 것을 싫어한다.
④ Sandra가 아르바이트를 여러 개 하고 있다.
⑤ Sandra는 당분간 모임에 나오지 못할 것이다.

M Why didn't Sandra <u>show up</u> for today's meeting?
W I don't know. She told me that she <u>couldn't come</u> to our meeting today.
M I wonder <u>what happened</u>. Is she sick again?
W I don't think so. I think she has <u>several part-time jobs</u>.
M Really? How do you know?
W I'm not sure, but she's been <u>so busy</u>. I'm only guessing.

남 Sandra가 오늘 모임에 왜 나오지 않았지?
여 모르겠어. 그녀가 오늘 내게 모임에 올 수 없다고 말했어.
남 무슨 일인지 궁금하네. 또 아픈가?
여 그건 아닐 거야. 내 생각에는 아르바이트를 여러 개 하는 것 같아.
남 정말? 어떻게 알아?
여 확실하지는 않지만 요즘 너무 바쁘더라고. 단지 추측일 뿐이야.

●●
show up 모습을 나타내다, 오다

09

대화를 듣고, 여자가 모자를 쓰지 않은 이유로 가장 적절한 것을 고르시오.

① 모자가 없어서
② 모자를 잃어버려서
③ 모자를 집에 두고 와서
④ 춥다고 생각하지 않아서
⑤ 모자가 잘 어울리지 않아서

W Can you believe <u>how cold it is</u> today?
M I know. It's unbelievable. I thought the weather was going to <u>get warmer</u>.
W Me, too. I think I should move to a <u>tropical country</u>.
M Why don't you have a <u>warm hat</u> for days like today?
W I have one, but I <u>left it at home</u>.
M I'm sure you <u>won't forget</u> the next time.
W You're right about that.

여 오늘이 얼마나 추운지 믿겨지니?
남 알아. 믿을 수 없을 정도지. 날씨가 더 따뜻해질 거라 생각했는데.
여 나도. 열대기후의 나라로 이사해야겠어.
남 왜 오늘 같은 날 겨울 모자를 안 쓰니?
여 하나 있는데, 집에 두고 왔어.
남 다음 번에는 절대로 잊지 않겠구나.
여 네 말이 맞아.

●●
unbelievable 믿을 수 없는, 믿기 힘든 **tropical** 열대의

10 대화를 듣고, 여자가 전화를 건 목적으로 가장 적절한 것을 고르시오.

① 제품을 사기 위해서
② 제품을 환불 받기 위해서
③ 제품 고장을 문의하기 위해서
④ 다른 제품으로 교환하기 위해서
⑤ A/S 센터의 위치를 물어보기 위해서

M Hello. Samil Electronics. How can I help you?
W Yes, I <u>bought</u> <u>a</u> <u>blender</u> from one of your stores last week, but it <u>doesn't</u> <u>work</u>.
M Have you <u>checked</u> <u>the</u> <u>electricity</u>?
W Yes, I have. The electricity is fine.
M I see. <u>Why</u> <u>don't</u> <u>you</u> take it to any A/S center near your house? If the blender has a problem, you can get a new one or <u>get</u> <u>your</u> <u>money</u> <u>back</u>.
W Okay. Thanks.

남 여보세요. 삼일전자입니다. 무엇을 도와드릴까요?
여 네, 지난 주에 귀사의 한 대리점에서 믹서기를 구입했는데 작동이 안됩니다.
남 전기는 확인해 보셨나요?
여 네, 확인해 봤어요. 전기는 괜찮아요.
남 알겠습니다. 댁에서 가까운 A/S 센터에 가지고 가시면 어떨까요? 믹서기에 문제가 있다면 새 것으로 받으시거나 환불 받으실 수 있습니다.
여 알겠습니다. 고맙습니다.

blender 믹서기 **work** 작동하다
electricity 전기

---

11 다음을 듣고, 남자가 제자들에게 부탁한 일로 가장 적절한 것을 고르시오.

① 질문을 많이 하자.
② 규칙을 준수하자.
③ 유머 감각을 키우자.
④ 서로 연락하고 지내자.
⑤ 긍정적인 태도를 갖자.

It was my pleasure to have you guys as my students. I'm <u>really</u> <u>proud</u> <u>of</u> you and your work. I want to <u>say</u> <u>thank</u> <u>you</u> to all of you. I'll miss your questions, your smiles, and your active and positive attitudes. You <u>paid</u> <u>attention</u> <u>to</u> my lessons and always agreed with me. All of you obeyed the <u>rules</u> and did your <u>duties</u> very well. Let's <u>keep</u> <u>in</u> <u>touch</u> <u>with</u> each other. I hope we meet again soon.

여러분을 제자로 둔 것이 제게는 기쁨이었습니다. 저는 정말 여러분과 여러분이 한 일들이 자랑스럽습니다. 저는 여러분 모두에게 감사를 전하고 싶습니다. 여러분의 질문, 미소, 그리고 활기차고 긍정적인 태도가 그리울 것입니다. 여러분은 제 수업에 집중해 주었고 항상 제 의견을 같이 했습니다. 여러분 모두 규칙을 준수하고 여러분의 의무를 잘 이행했습니다. 서로 연락하고 지냅시다. 저는 우리가 곧 다시 만나기를 바랍니다.

attitude 태도 **pay attention to** ~에 집중하다, 주의를 기울이다 **obey** 따르다, 준수하다
duty 의무 **keep in touch with** ~와 연락하고 지내다

---

12 대화를 듣고, 남자가 대화 직후에 할 일로 가장 적절한 것을 고르시오.

① 주유소에 간다.
② 택시를 부른다.
③ 엔진을 확인한다.
④ 정비사를 부른다.
⑤ 아버지에게 전화한다.

M Oh, no. My car <u>won't</u> <u>start</u>.
W What should we do? Did you <u>check</u> <u>the</u> <u>oil</u>? We don't have enough time to get to the <u>dinner</u> <u>party</u>.
M I'm really sorry. There's <u>something</u> <u>wrong</u> with my old car. This is my fault. I <u>should</u> <u>have</u> <u>checked</u> the engine.
W Well, let's <u>call</u> <u>the</u> <u>mechanic</u> first and then <u>call</u> <u>a</u> <u>taxi</u>.
M Okay, but first, I will call my father and tell him that we <u>will</u> <u>be</u> <u>late</u>.
W Okay. Then I will call the mechanic.

남 오, 안돼. 차가 시동이 안 걸려.
여 우리가 뭘 해야 하니? 기름은 점검해 봤어? 저녁 식사 파티에 가려면 시간이 충분치 않아.
남 정말 미안해. 차가 낡아서 이상이 생겼나 봐. 내 잘못이야. 엔진을 점검했었어야 했는데.
여 그럼, 먼저 정비사를 부른 다음 택시를 부르자.
남 좋아, 하지만 난 먼저 아버지께 전화해서 우리가 늦을 거라고 말씀 드려야겠어.
여 좋아. 그리고 나서 내가 정비사를 부를게.

fault 잘못 **mechanic** 정비사

13 대화를 듣고, 대화 내용과 일치하지 <u>않는</u> 것을 고르시오.

① 여자는 약 2년간 영어를 공부했다.
② 여자는 온라인 영어 강좌를 듣는다. ✓
③ 여자는 영자 신문을 잘 읽지 못한다.
④ 여자는 영어회화를 잘 못한다고 생각한다.
⑤ 남자는 여자가 영어회화를 잘한다고 생각한다.

M How long <u>have you</u> <u>studied</u> English?
W About two years.
M Are you taking an <u>online</u> <u>English</u> <u>course</u> or something?
W No, I study <u>on</u> <u>my</u> <u>own</u> with books.
M Can you read English newspapers?
W No, I can't read newspapers yet. I know the letters but not <u>what</u> <u>they</u> <u>mean</u>.
M How about <u>conversation</u>?
W I'm not <u>good</u> <u>at</u> <u>speaking</u> either.
M I thought you were really good at speaking.
W <u>Not</u> really. I can only say easy things well.

남 영어 공부를 얼마나 오랫동안 하셨나요?
여 2년 정도요.
남 온라인 영어 강좌나 뭐 그런 걸 수강하고 계신가요?
여 아뇨, 저는 책으로 독학합니다.
남 영자 신문을 읽을 수 있나요?
여 아니요, 아직 영자 신문은 못 읽어요. 글자들은 알지만 무슨 뜻인지 모르겠어요.
남 회화는 어떤가요?
여 말하는 것 역시 잘 하지는 못해요.
남 전 당신이 말하기를 정말 잘 한다고 생각했어요.
여 그렇지 않아요. 전 단지 쉬운 말들만 잘 할 수 있어요.

•• **on one's own** 혼자, 혼자 힘으로 **letter** 글자 **conversation** 대화, 회화 **be good at** ~을 잘하다

---

14 대화를 듣고, 남자의 마지막 말에 이어질 여자의 말로 가장 적절한 것을 고르시오.

① That sounds great.
② You'd better see a doctor.
③ Do well on your math test.
④ You'll do fine. Good luck to you. ✓
⑤ To be honest, I'm not interested in English.

W Where <u>are you</u> <u>heading</u> now? You seem to be <u>in a hurry</u>.
M I'm <u>on my</u> <u>way</u> to school. I have an exam in about 30 minutes.
W An exam? What exam? Finals are <u>over</u>.
M English. I missed the test last week because I was <u>sick</u> <u>in</u> <u>bed</u>.
W So are you taking a <u>make-up</u> <u>test</u>?
M That's right. I'm <u>worried</u> <u>about</u> the test because I <u>didn't</u> <u>study</u> enough.
W You'll do fine. Good luck to you.

여 지금 어디 가니? 급해 보이네.
남 학교에 가는 길이야. 30분 후에 시험이 있어.
여 시험? 무슨 시험? 기말고사는 끝났잖아.
남 영어. 지난 주에 아파 누워 있느라 시험을 보지 못했어.
여 그래서 재시험 보러 가니?
남 맞아. 충분히 공부를 안 했더니 시험이 걱정돼.
여 넌 잘 할거야. 행운을 빌어.

① 그거 좋겠다.
② 너는 병원에 가보는 것이 좋겠어.
③ 수학 시험 잘 봐.
⑤ 솔직히, 나는 영어에 관심이 없어.

•• **head** 가다, 향하다 **in a hurry** 바쁜, 서두르는 **on one's way to** ~에 가는 중인 **make-up test** 재시험

15

대화를 듣고, 여자의 마지막 말에 이어질 남자의 말로 가장 적절한 것을 고르시오.

① I'm afraid I can't. I'm busy.
② Let's play the game after school.
③ What kinds of games do you play?
④ My mom doesn't allow me to play computer games.
⑤ Well, I've tried to quit, but I can't stop thinking about it.

W You almost fell asleep in class. What's wrong with you?
M I'm very exhausted these days.
W Why?
M I've been staying up all night to play an online computer game.
W What game?
M It's called Great Power. It's a very exciting game.
W But staying up all night is very harmful to your health, and you can't concentrate on your studies.
M Well, I've tried to quit, but I can't stop thinking about it.

여 너는 수업 시간에 거의 자더라. 무슨 문제라도 있니?
남 요즘 굉장히 피곤해.
여 왜?
남 온라인 컴퓨터 게임을 하느라 밤을 새웠거든.
여 무슨 게임인데?
남 Great Power야. 정말 흥미진진한 게임이지.
여 하지만 밤을 새우는 것은 건강에 매우 해로운데다 공부에 집중할 수도 없어.
남 음, 나도 끊으려고 노력했지만 게임에 대한 생각을 멈출 수가 없어.

① 미안하지만 안돼. 바쁘거든.
② 방과 후에 그 게임을 하자.
③ 어떤 종류의 컴퓨터 게임을 하니?
④ 우리 엄마는 내가 컴퓨터 게임 하는 것을 허락하지 않으셔.

● ●
fall asleep 잠들다 **stay up all night** 밤을 새다 **harmful** 해로운 **concentrate on** ~에 집중하다

REVIEW TEST p. 39

A
① adult, 성인 ② empty, 비어 있는 ③ harmful, 해로운 ④ photography, 사진
⑤ duty, 의무 ⑥ thunderstorm, 뇌우 ⑦ electricity, 전기 ⑧ attitude, 태도
⑨ mechanic, 정비사 ⑩ make-up test, 재시험 ⑪ fall asleep, 잠들다 ⑫ concentrate on, ~에 집중하다

B
① looking for ② next train to ③ does it take
④ What, awake ⑤ show up ⑥ keep in touch
⑦ have you studied ⑧ staying up

문제 및 정답	받아쓰기 및 녹음내용	해석

01 다음을 듣고, 내일의 날씨로 가장 적절한 것을 고르시오.

① ②

③ ④

⑤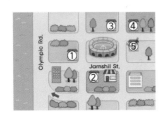

Good morning. This is Sam Scott with today's weather. I hope all of you <u>took</u> <u>advantage</u> <u>of</u> the sunshine today because it's not <u>going</u> <u>to</u> <u>last</u>. Tomorrow, the temperature will reach <u>a high of</u> 24°C, and it will be cloudy with <u>light</u> <u>rain</u>.

안녕하세요, 오늘의 날씨의 Sam Scott입니다. 여러분 모두 오늘의 화창한 날씨를 만끽하셨기를 바랍니다. 왜냐하면 화창한 날씨가 계속되지는 않을 테니까요. 내일은 최고 기온이 24도까지 올라가겠으며, 흐리고 약간 비가 내리겠습니다.

●●
take advantage of ~을 이용하다
last 계속되다, 지속하다 temperature 기온
high 최고 기온

02 대화를 듣고, 남자가 가려고 하는 장소를 고르시오.

W Hello?
M Sue, this is Jack. Sorry I'm late. I think we're <u>lost</u>.
W Well, where are you now?
M We're calling from the <u>entrance</u> of Olympic Road.
W Okay. <u>Go straight</u> down Olympic Road and <u>turn</u> <u>right</u> at Jamshil Street.
M Wait. Let me <u>repeat</u> <u>that</u>. Go down Olympic Road and make a right at Jamshil Street. Is that right?
W Yes. After that, turn left at the <u>second</u> <u>intersection</u>. You'll see Olympic Stadium on your left. My apartment is <u>across</u> <u>from</u> the stadium.
M I got it. Your house is on the <u>opposite</u> <u>side</u> of the stadium.
W That's correct. You <u>can't</u> <u>miss</u> <u>it</u>.
M Thanks a lot. See you soon.

여 여보세요?
남 Sue, 나 Jack이야. 늦어서 미안해. 우리가 길을 잃은 것 같아.
여 음, 지금 어디에 있는데?
남 지금 올림픽 대로 입구에서 전화하고 있어.
여 알았어. 올림픽 대로에서 쭉 직진해서 잠실로로 우회전해.
남 잠깐만. 내가 다시 말해볼게. 올림픽 대로를 따라 가다가 잠실로에서 우회전. 내 말 맞지?
여 맞아. 그 후에 두 번째 교차로에서 좌회전해. 왼편으로 올림픽 경기장이 보일 거야. 우리 아파트는 경기장의 맞은편에 있어.
남 이해했어. 너희 집은 운동장 반대편에 있다는 거지.
여 맞아. 쉽게 찾을 거야.
남 고마워. 금방 갈게.

●●
entrance 입구 repeat 되풀이해서 말하다
stadium 경기장 across from ~의 맞은편에
opposite 반대편의, 맞은편의 You can't
miss it. 쉽게 찾을 거예요.

03 대화를 듣고, 두 사람이 대화하는 장소로 가장 적절한 곳을 고르시오.

① 공항
② 우체국
③ 경찰서
④ 분실물 센터 ✓
⑤ 등산용품 가게

W Hello. Can I help you?

M I <u>lost</u> <u>my</u> <u>backpack</u> at the library. Did anyone <u>turn</u> one <u>in</u>?

W When did you lose it? <u>What</u> does it <u>look like</u>?

M I lost it yesterday. It's a brand-new blue backpack.

W <u>Let me check</u> first. Is this yours?

M Yes, that's it! Thank you very much.

W You're welcome. You <u>should be careful</u> from now on.

여 안녕하세요? 도와드릴까요?

남 도서관에서 가방을 잃어버렸습니다. 누군가가 돌려준 것이 있나요?

여 언제 잃어버리셨나요? 어떻게 생겼지요?

남 어제 잃어버렸어요. 신제품의 파란색 가방입니다.

여 먼저 확인해 볼게요. 이건가요?

남 네, 그거예요! 정말 고맙습니다.

여 별말씀을요. 앞으로는 조심하세요.

●● **backpack** 백팩, 배낭 **turn in** ~을 돌려주다 **brand-new** 완전 새 것의, 신제품의 **from now on** 앞으로는, 이제부터

---

04 대화를 듣고, 두 사람의 관계로 가장 적절한 것을 고르시오.

① boss – secretary ✓
② teacher – student
③ waiter – customer
④ police officer – driver
⑤ flight attendant – passenger

M Linda, could you <u>fax this</u> to Beijing for me?

W Sure. Oh, here are your <u>phone messages</u>.

M Ms. Graham called again?

W Yes, she wants the <u>financial data</u>.

M What did you tell her?

W I told her you'd <u>get back to her</u>.

M Thanks. I'd better work on that now.

남 Linda, 내 대신 베이징으로 팩스 좀 보내 주겠어요?

여 물론이죠. 아, 여기 전화 메시지가 있습니다.

남 Graham 씨가 다시 전화했나요?

여 네, 그녀는 재무 자료를 원해요.

남 그녀에게 뭐라고 말했나요?

여 당신이 다시 연락할 거라고 했어요.

남 고마워요. 지금 처리해야겠군요.

●● **financial data** 재무자료 **get back to** ~에게 다시 연락하다

---

05 대화를 듣고, 여자가 원하는 직업으로 가장 적절한 것을 고르시오.

① 과학자
② 무용가 ✓
③ 의사
④ 변호사
⑤ 프로게이머

M Jane, what do you <u>want to be</u>?

W Well, when I was a child, I wanted to be a scientist.

M Oh, <u>so did I</u>.

W But ever since I started high school, I have wanted to be a <u>dancer</u>.

M Right! You are <u>good at dancing</u>.

W But my parents <u>expect me</u> to be a doctor.

M That's interesting. My parents have <u>always wanted</u> <u>me</u> to be a lawyer, but I like to play computer games. So I want to be a <u>professional gamer</u>.

남 Jane, 넌 무엇이 되고 싶니?

여 글쎄, 나는 어렸을 때 과학자가 되고 싶었어.

남 오, 나도 그랬어.

여 하지만 고등학교 이후로는 계속 무용가가 되고 싶었어.

남 맞아! 넌 춤을 잘 추지.

여 하지만 우리 부모님은 내가 의사가 되기를 기대하셔.

남 흥미롭다. 우리 부모님은 항상 내가 변호사가 되기를 바라셨지만 나는 컴퓨터 게임 하기를 좋아해. 그래서 나는 프로게이머가 되고 싶어.

●● **ever since** ~ 이후로 계속 **expect** 기대하다, 예상하다 **lawyer** 변호사 **professional gamer** 프로게이머

06

대화를 듣고, 여자가 가지고 있는 만화책이 총 몇 권인지 고르시오.

① 21권
② 22권
③ 23권
④ 24권
⑤ 25권

M What do you have there?
W It's my comic book collection.
M Wow, that's cool.
W I have every book in the *Time Traveler* series except for the first and third ones.
M How many are there in the series?
W There are twenty-five. I've been collecting them for two years.

남 네가 가지고 있는 것이 뭐야?
여 만화책 수집한 거야.
남 와, 멋지다.
여 첫 번째와 세 번째 것만 빼고 〈시간 여행자 시리즈〉를 모두 가지고 있어.
남 그 시리즈가 총 몇 권인데?
여 25권이야. 난 그것들을 2년 동안 모았어.

●●
collection 수집품

07

대화를 듣고, 남자의 심정으로 가장 적절한 것을 고르시오.

① upset
② afraid
③ bored
④ pleased
⑤ thankful

W Brad, are you all right? Your face looks swollen.
M My tooth has been bothering me.
W You'd better see a dentist about it.
M I've always been fearful of dentists. I don't see one unless I absolutely have to.
W Really? It's not such a big deal. Besides, you'll feel better after he takes care of you.
M I know you're right. I'll make an appointment soon.

여 Brad, 너 괜찮니? 얼굴이 부은 것 같아.
남 이가 계속 불편해서.
여 음, 치과에 가 보는 게 좋겠다.
남 난 항상 치과 의사들이 무서워. 반드시 가야 할 때가 아니라면 가지 않아.
여 정말? 그렇게 대단한 것도 아닌데. 게다가 치과 의사가 치료해 주면 너도 괜찮아질 거야.
남 네 말이 맞는 거 알아. 곧 진료 예약해야겠다.

●●
swollen 부어오른 bother 괴롭히다, 신경 쓰이게 하다 dentist 치과 의사, 치과 fearful 무서운, 두려운 unless 만약 ~이 아니면 appointment 약속, 예약

08

대화를 듣고, 여자의 마지막 말의 의도로 가장 적절한 것을 고르시오.

① 칭찬
② 거절
③ 부탁
④ 비난
⑤ 후회

M Mom, we just ran out of milk. Could you get some, please?
W Sure. I will get some on my way home. What kind of milk do you want?
M I would like to have a carton of fat-free milk.
W Sure.
M Wait, Mom. If another kind is on sale, I would not mind getting that.
W What a wise son you are!

남 엄마, 우유가 막 떨어졌어요. 좀 사다 주실래요?
여 물론이지. 집에 가는 길에 좀 사올게. 어떤 종류의 우유를 원하니?
남 무지방 우유 한 팩 사다 주세요.
여 알겠어.
남 잠깐만요, 엄마. 만일 다른 종류의 우유가 할인 중이라면 전 아무거나 상관없어요.
여 우리 아들 참 현명하구나!

●●
run out of ~이 다 떨어지다 carton 곽, 통 wise 현명한

09 대화를 듣고, 남자가 일출을 보지 못한 이유로 가장 적절한 것을 고르시오.

① 차가 막혀서
② 날씨가 좋지 않아서
③ 일출 시간을 착각해서
④ 아침에 일찍 일어나지 못해서
⑤ 일출을 볼 수 있는 장소가 없어서

W Did you watch the sunrise on New Year's morning?
M No, I didn't. I planned to wake up, but I was just too tired.
W I thought about calling you, but I knew you were celebrating until very late at night.
M Yes, you're right. There was no way I could have woken up so early.
W Anyway, you missed an amazing sunrise. It was really nice.
M I'm sorry I missed it. There's always next year.

여 새해 아침에 일출 구경 했어?
남 아니, 못했어. 일어나려고 했는데 너무 피곤했어.
여 너한테 전화할 생각은 했는데, 네가 밤 늦게까지 신나게 놀았다는 것을 알았거든.
남 응, 네 말이 맞아. 그렇게 일찍 일어날 수 있는 방법이 없었어.
여 어쨌든, 넌 굉장한 일출을 놓친 거야. 정말 멋졌어.
남 나도 그걸 놓친 것이 아쉬워. 항상 내년은 있는 법이니까.

●●
sunrise 일출 celebrate 축하하다; 신나게 놀다 amazing 놀랄 만한, 굉장한

---

10 대화를 듣고, 무엇에 관한 내용인지 가장 적절한 것을 고르시오.

① 얼음
② 골프공
③ 바깥 날씨
④ 이웃집의 소음
⑤ 지붕 위의 도둑

M What is that noise on the roof?
W It sounds like someone is jumping on it. It's so loud.
M Look outside! There are huge balls of ice hitting the ground.
W I've never seen that before. They are as big as golf balls.
M Don't you think this weather is unbelievable?
W You're right. What do you call that?

남 지붕 위에서 나는 저 소리가 뭐니?
여 누가 저 위에서 뛰고 있는 것 같아. 정말 시끄럽다.
남 밖을 봐! 커다란 얼음 덩어리들이 땅으로 떨어지고 있어.
여 저런 것은 전에 한 번도 본 적이 없어. 골프공 만큼이나 크다.
남 믿기 힘든 날씨라고 생각하지 않아?
여 그래. 저걸 뭐라고 부르니?

●●
noise 소음

---

11 대화를 듣고, 남자가 여자에게 부탁한 일로 가장 적절한 것을 고르시오.

① 숙제 같이 하기
② 노트 빌려 주기
③ 수학 공부 도와주기
④ 영어로 편지 써주기
⑤ 영어 편지 교정 봐주기

M What's your favorite subject?
W English. What's yours?
M Math is my favorite. But I'm poor at English. So, I'd like to ask a favor of you.
W What's that?
M My English teacher gave me an assignment. I have to write a letter in English by next Monday. Will you please proofread my letter?
W Sure, I'll make a deal with you. You help me study math, and I'll correct your letter. Deal?
M Okay.

남 너는 좋아하는 과목이 뭐니?
여 영어야. 너는?
남 수학을 좋아해. 하지만 영어는 잘 못해. 저기, 너에게 부탁할 게 있는데.
여 뭔데?
남 영어 선생님이 나에게 과제를 내주셨어. 다음 주 월요일까지 영어로 편지를 써 가야 해. 내가 쓴 편지를 교정 봐 주겠니?
여 물론이지, 조건이 있어. 네가 내 수학 공부를 도와주면, 내가 네 편지를 고쳐줄게. 어때?
남 좋아.

●●
subject 과목 be poor at ~을 잘 못하다
ask a favor of ~에게 부탁하다
assignment 과제 proofread 교정보다
make a deal 거래하다

12

대화를 듣고, 두 사람이 대화 직후에 할 일로 가장 적절한 것을 고르시오.

① 농구 경기하기
② Bill과 Richard 만나기
③ 티셔츠 주문하기
④ 점심 식사 하기
⑤ 팀 이름 정하기

W Are you playing in the <u>basketball</u> <u>tournament</u> next week?

M Yes, Bill and Richard <u>promised</u> <u>to join</u> me.

W Bill and Richard? Oh, you will make a tough team.

M <u>By</u> <u>the</u> <u>way</u>, we don't have <u>uniforms</u>. So we're thinking of wearing simple black T-shirts. Do you think that's okay?

W Well, anything with the <u>same</u> <u>color</u> will be fine. And if it's possible, put the team name on it.

M Okay. Let's <u>have</u> <u>lunch</u> first and then think about the team name later.

여 다음 주에 농구 토너먼트전에 나갈 거니?

남 응, Bill과 Richard가 나와 함께 참가하기로 약속했어.

여 Bill과 Richard? 오, 너희는 상당히 센 팀이 되겠구나.

남 그런데, 우리는 유니폼이 없어. 그래서 단순한 검정색 티셔츠를 입을 생각이야. 괜찮을 것 같니?

여 응, 같은 색깔이면 뭐든 괜찮을 거야. 그리고 가능하면 팀 이름도 넣어.

남 그럴게. 먼저 점심을 먹고 나서 우리 팀 이름을 생각해 보자.

●●
tournament 토너먼트, 승자 진출전

13

다음을 듣고, 여자가 Jane의 생일 파티에 대해 언급하지 않은 것을 고르시오.

① 파티 요일
② 파티 장소
③ 파티 준비물
④ 초대 인원 수
⑤ 걱정하는 것

I'm planning to give Jane a big <u>surprise</u> <u>party</u> this Saturday. I prepared decorations, food, and <u>prizes</u> for games. I invited thirteen people, and everyone will <u>bring</u> <u>presents</u>. I'll ask everyone <u>not to tell</u> Jane about the surprise. But I'm <u>worried</u> <u>about</u> Rachael. Sometimes she can't <u>keep</u> <u>a</u> <u>secret</u>. I hope she doesn't tell Jane about the party.

나는 이번 주 토요일에 Jane에게 커다란 깜짝 파티를 해줄 계획이다. 나는 장식들, 음식, 그리고 게임에 쓸 상품들을 준비했다. 열세 명을 초대 했고, 모두 선물을 가지고 올 것이다. 나는 모두에게 깜짝 파티에 대해 Jane에게 말하지 말라고 부탁했다. 하지만 나는 Rachael이 걱정된다. 때때로 그녀는 비밀을 지키지 못하기 때문이다. 나는 그녀가 파티에 대해 Jane에게 말하지 않기를 바란다.

●●
decoration 장식, 장식품　**prize** 상, 상품
keep a secret 비밀을 지키다

14

대화를 듣고, 남자의 마지막 말에 이어질 여자의 말로 가장 적절한 것을 고르시오.

① No. Just bring yourself.
② I'm glad you could come.
③ How about some other time?
④ I'd love to, but I have to study.
⑤ You can come later. It finishes 10 p.m.

M Oh, hi, Ruth. How are you?

W Just fine. Listen. I'm having a <u>housewarming</u> <u>party</u> this Friday night. Would you like to come?

M Sure. What time?

W Any time <u>after</u> <u>five</u>. Here's an <u>invitation</u>.

M Thank you. Do you want me to <u>bring</u> <u>anything</u>?

W <u>No. Just bring yourself.</u>

남 오, 안녕, Ruth. 어떻게 지내니?

여 잘 지내. 저기 말이야. 금요일 밤에 집들이를 할 거야. 너도 올 거니?

남 물론이지. 몇 시야?

여 5시 이후로는 아무 때나 괜찮아. 여기 초대장이야.

남 고마워. 가져갈 것 없니?

여 ① <u>아니야. 그냥 몸만 와.</u>
② 네가 와 줘서 기뻐.
③ 다음에 하는 것이 어때?
④ 가고 싶지만, 공부를 해야 해.
⑤ 늦게 와도 돼. 파티는 10시에 끝나.

●●
housewarming party 집들이
invitation 초대, 초대장

30

15 대화를 듣고, 여자의 마지막 말에 이어질 남자의 말로 가장 적절한 것을 고르시오.

① I'm sure you'll like it.
② Sorry, ma'am. It's not refundable.
③ Yes, there's a one-year guarantee.
④ You can pay with cash or by credit card.
⑤ It's 300 dollars, but you can get a 10% discount.

M May I help you?
W Yes. I'd like to buy a gift for my son.
M Do you have anything special in mind?
W Yes, I'd like to see a smartwatch.
M We have several you might like. How about this one?
W Hmm... Can I see something a little better?
M I'm sorry. This is the most expensive one we have.
W Okay. Does it come with a guarantee?
M Yes, there's a one-year guarantee.

남 도와드릴까요?
여 네. 아들에게 줄 선물을 사고 싶은데요.
남 특별히 생각하고 계신 거라도 있습니까?
여 네, 스마트 시계를 보고 싶어요.
남 저희는 손님이 좋아하실 만한 것들을 여러 개 가지고 있습니다. 이것은 어떠세요?
여 음… 더 좋은 걸로 볼 수 있을까요?
남 죄송합니다. 이것이 여기서 가장 비싼 거예요.
여 알겠습니다. 보증은 되나요?
남 네, 1년 보증입니다.

① 틀림없이 마음에 드실 거예요.
② 죄송합니다, 손님. 환불은 안 됩니다.
④ 현금 또는 신용카드로 지불 가능합니다.
⑤ 그것은 300달러이지만 10%를 할인해드립니다.

• •
have ~ in mind ~을 생각하다[염두에 두다]
guarantee 보증 **refundable** 환불 가능한

▶ REVIEW TEST p. 47

A
① temperature, 기온 ② entrance, 입구 ③ stadium, 경기장 ④ lawyer, 변호사 ⑤ dentist, 치과 의사, 치과
⑥ appointment, 약속, 예약 ⑦ noise, 소음 ⑧ assignment, 과제 ⑨ tournament, 토너먼트, 승자 진출전
⑩ keep a secret, 비밀을 지키다 ⑪ invitation, 초대, 초대장 ⑫ guarantee, 보증

B
① across from ② miss it ③ wanted me to
④ How many, series ⑤ collecting them for ⑥ ask a favor
⑦ housewarming party ⑧ have, in mind

문제 및 정답	받아쓰기 및 녹음내용	해석

01

대화를 듣고, 여자의 손자가 누구인지 고르시오.

① ②

③ ④

⑤

W Could you please help me, officer? I <u>can't</u> <u>find</u> my grandson.

M When did you lose him, ma'am?

W While I was <u>making</u> <u>a</u> <u>phone</u> <u>call</u> a few minutes ago.

M How old is he, and <u>what</u> does he <u>look</u> <u>like</u>?

W He is five years old, and he has <u>short</u> <u>curly</u> <u>hair</u>.

M What is he wearing?

W He is wearing <u>glasses</u>, a blue shirt, and yellow <u>shorts</u>.

여 경관님, 좀 도와주실 수 있나요? 제 손자를 찾을 수가 없네요.

남 손자를 언제 잃어버리셨습니까, 부인?

여 몇 분전 제가 통화하는 사이에요.

남 몇 살이고 어떻게 생겼습니까?

여 다섯 살이고 짧은 곱슬머리를 하고 있어요.

남 어떤 차림을 하고 있습니까?

여 안경을 썼고 파란색 셔츠에 노란색 반바지를 입었어요.

●●
grandson 손자 **curly** 곱슬머리의
shorts 반바지

02

대화를 듣고, 남자가 가려고 하는 장소를 고르시오.

M Excuse me. I'm <u>looking</u> <u>for</u> the West Town Mall on Pine Avenue.

W Let's see… Pine Avenue… Ah, yes, I know. Take a left at the <u>gas</u> <u>station</u>, and walk up to First Street.

M Up to First Street. Okay. Then, do I turn left or right?

W Turn right. Go down First Street until you <u>come</u> <u>to</u> <u>the</u> <u>crosswalk</u>. Just before you come to it, there's a street <u>on</u> <u>the</u> <u>left</u>. That's Pine Avenue.

M That's Pine Avenue. Okay.

W Then, go down Pine Avenue for two blocks. You'll find it <u>on</u> <u>your</u> <u>right</u>.

M Okay. I got it. You're so kind. Thank you.

W No problem.

남 실례합니다. 파인가에 있는 웨스트타운 몰을 찾고 있는데요.

여 어디 봅시다… 파인가라… 아, 네, 알겠어요. 주유소에서 왼쪽으로 돌아서 1번가까지 걸어가세요.

남 1번가까지요. 알겠습니다. 거기서 왼쪽으로 도나요 오른쪽으로 도나요?

여 오른쪽으로 도세요. 횡단보도가 나올 때까지 1번가를 따라 가세요. 횡단보도가 나오기 바로 전에 왼쪽에 도로가 하나 있어요. 그곳이 파인가예요.

남 그곳이 파인가군요. 알겠습니다.

여 그리고 파인가를 따라 두 블록 가세요. 오른편에 몰이 보일 겁니다.

남 네. 알겠습니다. 너무 친절하시군요. 감사합니다.

여 천만에요.

●●
avenue ~가, 대로 **crosswalk** 횡단보도

03 대화를 듣고, 두 사람이 고른 점심 메뉴가 **아닌** 것을 고르시오.

① 스테이크
② 샌드위치
③ 샐러드
④ 아이스크림
⑤ 차

W I'm hungry. <u>Shall</u> <u>we</u> <u>have</u> some steak?

M I want <u>something</u> <u>light</u> today. How about going to the Baker's Table? It serves <u>fresh</u> <u>sandwiches</u> and salads.

W All right. I'll have an egg sandwich and a Greek salad then. But the next time, let's eat what I want to eat.

M Okay. <u>That's fair</u>. Let's go to the restaurant. I also <u>feel</u> <u>like having</u> some ice cream and a cup of tea after our meal.

W Well, that <u>sounds</u> <u>good</u> <u>to</u> me.

여 배고파. 우리 스테이크 먹을래?

남 오늘은 가벼운 걸로 먹었으면 좋겠어. Baker's Table에 가는 것이 어때? 그곳은 신선한 샌드위치와 샐러드를 제공해.

여 좋아. 그럼 난 달걀 샌드위치와 그리스식 샐러드를 먹을래. 하지만 다음 번에는 내가 원하는 것으로 먹는 거야.

남 그래. 그게 공평하지. 식당으로 가자. 그리고 식사 후에는 아이스크림을 먹고 차 한잔을 마시고 싶어.

여 음, 나도 좋아.

●●
fair 공평한 **feel like -ing** ~하고 싶다

---

04 대화를 듣고, 두 사람의 관계로 가장 적절한 것을 고르시오.

① 은행원 - 지점장
② 재단사 - 디자이너
③ 세탁소 주인 - 손님
④ 옷가게 직원 - 손님
⑤ 자동차 정비사 - 운전자

W Good morning. Can I help you?

M Yes, I bought a <u>sweater</u> here last week, but I don't really like the <u>color</u>. It looked okay here, but when I got home, it looked <u>different</u>. I want to <u>return it</u>.

W Yes, sir. Do you have the <u>receipt</u>?

M Uh, yeah. Here it is.

W Okay. Uh-oh. Sir, this was <u>on sale</u> when you bought it. I'm sorry, but sale items <u>can't be returned</u>.

M What?

W I'm sorry, but that's the <u>store policy</u>.

여 좋은 아침이에요. 도와드릴까요?

남 네, 여기서 지난 주에 스웨터를 샀는데 색깔이 정말 마음에 안 들어요. 여기서는 괜찮아 보였는데, 집에 가서 보니 다르더라고요. 반품하고 싶어요.

여 알겠습니다, 손님. 영수증을 가지고 계신가요?

남 음, 네. 여기 있어요.

여 좋습니다. 이런. 손님, 이것을 사실 때 할인 중이었네요. 죄송하지만 할인 품목들은 반품이 안 됩니다.

남 뭐라고요?

여 죄송합니다만, 저희 가게 방침이라서요.

●●
return 반납하다, 반품하다 **receipt** 영수증

---

05 다음을 듣고, 여자가 오늘 한 일로 언급하지 **않은** 것을 고르시오.

①
②
③
④
⑤

What a <u>busy</u> <u>day</u>! First, I woke up early and <u>vacuumed</u> the whole house. Then, I drove to work through a horrible <u>traffic jam</u>. At the office, all I did was type all day because my team's final report is <u>due tomorrow</u>. I didn't even take a <u>lunch break</u>. I was so nervous about not finishing it <u>on time</u>. Finally, after work, I went to the airport to <u>pick up</u> my parents.

정말 바쁜 하루였어요! 먼저, 저는 일찍 일어나서 집 전체를 진공청소기로 청소했어요. 그리고 나서 혼잡한 교통을 뚫고 운전해서 출근했지요. 사무실에서 제가 한 것이라곤 우리 팀 최종 보고서가 내일까지여서 하루 종일 컴퓨터 자판을 두드린 것뿐이었어요. 점심 시간조차 갖지 못했어요. 제시간에 끝내지 못할까 봐 불안했거든요. 마지막으로 퇴근 후에는 부모님을 모시러 공항에 갔었답니다.

●●
vacuum 진공청소기로 청소하다 **horrible** 끔찍한 **traffic jam** 교통 체증 **due** ~까지 하기로 되어 있는 **on time** 제시간에 **pick up** (차로) 태우다, 태우러 가다

06

대화를 듣고, 남자가 지불해야 할 금액으로 가장 적절한 것을 고르시오.

① $2
② $3
③ $4
④ $5
⑤ $6

M Guess what? My class is going on a field trip.

W Where are you going?

M We're going to the National Museum. Then, we're having a picnic in the park.

W It sounds like it'll be a lot of fun.

M It really does. And the weather forecast says it will be sunny that day.

W Do you have to pay for that?

M Yes. Admission to the museum is 4 dollars per person, but students can get a 50% discount.

남 그거 알아? 우리 반 견학 간대.

여 어디로 가는데?

남 국립 박물관으로 갈 거야. 그리고 공원으로 소풍도 갈 거야.

여 정말 재미있을 것 같다.

남 정말 그래. 그리고 일기예보에서 그 날은 화창할거래.

여 돈을 내야 하니?

남 응. 박물관 입장료는 1인당 4달러인데, 학생들은 50% 할인을 받을 수 있어.

●●
field trip 견학, 현장 학습 **the National Museum** 국립 박물관 **admission** 입장료

07

대화를 듣고, 여자의 심정으로 가장 적절한 것을 고르시오.

① sad
② bored
③ pleased
④ nervous
⑤ annoyed

W Chris, please turn it down.

M What did you say, Mom?

W Turn down the music!

M I just love to turn it up loud.

W There are other people in the house, too. I can't concentrate on my work because of the music.

M Okay. Then I'll put on my headphones.

여 Chris, 소리 좀 줄여 줘.

남 뭐라고요, 엄마?

여 음악 소리 좀 줄이라고!

남 전 크게 트는 것이 좋은데요.

여 이 집에 너 말고 다른 사람들도 있잖니. 음악 때문에 일에 집중을 할 수가 없구나.

남 알겠어요. 그럼 헤드폰을 쓸게요.

●●
turn down 낮추다, 줄이다 **put on** 입다, 쓰다

08

대화를 듣고, 여자가 묻고 있는 것으로 가장 적절한 것을 고르시오.

① 환승역의 위치
② 지하철 환승 방법
③ 목적지까지 소요 시간
④ 목적지까지 가는 방법
⑤ 가장 가까운 지하철역의 위치

M Excuse me. Do you need any help?

W Yes, thank you. I'm looking for Yeoksam Station on this map.

M That's easy. Just find the green line. It's line number 2.

W Thank you, sir.

M We're on line number 5 now, which means you must change trains at Yeongdeungpo-gu Office Station.

W You've been so helpful, sir.

M No problem at all.

남 실례합니다. 도움이 필요하세요?

여 네, 고맙습니다. 이 지도에서 역삼역을 찾고 있는데요.

남 그건 쉬워요. 녹색 선을 찾으면 돼요. 2호선이요.

여 고맙습니다.

남 지금 우리가 5호선에 있으니까 영등포구청역에서 열차를 갈아타야 한다는 말이지요.

여 정말 도움이 많이 되었습니다.

남 별말씀을요.

09 대화를 듣고, 여자가 화가 난 이유로 가장 적절한 것을 고르시오.

① 미용사가 불친절해서
② 미용실 가격이 너무 비싸서
③ 미용실 예약에 착오가 생겨서
④ 미용실에서 너무 오래 기다려서
⑤ 미용사가 해 준 머리가 마음에 들지 않아서

M What's wrong, Linda? You <u>seem</u> <u>angry</u>.
W I went to the beauty shop, and the person cut my hair <u>too</u> <u>short</u>.
M I don't think it's too short. You look great.
W You're just saying that to <u>make</u> <u>me</u> <u>feel</u> <u>better</u>.
M I'm <u>serious</u>. You look better with short hair. It <u>highlights</u> your face.
W Do you really think so?
M I <u>wouldn't</u> <u>say</u> <u>that</u> if I didn't.

남 무슨 일이야, Linda? 화난 것 같다.
여 미용실에 갔는데, 미용사가 머리카락을 너무 짧게 잘라 놓았어.
남 내 생각에는 너무 짧은 것 같지 않은데. 아주 좋아 보여.
여 나 기분 좋으라고 그렇게 말하는 거잖아?
남 진짜야. 너는 짧은 머리가 잘 어울려. 네 얼굴을 돋보이게 한다니까.
여 정말 그렇게 생각해?
남 그렇지 않으면 너에게 이런 말도 안 하지.

●●
highlight 돋보이게 하다

---

10 대화를 듣고, 무엇에 관한 내용인지 가장 적절한 것을 고르시오.

① 겨울 축제
② 이상 기후
③ 강릉의 명소
④ 여자의 고향 학교
⑤ 남자의 고향 사람들

M Did you hear that Gangneung received 70 centimeters of snow today? It was <u>quite a</u> <u>shock</u> to the people there.
W 70 centimeters? That's <u>nothing</u>. Where I'm from, it's not <u>unusual</u> to get several hundred centimeters of snow <u>at</u> <u>one</u> <u>time</u>.
M You <u>must</u> <u>be</u> <u>kidding</u>. I can't imagine that.
W Well, the <u>climate</u> can be very different in other parts of the world.
M I know, but it's <u>hard</u> <u>to</u> <u>believe</u> that much snow can fall at one time.
W It's true. Sometimes the schools <u>are</u> <u>closed</u> for several days.

남 오늘 강릉에 70센티미터의 눈이 왔다는 얘기 들었니? 거기 사는 사람들에게는 꽤 충격이었대.
여 70센티미터? 그건 아무 것도 아니야. 내가 살던 곳은 한 번에 눈이 몇 백 센티미터 오는 게 드문 일이 아니야.
남 농담이겠지. 상상할 수가 없는 걸.
여 세계의 다른 곳에서는 기후가 매우 다를 수 있어.
남 알아, 하지만 그렇게 많은 눈이 한 번에 온다는 것은 믿기 힘들어.
여 정말이야. 가끔은 학교들이 며칠 동안 문을 닫기도 해.

●●
unusual 특이한, 드문 **climate** 기후

---

11 대화를 듣고, 여자가 남자에게 부탁한 일로 가장 적절한 것을 고르시오.

① 치즈 사 오기
② 사진 찍어 주기
③ 초상화 그려 주기
④ 종탑까지 가는 길 알려 주기
⑤ 자동 사진기 종류 보여 주기

W <u>Would</u> <u>you</u> <u>mind</u> taking my picture in front of this tower?
M No, not at all.
W <u>Just</u> <u>press</u> this red button.
M Do I need to <u>focus</u>?
W No, it will focus <u>automatically</u>. Please try to get the top of the <u>bell</u> <u>tower</u> and also <u>those</u> <u>houses</u> on the left.
M Okay. I think I can do that. Ready? <u>Say</u> <u>cheese</u>.

여 이 탑 앞에서 제 사진 좀 찍어 주실 수 있나요?
남 네, 그러죠.
여 이 빨간 버튼을 누르시기만 하면 됩니다.
남 초점을 맞춰야 하나요?
여 아니요, 자동으로 초점이 맞춰집니다. 종탑의 윗부분과 왼편에 있는 저 집들도 넣어 주세요.
남 알겠어요. 그렇게 할 수 있겠네요. 준비됐나요? 웃으세요.

●●
take a picture 사진을 찍다 **focus** 초점을 맞추다 **automatically** 자동으로

12 대화를 듣고, 남자가 대화 직후에 할 일로 가장 적절한 것을 고르시오.

① 옷을 포장한다.
② 옷을 수선한다.
③ 돈을 거슬러 준다.
④ 여자가 주문한 옷을 보여 준다.
⑤ 여자에게 새로운 옷을 보여 준다.

M May I help you, madam?
W I would like to <u>pick up</u> my suit.
M Oh, yes. Here you are. Please <u>try it on</u>. How do you like it?
W It's a bit <u>too tight</u> under the arms, I think, and around the waist, too.
M All right. That's easily fixed. How about the <u>shoulders</u>?
W They're fine. <u>How much</u> is the total?
M The total is 300 dollars. Wait here. I'll <u>fix it right now</u>.

남 무엇을 도와드릴까요. 사모님?
여 제 옷을 가지러 왔어요.
남 아, 네. 여기 있습니다. 입어 보세요. 어떠세요?
여 팔 아래 부분과 허리 주변이 너무 꼭 끼네요.
남 알겠습니다. 쉽게 수선할 수 있어요. 어깨 부분은 어떠십니까?
여 좋아요. 모두 얼마죠?
남 모두 300달러입니다. 여기서 기다리세요. 지금 바로 고쳐 오겠습니다.

●●
try on (옷·신발 등을) 입어[신어] 보다
tight 꼭 끼는 **fix** 고치다, 수선하다

---

13 대화를 듣고, 여자가 주말에 한 일과 시간이 일치하지 <u>않는</u> 것을 고르시오.

① 토요일 오전 – 방 청소
② 토요일 오전 – 식물에 물주기
③ 토요일 오후 – 숙제하기
④ 일요일 오전 – 체육관에서 운동하기
⑤ 일요일 오후 – TV 보기

M What did you do <u>on Saturday</u>?
W I did <u>a lot of housework</u> like cleaning my room and watering the plants in the morning.
M What did you do in the afternoon?
W I did my homework.
M You <u>must have been tired</u>. What about Sunday?
W I exercised at the gym in the morning and <u>went shopping</u> in the afternoon. What about you?
M Well, I <u>sat around</u> the house and watched TV <u>all day</u>.
W Do you want to go to the gym together next week?
M Yes, I'd love to go there.

남 토요일에 뭐 했니?
여 오전에는 방 청소와 식물에 물주기 같은 집안일을 많이 했어.
남 오후에는 뭐 했니?
여 숙제 했어.
남 피곤했겠다. 일요일에는?
여 오전에는 체육관에서 운동하고 오후에는 쇼핑하러 갔지. 너는?
남 음, 난 집에서 빈둥거리며 하루 종일 TV를 봤어.
여 다음 주에는 체육관에 같이 갈래?
남 응, 나도 가고 싶어.

●●
water 물을 주다 **sit around** 빈둥거리다

---

14 대화를 듣고, 남자의 마지막 말에 이어질 여자의 말로 가장 적절한 것을 고르시오.

① I couldn't agree more.
② Okay. We'll see you there.
③ What will you do after graduation?
④ Cheer up. You'll do better the next time.
⑤ Don't worry about it, and thanks for the gift.

M Sandy, I have <u>something for you</u>.
W Really? What is it?
M It's a gift for your <u>graduation</u>.
W But I graduated from university <u>two months ago</u>.
M I know. It's a <u>late</u> graduation present.
W You <u>don't have to</u> do this.
M I'm sorry for <u>forgetting</u> your graduation.
W <u>Don't worry about it, and thanks for the gift.</u>

남 Sandy, 너에게 줄 게 있어.
여 정말? 뭔데?
남 졸업 선물이야.
여 하지만 난 두 달 전에 대학을 졸업했잖아?
남 알아. 늦은 졸업 선물이야.
여 이렇게 할 필요까진 없는데.
남 네 졸업을 잊어서 미안해.
여 <u>그건 걱정하지마, 그리고 선물 고마워.</u>

① 전적으로 동의해.
② 좋아. 거기서 보자.
③ 졸업하고 뭘 할거야?
④ 기운 내. 다음엔 더 잘할 거야.

●●
graduation 졸업

15 대화를 듣고, 여자의 마지막 말에 이어질 남자의 말로 가장 적절한 것을 고르시오.

① I wish I had more time.
② Can you wake me up in an hour?
③ I usually go to bed around 10 o'clock.
④ I will try, but it's not going to be easy.
⑤ I just didn't hear the alarm this morning.

W Whattime did you go to bed last night?
M I am not sure, but I think it was close to midnight. I had lots of homework to do.
W You'd better go to bed early. Do you think you can do your homework during the day?
M I am too tired to do it right after school.
W I noticed that you take naps these days. Can you try not to take naps anymore?
M I will try, but it's not going to be easy.

여 어젯밤에 몇 시에 잤니?
남 확실치 않지만 거의 자정 가까이 된 것 같아요. 해야 할 숙제가 많았거든요.
여 일찍 잠자리에 드는 게 좋겠구나. 낮 동안에 숙제를 할 수 있겠니?
남 방과 후에 바로 하기에는 너무 피곤해요.
여 요즘 너 낮잠을 자던데. 더 이상 낮잠을 자지 않도록 해볼 수 있겠어?
남 노력은 해보겠지만, 쉽지는 않을 거예요.

① 시간이 더 많았으면 좋겠어요.
② 한 시간 후에 깨워주실래요?
③ 저는 보통 10시쯤 잠자리에 들어요.
④ 오늘 아침에 알람 소리를 못 들었어요.

•• midnight 자정 take a nap 낮잠을 자다

REVIEW TEST p. 55

A
① shorts, 반바지 ② avenue, ~가, 대로 ③ fair, 공평한 ④ receipt, 영수증
⑤ vacuum, 진공청소기로 청소하다 ⑥ field trip, 견학, 현장 학습 ⑦ admission, 입장료 ⑧ climate, 기후
⑨ automatically, 자동으로 ⑩ traffic jam, 교통 체증 ⑪ on time, 제시간에 ⑫ take a nap, 낮잠을 자다

B
① short curly hair ② feel like ③ returned
④ due tomorrow ⑤ wouldn't say ⑥ be kidding
⑦ sat around, watched ⑧ don't have to

문제 및 정답	받아쓰기 및 녹음내용	해석

01

다음을 듣고, 다음 주 화요일의 날씨로 가장 적절한 것을 고르시오.

① ②

③ ④

⑤

Good evening. This is Max Morris from CNB. Here is the <u>weather report</u> for next week. On Monday, it is going to snow <u>all</u> day <u>long</u>. Tuesday won't see <u>any</u> sunshine because of the cloudy skies. On Wednesday, we will have <u>clear skies</u>, but it will be cold. It'll be sunny and <u>a little windy</u> on Thursday and Friday. Thank you.

안녕하세요, 저는 CNB의 Max Morris입니다. 다음주 일기예보입니다. 월요일에는 하루 종일 눈이 내리겠습니다. 화요일은 흐린 하늘 때문에 햇빛이 보이지 않겠습니다. 수요일은 하늘이 맑아지겠으나 쌀쌀하겠습니다. 목요일과 금요일에는 화창하고 바람이 약간 불 것입니다. 감사합니다.

02

대화를 듣고, 남자가 가려고 하는 장소를 고르시오.

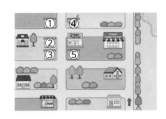

M Excuse me. I think I'm <u>lost</u>.

W What are you looking for?

M I'd like to go to the city library. <u>Could you tell me</u> how to get there, please?

W Well… It is a little far from here, but I think you can go <u>on foot</u>.

M I <u>do</u> <u>not</u> <u>mind</u> walking there.

W Oh, then go straight two blocks until you get to Green Supermarket. <u>Turn left</u> just after the supermarket, and <u>keep going straight</u>.

M After Green Supermarket, make a left and go straight.

W Yes, it's on your right. It is <u>across from</u> the Green Theater. You <u>can't miss it</u>.

M Thank you, ma'am.

W My pleasure. Have a nice day.

남 실례합니다. 길은 잃은 것 같아요.

여 어디를 찾으시는데요?

남 시립 도서관이요. 그곳에 어떻게 가는지 알려 주시겠어요?

여 음… 여기서 조금 멀긴 하지만 걸어서 가실 수 있을 거예요.

남 걸어가도 상관 없어요.

여 아, 그러면 그린 슈퍼마켓에 도착할 때까지 두 블록을 곧장 가세요. 슈퍼마켓을 지나면 바로 좌회전하고, 계속 직진하세요.

남 그린 슈퍼마켓을 지나 좌회전하고 직진하라고요.

여 네, 도서관은 오른편에 있어요. 그린 극장의 맞은편이에요. 쉽게 찾으실 거예요.

남 감사합니다, 부인.

여 천만에요. 좋은 하루 보내세요.

● ●
on foot 걸어서, 도보로

03 대화를 듣고, 두 사람이 대화하는 장소로 가장 적절한 곳을 고르시오.

① 약국
② 경찰서
③ 동물 병원
④ 동물 보호소
⑤ 분실물 센터

W What seems to be the problem with your pet?
M Well, every time I give something to Spot, he only eats a little, and he has diarrhea, too.
W I see. How long has he had these symptoms?
M I guess for about a week or so.
W You should have brought him to my office earlier.
M What's wrong with him? Is he really sick?
W Well... You had better leave Spot here for a couple of days.
M Okay. Please take good care of him.

여 애완동물에게 어떤 문제가 있으세요?
남 글쎄요, 제가 Spot에게 뭔가를 줄 때마다 조금 밖에 먹지 않고 설사도 해요.
여 알겠어요. 이런 증상들을 보인 지는 얼마나 됐나요?
남 한 일주일 정도 된 것 같아요.
여 병원에 더 일찍 데리고 오셨어야 했어요.
남 무슨 문제라도 있나요? 정말로 많이 아픈가요?
여 음… Spot을 이곳에 이틀 정도 두고 가시는 것이 좋겠어요.
남 알겠습니다. 잘 좀 보살펴 주세요.

●●
diarrhea 설사 **symptom** 증상

---

04 대화를 듣고, 두 사람의 관계로 가장 적절한 것을 고르시오.

① 경찰관 - 시민
② 연예인 - 매니저
③ 사진 작가 - 모델
④ 매표소 직원 - 손님
⑤ 관광 가이드 - 여행객

W Now, coming up on our left is John Paul Jones's house.
M Is it open to the public?
W Yes. You can visit it after we finish this tour if you want.
M There's so much history in this city.
W If you like historical buildings, you should visit the Banks Museum.
M What's that?
W It's an open-air museum full of old houses.
M It sounds interesting.

여 이제, 우리 왼편으로 John Paul Jones의 집이 보이네요.
남 그 집은 일반 사람들에게 공개되나요?
여 네. 원하시면 이 투어가 끝난 후에 방문하실 수 있습니다.
남 이 도시에는 아주 많은 역사가 있네요.
여 역사적인 건물들을 좋아하시면 Banks Museum을 방문해 보세요.
남 그게 뭐죠?
여 오래된 집들로 가득한 야외 박물관이에요.
남 재미있을 것 같네요.

●●
public 일반 사람들, 대중 **historical** 역사적인 **open-air** 옥외의, 야외의

---

05 대화를 듣고, 남자가 가장 좋아하는 배우가 누구인지 고르시오.

M I can't believe it! That's my favorite actor over there.
W Where?
M See? He's sitting with his girlfriend at a table for two.
W Do you mean the guy drinking beer?
M No, the one wearing the suit and glasses.
W Oh, I see him. He's eating a steak, right?
M That's him. I'm going to ask him for his autograph.
W Can you get one for me, too?

남 믿을 수가 없어! 저기 있는 사람이 내가 가장 좋아하는 배우야.
여 어디?
남 보여? 그는 여자 친구와 2인용 탁자에 앉아 있어.
여 맥주 마시는 남자 말이야?
남 아니, 양복을 입고 안경을 쓰고 있는 사람.
여 아, 나도 보여. 그는 스테이크를 먹고 있어, 그렇지?
남 바로 그 사람이야. 그에게 사인해 달라고 부탁할 거야.
여 내 것도 하나 받아 줄 수 있어?

●●
autograph 사인

06 대화를 듣고, 여자의 운동을 시작하기 전 몸무게로 가장 적적할 것을 고르시오.

① 47kg
② 48kg
③ 51kg
④ 53kg
⑤ 54kg

M So I hear you're <u>working out</u> these days.
W Yeah. I feel great.
M Your skin seems to have <u>cleared up</u>, too.
W I know. I'm so happy.
M Have you <u>lost weight</u>?
W No. <u>Believe it or not</u>, I recently gained 3 kilograms.
M You're <u>kidding</u>.
W No. It's all muscle though. Now I <u>weigh</u> 51 kilograms.

남 요즘 운동한다고 들었어.
여 응. 기분이 아주 좋아.
남 피부도 아주 깨끗해진 것 같아.
여 맞아. 너무 행복해.
남 체중도 줄었니?
여 아니. 믿거나 말거나, 최근 3킬로그램이 늘었어.
남 농담이겠지.
여 정말이야. 하지만 전부 근육이야. 지금은 체중이 51킬로그램이야.

•• **work out** 운동하다 **lose weight** 체중이 줄다, 살이 빠지다 **believe it or not** 믿거나 말거나, 믿기 힘들겠지만 **muscle** 근육

---

07 대화를 듣고, 남자의 심정으로 가장 적절한 것을 고르시오.

① 기쁘다
② 피곤하다
③ 재미없다
④ 흥미롭다
⑤ 혼란스럽다

M Do you like football?
W <u>That</u> <u>depends</u>. If you mean <u>soccer</u>, then the answer is yes. If you mean <u>American</u> <u>football</u>, the answer is no.
M Now I'm <u>confused</u>.
W In England, they <u>call</u> soccer "<u>football</u>."
M To me, the word "football" is strange. <u>Anyway</u>, do you like soccer?
W Oh, yes. I like soccer very much.

남 넌 축구(football)를 좋아하니?
여 그건 상황에 따라 달라. 축구를 뜻하는 거라면 그 대답은 "예"야. 미식 축구를 뜻하는 거라면 그 대답은 "아니오"야.
남 나 지금 조금 헷갈린다.
여 영국에서는 축구를 "football"이라고 부르지.
남 나에게 "football"이라는 단어는 좀 이상해. 어쨌든, 넌 축구(soccer)를 좋아하니?
여 응, 좋아해. 난 축구를 아주 많이 좋아해.

•• **That depends.** 상황에 따라 다르다. **confused** 혼란스러운, 헷갈리는

---

08 대화를 듣고, 여자의 마지막 말의 의도로 가장 적절한 것을 고르시오.

① 불평
② 사과
③ 칭찬
④ 동의
⑤ 감사

M Do you live <u>near</u> <u>here</u>?
W Yes, I live in one of those <u>apartments</u> <u>over</u> <u>there</u>. What about you?
M Oh, I'm staying with a family near the station.
W Are you <u>on vacation</u>?
M <u>Not</u> <u>really</u>. I'm here to study English. I'm from Korea.
W I don't think you need to study English <u>anymore</u>. Your English is <u>good</u> <u>enough</u>.

남 이 근처에 사세요?
여 네, 저기 있는 아파트들 중 한 곳에 살아요. 당신은요?
남 아, 저는 가족과 함께 역 근처에 머물고 있어요.
여 휴가 중이신가요?
남 그렇진 않아요. 이곳에는 영어를 공부하러 왔어요. 저는 한국인이에요.
여 영어 공부는 더 이상 할 필요가 없을 것 같은데요. 당신의 영어는 충분히 좋아요.

•• **on vacation** 휴가 중인

09 대화를 듣고, 남자가 화가 난 이유로 가장 적절한 것을 고르시오.

① 여자가 짜증을 내서
② 라디오를 켤 수 없어서
③ 몸을 움직일 수 없어서
④ 교통 체증이 너무 심해서
⑤ 부모님을 만나 뵐 수 없어서

M Oh, no, another traffic jam. I <u>can't</u> <u>stand</u> this.
W Take it easy, George. Don't be upset <u>for</u> <u>no</u> <u>reason</u>.
M It just seems it <u>takes</u> <u>so</u> <u>long</u> to get everywhere.
W Let's <u>turn</u> <u>on</u> the radio to see how long it will take.
M There's a traffic jam every year <u>during</u> <u>the</u> <u>holidays</u>.
W Just relax. I'm sure the traffic will move soon. Do you see? It's <u>starting</u> <u>to</u> <u>move</u> now.

남 오, 안돼, 또 정체야. 이건 참을 수 없어.
여 진정해, George. 아무 이유 없이 화내지 마.
남 어딜 가든지 너무 오래 걸리는 것 같아서.
여 얼마나 오래 걸릴지 보기 위해 라디오를 켜보자.
남 연휴 기간에는 매년 이렇게 정체야.
여 여유를 가져. 정체는 금방 풀릴 거야. 보여? 이제 움직이기 시작하잖아.

••
stand 참다, 견디다　**Take it easy.** 진정해.
it seems ~ ~인 것 같다　**turn on** 켜다
relax 쉬다, 긴장을 풀다

---

10 대화를 듣고, 남자가 병원을 방문한 목적으로 가장 적절한 것을 고르시오.

① 약을 처방 받기 위해서
② 건강검진을 받기 위해서
③ 입원 환자를 만나기 위해서
④ 엘리베이터를 수리하기 위해서
⑤ 부러진 다리를 치료받기 위해서

W Hello, sir. What can I <u>do</u> <u>for</u> <u>you</u>?
M I'm here to <u>see</u> <u>a</u> <u>patient</u>.
W What's the name?
M Edward Cane. He came in with a <u>broken</u> <u>leg</u>.
W Oh, yes. Mr. Cane is <u>on</u> <u>the</u> <u>ninth</u> <u>floor</u>.
M Thank you.

여 안녕하세요. 무엇을 도와드릴까요?
남 환자를 만나러 왔는데요.
여 성함이 어떻게 되죠?
남 Edward Cane입니다. 다리를 다쳐서 들어 왔어요.
여 아, 네. Cane 씨는 9층에 있습니다.
남 고맙습니다.

••
patient 환자　**broken leg** 골절된 다리
floor (건물의) 층

---

11 대화를 듣고, 여자가 영어 숙제에 대해 걱정하는 것으로 가장 적절한 것을 고르시오.

① 조사해야 할 자료가 많다.
② 숙제를 영어로 작성해야 한다.
③ 반 친구들 앞에서 발표해야 한다.
④ 셰익스피어에 관한 지식이 전혀 없다.
⑤ 팀원들의 의견을 하나로 모아야 한다.

M That is <u>interesting</u> <u>homework</u> we have for English class.
W Interesting? It's going to be <u>a</u> <u>lot</u> <u>of</u> <u>work</u>.
M What's so hard about it? We just have to do some research on Shakespeare and <u>give</u> <u>a</u> <u>presentation</u> in class.
W <u>Doing</u> <u>some</u> <u>research</u> isn't so hard. But we have to give a speech in class.
M That actually sounds like fun to me.
W That's <u>good</u> <u>for</u> <u>you</u>. But it doesn't seem like fun to me.

남 영어 수업 숙제가 재미있어.
여 재미있다고? 그건 아주 힘들 거야.
남 그게 뭐가 힘들어? 우린 그냥 셰익스피어에 대해 조사하고 수업 시간에 발표만 하면 되는데.
여 조사하는 건 별로 어렵지 않아. 하지만 수업 시간에 이야기를 해야 하잖아.
남 사실 나는 재미있을 것 같아.
여 잘됐네. 하지만 나는 재미없을 것 같아.

••
research 조사　**speech** 연설, 이야기

12

대화를 듣고, 남자의 충고를 들은 여자가 할 일로 가장 적절한 것을 고르시오.

① 룸메이트에게 편지를 쓴다.
② 룸메이트와 옷을 사러 간다.
③ 룸메이트를 바꿔달라고 말한다.
④ 룸메이트와 문제에 대해 이야기한다.
⑤ 룸메이트 없이 혼자 방을 쓰기로 한다.

M How are things going with you and your roommate?
W Not very well. She's the worst roommate I've ever had.
M It can't be that bad. What's wrong with your new roommate?
W She always makes loud noises at night and throws her clothes and shoes everywhere.
M I know how you feel. I used to have a roommate like that. Why don't you have a heart-to-heart chat with her?
W I will try. I would like to talk things out with her.
M I think that's a good idea. I hope things go well.

남 너와 룸메이트 사이는 어떻게 되어 가니?
여 별로 좋지 않아. 그녀는 지금까지 내가 겪어본 최악의 룸메이트야.
남 그렇게 나쁘지만은 않을 거야. 새 룸메이트의 뭐가 문제니?
여 그녀는 항상 밤에 큰 소리를 내고 옷과 신발을 여기저기 던져 놔.
남 네가 어떤 기분인지 알아. 나도 그런 룸메이트가 있었어. 그녀와 마음을 터놓고 대화해보지 그러니?
여 그래야겠어. 나는 이 문제를 대화로 풀고 싶거든.
남 좋은 생각인 것 같아. 일이 잘 되길 바라.

heart-to-heart 마음을 터놓고
talk things out 대화로 풀다

13

대화를 듣고, 남자의 이야기에서 친구들이 아픈 소년을 위해 한 일로 가장 적절한 것을 고르시오.

① 헌혈을 해 주었다.
② 수술비를 모금해 주었다.
③ 깜짝 파티를 열어 주었다.
④ 자신들도 머리를 삭발했다.
⑤ 소년의 머리카락을 잘라 주었다.

M I heard a heartwarming story on the radio.
W What was it about?
M A boy who was suffering from cancer. The harmful effects of the medication caused the boy to lose all his hair and become bald. So the once cheerful boy became very depressed.
W What a shame!
M Guess what? All his classmates went to the barber and got their heads shaved. Since then, the boy has regained his cheerfulness.
W What an amazing story!

남 라디오에서 마음이 따뜻해지는 이야기를 들었어.
여 무슨 이야기인데?
남 암으로 고통받고 있던 소년의 이야기야. 그 소년은 약물 치료의 부작용으로 머리카락이 다 빠지고 대머리가 되었대. 그래서 한때 활발했던 소년은 매우 의기소침해졌대.
여 그것 참 안됐구나!
남 그런데 그거 알아? 소년의 반 친구들 모두 이발소에 가서 자신들의 머리를 삭발했대. 그 이후로 소년은 활기를 되찾았대.
여 정말 놀라운 이야기다!

heartwarming 마음이 따뜻해지는
suffer from ~로 고통 받다 **cancer** 암
medication 약, 약물 치료 **bald** 대머리의
shame 애석한 일, 유감스러운 일
barber 이발사, 이발소 **shave** 깎다, 면도하다
regain 회복하다

14 대화를 듣고, 남자의 마지막 말에 이어질 여자의 말로 가장 적절한 것을 고르시오.

① I'm sorry to hear that.
② No thanks. It tastes terrible.
③ My father is a professor of history.
④ Thanks. I'm glad you think it's nice.
⑤ Thanks. I enjoyed the meal very much.

M Thank you for inviting me to your <u>housewarming</u> <u>party</u>.
W Thank you for coming.
M When did you <u>move in</u>?
W I moved in a month ago.
M Well, I have to say your house looks fabulous. Did you <u>decorate</u> and <u>furnish</u> it yourself?
W Yes, I did. It took me quite a lot of time.
M Well, you have <u>such good taste</u> in interior decorating. You're better than a professional designer.
W <u>Thanks. I'm glad you think it's nice.</u>

남 집들이에 초대해 줘서 고마워.
여 와 줘서 고마워.
남 언제 이사 왔니?
여 한달 전에 이사 왔어.
남 음, 네 집이 아주 멋져 보이는구나. 네가 직접 장식하고 가구를 놓은 거야?
여 응, 내가 했어. 꽤 많은 시간이 들었지.
남 음, 넌 실내 장식에 뛰어난 안목이 있구나. 전문 디자이너 보다 낫네.
여 <u>고마워. 네가 좋은 것 같다니 기뻐.</u>

① 그것 참 안됐구나.
② 사양할게. 그건 너무 맛이 없어.
③ 우리 아버지는 역사학 교수야.
⑤ 고마워. 맛있게 잘 먹었어.

move in 이사 오다 **furnish** 가구를 놓다 [비치하다] **have good taste in** ~에 뛰어난 안목이 있다 **interior decorating** 실내 장식

---

15 대화를 듣고, 여자의 마지막 말에 이어질 남자의 말로 가장 적절한 것을 고르시오.

① I've worked in a plant for five years.
② Oh, my God. You've killed a lot of plants.
③ If you like, I will tell you my special secret.
④ Well, I'm sure you have a talent for gardening.
⑤ That's great. I envy your ability to raise animals.

M You are good at <u>growing plants</u>. What's your <u>secret</u>?
W If I had one, I'd tell you. Maybe it's just luck.
M I don't understand it! I've <u>tried everything</u> with mine, but they are all still dying. I <u>envy your ability</u>.
W But I don't do <u>anything special</u>. I just know when they need to <u>be watered</u> and where they get the best sun in the house.
M <u>Well, I'm sure you have a talent for gardening.</u>

남 식물을 잘 키우시네요. 비결이 뭐죠?
여 비결이 있으면 말했죠. 아마도 그냥 운일 거예요.
남 이해할 수가 없어요! 전 제 식물을 가지고 모든 것을 해봤지만 여전히 모두 죽어버려요. 당신의 재능이 부럽군요.
여 하지만 제가 특별히 한 건 없어요. 전 단지 언제 물을 줘야 하고 집안 어디에 햇볕이 가장 잘 드는지를 알 뿐이에요.
남 <u>글쎄요, 당신에게는 틀림없이 정원을 가꾸는 재능이 있어요.</u>

① 저는 공장에서 5년 동안 일했어요.
② 오, 이런. 당신은 많은 식물을 죽였군요.
③ 원하시면 제가 당신에게 특별한 비밀을 말해 줄게요.
⑤ 잘됐네요. 저는 당신의 동물 키우는 능력이 부러워요.

envy 부러워하다 **raise** 키우다, 기르다

REVIEW TEST p. 63

A ① diarrhea, 설사 ② symptom, 증상 ③ open-air, 옥외의, 야외의 ④ autograph, 사인

⑤ muscle, 근육 ⑥ patient, 환자 ⑦ heartwarming, 마음이 따뜻해지는 ⑧ bald, 대머리의

⑨ research, 조사 ⑩ on foot, 걸어서, 도보로 ⑪ turn on, 켜다 ⑫ lose weight, 체중이 줄다, 살이 빠지다

B ① do not mind ② a couple of ③ take, care of

④ Believe it or not ⑤ on vacation ⑥ turn on

⑦ the worst roommate ⑧ good taste

문제 및 정답	받아쓰기 및 녹음내용	해석

01 다음을 듣고, 월요일 아침의 날씨로 가장 적절한 것을 고르시오.

①   ②

③   ④

⑤

This is the weather channel. We're <u>looking ahead</u> to the weekend. It's going to be a good night heading into tonight. <u>Take a look</u> outside. You can see clear skies and feel the <u>warm temperature</u>. This will continue for the next 24 hours. However, <u>starting on</u> Sunday morning, we are going to get <u>heavy rainfall</u>. It is going to affect your Monday morning <u>commute</u>, so please <u>take an umbrella</u> with you.

날씨 채널입니다. 주말을 앞두고 있는데요. 오늘 밤에는 날씨가 좋을 것 같습니다. 밖을 한번 내다보세요. 맑은 하늘을 보실 수 있고 따뜻한 기온을 느끼실 수 있습니다. 이것은 앞으로 24시간 동안 계속될 것입니다. 하지만, 일요일 아침부터는 폭우가 내리겠습니다. 월요일 아침 출근 길에도 영향을 미칠 것이니 우산을 가져가시기 바랍니다.

● ●
look ahead to ~을 앞두다 **take a look** 한번 보다 **rainfall** 강우 **affect** 영향을 미치다 **commute** 통근, 출퇴근

02 대화를 듣고, 남자가 가려고 하는 장소를 고르시오.

M Wow! You got a <u>new</u> <u>backpack</u>, didn't you? It looks great.

W I got it as a <u>birthday</u> <u>present</u> from my father.

M Where did he buy it?

W At World Store on Main Street.

M Please tell me <u>where</u> <u>it is</u>.

W You know where Main Street is. <u>Go</u> <u>straight</u> <u>toward</u> Main Street and turn left.

M Turn left on Main Street?

W Right. Walk down the street, and you'll see a <u>stationery store</u> on your right. World Store is <u>behind</u> it.

남 와! 새 책가방 샀구나, 그렇지? 정말 멋지다.

여 아버지께 생일 선물로 받았어.

남 그거 어디서 샀니?

여 메인가에 있는 World Store에서.

남 어디인지 좀 알려 줘.

여 메인가가 어디인지 알지. 메인가 쪽으로 곧장 가서 왼쪽으로 돌아.

남 메인가에서 왼쪽으로 돌라고?

여 맞아. 길을 따라 걸으면 오른쪽에 문구점이 보일 거야. World Store는 문구점 뒤편에 있어.

● ●
stationery store 문구점

03 대화를 듣고, 두 사람이 대화하는 장소로 가장 적절한 곳을 고르시오.

① home
② office
③ coffee shop
④ computer store
⑤ stationery store

M Have you <u>finished</u> <u>inputting</u> that new data?

W Almost. What should I do with the <u>printout</u> when it's <u>completed</u>?

M Make several copies and <u>distribute</u> <u>them</u> to the people on this list.

W Okay, but the copier <u>is being</u> <u>serviced</u> right now. Do I need to print these right away?

M The meeting will be in <u>half</u> <u>an hour</u>. You can finish them before the meeting.

W Sure. I can do that, sir.

남 새로운 자료 입력을 끝마쳤나요?

여 거의 끝냈습니다. 완료되면 인쇄된 것을 어떻게 할까요?

남 몇 부 복사해서 이 명단에 있는 사람들에게 나누어 주세요.

여 네, 그런데 복사기는 지금 수리 중이에요. 지금 바로 이것들을 복사해야 하나요?

남 회의는 30분 후에 있어요. 회의 전까지만 끝내면 됩니다.

여 네. 그렇게 하겠습니다.

input 입력하다 **printout** 인쇄된 것, 인쇄물 **distribute** 나누어주다, 분배하다 **copier** 복사기 **service** 점검하다, 수리하다

---

04 대화를 듣고, 두 사람의 관계로 가장 적절한 것을 고르시오.

① friend - friend
② clerk - customer
③ baker - customer
④ bus driver - passenger
⑤ plumber - home owner

M What <u>seems</u> <u>to be</u> the problem?

W The sink in the bathroom <u>is</u> <u>clogged</u>.

M That shouldn't be too difficult. I'll just <u>clean out</u> the pipe for you.

W Thank you. While you're working on it, could you <u>check</u> <u>the tub</u>, too?

M Is the bathtub drain clogged <u>as</u> <u>well</u>?

W Not completely, but it drains <u>awfully</u> <u>slowly</u>.

M I see. Well, I'll take a look at it.

남 무엇이 문제인 것 같으세요?

여 화장실 세면대가 막혔어요.

남 그리 힘들지는 않겠네요. 그냥 파이프 속을 청소해 드릴게요.

여 고맙습니다. 작업하시는 동안 욕조도 확인해 주시겠어요?

남 욕조 배수구도 막혔나요?

여 완전히는 아니지만, 그곳도 너무 천천히 물이 빠져서요.

남 알겠어요. 그럼, 그것도 살펴볼게요.

be clogged 막히다 **tub** 욕조 **drain** 배수구; 물이 빠지다 **awfully** 몹시, 대단히 **clerk** 점원 **baker** 제빵사, 빵집 주인 **plumber** 배관공

---

05 대화를 듣고, 여자의 모습 중 최근에 달라진 부분을 고르시오.

W Don't you notice <u>anything</u> <u>different</u> about me?

M Uh, I don't know. Did you get a <u>new</u> <u>haircut</u>?

W No, guess again.

M Aha! I know. It's your dress. That's a new dress, <u>isn't it</u>?

W I've had this dress <u>for ages</u>. Don't tell me you don't <u>recognize</u> it.

M Oh, of course. I knew that. Ah… how about a <u>hint</u>?

W Look deep into my eyes.

M Your glasses are <u>gone</u>! When did you get <u>contact lenses</u>?

여 나한테 달라진 거 없니?

남 어, 모르겠는데. 머리 새로 했니?

여 아니, 다시 맞춰봐.

남 아! 알겠다. 네 원피스야. 그거 새 옷이지, 그렇지 않니?

여 난 이 옷을 오랫동안 가지고 있었어. 이 옷을 못 알아 보겠다고는 말하지마.

남 오, 물론이지. 그 옷 알아. 아… 힌트 좀 줄래?

여 내 눈을 깊이 들여다 봐.

남 네 안경이 없네! 언제 콘택트렌즈 했어?

notice 알아채다 **haircut** 이발, 머리 모양 **for ages** 오랫동안 **recognize** 알아보다 **contact lenses** 콘택트렌즈

06 대화를 듣고, 올해가 몇 년도인지 고르시오.

① 2000년
② 2010년
③ 2012년
④ 2022년 ✓
⑤ 2025년

M Carrie, is that you?
W James? <u>How</u> <u>long</u> has it been?
M It's been too long. <u>How</u> <u>have</u> <u>you</u> <u>been</u>?
W Very well. Thanks. When was the <u>last</u> <u>time</u> we saw each other?
M At our high school <u>graduation</u>, I think. We were the class of <u>2012</u>.
W It has already been 10 years since then. <u>Time</u> <u>flies</u>, doesn't it?

남 Carrie, 너니?
여 James? 이게 얼마만이야?
남 정말 오래됐지. 어떻게 지냈어?
여 잘 지내. 고마워. 우리가 서로 마지막으로 본 것이 언제였더라?
남 내 생각엔 고등학교 졸업식인 것 같다. 우리는 2012년 졸업반이었잖아.
여 그 후로 벌써 10년이 지났구나. 시간 정말 빠르다, 그렇지 않니?

●● **the class of 2012** 2012년 졸업반

---

07 대화를 듣고, 남자가 한국 문화에 대해 어떻게 생각하는지 고르시오.

① 지루하다
② 흥미롭다 ✓
③ 이상하다
④ 독특하다
⑤ 관심 없다

W Have you watched the video that I <u>recommended</u>?
M I never knew Korean <u>folk</u> <u>dancing</u> was so beautiful.
W There is a lot you don't know about Korea.
M You're right. Where can I learn more about <u>Korean</u> <u>culture</u>?
W We could go to the <u>bookstore</u>.
M Let's go now. I want to learn more.
W <u>Slow</u> <u>down</u>. It's 10:00 p.m. It's already closed. You'll have to <u>wait</u> <u>until</u> <u>morning</u> to go there.
M Okay. Maybe I can find some information <u>on</u> <u>the</u> <u>Internet</u>.

여 내가 추천해 준 영상 봤니?
남 난 한국 민속춤이 그렇게 아름다운지 전혀 몰랐어.
여 한국에 대해 네가 모르는 것이 많이 있어.
남 맞아. 한국 문화에 대해 어디서 더 많이 배울 수 있지?
여 서점에 가면 되지.
남 지금 가자. 더 알고 싶거든.
여 천천히 해. 지금 밤 10시야. 이미 문 닫았어. 거기 가려면 아침까지 기다려야 해.
남 알았어. 아마 인터넷에서 정보를 좀 찾을 수 있을 거야.

●● **folk dancing** 민속춤 **information** 정보

---

08 대화를 듣고, 남자가 하는 일로 가장 적절한 것을 고르시오.

① 도넛 만들기 ✓
② 도넛 판매하기
③ 도넛 포장하기
④ 도넛 배달하기
⑤ 도넛 가게 청소하기

W So what do you do <u>for</u> <u>a</u> <u>living</u>?
M I make donuts at a donut shop.
W <u>How</u> <u>delicious</u>! Do you ever eat on the job?
M I <u>used</u> <u>to</u> in the beginning, but now I'm kind of <u>tired</u> <u>of</u> donuts.
W I understand. You <u>must</u> <u>be</u> <u>good</u> <u>at</u> what you do.
M I'm not bad. <u>I've</u> <u>been</u> <u>doing</u> this job for several years now.

여 어떤 일을 하시나요?
남 도넛 가게에서 도넛을 만들어요.
여 정말 맛있겠어요! 일하면서 드시기도 하나요?
남 처음에는 그랬는데, 지금은 도넛에 조금 질렸어요.
여 이해가 가요. 하시는 일에는 능숙하시겠어요.
남 못하는 편은 아니에요. 지금 몇 년째 이 일을 해오고 있거든요.

●● **for a living** 생계를 위해 **on the job** 근무 중에 **be tired of** ~에 질리다

09 대화를 듣고, 창문이 열리지 않는 이유로 가장 적절한 것을 고르시오.

① 창문이 고장 나서
② 밖이 너무 추워서
③ 창문이 오래 되어서
④ 방 안이 너무 추워서
⑤ 밖에서 창문을 잠가 두어서

W Please open the window. It's <u>hot</u> <u>in</u> <u>here</u>.
M All right. It's... uh... stuck. It must be very <u>cold</u> <u>outside</u> today.
W Let me <u>give</u> <u>it</u> <u>a</u> <u>try</u>. You're right. It's stuck. It must be <u>frozen</u>.
M We may have to wait until the weather <u>gets</u> <u>warmer</u> to open it.
W I can't <u>wait</u> <u>that</u> <u>long</u>. I'm going to the library where the <u>air</u> <u>is</u> <u>better</u>.
M Wait for me. I'll go with you.

여 창문 좀 열어 줘. 이 안은 너무 더워.
남 알았어. 이게… 어… 움직이지를 않아. 오늘 밖이 아주 추운가 봐.
여 내가 한번 해 볼게. 네 말이 맞아, 움직이질 않네. 얼어붙은 것이 틀림 없어.
남 날씨가 더 따뜻해져서 그걸 열 수 있을 때까지 기다려야 할 것 같아.
여 그렇게 오래는 못 기다려. 공기가 더 좋은 도서관으로 가야겠어.
남 기다려. 나도 같이 갈래.

●● **give it a try** 한번 해 보다 **frozen** 얼어붙은

---

10 대화를 듣고, 여자의 증상으로 가장 적절한 것을 고르시오.

① 콧물
② 두통
③ 변비
④ 설사
⑤ 구토

W I've been running to the bathroom <u>all</u> <u>day</u>.
M What's wrong? Are you sick?
W I ate potato salad for lunch, and it really <u>upset</u> <u>my</u> <u>stomach</u>.
M You mean...
W That's right. <u>Diarrhea</u>.
M Try to relax. It will <u>stop</u> <u>eventually</u>.

여 하루 종일 화장실을 들락날락거리고 있어.
남 무슨 일이야? 어디 아파?
여 점심으로 감자 샐러드를 먹었는데 배탈이 났어.
남 그렇다면…
여 맞아. 설사야.
남 긴장을 풀어 봐. 결국은 멈출 거야.

●● **upset one's stomach** 배탈이 나게 하다 **eventually** 결국

---

11 대화를 듣고, 여자가 남자에게 해 준 조언으로 가장 적절한 것을 고르시오.

① 운동을 해라.
② 휴식을 취해라.
③ 취미를 가져라.
④ 공부를 열심히 해라.
⑤ 선생님께 도움을 요청해라.

M Aw, I'm so upset!
W What are you <u>worried</u> <u>about</u>?
M I <u>didn't</u> <u>do</u> <u>well</u> on the midterm exam. Now I am very worried and upset.
W Listen. You <u>tend</u> <u>to</u> <u>make</u> big things <u>out</u> <u>of</u> little things.
M No, it's not a little thing. It's <u>serious</u> to me.
W <u>Take</u> <u>it</u> <u>easy</u>. You will get a good grade because you always study hard.
M But I <u>will</u> <u>be</u> <u>disappointed</u> if I don't get a good grade.
W You <u>studied</u> <u>so</u> <u>hard</u> for the midterm and it's over. You should stop thinking about it and <u>get</u> <u>some</u> <u>rest</u>.

남 이런, 너무 속상해!
여 뭐가 걱정이니?
남 중간고사를 잘 못 봤어. 난 지금 너무 걱정되고 속상해.
여 들어 봐. 너는 작은 일을 크게 만드는 경향이 있어.
남 아니야, 이건 작은 일이 아니야. 내게는 심각한 일이야.
여 편안하게 생각해. 넌 항상 열심히 공부하니까 좋은 성적을 받을 거야.
남 하지만 좋은 성적을 받지 못하면 실망할 거야.
여 넌 중간고사를 위해 열심히 공부했고 이제는 끝났어. 그만 생각하고 좀 쉬어.

●● **tend to** ~하는 경향이 있다 **grade** 성적 **serious** 심각한, 진지한

12 대화를 듣고, 두 사람이 대화 직후에 할 일로 가장 적절한 것을 고르시오.

① 커피 마시기
② 잔돈 바꾸기
③ 약속 정하기
④ 저녁 식사 하기
⑤ 식당 예약 하기

M That was a <u>wonderful</u> <u>meal</u>.
W I thought you would like that <u>restaurant</u>.
M We should go there again.
W Of course. Whenever you want to go, <u>let</u> <u>me</u> <u>know</u>.
M Would you like <u>a cup of</u> <u>coffee</u>?
W Yes, but I don't have <u>any</u> <u>change</u>.
M Don't worry. I have enough.
W Thank you. The next time, I'll <u>treat</u> <u>you</u>.

남 훌륭한 식사였어요.
여 당신이 그 식당을 좋아할 거라고 생각했어요.
남 우리 거기 또 가야겠어요.
여 물론이죠. 가고 싶을 때 언제든지 알려 주세요.
남 커피 마실래요?
여 네, 그런데 잔돈이 하나도 없네요.
남 걱정 마세요. 저한테 충분히 있어요.
여 <u>고마워요. 다음엔 제가 살게요.</u>

●●
change 잔돈 **treat** 한턱 내다

---

13 대화를 듣고, TV 채널과 프로그램이 일치하는 것을 고르시오.

① Channel 4 - *The Animal Kingdom*
② Channel 5 - Talk show
③ Channel 7 - Basketball
④ Channel 8 - *Frozen*
⑤ Channel 11 - *Spiderman*

W What's <u>on TV</u>? Is there anything interesting?
M I don't know. I'm <u>watching</u> <u>basketball</u> on channel 5.
W I hate sports. <u>How</u> <u>about</u> <u>watching</u> a talk show on channel 7?
M That's too <u>serious</u>.
W <u>Let</u> <u>me</u> <u>check</u> the TV programs. Oh! *Frozen* is showing on channel 4, *Spiderman* is on channel 11, and *The Animal Kingdom* is on channel 8.
M Then let's watch *Frozen*. I <u>haven't</u> <u>seen</u> <u>it</u>.
W Okay.

여 TV에서 뭐하니? 뭐 재미있는 거라도 해?
남 모르겠는데. 나는 5번에서 하는 농구를 보고 있어.
여 난 스포츠가 싫어. 7번에서 하는 토크쇼를 보는 것이 어때?
남 그건 너무 진지해.
여 TV 편성표를 확인해볼게. 아! 4번에서는 〈겨울왕국〉, 11번에서는 〈스파이더맨〉, 그리고 8번에서는 〈동물의 왕국〉을 하네.
남 그러면 〈겨울왕국〉을 보자. 나 그거 안 봤거든.
여 좋아.

---

14 대화를 듣고, 남자의 마지막 말에 이어질 여자의 말로 가장 적절한 것을 고르시오.

① Oh, yes. Every day.
② I am a night person.
③ I hate getting up early.
④ I usually go to school by bus.
⑤ Yes, I try to exercise every day.

M <u>What</u> <u>time</u> do you get up?
W I get up around six.
M What <u>wakes</u> <u>you</u> <u>up</u>? Does your mother wake you up?
W No. My alarm clock wakes me up.
M Do you get up <u>immediately</u>?
W No, I <u>lie</u> <u>in</u> <u>bed</u> for a few minutes because it takes me a while to <u>get</u> <u>motivated</u>.
M Is this your <u>normal</u> <u>routine</u>?
W <u>Oh, yes. Every day.</u>

남 몇 시에 일어나니?
여 6시쯤 일어나.
남 어떻게 일어나니? 어머니가 깨워 주시니?
여 아니. 내 자명종 시계가 날 깨워 주지.
남 즉시 일어나?
여 아니, 정신이 들려면 시간이 걸려서 침대에 몇 분 동안 누워 있어.
남 항상 그러니?
여 어, 그래. 매일.

② 나는 저녁형 인간이야.
③ 나는 일찍 일어나는 것이 싫어.
④ 나는 보통 버스로 학교에 가.
⑤ 응, 나는 매일 운동하려고 노력해.

●●
immediately 곧, 즉시 **lie in bed** 침대에 누워 있다 **get motivated** 의욕이 생기다 **routine** 일상

15 대화를 듣고, 여자의 마지막 말에 이어질 남자의 말로 가장 적절한 것을 고르시오.

① What a bad sister you are!
② Your son should be punished.
③ Then everything is all right now.
④ I'm really sorry about your sister.
⑤ I think you should go and apologize to her.

W I've been <u>worried</u> <u>all</u> <u>day</u>.
M What happened?
W I <u>quarreled</u> <u>with</u> my sister. I felt terrible about it later.
M Why did you <u>argue</u>?
W My son Sam did <u>something</u> <u>wrong</u>, and I <u>punished</u> him. My sister defended Sam. I told her <u>not</u> <u>to</u> <u>bother</u>.
M What did your sister say?
W She <u>apologized</u>. Then, of course, I apologized, too.
M <u>Then everything is all right now.</u>

여 하루 종일 걱정했어요.
남 무슨 일 있어요?
여 여동생하고 말다툼을 했어요. 나중에는 그것 때문에 기분이 안 좋아졌어요.
남 왜 싸웠나요?
여 제 아들 Sam이 잘못을 해서 벌을 줬어요. 제 여동생은 그 애를 감쌌지요. 난 그녀에게 참견하지 말라고 했어요.
남 여동생이 뭐라고 말했죠?
여 그녀는 사과했어요. 그 다음에 나도 물론 사과했죠.
남 <u>그러면 이제 모든 일이 잘됐네요.</u>

① 당신은 정말 나쁜 언니군요!
② 당신 아들은 벌을 받아야 해요.
④ 당신 여동생에 대해 정말 유감이군요.
⑤ 저는 당신이 그녀에게 사과해야 한다고 생각해요.

quarrel 말다툼하다　**argue** 논쟁하다
punish 벌 주다　**defend** 방어하다
apologize 사과하다

▶ REVIEW TEST p. 71

A
① commute, 통근, 출퇴근　② stationary store, 문구점　③ distribute, 나누어주다, 분배하다
④ drain, 배수구; 물이 빠지다　⑤ for ages, 오랫동안　⑥ recognize, 알아보다　⑦ information, 정보
⑧ eventually, 결국　⑨ grade, 성적　⑩ routine, 일상　⑪ quarrel, 말다툼하다　⑫ apologize, 사과하다

B
① half an hour　② the last time　③ Time flies
④ for a living　⑤ give it, try　⑥ do well
⑦ tend to, out of　⑧ treat you

문제 및 정답	받아쓰기 및 녹음내용	해석

01 대화를 듣고, 남자가 구입할 의상으로 가장 적절한 것을 고르시오.

① ②

③ ④

⑤

M Mom, can I <u>order</u> a Halloween <u>costume</u> online?

W Which one?

M I want <u>either</u> a Spiderman <u>or</u> skeleton costume.

W Let me see. I like <u>both</u>, but I don't think they have <u>the right size</u> for you. These are all for small kids.

M I can <u>keep looking</u>. How about this ghost?

W It looks <u>pretty scary</u>.

M I like it, but I think I have a <u>similar one</u> at home. I want to try a <u>pirate one</u> this year.

W I think a pirate one <u>should be fine</u>.

남 엄마, 온라인으로 핼러윈 의상 주문해도 돼요?

여 어떤 것 말이니?

남 스파이더맨이나 해골 의상을 주문하고 싶어요.

여 한번 보자. 엄마는 둘 다 마음에 들어, 그런데 너한테 맞는 사이즈가 없는 것 같네. 이것들은 모두 어린 아이들 거야.

남 계속 찾아볼게요. 이 유령은 어때요?

여 아주 무서워 보이네.

남 마음에 들긴 하지만 집에 비슷한 것이 있는 것 같아요. 올해는 해적 의상을 입어보고 싶어요.

여 해적 의상이 좋을 것 같구나.

●●
order 주문하다 **costume** 의상 **either A or B** A나 B 중 하나 **skeleton** 해골 **ghost** 유령 **pirate** 해적

02 대화를 듣고, 남자가 가려고 하는 장소를 고르시오.

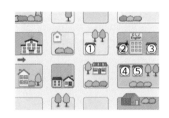

M Hello. May I speak to Ana?

W <u>This is she</u>. Who am I speaking to?

M It's Tom. Ana, do you remember that strawberry pie you gave me <u>the other day</u>? Where did you buy it?

W At Jimmy's Bakery. Why?

M Oh, it was very delicious. So I want to buy one for my mother. Where is it <u>located</u>?

W It's just <u>three blocks away</u> from our school. It's near the CLJ English Institute.

M I know where that is. If I am <u>facing the institute</u>, should I go left or right?

W Go left. You can't miss it. Just <u>follow the smell</u>.

M Thanks, Ana.

남 여보세요. Ana와 통화 할 수 있을까요?

여 전데요. 누구세요?

남 나 Tom이야. Ana, 지난번에 네가 나한테 줬던 딸기 파이 기억나? 그거 어디서 샀었니?

여 Jimmy's 제과점에서. 왜?

남 아, 그거 너무 맛있더라. 그래서 우리 엄마한테 하나 사다 드리고 싶어서. 위치가 어디야?

여 우리 학교에서 세 블록 떨어져 있어. CLJ 영어 학원 근처에 있지.

남 그 학원 어디에 있는지 알아. 학원을 바라봤을 때 왼쪽으로 가야 해 오른쪽으로 가야 해?

여 왼쪽으로 가. 쉽게 찾을 거야. 그냥 냄새를 따라가.

남 고마워, Ana.

●●
the other day 지난번에 **institute** 학회. 연구소; 학원

03

대화를 듣고, 두 사람이 대화하는 장소로 가장 적절한 곳을 고르시오.

① shoe store
② beauty salon
③ jewelry store
④ grocery store
⑤ movie theater

W Good evening. Can I help you, sir?
M Yes. May I take a look at the bracelet on display over there?
W Do you mean the one on the left?
M No, the second one on the right.
W That's a very good bracelet, sir. It's really popular these days.
M How much is it?
W The price is 125 dollars. It's on sale. You can get 20% off.
M Good. I'd like to have it.

여 안녕하세요. 도와드릴까요, 손님?
남 네. 저기 진열되어 있는 팔찌를 한번 볼 수 있을까요?
여 왼쪽에 있는 것 말씀이세요?
남 아니요, 오른쪽 두 번째에 있는 거요.
여 저건 정말 좋은 팔찌입니다, 손님. 요즘 정말 인기가 있어요.
남 얼마에요?
여 가격은 125달러입니다. 지금 할인 판매 중이에요. 20% 할인 받으실 수 있어요.
남 좋아요. 그걸로 주세요.

●●
bracelet 팔찌 **on display** 전시된, 진열된

04

대화를 듣고, 두 사람의 관계로 가장 적절한 것을 고르시오.

① mother - son
② husband - wife
③ teacher - student
④ boyfriend - girlfriend
⑤ travel agent - customer

W Honey, it's our 10th wedding anniversary.
M Yes, we should take a special trip.
W Really? Where do you want to go? Can we go to Hawaii?
M Hawaii… That's very expensive and far away.
W I know, but I really want to go there. Maybe someday…
M Well… How about going to Phuket? It'll be less expensive and closer than Hawaii.
W Really? That's another place that I want to go to. You're so wonderful.
M I'm happy you like it.

여 여보, 우리의 결혼 10주년이에요.
남 그래요, 특별한 여행을 가야겠어요.
여 정말이요? 어디로 가고 싶은데요? 하와이로 갈까요?
남 하와이라… 거긴 너무 비싸고 멀어요.
여 알아요, 하지만 정말 거기에 가보고 싶어요. 아마도 언젠가는…
남 그럼… 푸켓에 가는 건 어때요? 비용도 덜 비싸고 하와이보다 더 가까울 거예요.
여 정말이요? 그곳도 내가 가고 싶었던 곳이에요. 당신은 정말 멋져요.
남 당신이 좋아하니 기쁘네요.

●●
wedding anniversary 결혼기념일
travel agent 여행사 직원

05

대화를 듣고, 여자가 여가 시간에 하는 일로 가장 적절한 것을 고르시오.

① 식물 기르기
② 자원봉사하기
③ 과학 만화 읽기
④ 공원에서 쓰레기 줍기
⑤ 환경 다큐멘터리 시청하기

M What do you do in your spare time?
W I volunteer by teaching children about environmental problems.
M That's incredible! Is it rewarding?
W Oh, yes. They love to learn about the air, soil, and water.
M Well, the children are the future.
W That is certainly true.

남 여가 시간에 뭐하세요?
여 아이들에게 환경 문제에 대해 가르치는 자원봉사를 해요.
남 멋지군요! 보람이 있나요?
여 네, 그럼요. 아이들은 공기, 토양, 그리고 물에 대해 배우는 것을 아주 좋아해요.
남 그래요, 아이들은 미래잖아요.
여 정말 그래요.

●●
spare time 여가 시간 **volunteer** 자원봉사하다 **environmental** 환경의 **rewarding** 보람 있는 **certainly** 확실히, 틀림없이

06 다음을 듣고, 내일의 최고 기온으로 가장 적절한 것을 고르시오.

① 10℃
② 12℃
③ 15℃
④ 20℃
⑤ 25℃

Good morning. This is Ann Smith here with your <u>weekend</u> <u>weather</u> <u>report</u>. Right now, it is 25℃ and clear. But toward the end of the day, it will start to <u>cool</u> <u>off</u>, and we can expect <u>a</u> <u>low</u> <u>of</u> 12℃ tonight. Tomorrow, the temperature will only reach <u>a</u> <u>high</u> <u>of</u> 20℃, and we will see some rain in the afternoon. Next week, we can <u>expect</u> <u>more</u> <u>rain</u>, and the temperatures will be in the high 20s to low 10s.

안녕하세요. 주말 일기예보를 말씀드릴 Ann Smith입니다. 지금은 25도이고 맑은 날씨입니다. 하지만 날이 저물면서 서늘해지기 시작해서 오늘 밤은 최저 12도까지 내려갈 것으로 예상됩니다. 내일은 최고 기온이 20도에 불과할 것이며, 오후에는 비가 내리겠습니다. 다음 주에는 더 많은 비가 내리겠으며, 기온은 20도에서 10도를 웃돌겠습니다.

●●

cool off 서늘해지다 **low** 최저 기온

---

07 대화를 듣고, 남자의 심정으로 가장 적절한 것을 고르시오.

① bored
② nervous
③ unhappy
④ confident
⑤ disappointed

W Don, could you <u>tell</u> <u>me</u> <u>the</u> <u>time</u>?
M Why don't you look at the clock <u>yourself</u>?
W Why are you in <u>such</u> <u>a</u> <u>bad</u> <u>mood</u>?
M I guess I'm just tired. I'm sorry.
W You'd better <u>get</u> <u>some</u> <u>rest</u>. That'll make you feel better.
M I wish <u>I</u> <u>could</u>. But I have so many <u>things</u> <u>to</u> <u>do</u>.

여 Don, 지금 몇 시인지 좀 말해 줄래?
남 네가 시계 좀 보지 그래?
여 너 왜 그렇게 기분이 안 좋아?
남 좀 피곤한가 봐. 미안해.
여 좀 쉬는 게 좋겠어. 그러면 기분이 좀 나아질 거야.
남 나도 그랬으면 좋겠어. 하지만 할 일이 너무 많아.

●●

confident 자신 있는

---

08 대화를 듣고, 남자의 마지막 말의 의도로 가장 적절한 것을 고르시오.

① 사과
② 동의
③ 조언
④ 감사
⑤ 거절

W Don't you have a <u>math</u> <u>test</u> tomorrow?
M Yes, I do.
W Then you should study now.
M Just wait. I've <u>almost</u> <u>completed</u> this level.
W When are you <u>going</u> <u>to</u> <u>finish</u> that computer game?
M After this level, there is only one more level.
W Tony, you can play the game <u>whenever</u> you want to after the test is <u>over</u>. Please study first.
M Okay, Mom. <u>I</u> <u>had</u> <u>better</u> start studying before it's <u>too</u> <u>late</u>.

여 내일 수학 시험 보지 않니?
남 네, 그래요.
여 그럼 지금 공부해야겠구나.
남 잠깐만요. 이번 판은 거의 끝났어요.
여 그 컴퓨터 게임이 언제 끝나는데?
남 이번 판 다음에 한 판밖에 안 남았어요.
여 Tony, 게임은 시험 끝나고 네가 원할 때 언제든지 할 수 있잖아. 공부 먼저 하렴.
남 알겠어요, 엄마. 너무 늦기 전에 공부를 시작하는 게 낫겠어요.

09 대화를 듣고, 남자가 난처해하는 이유로 가장 적절한 것을 고르시오.

① 집에 일찍 가야 해서
② 여자의 질문을 이해하지 못해서
③ 저녁 식사 초대에 응하고 싶지 않아서
④ 요리 방법을 몰라 대답해 줄 수 없어서
⑤ 음식에 대해 솔직하게 말하기 어려워서

W I want to thank you all for <u>coming</u> <u>to</u> <u>dinner</u>. Did you like the soup, Dick?

M Uh… it was… uh… good.

W Are you sure? You <u>sound</u> <u>uncertain</u>.

M I can see you put <u>a</u> <u>lot</u> <u>of</u> <u>time</u> into it. Thank you, but…

W But what?

M It needed just a little more <u>salt</u>. Then it <u>would</u> <u>have</u> <u>been</u> <u>perfect</u>.

W Were you disappointed?

M No. Please <u>don't</u> <u>be</u> <u>offended</u>. I really enjoyed the food.

여 모두 저녁 식사에 와 줘서 고마워. Dick, 수프 맘에 들었니?

남 어… 그게… 어… 좋았어.

여 정말이야? 확실치 않은 것처럼 들리는데.

남 네가 그것에 많은 시간을 투자했다는 걸 알겠어. 고마워, 하지만…

여 하지만 뭐?

남 소금을 조금 더 넣었어야 했어. 그랬다면 완벽했을 거야.

여 실망했니?

남 아니야. 기분 나쁘게 생각하지 마. 정말로 맛있게 먹었어.

●●
uncertain 불확실한 **put time into** ~에 시간을 투자하다 **offend** 기분 상하게 하다

---

10 대화를 듣고, 여자가 이용한 교통수단으로 가장 적절한 것을 고르시오.

① bus
② train
③ ferry
④ plane
⑤ subway

M I heard you went to Japan for the <u>holidays</u>.

W That's right. I went to Tokyo <u>for</u> <u>a</u> <u>change</u>.

M What was it like?

W It was great. <u>Foreign</u> <u>countries</u> are always interesting.

M How did you get there, <u>by</u> <u>plane</u> or <u>by</u> <u>ferry</u>?

W You know, I prefer <u>not</u> <u>to</u> <u>fly</u>.

남 너 휴가 기간 동안 일본에 갔었다며?

여 맞아. 기분 전환하러 도쿄에 갔었어.

남 어땠어?

여 좋았어. 외국은 항상 흥미롭잖아.

남 어떻게 갔니, 비행기로 아니면 여객선으로?

여 너도 알다시피 내가 비행기 타는 걸 선호하지 않잖니.

●●
for a change 기분 전환으로 **foreign country** 외국 **ferry** 페리, 여객선

---

11 대화를 듣고, 남자가 여자에게 해 준 조언으로 가장 적절한 것을 고르시오.

① 다이어트 하기
② 성형 수술 하기
③ 미용 기술 배우기
④ 머리 모양 바꾸기
⑤ 건강에 좋은 음식 먹기

W I'm thinking about having <u>plastic</u> surgery.

M Are you sure? I don't understand. You look great just <u>the</u> <u>way</u> <u>you</u> <u>are</u>.

W Well, I'm pleased with my eyes and nose, but I'm not <u>satisfied</u> <u>with</u> my lips. They're too thin.

M That's <u>ridiculous</u>. You've got a nice face that makes people <u>feel</u> <u>comfortable</u>. Having plastic surgery is not a good idea.

W Do you really <u>think</u> <u>so</u>?

M Yes. But if you want to <u>change</u> <u>something</u> about yourself, why don't you change your <u>hairstyle</u>?

W Maybe I should. Thanks for <u>your</u> <u>advice</u>.

여 나 성형수술을 할까 해.

남 정말? 이해할 수 없어. 너는 지금 있는 그대로로 보기 좋아.

여 글쎄, 난 눈과 코는 만족하지만 입술이 마음에 들지 않아. 너무 얇아.

남 말도 안돼. 너는 사람들을 편안하게 해주는 좋은 인상을 가지고 있어. 성형수술을 하는 건 좋은 생각이 아니야.

여 정말 그렇게 생각하니?

남 그럼. 그래도 네 자신을 바꾸고 싶다면 머리 모양을 바꾸는 것이 어떻겠니?

여 그래야겠다. 조언 고마워.

●●
be pleased with ~에 기뻐하다, ~에 만족하다 **be satisfied with** ~에 만족하다 **ridiculous** 웃기는, 말도 안 되는 **advice** 충고, 조언

12 대화를 듣고, 대화에서 credits가 의미하는 것으로 가장 적절한 것을 고르시오.

① 영화 제작 회사
② 영화의 관람 등급
③ 영화의 평가 점수
④ 영화에 투자한 사람들의 명단
⑤ 영화 제작에 도움을 준 사람들의 명단

M Come on. Let's go. The movie's over.

W No, wait. I want to see the credits right through to the end.

M The credits?

W The credits are the list of people who help make a film, record, or television program.

M Oh, I know what they are. But do you really want to see them?

W My sister's in the movie business, and she worked on this movie.

M Really? What does she do?

W She's a costume designer. Look. There she is. That's her name just coming up now.

남 이봐, 가자. 영화 끝났어.

여 안돼, 잠시만. 난 크레딧을 끝까지 보고 싶어.

남 크레딧이라고?

여 영화, 음반, 또는 텔레비전 프로그램을 만드는 데 도움을 준 사람들의 명단이야.

남 아, 나도 그게 뭔지 알아. 하지만 정말 그걸 보고 싶어?

여 언니가 영화 쪽 일을 하는데 이 영화에서 작업 했거든.

남 정말? 뭐 하시는데?

여 의상 디자이너야. 봐, 저기 있어. 지금 막 나오는 이름이야.

---

13 대화를 듣고, 두 사람이 이번 주말에 가려고 하는 곳을 고르시오.

① 시장
② 백화점
③ 이마트
④ 월마트
⑤ 볼링장

M Where did you buy that dress?

W Do you like it? I got it at the new department store.

M Where is it?

W It's just across the street from that E-Mart where we went shopping last month. Do you remember?

M Yes, I remember that. Hmm... It may be next to the post office.

W No, that's Wal-Mart. The department store is on Main Street.

M Oh, I see. You mean the bowling alley that used to be there before it closed down.

W That's right. They tore down the bowling alley and put up a brand-new building for the department store. We should go there this weekend.

남 그 원피스 어디에서 샀니?

여 맘에 드니? 새로 생긴 백화점에서 샀어.

남 어디에 있는데?

여 우리가 지난 달 쇼핑하러 갔던 이마트의 바로 맞은 편에 있어. 기억 나니?

남 응, 기억나. 흠… 그건 아마도 우체국 옆에 있었지.

여 아니야, 그건 월마트지. 백화점은 메인가에 있어.

남 아, 알겠어. 문 닫기 전에 거기에 있었던 볼링장 말하는 거구나.

여 맞아. 볼링장은 허물고 백화점으로 할 새 건물을 세웠어. 이번 주말에 한번 가 보자.

●●
bowling alley 볼링장 **tear down** 허물다
put up 세우다

14 대화를 듣고, 남자의 마지막 말에 이어질 여자의 말로 가장 적절한 것을 고르시오.

① Of course not! I promise.
② I forget things all the time.
③ It was nice to see you again.
④ Let's talk about something else.
⑤ I've always wanted to study abroad.

W Thanks for having this <u>farewell party</u> for me, Mark. I really <u>appreciate</u> it.
M Oh, no problem. I just wanted you to know how much I'm going to <u>miss you</u>. Are you excited about moving?
W I am a little nervous, but I'm <u>looking forward to</u> it, too. The school there <u>is supposed to be</u> good, and I'm sure I'll make some <u>new friends</u>.
M Don't forget your old friends!
W <u>Of course not! I promise.</u>

여 날 위해 송별회를 해 줘서 고마워, Mark. 정말 고맙게 생각해.
남 아, 천만에. 난 단지 내가 널 얼마나 보고 싶어 할지 네가 알아줬으면 해서. 이사하는 것에 들떠있니?
여 좀 긴장이 되긴 하지만 몹시 기대되기도 해. 그곳의 학교는 좋을 거고 새 친구들도 사귈 테니까.
남 너의 옛 친구들을 잊지 마!
여 <u>물론 잊지 않지! 약속할게.</u>

② 나는 늘 뭘 잊어.
③ 다시 만나서 반가웠어.
④ 다른 얘기를 하자.
⑤ 나는 항상 유학을 하고 싶었어.

farewell party 송별회 **look forward to** ~을 몹시 기다리다 **be supposed to** ~하기로 되어 있다

---

15 대화를 듣고, 여자의 마지막 말에 이어질 남자의 말로 가장 적절한 것을 고르시오.

① I have something in my eye.
② Really? I have double vision.
③ My sister has good eyesight.
④ The glasses look good on you.
⑤ Then you'd better see a doctor.

M Your eyes are <u>red</u>. They look <u>painful</u>. Are you okay?
W My eyes <u>hurt</u>, and they <u>water</u>.
M Do you wear contact lenses?
W Yes, how did you know?
M My sister wears them, so I've <u>seen your condition</u> before.
W My eyesight seems to be <u>gradually worsening</u>.
M <u>Then you'd better see a doctor.</u>

남 네 눈이 빨갛다. 아파 보여. 괜찮니?
여 눈이 아프고 눈물이 나.
남 콘택트렌즈를 착용했니?
여 응, 어떻게 알았어?
남 내 여동생도 그걸 쓰기 때문에 전에 너와 같은 상태를 본 적이 있어.
여 내 시력이 점점 나빠지는 것 같아.
남 <u>그럼 의사한테 가 보는 게 좋겠다.</u>

① 내 눈에 뭐가 들어갔어.
② 정말? 나는 사물이 두 개로 보여.
③ 내 여동생은 시력이 좋아.
④ 그 안경은 너에게 잘 어울려.

painful 고통스러운 **water** 눈물이 나다 **gradually** 점점, 서서히 **worsen** 나빠지다

REVIEW TEST p. 79

A
① order, 주문하다 ② costume, 의상 ③ pirate, 해적 ④ the other day, 지난번에
⑤ bracelet, 팔찌 ⑥ wedding anniversary, 결혼기념일 ⑦ volunteer, 자원봉사하다 ⑧ rewarding, 보람 있는
⑨ ferry, 페리, 여객선 ⑩ ridiculous, 웃기는, 말도 안 되는 ⑪ farewell party, 송별회 ⑫ worsen, 나빠지다

B
① speaking to ② facing, left, right ③ bad mood
④ offended ⑤ for a change ⑥ having plastic surgery
⑦ the way you are ⑧ looking forward to

문제 및 정답	받아쓰기 및 녹음내용	해석

01 다음을 듣고, 여자의 직업으로 가장 적절한 것을 고르시오.

①  ②

③ ④

⑤

Well, it's a tough job. Being a woman in the military is never easy, but I enjoy the challenge. I've always liked physical exercise, and with practice, I've become pretty good with weapons, too. But most of all, I like the feeling of knowing I'm serving my country.

글쎄요, 그건 힘든 직업이죠. 군대에서 여자인 것은 결코 쉬운 일이 아니지만 저는 도전을 즐깁니다. 저는 항상 신체 운동을 좋아했고, 연습을 통해 무기도 꽤 잘 다루게 되었습니다. 하지만 무엇보다도, 제가 조국에 봉사하고 있다는 것을 아는 것을 안다는 느낌이 좋습니다.

●●
military 군대 **challenge** 도전 **physical** 육체적인 **be good with** ~을 잘 쓰대[다루다] **weapon** 무기

---

02 대화를 듣고, 여자가 가려고 하는 장소를 고르시오.

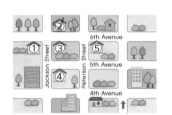

W Excuse me. How do I get to ABC Mart from here?

M ABC Mart? Yes, that's on 6th Avenue. Go two blocks and then turn left. Walk till you get to Peterson Street... Oh, no. I mean Jackson Street. It's on your right.

W Let me see if I've got that. Go straight two blocks and turn left. Then, go to Jackson Street. It's on my right.

M That's correct. You can't miss it.

W Thank you.

여 실례합니다. 여기서 ABC 마트에 어떻게 가나요?

남 ABC 마트요, 네, 그건 6번가에 있어요. 두 블록 가서 왼쪽으로 도세요. 피터슨가에 닿을 때까지 걸어가서… 오, 아니예요. 제 말은 잭슨가예요. 그것은 오른편에 있어요.

여 제가 이해했는지 볼게요. 곧장 두 블록을 가서 왼쪽으로 돌고요. 그 다음에 잭슨가까지 가요. 그럼 오른편에 있고요.

남 맞아요. 쉽게 찾으실 거예요.

여 고맙습니다.

---

03 대화를 듣고, 두 사람이 대화하는 장소로 가장 적절한 곳을 고르시오.

① 버스
② 식당
③ 공원
④ 지하철
⑤ 엘리베이터

W Ow! Hey!

M Oh, I'm sorry. Did I hurt you?

W Watch where you're going.

M I'm really sorry. It was an accident. The bus suddenly made a stop. Are you okay?

W Never mind.

M I was careless, and I didn't see you there. Really sorry.

W That's okay. Just be careful in the future.

여 아야! 이봐요!

남 아, 죄송합니다. 다치셨나요?

여 앞 좀 보고 다니세요.

남 정말 죄송합니다. 고의가 아니었어요. 버스가 갑자기 멈췄거든요. 괜찮으세요?

여 신경 쓰지 마세요.

남 제가 부주의해서 그곳에 계신 걸 보지 못했습니다. 정말 죄송합니다.

여 괜찮아요. 앞으로는 조심하세요.

●●
accident 사고, 우발적인 일 **suddenly** 갑자기 **make a stop** 멈추다 **careless** 부주의한

04

대화를 듣고, 두 사람의 관계로 가장 적절한 것을 고르시오.

① 의사 - 환자
② 구급대원 - 시민
③ 승무원 - 탑승객
④ 자동차 정비사 - 손님
⑤ 렌터카 회사 직원 - 손님

W My car sounds a bit strange. What <u>do you think</u> is wrong with it?

M Well, your brakes are old.

W How long <u>will it take</u> to repair it?

M I'll be able to get it done by <u>the day after tomorrow</u>.

W <u>How come</u> it will take so long?

M We don't have the parts, so we <u>have to order</u> them. That will take <u>a couple of</u> days.

W Okay. How much <u>will it cost</u>?

M 200 dollars.

여 제 자동차에서 좀 이상한 소리가 나는데요. 어디가 잘못된 것 같나요?
남 음, 제동 장치가 낡았어요.
여 수리하는 데 얼마나 걸릴까요?
남 내일 모레까지는 고칠 수 있을 거예요.
여 왜 그렇게 오래 걸리는 건가요?
남 부품이 없어서 주문해야 해요. 그게 이틀 정도 걸릴 거예요.
여 알겠습니다. 비용은 얼마나 들까요?
남 200달러입니다.

●●
brake 브레이크, 제동 장치 **repair** 수리하다
how come 왜, 어째서 **part** 부품

05

대화를 듣고, 여자가 취해야 할 동작으로 가장 적절한 것을 고르시오.

① 　②

③ 　④

⑤

W Do you know any good exercises for the <u>outer thighs</u>?

M Sure. Start by <u>lying down</u> on your left side.

W Can I <u>lean on</u> my elbow like this?

M Yeah, okay. Now lift your right leg up at about a 35-degree <u>angle</u>.

W Is this right?

M Uh-huh. Keep your <u>knee straight</u> though.

W This is hard. Can I put my leg down now?

M Of course. Just keep slowly <u>raising and lowering</u> it.

여 바깥쪽 허벅지에 좋은 운동을 알고 있니?
남 물론이지. 왼쪽 옆으로 눕는 것으로 시작해.
여 이렇게 팔꿈치에 기대도 돼?
남 응, 좋아. 이제 오른쪽 다리를 약 35도 각도로 들어 올려.
여 이게 맞아?
남 아니. 무릎을 일직선으로 유지해야 해.
여 이거 힘들다. 이제 다리를 내려도 될까?
남 물론이지. 그냥 계속해서 천천히 올렸다 내렸다 하면 돼.

●●
thigh 허벅지 **lie down on one's side**
옆으로 눕다 **lean on** ~에 기대다 **elbow**
팔꿈치 **angle** 각도 **knee** 무릎 **raise** 올리다
lower 내리다

06

대화를 듣고, 지난 달과 이번 달에 낸 가스 요금의 차액을 고르시오.

① $15
② $20
③ $35
④ $45
⑤ $50

W Wow, our <u>gas bill</u> this month is <u>50</u> dollars. That's <u>higher than</u> last month.

M Really? How much was the bill last month?

W Last month it was only <u>35</u> dollars.

M <u>Don't forget</u> that it's January and that it's winter.

W I know. I know. I just didn't expect <u>such an increase</u>.

M All prices are going up these days. They're <u>out of control</u>.

W <u>Tell me about it</u>. I think I may have to get a second job.

여 와, 이번 달 가스 요금이 50달러네. 지난 달 보다 더 많이 나왔어.
남 정말? 지난 달 가스 요금은 얼마였는데?
여 지난 달에는 35달러 밖에 안 나왔어.
남 지금은 1월이고 겨울이라는 것을 잊지마.
여 알아. 난 단지 이렇게나 더 많이 나올 줄은 몰랐어.
남 요즘 모든 가격이 오르고 있잖아. 어쩔 수 없어.
여 그러게 말이야. 직장을 하나 더 구해야 할지도 모르겠다.

●●
gas bill 가스 요금 **increase** 증가
out of control 통제 불가능한, 어쩔 수 없는
Tell me about it. 그러게 말이야., 내 말이.

07

대화를 듣고, 여자의 심정으로 가장 적절한 것을 고르시오.

① sad ✓
② tired
③ proud
④ nervous
⑤ cheerful

M Jane, I am so sorry <u>for your loss</u>. My condolences.

W Thank you.

M Were you very <u>close to</u> your grandmother?

W Yes, I was. She taught me a lot of <u>wonderful things</u>. I will miss her very much.

M Please <u>let me know</u> if you need any help from me. I am <u>here for you</u>.

W Thank you so much for your kindness.

• •

loss 상실, 죽음 **condolences** 애도, 조의
close 가까운, 친밀한

남 Jane, 상심이 정말 크시겠어요. 삼가 고인의 명복을 빌어요.

여 감사해요.

남 할머니와는 많이 가까웠어요?

여 네, 그래요. 할머니는 제게 많은 멋진 것들을 가르쳐 주셨어요. 할머니가 아주 많이 그리울 거예요.

남 제 도움이 필요하시면 알려주세요. 제가 여기 있잖아요.

여 친절에 감사 드립니다.

08

다음을 듣고, 두 사람의 대화가 <u>어색한</u> 것을 고르시오.

①   ② ✓   ③   ④   ⑤

① W These new shoes are <u>hurting my feet</u>.
 M Then why don't you buy a new pair of shoes?

② M The weather is <u>warming up</u>, isn't it?
 W I prefer science-fiction novels.

③ W Can I use this telephone?
 M Sure, you <u>have to press</u> 9 to get an outside line.

④ M Can you name five Korean presidents?
 W Yes, that's <u>a piece of cake</u>.

⑤ W What would you <u>like to order</u>?
 M I'll have a tuna sandwich, please.

① 여 이 새 신발 때문에 발이 아파요.
 남 그러면 새 신발을 사는 게 어때요?

② 남 날씨가 따뜻해지고 있구나, 그렇지 않니?
 여 난 공상 과학 소설을 더 좋아해.

③ 여 이 전화 좀 사용해도 될까요?
 남 물론이죠, 외부로 전화하려면 9번을 누르셔야 해요.

④ 남 한국 대통령 다섯 분의 이름을 댈 수 있니?
 여 그럼, 식은 죽 먹기지.

⑤ 여 무엇을 주문하시겠어요?
 남 참치 샌드위치로 할게요.

• •

science-fiction novel 공상 과학 소설
outside line 외선, 외부 전화 **name** 이름을 대다 **a piece of cake** 식은 죽 먹기, 아주 쉬운 일

09

대화를 듣고, 여자가 박물관에 가고 싶어 하는 이유로 가장 적절한 것을 고르시오.

① 흥미로운 그림들이 있어서 ✓
② 한 번도 가 본 적이 없어서
③ 무료 전시회가 열리고 있어서
④ 에어컨 시설이 잘 되어 있어서
⑤ 유명 화가의 전시가 열리고 있어서

W Let's sit on this bench <u>for a while</u>. It's very hot today.

M All right. Let's <u>take a break</u>. What should we do next?

W We could <u>go to the museum</u>. I heard it has some interesting paintings.

M That sounds good. I've <u>never been to</u> a museum before.

W Great. Let's go!

M <u>Let's rest</u> for just a few minutes longer. Okay?

여 이 벤치에 잠깐 앉자. 오늘 너무 덥다.

남 그래. 잠시 쉬자. 다음은 뭘 해야 하지?

여 박물관에 가면 되지. 거기에 흥미로운 그림들이 있다고 들었어.

남 그거 좋겠다. 난 박물관에 한 번도 가 본 적이 없거든.

여 좋아. 가자!

남 몇 분만 더 쉬었다 가자. 괜찮지?

• •

take a break 잠시 휴식을 취하다 **rest** 쉬다

10

대화를 듣고, 남자가 전화를 건 목적으로 가장 적절한 것을 고르시오.

① 장난감을 사기 위해서
② 장난감을 환불받기 위해서 ✓
③ 장난감을 수리하기 위해서
④ 건전지를 교환하기 위해서
⑤ 다른 장난감으로 교환하기 위해서

W Hello. Toys For You. May I help you?
M Yes. I bought a robot toy for my son at your store, but it doesn't work.
W Have you checked the batteries?
M Yes, I am sure the batteries aren't dead. I put new ones in yesterday. Can I get a refund, please?
W Certainly. If you bring us your toy and receipt, we'll give you your money back.
M Thank you very much. I'll be in today.

여 안녕하세요. 〈Toys For You〉입니다. 무엇을 도와드릴까요?
남 네. 그 가게에서 우리 아들에게 장난감 로봇을 사줬는데 작동이 안되네요.
여 건전지를 확인해 보셨나요?
남 네, 건전지가 다 돼서 그런 것이 아니라는 건 확실합니다. 어제 새 것으로 넣었거든요. 환불받을 수 있을까요?
여 물론이죠. 장난감과 영수증을 가져오시면 환불해 드리겠습니다.
남 감사합니다. 오늘 가겠습니다.

●●
battery 건전지, 배터리 **get a refund** 환불받다

11

대화를 듣고, 남자가 여자에게 해 준 조언으로 가장 적절한 것을 고르시오.

① 이사하기
② 새 옷 사기
③ 옷 입어 보기
④ 오래된 옷 버리기 ✓
⑤ 안 입는 옷 기부하기

M What can I do for you?
W Would you give me a hand with this box? I want to move it.
M Sure. It's so heavy! No wonder you couldn't lift it by yourself. What's in it?
W Oh, just some old clothes. I don't know what to do with them.
M You know, you really should throw away some of these things. You never wear them.
W You're right. I think I'll start with this old blouse.

남 무엇을 도와줄까?
여 이 상자 좀 도와줄래? 옮기고 싶어서 말이야.
남 물론이지. 너무 무겁다! 네가 그걸 혼자 들 수 없었던 게 당연하네. 안에 뭐가 들었니?
여 아, 그냥 오래된 옷들이 좀 들어 있어. 그것들을 어떻게 해야 할지 모르겠어.
남 있잖아, 이것들 중 몇 벌은 정말 버려야 해. 절대 안 입으니까.
여 네 말이 맞아. 이 낡은 블라우스부터 시작해야겠다.

●●
no wonder 당연히 ~하다 **lift** 들어올리다
(all) by oneself 혼자, 도움을 받지 않고
throw away 버리다 **blouse** 블라우스

12

대화를 듣고, 여자가 대화 직후에 할 일로 가장 적절한 것을 고르시오.

① 안내 방송 하기
② 기내 영화 보기
③ 화장실 다녀오기
④ 안전벨트 착용하기
⑤ 오렌지주스 가져다 주기 ✓

M Excuse me. Why is the plane shaking?
W Don't worry. It happens a lot. Just keep your seatbelt on.
M This is my first time flying, so I'm a little nervous.
W I understand. Can I get you something to drink?
M Orange juice, please.
W I'll be right back. Just sit back and enjoy the in-flight movie.

남 실례합니다. 비행기가 왜 흔들리죠?
여 걱정 마세요. 흔히 있는 일이에요. 안전벨트를 계속 착용하고 계세요.
남 비행기 타는 것이 처음이라 조금 떨려요.
여 이해합니다. 마실 거라도 드릴까요?
남 오렌지주스 주세요.
여 바로 가져다 드리죠. 편안히 앉으셔서 기내 영화를 즐기시기 바랍니다.

●●
shake 흔들리다 **sit back** 편안히 앉다
in-flight movie 기내 영화

13 대화를 듣고, 대화 내용과 일치하지 <u>않는</u> 것을 고르시오.

① 여자는 초조할 때면 손톱을 물어 뜯는다.

② 여자는 요리를 잘하지는 못한다.

③ 여자의 직장 동료들이 여자의 집을 방문할 것이다.

④ 여자는 중국 음식점에서 요리를 주문할 것이다.

⑤ 여자는 직장 동료들을 위해 직접 요리를 할 것이다.

M Why are you <u>biting</u> <u>your</u> <u>fingernails</u>?

W When I am nervous, I always bite my nails.

M What's <u>making</u> <u>you</u> <u>nervous</u>?

W My co-workers are visiting my house this Saturday.

M <u>What's</u> <u>wrong</u> with that?

W That means I have to cook. I know <u>how</u> <u>to</u> <u>cook</u>, but I can't cook very well.

M I have an idea. <u>Why</u> <u>don't</u> <u>you</u> order food from a Chinese restaurant?

W That's a good idea! Thanks.

남 왜 그렇게 손톱을 물어뜯니?

여 난 초조하면 항상 손톱을 물어뜯어.

남 뭐가 그렇게 초조한데?

여 직장 동료들이 이번 토요일에 집에 방문할거야.

남 그게 무슨 문제야?

여 그건 내가 요리를 해야 한다는 거지. 난 요리할 줄은 알지만 잘하지는 못하거든.

남 내게 생각이 있어. 중국 음식점에서 요리를 주문하는 건 어때?

여 좋은 생각이다! 고마워.

bite 물다 **fingernail** 손톱 **co-worker** 동료

---

14 대화를 듣고, 남자의 마지막 말에 이어질 여자의 말로 가장 적절한 것을 고르시오.

① You are such a wonderful pianist.

② I'm afraid I can't go to your concert.

③ When did you start playing the cello?

④ Can you tell me where I can buy a guitar?

⑤ I can't believe you can play two instruments.

W Can you come to my <u>birthday</u> <u>party</u> this Saturday?

M <u>At</u> <u>what</u> <u>time</u>?

W Six.

M I'm sorry. I <u>can't</u> <u>make</u> <u>it</u>.

W Why? You should come.

M I play in the school orchestra, and we <u>have</u> <u>practice</u> every Saturday.

W Do you play in the orchestra? <u>What</u> <u>instrument</u> do you play?

M I play the violin, and I also play the clarinet.

W <u>I can't believe you can play two instruments.</u>

여 이번 주 토요일 내 생일 파티에 올 수 있니?

남 몇 시에?

여 6시.

남 미안해. 못 갈 것 같아.

여 왜? 너는 꼭 와야 해.

남 내가 학교 관현악단에서 연주를 하는데, 매주 토요일에 연습이 있어.

여 너 관현악단에서 연주하니? 무슨 악기를 하는데?

남 바이올린을 연주하고 클라리넷도 불어.

여 <u>네가 악기 두 개를 연주한다는 게 믿어지지 않아.</u>

① 너는 정말 멋진 피아노 연주자야.

② 미안하지만, 네 연주회에는 갈 수 없어.

③ 언제부터 첼로를 연주하기 시작했니?

④ 어디에서 기타를 살 수 있는지 알려줄 수 있니?

make it (모임 등에) 가다 **orchestra** 오케스트라, 관현악단 **instrument** 악기 **violin** 바이올린 **clarinet** 클라리넷

15

대화를 듣고, 여자의 마지막 말에 이어질 남자의 말로 가장 적절한 것을 고르시오.

① That's 23 dollars, please.
② Sorry. I don't know that place.
③ I'll put your luggage in the trunk.
④ Thanks. Don't forget your things.
⑤ It will take about one hour to get there.

M Where can I take you, ma'am?
W Please take me to the King Bookstore.
M Which one do you want, the one in Gwanghwamun or Gangnam?
W Are there two King Bookstores? I didn't know that.
M Yes, the Gangnam branch is a new one.
W Please go to the Gangnam branch.
M Sure. Would you please fasten your seatbelt? It's for your safety.
W Of course. How long will it take to get there?
M It will take about one hour to get there.

남 어디로 모실까요, 손님?
여 King 서점으로 가 주세요.
남 어떤 King 서점으로 갈까요? 광화문이요 아니면 강남이요?
여 King 서점이 두 곳이었나요? 몰랐어요.
남 네, 강남점이 새로 개점한 곳입니다.
여 강남점으로 가 주세요.
남 알겠습니다. 안전벨트를 매 주시겠습니까? 손님의 안전을 위해서 입니다.
여 물론이죠. 그곳까지 가는데 시간이 얼마나 걸릴까요?
남 그곳까지 가는데 1시간 정도 걸릴 거예요.

① 요금은 23달러입니다.
② 죄송합니다. 그곳을 잘 모르겠어요.
③ 짐은 트렁크에 실을게요.
④ 감사합니다. 놓고 내리시는 물건이 없는지 확인하세요.

●●
branch 지점 **safety** 안전

▶ REVIEW TEST p. 87

A
① military, 군대 ② weapon, 무기 ③ accident, 사고, 우발적인 일 ④ repair, 수리하다
⑤ thigh, 허벅지 ⑥ elbow, 팔꿈치 ⑦ increase, 증가 ⑧ take a break, 잠시 휴식을 취하다
⑨ battery, 건전지, 배터리 ⑩ throw away, 버리다 ⑪ fingernail, 손톱 ⑫ instrument, 악기

B
① How come ② lying down, side ③ Keep, straight
④ let me know ⑤ piece of cake ⑥ get a refund
⑦ No wonder ⑧ first time flying

문제 및 정답	받아쓰기 및 녹음내용	해석

01 대화를 듣고, 남자가 그린 그림으로 가장 적절한 것을 고르시오.

 ① ②

③ ④

⑤

M Mom, <u>look at this</u>! I made this card at school today.

W Great! It's really cute. What does this letter S mean?

M It is the <u>first letter</u> of dad's name, Steve, and his <u>favorite animal</u> is the dog.

W Oh, so you put the S right <u>next to</u> the dog.

M Yes. I put a J next to the cat here because your favorite animal is a cat.

W I didn't know this card was <u>for us</u>.

M Tomorrow is <u>Parents' Day</u>.

남 엄마 이것 좀 보세요! 오늘 학교에서 이 카드 만들었어요.

여 멋지구나! 너무 귀엽네. 이 S는 무슨 뜻이니?

남 그건 아빠 이름 Steve의 첫 글자이고, 아빠가 가장 좋아하는 동물이 강아지잖아요.

여 아, 그래서 강아지 바로 옆에 S라고 쓴 것이구나.

남 네. 여기 고양이 옆에는 J라고 썼어요. 왜냐하면 엄마가 가장 좋아하는 동물이 고양이라서요.

여 이 카드를 우리를 위해 만든 것인지 몰랐구나.

남 내일이 어버이날이잖아요.

02 대화를 듣고, 여자가 가려고 하는 장소를 고르시오.

W Excuse me. I'm looking for the new <u>children's hospital</u> near here. Could you help me find it?

M Sure, it's easy. Just <u>walk down</u> this street and <u>pass</u> the convenience store. Then, turn right.

W So go down the street until I see the convenience store, and then <u>as soon as</u> I pass the convenience store, turn right?

M Yes. <u>The third building</u> on your right is the hospital.

W Thank you very much. You've been <u>a great help</u>.

M <u>Don't mention it</u>.

여 실례합니다. 이 근처에 새로 개업한 어린이 병원을 찾고 있는데요. 찾는 것을 도와주실 수 있나요?

남 그럼요, 찾기 쉬워요. 그냥 이 길을 따라 쭉 걸어가서 편의점을 지나가세요. 그런 다음 오른쪽으로 도세요.

여 그러니까 편의점이 보일 때까지 이 길을 따라 쭉 가서, 편의점을 지나자마자 오른쪽으로 도는 거죠?

남 네. 오른편의 세 번째 건물이 병원입니다.

여 정말 고맙습니다. 많은 도움이 됐어요.

남 별말씀을요.

03	대화를 듣고, 두 사람이 대화하는 장소로 가장 적절한 곳을 고르시오.	W Mike... Mike! You'd better <u>turn off</u> the TV now.	여 Mike… Mike! 지금 TV를 끄는 게 좋을 거야.

03 대화를 듣고, 두 사람이 대화하는 장소로 가장 적절한 곳을 고르시오.

① 집
② 극장
③ 학교
④ 상점
⑤ 도서관

W Mike... Mike! You'd better <u>turn off</u> the TV now.

M Oh, no. This is one of my <u>favorite</u> <u>TV</u> <u>programs</u>!

W I know. But you've watched too much TV today. You should <u>finish</u> <u>your</u> <u>homework</u> before you go to bed.

M Can I finish watching this first?

W No. And now <u>pick up your things</u>. They're all over the living room floor.

M Okay. I'll turn it off. <u>Just a minute</u>.

W Good boy. I can help you.

M Thank you, Mom.

여 Mike… Mike! 지금 TV를 끄는 게 좋을 거야.

남 어, 안돼요. 이건 제가 가장 좋아하는 TV 프로그램들 중 하나란 말이에요!

여 알고 있어. 하지만 오늘 TV를 너무 많이 봤잖아. 잠자리에 들기 전에 숙제를 끝마쳐야 한다.

남 이것 먼저 보고 하면 안 될까요?

여 안돼. 그리고 지금 네 물건들을 치워라. 거실 바닥에 온통 흩어져 있잖아.

남 알았어요. 끌게요. 잠깐만요.

여 착한 우리 아들. 엄마가 도와줄게.

남 고마워요, 엄마.

●●
turn off 끄다　**pick up** (어질러진 물건들을) 치우다, 정리하다　**Just a minute.** 잠깐만요.

---

04 대화를 듣고, 두 사람의 관계로 가장 적절한 것을 고르시오.

① boss – staff
② doctor – patient
③ foreigner – passerby
④ professor – instructor
⑤ receptionist – student

M Hello. How can I help you?

W I want to <u>learn</u> <u>English</u>.

M <u>What</u> <u>skills</u> do you want to learn?

W I want to learn <u>how</u> <u>to</u> <u>speak</u> English well.

M <u>Have</u> <u>you</u> <u>taken</u> any English conversation classes before?

W Yes, but I can speak <u>only a little</u> English and make simple sentences.

M Okay, I see. Then you have to take a <u>placement</u> <u>test</u>.

W Where should I do that?

M Go to room number 505 on the <u>fifth</u> <u>floor</u>.

남 안녕하세요. 무엇을 도와드릴까요?

여 영어를 배우고 싶습니다.

남 어떤 분야를 배우고 싶으세요?

여 영어 말하기를 배우고 싶습니다.

남 전에 영어 회화 수업을 수강한 적이 있습니까?

여 네, 하지만 영어는 조금만 할 수 있고, 간단한 영어 문장을 만들 수 있을 정도예요.

남 네, 알겠습니다. 그러면 반 편성 시험을 보셔야 합니다.

여 어디에서 하면 되지요?

남 네, 5층의 505호 강의실로 가시면 됩니다.

●●
placement test 반 편성 시험　**foreigner** 외국인　**passerby** 행인　**instructor** 강사　**receptionist** 접수 담당자

---

05 대화를 듣고, 남자의 형이 누구인지 고르시오.

M Here's a <u>picture</u> of my brother's old heavy metal band.

W <u>Which</u> <u>one</u> is your brother?

M I'll <u>give</u> <u>you</u> <u>a hint</u>. He has long hair.

W <u>All</u> <u>but</u> two of them have long hair.

M He's also tall, like me.

W Is this him? The one <u>holding the guitar</u>?

M Yeah, that's my brother.

남 여기 우리 형의 옛날 헤비메탈 밴드 사진이 있어.

여 누가 네 형이야?

남 내가 힌트를 줄게. 그는 머리카락이 길어.

여 그들 중 두 명만 빼고 다 긴 머리야.

남 그는 또한 나처럼 키가 커.

여 이 사람이 형이야? 기타 들고 있는 사람?

남 응, 그 사람이 우리 형이야.

●●
heavy metal (음악 장르) 헤비메탈　**all but** ~외에 모두

06 대화를 듣고, 남자가 지불해야 할 금액으로 가장 적절한 것을 고르시오.

① $3
② $6
③ $12
④ $30
⑤ $36

W Welcome to my flower shop. How can I help you?
M I'd like to get some flowers for my wife. It is our wedding anniversary.
W What kind of flowers are you thinking of?
M I don't know. Maybe some roses?
W That's a good choice. They are three dollars each.
M Great. I'll take a dozen.
W I'm sure your wife will love these.
M I hope so. Thanks.

여 저희 꽃집을 찾아 주셔서 고맙습니다. 무엇을 도와드릴까요?
남 아내를 위해 꽃을 좀 사고 싶은데요. 결혼기념일이거든요.
여 어떤 종류의 꽃을 생각하고 계세요?
남 모르겠어요. 아마도 장미가 좋을 듯 한데요?
여 훌륭한 선택이세요. 장미는 한 송이에 3달러예요.
남 좋습니다. 열 두 송이 주세요.
여 부인께서 아주 좋아하실 거예요.
남 그러길 바래요. 고맙습니다.

●●
dozen 12개

07 대화를 듣고, 두 사람의 심정으로 가장 적절한 것을 고르시오.

① upset
② bored
③ scared
④ relieved
⑤ confident

W It is dark now. I think we are lost.
M I am not sure where we are now.
W We're in an unfamiliar part of town.
M Do you hear the sounds of wild animals roaring?
W Let's walk down this street.
W Sure. I hope we can see people or a town on our way.

여 해가 져 버렸어. 우린 길을 잃은 것 같아.
남 우리가 지금 어디에 있는지 모르겠어.
여 우리는 마을의 낯선 곳에 있어.
남 야생 동물들이 으르렁거리는 소리 들리니?
여 이 길로 걸어 내려가자.
남 그러자. 가는 길에 사람들이나 마을을 볼 수 있다면 좋겠어.

●●
roar 으르렁거리다

08 대화를 듣고, 남자의 마지막 말의 의도로 가장 적절한 것을 고르시오.

① 실망
② 사과
③ 비난
④ 후회
⑤ 기대

M When will it stop snowing?
W The weather forecast said even more snow is expected over the weekend.
M Do you think we can still travel this weekend?
W I think it will be very dangerous to drive in snow.
M Well, we planned this trip almost two months ago.
W I know, but I think we should postpone it.
M That's too bad. I was really looking forward to it.

남 눈이 언제 멈출까?
여 일기예보에서는 주말에 훨씬 더 많은 눈이 예상된다.
남 이번 주말에 우리 여행갈 수 있을까?
여 눈이 오는데 운전하는 건 아주 위험할 것 같아.
남 음, 우리는 이 여행을 거의 두 달 전에 계획했잖아.
여 알아, 하지만 연기를 해야 할 것 같아.
남 그거 아쉽네. 정말 기대하고 있었거든.

●●
postpone 연기하다

09 대화를 듣고, Kevin의 다리가 부러진 이유로 가장 적절한 것을 고르시오.

① 학교 친구와 싸워서
② 축구 경기 중에 다쳐서
③ 학교 운동장에서 넘어져서
④ 자전거를 타다가 넘어져서
⑤ 발이 걸려 계단에서 넘어져서

W Did you see Kevin?
M Yes, I did. He <u>broke</u> <u>his</u> <u>leg</u>.
W Do you know <u>what</u> <u>happened</u> <u>to</u> him?
M I heard that he <u>tripped</u> and <u>fell</u> <u>down</u> the school steps last Thursday.
W <u>That's</u> <u>how</u> he broke his leg?
M That's what happened.
W I <u>feel</u> <u>sorry</u> for him.

여 Kevin 봤니?
남 응, 봤어. 다리가 부러졌더라.
여 그에게 무슨 일이 있었는지 알고 있니?
남 지난 목요일에 발이 걸려서 학교 계단에서 넘어졌다고 들었어.
여 그렇게 해서 다리가 부러진 거야?
남 그렇대.
여 안됐구나.

●●
trip (발이) 걸리다   fall down 넘어지다
step 계단

10 대화를 듣고, 여자의 증상으로 가장 적절한 것을 고르시오.

① 감기
② 일사병
③ 뾰루지
④ 알레르기
⑤ 소화불량

W Do you know what? I feel <u>a</u> <u>little</u> <u>sick</u>.
M Sick? How long have you been out <u>in</u> <u>the</u> <u>sun</u>?
W Oh, a few hours. Maybe four.
M But it's over 30 degrees. You probably have been in the sun for too long. You need to <u>drink</u> <u>some</u> <u>water</u> right away and <u>get</u> <u>out</u> <u>of</u> the sun.
W Yes. It <u>wasn't</u> <u>very</u> <u>smart</u> to be out in the sun for so long.
M Well, you have to be <u>more</u> <u>careful</u> these days.

여 있잖아. 나 조금 아픈 것 같아.
남 아프다고? 밖에서 햇볕에 얼마나 오래 있었니?
여 아, 몇 시간 정도. 아마도 네 시간.
남 하지만 30도가 넘잖아. 너무 오랫동안 햇볕에 있었나 보다. 지금 당장 물을 마시고 햇볕에서 나와야 해.
여 응. 햇볕에 그렇게 오랫동안 있는 것은 현명하지 못했어.
남 그래, 요즘은 더 조심해야 돼.

●●
get out of ~에서 나오다

11 대화를 듣고, 남자가 여자에게 해 준 조언으로 가장 적절한 것을 고르시오.

① 동물 병원에 데려가기
② 고양이 사료 바꿔주기
③ 너무 많이 먹이지 않기
④ 고양이의 털 자주 빗어주기
⑤ 고양이가 마시는 물 바꿔주기

W My cat <u>is</u> <u>not</u> <u>eating</u> these days. What should I do?
M <u>Have</u> <u>you</u> <u>tried</u> changing its cat food?
W No, I haven't.
M My aunt's cat had the same problem, and <u>all</u> <u>she</u> <u>did</u> was change the food.
W I'll <u>give</u> <u>it</u> <u>a</u> <u>try</u>.
M You know, cats can be <u>very</u> <u>picky</u>.

여 요즘 제 고양이가 아무 것도 안 먹어요. 어떻게 하죠?
남 고양이 사료를 바꿔봤어요?
여 아니요.
남 저희 이모네 고양이도 같은 문제를 가지고 있었는데, 이모가 한 거라곤 사료를 바꾼 것뿐이거든요.
여 한번 해 봐야겠어요.
남 아시다시피 고양이들은 매우 까다로울 수 있어요.

●●
picky 까다로운

12 대화를 듣고, 두 사람이 조깅하기 전에 해야 할 일로 가장 적절한 것을 고르시오.

① 물 마시기
② 근육 풀어 주기
③ 화장실 다녀오기
④ 숨을 깊이 들이쉬기
⑤ 알맞은 조깅복 입기

M Are you ready for our morning jog?
W Yes, I am. What are you doing there?
M We should do some warm-up exercises before we start. Our muscles are still too cold for jogging.
W I see. I'm sure I can learn a lot from you.
M After our warm-up, we should then stretch our muscles.
W I got it. Then we jog, right?
M That's right.

남 아침 조깅할 준비됐어?
여 그래, 됐어. 넌 거기서 뭐하고 있니?
남 시작하기 전에 준비 운동을 해야 해. 우리 근육은 조깅을 하기에는 아직 너무 굳어 있거든.
여 그렇구나. 너한테 많은 것을 배울 수 있을 것 같다.
남 준비 운동 후에는 근육을 스트레칭해야 해.
여 알겠어. 그런 다음에 조깅하는 거지?
남 맞아.

• •
jog 조깅: 조깅하다 warm-up exercise 준비 운동 stretch 펴다, 늘이다

---

13 대화를 듣고, 대화 내용과 일치하지 <u>않는</u> 것을 고르시오.

① 여자는 서울에서 태어났다.
② 여자는 서울에서 고등학교를 마칠 때까지 살았다.
③ 여자는 부산에서 몇 년 동안 살았다.
④ 여자는 1년 전에 서울로 돌아왔다.
⑤ 여자의 자매들은 모두 서울에 살고 있다.

M So tell me a little about yourself.
W I was born right here in Seoul and lived here until I finished high school. I lived in Busan for several years, and then I moved back here two years ago.
M Do you have any brothers or sisters?
W Yes. I have two sisters. They both live in Seoul.

남 당신에 대해 이야기 좀 해 봐요.
여 저는 이곳 서울에서 태어났고 고등학교를 마칠 때까지 여기 살았어요. 부산에서 몇 년 동안 살았고, 그리고 나서 2년 전에 다시 이곳으로 이 사왔죠.
남 형제나 자매는 있나요?
여 네, 자매가 둘 있어요. 그들 모두 서울에 살아요.

---

14 대화를 듣고, 남자의 마지막 말에 이어질 여자의 말로 가장 적절한 것을 고르시오.

① Okay, I'll see you then.
② I hope he gets well soon.
③ You seem very happy today.
④ Do you want some more soup?
⑤ Oh, now I know why you're in a bad mood.

M This soup is terrible! What did you do to it?
W Nothing different.
M And the tea is cold. Why didn't you heat it up?
W John, I know you are in a bad mood this morning, but don't yell at me.
M I'm sorry. I didn't get enough sleep last night, so I'm pretty moody now.
W Oh, now I know why you're in a bad mood.

남 이 수프는 너무 맛이 없네. 어떻게 한 거예요?
여 다를 거 없는데요.
남 그리고 차가 너무 차가워요. 왜 데우지 않았어요?
여 John, 오늘 아침에 당신 기분이 좋지 않은 것은 알겠지만 나에게 소리치지는 마세요.
남 미안해요. 지난 밤에 충분히 자지 못해서 지금 기분이 좋지 않아요.
여 <u>오, 왜 기분이 좋지 않은지 이제야 알겠네요.</u>

① 좋아요, 그때 봐요.
② 그가 빨리 낫기를 바래요.
③ 당신 오늘 아주 행복해 보여요.
④ 수프 좀 더 먹을래요?

• •
yell 소리치다 moody 기분이 좋지 않은, 침울한

15 대화를 듣고, 여자의 마지막 말에 이어질 남자의 말로 가장 적절한 것을 고르시오.

① You have to finish this tonight.
② Well, I don't know what to do first.
③ You must be very proud of yourself.
④ Then I'll help you with one of your projects.
⑤ Tell me whatever you want to say. I'll listen.

M Jessica, you <u>look pale</u>. What happened?

W I didn't <u>sleep a wink</u> last night.

M Did you have something <u>on your mind</u>? You look worried.

W Well, I'm under <u>a lot of pressure</u>. My boss assigned me three projects. Now the deadlines are near, and I still <u>haven't finished</u> any of my projects.

M <u>Is there anything</u> I can do to help you?

W Well, I guess no one can help me <u>but myself</u>. For the moment, I just need <u>someone to talk to</u> so that I can <u>relieve my stress</u>.

M <u>Tell me whatever you want to say. I'll listen.</u>

남 Jessica, 창백해 보여. 무슨 일이니?

여 지난 밤에 한잠도 못 잤어.

남 마음에 걸리는 거라도 있니? 걱정스러워 보여.

여 글쎄, 난 너무 부담스러워. 상사가 나에게 세 개의 과제를 맡겼어. 이제 최종 기한이 다가오는데 난 아직 어떤 과제도 끝내지 못했어.

남 내가 도와줄 일이 있을까?

여 글쎄, 내 자신 외에는 아무도 날 도울 수 없을 거야. 지금은 그냥 스트레스를 좀 덜 수 있도록 이야기할 누군가가 필요할 뿐이야.

남 말하고 싶은 게 있으면 내게 뭐든지 말해. 내가 들어 줄게.

① 너는 오늘 밤에 이 일을 끝내야 해.
② 음, 뭘 먼저 해야 할지 모르겠어.
③ 네 자신이 정말 자랑스럽겠구나.
④ 그렇다면 내가 네 과제들 중 하나를 도와 줄게.

●●
pale 창백한 **sleep a wink** 한잠 자다
assign 맡기다, 할당하다 **deadline** 마감일
relieve 경감하다, 덜다

▶ REVIEW TEST p. 95

A
① turn off, 끄다 ② roar, 으르렁거리다 ③ postpone, 연기하다 ④ fall down, 넘어지다
⑤ picky, 까다로운 ⑥ jog, 조깅, 조깅하다 ⑦ stretch, 펴다, 늘이다 ⑧ yell, 소리치다
⑨ pale, 창백한 ⑩ sleep a wink, 한잠 자다 ⑪ deadline, 마감일 ⑫ relieve, 경감하다, 덜다

B
① mention it ② Have you taken ③ dozen
④ dangerous to drive ⑤ what happened to ⑥ How long
⑦ brothers or sisters ⑧ under, pressure

문제 및 정답	받아쓰기 및 녹음내용	해석

01 대화를 듣고, 남자가 가장 귀엽게 생각하는 원숭이를 고르시오.

W Which monkey <u>do you</u> <u>think</u> is the cutest?

M I like the one over there <u>on the</u> <u>rock</u>.

W That one? You think he's cute?

M Yeah. See how he's <u>balancing</u> <u>that</u> <u>ball</u> on his head.

W I think his friend is about to <u>steal</u> it from him.

M Monkeys are so much <u>fun</u> <u>to</u> <u>watch</u>.

W I'm glad you're having a good time.

여 네 생각엔 어떤 원숭이가 가장 귀엽니?

남 나는 저기 바위 위에 있는 원숭이가 좋아.

여 저거? 저게 귀엽다고 생각해?

남 응. 그가 어떻게 머리 위의 공이 떨어지지 않게 균형을 잡고 있는지 봐.

여 내 생각에는 그 원숭이의 친구가 그에게서 공을 빼앗으려고 하는 것 같은데.

남 원숭이들을 보니 참 재미있다.

여 좋은 시간이 되고 있다니 기뻐.

● ●
balance 균형을 잡다 **steal** 훔치다, 빼앗다

02 대화를 듣고, 여자가 가려고 하는 장소를 고르시오.

W Excuse me. Can you tell me <u>the</u> <u>way</u> <u>to</u> the COEX Mall?

M Sure. Walk along Samsung Avenue <u>till</u> <u>you</u> <u>come</u> <u>to</u> Bongeunsa Street.

W So I should go to Bongeunsa Street, right?

M Yes, that's right. <u>Turn</u> <u>left</u> there. Then, go one block, and turn right onto Teheran Street. It's <u>on</u> <u>your</u> <u>right</u>.

W Turn left on Bongeunsa Street and go one block. Then, turn right onto Teheran Street, and it's on my right?

M <u>That's</u> <u>it</u>. You can't miss it.

여 실례합니다. 코엑스몰 가는 길 좀 가르쳐 주시겠어요?

남 네. 봉은사로가 나올 때까지 삼성로를 따라 걸어가세요.

여 그러니까 봉은사로까지 가야 한다는 말씀이시죠?

남 네, 맞아요. 거기서 왼쪽으로 도세요. 그런 다음 한 블록 가서 테헤란로에서 오른쪽으로 도세요. 코엑스몰은 오른편에 있어요.

남 봉은사로에서 좌회전해서 한 블록 가고요. 그런 다음, 테헤란로에서 우회전하면 오른편에 있다고요?

여 맞아요. 쉽게 찾으실 거예요.

03 대화를 듣고, 두 사람이 대화하는 장소로 가장 적절한 곳을 고르시오.

① 공항
② 경찰서
③ 여행사
④ 학교 기숙사
⑤ 분실물 센터

M Where are you from?

W I'm from Korea.

M <u>Passport</u>, please. What's the <u>purpose</u> of your visit?

W I'm here to <u>study</u> <u>English</u> at the University of Chicago for one year.

M What is your <u>address</u> while you're here?

W I'm going to stay in the <u>school</u> <u>dormitory</u>.

M All right. Here is your passport. <u>Good</u> <u>luck</u> with your studies.

W Thank you. Goodbye.

남 어디에서 오셨습니까?

여 한국에서 왔어요.

남 여권을 주십시오. 방문 목적이 뭔가요?

여 저는 시카고 대학에서 1년 동안 영어를 공부하러 왔어요.

남 여기 계시는 동안 주소가 어떻게 되나요?

여 학교 기숙사에 있을 예정입니다.

남 알겠습니다. 여기 여권 받으세요. 학업에 행운을 빕니다.

여 감사합니다. 안녕히 계세요.

●●
passport 여권 **purpose** 목적 **address** 주소 **dormitory** 기숙사

---

04 대화를 듣고, 두 사람의 관계로 가장 적절한 것을 고르시오.

① 감독 - 선수
② 교사 - 학생
③ 점원 - 고객
④ 경찰관 - 행인
⑤ 버스 기사 - 승객

M Excuse me. Do you know <u>what</u> <u>you</u> <u>just</u> <u>did</u>?

W No, I'm sorry. I don't.

M You are supposed to <u>use</u> <u>the</u> <u>crosswalks</u>. That's why they are there.

W I still <u>don't</u> <u>follow</u> <u>you</u>.

M You crossed the street in the middle of the road. You could <u>injure</u> <u>yourself</u> or cause a <u>traffic</u> <u>accident</u>.

W I'm sorry. I just wasn't thinking. I'm <u>late</u> <u>for</u> work.

M I won't <u>give</u> <u>you</u> <u>a</u> <u>ticket</u> this time, but I will if I catch you again.

남 실례합니다. 당신이 지금 막 무엇을 했는지 아십니까?

여 아니오, 죄송합니다. 모르겠어요.

남 당신은 횡단보도를 이용해야 합니다. 그게 바로 횡단보도가 거기에 있는 이유이고요.

여 무슨 말씀이신지 여전히 모르겠어요.

남 도로 한가운데에서 길을 건너셨어요. 다칠 수도 있었고 교통사고가 날 수도 있었습니다.

여 죄송해요. 제가 생각을 못 했네요. 회사에 늦었거든요.

남 이번에는 딱지를 떼지 않겠습니다만, 한 번 더 발견되면 딱지를 떼겠습니다.

●●
follow 이해하다, (설명 등을) 따라가다 **injure** 부상을 입히다 **ticket** (위반) 딱지

---

05 대화를 듣고, 여자가 좋아하는 운동으로 가장 적절한 것을 고르시오.

① 축구
② 배구
③ 탁구
④ 테니스
⑤ 배드민턴

M What time is that soccer game <u>on</u>? I thought it started at two.

W We must have gotten the <u>time</u> <u>wrong</u>. Oh, well. Soccer is not my favorite sport anyway. I <u>much</u> <u>prefer</u> badminton.

M Really? I thought your favorite sport was tennis. I'm <u>a</u> <u>big</u> <u>fan</u> <u>of</u> badminton, too.

W How about <u>playing</u> <u>it</u> <u>together</u> sometime?

M Sure. Why don't we play now since the soccer game <u>isn't</u> <u>on</u>?

W That's great! Let's go.

남 그 축구 경기는 몇 시에 하지? 2시에 시작할 거라고 생각했는데.

여 우리가 시간을 잘못 안 게 틀림없어. 아, 뭐. 어쨌든 축구는 내가 가장 좋아하는 운동이 아니야. 난 배드민턴을 훨씬 더 좋아해.

남 정말? 나는 네가 가장 좋아하는 운동이 테니스인 줄 알았어. 나도 배드민턴의 열렬한 팬이야.

여 언제 한번 같이 치는 건 어때?

남 좋지. 축구 경기가 없으니 지금 하는 게 어때?

여 좋아! 가자.

●●
on 진행 중인, 시작된

06 대화를 듣고, 남자의 학급 학생 수로 가장 적절한 것을 고르시오.

① 5명
② 6명
③ 20명
④ 30명
⑤ 40명

W Do you like your class?
M Not really. There are too many students in my class.
W Really? How many are there?
M Hmmm... There are six rows, with five students in each row...
W You're right. There really are a lot of students in your class.
M There's also too much noise. It's hard to concentrate.
W My class is the same.

여 너희 반 좋아?
남 아니. 우리 반은 학생 수가 너무 많아.
여 정말? 몇 명이나 되는데?
남 음… 6줄에 5명씩 있으니까…
여 네 말이 맞다. 너희 반 학생 수가 정말 많구나.
남 그리고 정말 시끄러워. 집중하기가 힘들 정도야.
여 우리 반도 똑같아.

●● **row** 줄, 열

---

07 대화를 듣고, 남자의 성격으로 가장 적절한 것을 고르시오.

① shy
② lazy
③ polite
④ energetic
⑤ responsible

W Let's clean up before our parents get home.
M Why don't you start first, and I'll help you later?
W No way! We both made this mess, so both of us will clean it up.
M I don't want to. I'd rather watch TV.
W Don't be a couch potato. Come on. We don't have much time.
M I said I don't want to. Stop bothering me.

여 부모님이 집에 도착하시기 전에 우리 같이 청소하자.
남 네가 먼저 시작하면 내가 나중에 도와주는 거 어때?
여 안 돼! 우리 둘이 이렇게 어지럽혀 놨잖아, 그러니까 같이 청소해야지.
남 하기 싫어. 나는 TV 볼래.
여 게으른 소리 좀 하지마. 제발. 시간이 별로 없어.
남 하기 싫다고 말했잖아. 귀찮게 좀 하지 마.

●● **make a mess** 어지럽히다　**couch potato** 소파에 앉아 TV만 보며 많은 시간을 보내는 사람

---

08 대화를 듣고, 오늘 저녁과 내일 점심 메뉴로 가장 적절한 것을 고르시오.

	오늘 저녁	내일 점심
①	fish	pizza
②	pizza	spaghetti
③	hamburger	pizza
④	spaghetti	pizza
⑤	spaghetti	fish

M Mom, Paul is coming to stay with us for two days before school starts.
W Oh, really? Do you want fish for dinner?
M Oh, no, Mom. Don't cook fish.
W Why not? You like fish.
M But Paul doesn't. He hates fish.
W Well, what does he like?
M He likes spaghetti, and he loves pizza.
W Okay, let's have spaghetti for dinner tonight.
M And pizza for lunch tomorrow.
W All right, Mike. All right.

남 엄마, Paul이 개학하기 전 이틀 동안 우리와 함께 지낼 거예요.
여 오, 정말? 저녁 식사로 생선 요리를 할까?
남 오, 안돼요, 엄마. 생선 요리는 하지 마세요.
여 왜 그래? 너는 생선을 좋아하잖아.
남 하지만 Paul은 아니에요. 그는 생선 요리를 싫어해요.
여 그러면 그 애는 뭘 좋아하니?
남 스파게티를 좋아하고 피자도 아주 좋아해요.
여 그래, 오늘 저녁에는 스파게티를 먹자꾸나.
남 그리고 내일 점심은 피자로요.
여 알았다, Mike. 알았어.

●● **spaghetti** 스파게티

09

대화를 듣고, 남자가 집중할 수 없는 이유로 가장 적절한 것을 고르시오.

① 잠을 자지 못해서
② 음식을 먹지 못해서
③ 할 일이 너무 많아서
④ 커피를 너무 많이 마셔서
⑤ 좋아하는 여자가 도서관에 있어서

W Are you going to the library to study tonight?
M I'm sorry. I can't. I haven't slept for several days, so I need to go directly to bed.
W Oh, that's too bad. How do you feel?
M I can't concentrate, and I feel kind of weak.
W Some people function well without sleep while others can't function at all. What type of person are you?
M I'm definitely in the second group. Sleep is essential to me.

여 오늘 밤에 공부하러 도서관에 갈 거니?
남 미안해. 못 가. 며칠 동안 잠을 못 자서 바로 자러 가야겠어.
여 저런, 안됐구나. 기분은 좀 어때?
남 집중이 안되고 힘이 없는 것 같아.
여 어떤 사람들은 잠을 못 자도 잘 활동하는 반면에 다른 사람들은 전혀 그렇지 않아. 너는 어느 쪽이니?
남 난 확실히 후자 쪽이지. 잠은 나에게 꼭 필요한 것이야.

••
directly 곧장 **function** 기능하다, 활동하다
definitely 분명히, 확실히 **essential** 필수적인

10

대화를 듣고, 여자가 생각하는 남자의 증상으로 가장 적절한 것을 고르시오.

① 독감
② 빈혈
③ 식중독
④ 불면증
⑤ 우울증

W What made you come here today?
M I have some sharp pain in my stomach.
W I see. What did you eat today?
M Well, I only ate a sandwich I bought at a convenience store.
W That might be the problem. Please be careful of what you eat.

여 무슨 일로 오셨나요?
남 위가 찌르는 것처럼 아파요.
여 알겠어요. 오늘 뭘 드셨죠?
남 음, 편의점에서 산 샌드위치를 먹은 게 다에요.
여 아마 그게 문제였나 보군요. 먹는 것에 주의 하셔야 해요.

••
sharp pain 찌를듯한 통증

11

대화를 듣고, 여자가 남자에게 부탁한 일로 가장 적절한 것을 고르시오.

① 동생 돌봐 주기
② 동생과 같이 놀아주기
③ 동생의 숙제 도와주기
④ 동생에게 게임기 양보하기
⑤ 동생에게 게임 하는 법 알려주기

M Mom! Tell her to give me back my game player.
W Why don't you let your sister play it for a while?
M I didn't say she could play with it.
W Well, if she asks you, will you let her play it?
M If she asks me… well… Okay.
W That's a good boy. It's important to learn to share, isn't it?
M You're right, Mom.

남 엄마! 동생한테 내 게임기 돌려 주라고 말해 주세요.
여 동생 좀 잠깐 하게 해주지 그러니?
남 난 동생한테 가지고 놀 수 있다고 말하지 않았어요.
여 그럼, 동생이 너한테 물어보면 하라고 할 거니?
남 물어 본다면… 글쎄요… 그렇게 할게요.
여 착하구나. 함께 나누는 것을 배우는 건 중요한 거야, 그렇지 않니?
남 엄마 말씀이 맞아요.

12 대화를 듣고, 여자가 대화 직후에 할 일로 가장 적절한 것을 고르시오.

① 시험공부하기
② 시험 보러 가기
③ Helen에게 전화하기
④ 남자와 함께 산책하기
⑤ 창문 열어 환기시키기

W Do you know what Helen did?
M No. Did she do <u>something wrong</u>?
W Yeah, she did. She borrowed my biology notes, and then she <u>lost mine</u>.
M She lost your biology notes?
W Yes, we have a test tomorrow. I feel like telling her <u>how angry I am</u>.
M Calm down. You'd better <u>count to ten</u> before you do anything.
W I'll be all right <u>after</u> a <u>while</u>, but I'm so mad right now.
M Why don't you <u>go for</u> a <u>walk</u> with me before you call her?
W That's a good idea. I need some <u>fresh air</u>.

여 Helen이 무슨 짓을 했는지 아니?
남 아니. 무슨 잘못이라도 했어?
여 맞아. 그녀가 내 생물 공책을 빌려 가서 그것을 잃어버렸어.
남 너의 생물 공책을 잃어버렸다고?
여 응, 시험이 내일인데. 난 그녀에게 내가 얼마나 화가 났는지 말해 주고 싶어.
남 진정해. 네가 뭔가를 하기 전에 열까지 세어 봐.
여 잠시 후면 괜찮아 지겠지만 지금은 너무 화가 나.
남 그녀에게 전화하기 전에 나랑 산책 가는 게 어떠니?
여 좋은 생각이야. 나에게는 신선한 공기가 좀 필요해.

●●
borrow 빌리다 **biology** 생물학 **count** 세다
after a while 잠시 후에 **go for a walk** 산책 하러 가다

13 대화를 듣고, 대화 내용과 일치하지 <u>않는</u> 것을 고르시오.

① 남자는 예약을 하지 않았다.
② 남자는 2인실에 묵을 예정이다.
③ 남자는 80달러를 지불해야 한다.
④ 남자는 작은 서류 가방만 가지고 있다.
⑤ 호텔 직원이 방까지 안내해 줄 것이다.

W Good afternoon. May I help you?
M Do you have a <u>room for tonight</u>? I don't have a <u>reservation</u>.
W Yes, we do. A single room or a <u>double room</u>?
M A single room with a <u>nice view</u>, please. And what is the <u>room rate</u>?
W 80 dollars <u>a day</u>.
M That's good. I'll take it.
W Please <u>fill out</u> this card. Do you need help <u>with your bags</u>?
M No, I just have a small <u>briefcase</u>.
W Okay. Our bellman will take you up to your room.

여 안녕하세요. 무엇을 도와드릴까요?
남 오늘 밤에 묵을 방이 있나요? 예약은 하지 않았는데요.
여 네, 있습니다. 1인실 인가요, 아니면 2인실 인가요?
남 전망 좋은 1인실로 부탁드립니다. 숙박료는 얼마인가요?
여 하루에 80달러입니다.
남 좋아요. 그걸로 할게요.
여 이 카드를 작성해 주세요. 가방 드는 것을 도와드릴까요?
남 아니요, 작은 서류 가방뿐이에요.
여 알겠습니다. 저희 직원이 방까지 안내해 드릴 겁니다.

●●
have a reservation 예약되어 있다 **single room** 1인실 **double room** 2인실 **rate** 요금 **fill out** 작성하다 **briefcase** 서류 가방 **bellman** (호텔에서 객실까지 안내해주는) 벨맨

14 대화를 듣고, 남자의 마지막 말에 이어질 여자의 말로 가장 적절한 것을 고르시오.

① I had a great time in Seoul.
② I don't like traveling by plane.
③ I hope you visit there sometime.
④ Wow! It must have been beautiful!
⑤ How long will you stay on Jeju Island?

W Have you ever traveled <u>by plane</u>?
M Yes, I went to Jeju Island by air last summer.
W How long <u>did it take</u> from Seoul to Jeju Island?
M Only an hour.
W Did you get a <u>good view</u> of Jeju Island?
M I did. The sky was very clear, so we could see for <u>miles and miles</u>.
W <u>Wow! It must have been beautiful!</u>

여 비행기로 여행해 봤니?
남 응, 지난 여름에 비행기로 제주도에 다녀왔어.
여 서울에서 제주도까지 얼마나 걸렸니?
남 겨우 1시간.
여 제주도의 아름다운 풍경을 봤니?
남 봤어. 하늘이 너무 맑아서 아주 멀리까지 볼 수 있었어.
여 와! 아름다웠겠다!

① 나는 서울에서 즐거운 시간을 보냈어.
② 나는 비행기로 여행하는 것을 좋아하지 않아.
③ 언젠가 네가 그곳에 가보길 바라.
⑤ 제주도에는 얼마나 오래 있을 거니?

●●
by air[plane] 비행기로   **miles and miles** 아주 멀리

15 대화를 듣고, 여자의 마지막 말에 이어질 남자의 말로 가장 적절한 것을 고르시오.

① I'm sorry, maybe next time.
② I really hate mathematics class.
③ Well, I know I am good at writing.
④ No, I can't. I handed in my essay yesterday.
⑤ Okay, I will do that. Thanks for your advice.

W Are you <u>done with</u> your essay for English class?
M I finished it this morning, and I'm about to <u>turn it in</u>.
W Do you mind if I <u>take a look</u> at it?
M Sure. I need <u>someone to read</u> it. How is it?
W Honestly? I don't think you should <u>hand this in</u> now.
M Why?
W I think you should add <u>more examples</u> in the body of the paper.
M <u>Okay, I will do that. Thanks for your advice.</u>

여 영어 에세이 다 썼니?
남 오늘 아침에 끝내서 제출하려고 해.
여 한번 봐도 되겠니?
남 물론이지. 누군가 읽어 줄 사람이 필요하거든. 어때?
여 솔직하게? 난 네가 이걸 지금 제출해서는 안 된다고 생각해.
남 왜?
여 글의 본문에 예를 더 추가해야 할 것 같아.
남 좋아, 그렇게 할게. 조언 고마워.

① 미안해, 다음에 가자.
② 나는 수학 시간이 정말 싫어.
③ 음, 나도 내가 글쓰기를 잘하는 걸 알아.
④ 안돼. 어제 에세이를 제출했거든.

●●
hand[turn] in 제출하다

▶ REVIEW TEST p. 103

A
① balance, 균형을 잡다 ② steal, 훔치다, 빼앗다 ③ passport, 여권 ④ address, 주소
⑤ dormitory, 기숙사 ⑥ injure, 부상을 입히다 ⑦ make a mess, 어지럽히다 ⑧ function, 기능하다, 활동하다
⑨ essential, 필수적인 ⑩ briefcase, 서류 가방 ⑪ by air, 비행기로 ⑫ hand in, 제출하다

B
① the way ② purpose, your visit ③ must have, wrong
④ big fan ⑤ sharp pain ⑥ reservation
⑦ fill out ⑧ take a look

문제 및 정답	받아쓰기 및 녹음내용	해석

01

대화를 듣고, 두 사람이 구입할 스웨터로 가장 적절한 것을 고르시오.

①   ②

③   ④

⑤

M Let's get one of the sweaters here for Peter's <u>birthday</u> <u>gift</u>.

W Great idea! How about this one? It has the <u>letter P</u> on it.

M It is nice, but it looks <u>too</u> <u>simple</u> without any pictures.

W Peter likes monkeys. He <u>may</u> <u>like</u> <u>this</u> because it has a monkey picture.

M It is cute, but he likes dogs, too.

W That's right. <u>Either</u> <u>one</u> looks good, so you pick one.

M Let's buy the sweater with the <u>monkey</u> picture and the letter <u>M</u>.

W Sounds good.

남 Peter의 생일 선물로 여기 있는 스웨터 중에서 하나 고르자.

여 좋은 생각이다! 이건 어때? 글자 P가 있는데.

남 좋긴 한데, 아무 그림이 없어서 너무 단조로운 것 같아.

여 Peter가 원숭이를 좋아하잖아. 이것은 원숭이 그림이 있어서 피터가 좋아할지도 모르겠다.

남 귀엽네, 하지만 Peter는 개도 좋아해.

여 맞다. 둘 다 좋아 보이니까 네가 골라.

남 원숭이 그림이 있고 글자 M이 있는 이 스웨터로 사자.

여 좋아.

02

다음을 듣고, 남자가 하는 말의 내용으로 가장 적절한 것을 고르시오.

① 매장 위치 안내
② 매장 운영 시간
③ 할인 행사 안내
④ 할인 쿠폰 사용
⑤ 신규 회원 모집

Hello, and <u>welcome to</u> S-Mart. We have good news for <u>shoppers</u> today. We are having a big sale now. A <u>dozen</u> eggs are only $1.00, <u>strawberries</u> are only $2.50 a pound, and ramen is only $5.50 a box. <u>Don't miss</u> this chance. Thank you for shopping at S-Mart.

안녕하세요, S-Mart에 오신 것을 환영합니다. 오늘 쇼핑하시는 분들께 좋은 소식을 알려 드리겠습니다. 지금 저희는 특별 할인 행사를 하고 있습니다. 12개 들이 달걀이 단돈 1달러, 딸기는 1파운드당 단돈 2달러 50센트, 라면은 한 상자당 단돈 5달러 50센트입니다. 이번 기회를 놓치지 마세요. S-Mart를 이용해 주셔서 감사 합니다.

●●
pound (무게 단위) 파운드

03

다음을 듣고, 여자가 설명하는 운동으로 가장 적절한 것을 고르시오.

① soccer
② fishing
③ skating
④ swimming
⑤ water-skiing

My father helped me by holding my hands as I <u>kicked</u> <u>in</u> <u>the</u> <u>water</u>. Sometimes he would <u>let</u> <u>go</u> <u>of</u> me. Then, I would get scared and <u>grab</u> <u>on</u> to him. But he just kept saying that I could <u>float</u> if I'd kick my feet and move my arms. One day, I just did it. I was moving around the pool <u>all</u> <u>by</u> <u>myself</u>, and my father was very <u>proud</u> of me.

우리 아버지는 내가 물장구를 칠 때 내 손을 잡아서 나를 도와주셨다. 가끔씩 그는 나를 손에서 놓기도 했다. 그러면 나는 겁이 나서 그를 꼭 붙잡았다. 하지만 그는 내가 발을 차면서 팔을 움직이면 뜰 수 있다고 계속 말씀하셨다. 어느 날 나는 해냈다. 나는 혼자 힘으로 수영장 주위를 헤엄쳤고 아빠는 나를 매우 자랑스러워 하셨다.

●●
kick (발로) 차다 **let go of** ~을 놓다 **grab** 붙잡다 **float** 뜨다

04 대화를 듣고, 두 사람의 관계로 가장 적절한 것을 고르시오.

① 교사 - 학생
② 승무원 - 탑승객
③ 은행 직원 - 고객
④ 매표소 직원 - 손님
⑤ 컴퓨터 수리 기사 - 고객

W Excuse me. Could you please tell me how to use this machine?

M Well, first put your card in the slot. Then, enter your secret number. Okay?

W Okay. First I put my card in the slot. Next I enter my secret number. Then what?

M Next, push "withdrawal" and the amount of money you want. Take your card out. Then, get your money.

W I see. That doesn't sound very hard. I think I've got it.

여 실례합니다. 이 기계를 어떻게 사용하는지 말씀해 주실 수 있나요?

남 음, 먼저 투입구에 카드를 집어넣으세요. 그런 다음 비밀 번호를 누르세요. 아시겠어요?

여 네. 먼저 투입구에 카드를 넣고요. 그 다음 비밀 번호를 눌러요. 그 다음은요?

남 그런 다음 "인출"을 누르고 원하시는 금액을 누르세요. 카드를 빼세요. 그리고 돈을 가져가세요.

여 알겠습니다. 아주 어려운 것 같지는 않네요. 할 수 있을 것 같아요.

● ●
slot (가느다란) 구멍, 투입구 **withdrawal** 인출

---

05 대화를 듣고, 여자가 방문한 나라로 언급하지 않은 곳을 고르시오.

① 영국
② 프랑스
③ 스페인
④ 독일
⑤ 이탈리아

M So you're back from abroad. How was it?

W It was a lot of fun. I'd never been to Europe before. It was my first time there.

M I've been there about three times. I never get tired of going there. Where did you go in particular?

W I went to France, Spain, and Germany. I had a really great time.

M You didn't go to Italy?

W Oh, yes, I did. I took a lot of photos there, too.

남 너 해외에서 돌아왔구나. 어땠어?

여 정말 재미있었어. 전에 유럽을 가 본 적이 한 번도 없었거든. 이번이 처음이었어.

남 난 세 번쯤 다녀왔어. 난 그곳에 가는 것이 절대 질리지 않아. 넌 특별히 어디를 갔었니?

여 프랑스, 스페인, 그리고 독일에 갔어. 정말 좋은 시간을 보냈지.

남 이탈리아는 안 갔어?

여 아, 갔었어. 거기서도 사진 많이 찍었어.

● ●
abroad 해외, 해외로 **in particular** 특히, 특별히

06 대화를 듣고, 사진 속에 있는 사람들이 모두 몇 명인지 고르시오.

① 4명
② 5명
③ 6명
④ 7명
⑤ 8명

M Hey, is this a picture of your family?
W Yes, it is. These are all my <u>family</u> <u>members</u>.
M It looks like you have a <u>big</u> <u>family</u>.
W Yes. Here are my mom, my dad, my two sisters, and one brother.
M It's a very nice picture. But <u>what</u> <u>about</u> <u>you</u>? You are not <u>in</u> <u>this</u> <u>picture</u>.
W I was in Tokyo studying Japanese when they <u>took</u> <u>this</u>.
M Did you feel sorry that you <u>missed</u> <u>the</u> <u>moment</u>?
W Yes, but it's okay. We are going to take <u>another</u> <u>family</u> <u>picture</u> this year.

남 이봐, 이것이 너희 가족 사진이니?
여 응. 모두 우리 가족들이야.
남 가족이 많은 것 같다.
여 응. 여기 우리 엄마, 아빠, 두 여동생, 그리고 남동생이야.
남 사진 정말 잘 나왔다. 그런데, 너는 어디 있니? 너는 이 사진 속에 없네.
여 식구들이 이 사진을 찍을 때 나는 일본어 공부하느라 도쿄에 있었어.
남 그 순간을 놓쳐서 아쉬웠니?
여 응, 그렇지만 괜찮아. 올해 가족 사진을 또 찍기로 했거든

●●
moment 순간

---

07 대화를 듣고, 여자의 심정으로 가장 적절한 것을 고르시오.

① angry
② proud
③ thankful
④ disappointed
⑤ embarrassed

M Susan, please answer question four.
W I'm sorry, but I <u>didn't</u> <u>do</u> question four.
M Did you do any of the questions?
W I'm <u>ashamed</u> <u>to</u> <u>say</u> that I did not. I was so <u>tired</u> last night that I just <u>went</u> <u>to</u> <u>bed</u>.
M That's not a very <u>good</u> <u>excuse</u>.
W I'm sorry. I won't <u>do</u> <u>it</u> <u>again</u>.

남 Susan, 4번 문항에 대한 정답을 말해 보겠니.
여 죄송합니다만 4번을 안 풀었는데요.
남 다른 문제는 풀었니?
여 말씀드리기 부끄럽지만 안 했어요. 어젯밤에 너무 피곤해서 그냥 잤거든요.
남 그리 좋은 변명은 아니구나.
여 죄송합니다. 다시는 안 그럴게요.

●●
ashamed 부끄러운   **excuse** 변명

---

08 대화를 듣고, 남자의 마지막 말의 의도로 가장 적절한 것을 고르시오.

① 격려
② 조언
③ 부탁
④ 동의
⑤ 불평

M You <u>look</u> <u>lost</u>. May I help you?
W Yes, I've been <u>trying</u> <u>to</u> <u>find</u> the Grace Hotel for an hour.
M Well, you're going the <u>wrong</u> <u>way</u>. I think that the hotel is on Lenox Avenue.
W <u>How</u> <u>far</u> is it from here?
M Let me see. It's about four blocks <u>to</u> <u>the</u> <u>south</u>.
W How can I get there?
M Why don't you go there <u>by</u> <u>taxi</u>?

남 길을 잃은 것 같군요. 도와드릴까요?
여 네, Grace 호텔을 한 시간 동안 찾고 있었어요.
남 음, 길을 잘못 드신 것 같군요. 저는 그 호텔이 레녹스가에 있는 걸로 아는데요.
여 여기서 얼마나 먼가요?
남 어디 보자. 남쪽으로 네 블록 정도네요.
여 거기에는 어떻게 가죠?
남 택시를 타고 가시는 게 어때요?

09

대화를 듣고, 쓰레기를 저녁 6시 이후에 버려야 하는 이유로 가장 적절한 것을 고르시오.

① 행인들의 안전을 위해서
② 낮 동안 악취가 날 수 있어서
③ 차량 통행을 원활하게 하기 위해서
④ 청소 업체가 밤 사이에 운영을 해서
⑤ 도시가 지저분해 보이지 않게 하기 위해서

W Don't forget that the <u>garbage goes out</u> after six o'clock in the evening.
M Sure, thanks. <u>By the way</u>, why do we have to wait?
W That law was made to ensure the city <u>doesn't look dirty</u> during the day.
M Oh, that <u>makes sense</u>. I never thought about that before.
W There are reasons for rules, you know.
M I <u>realize that</u> now.

여 쓰레기는 저녁 6시 이후에 버려야 한다는 것 잊지마.
남 알았어, 고마워. 그런데, 왜 기다려야 하는 거지?
여 낮 동안에 도시가 지저분해 보이지 않도록 하기 위해서 그 법이 만들어진 거야.
남 오, 이해가 되네. 전혀 그렇게 생각하지 못했어.
여 너도 알다시피 규칙에는 이유가 있기 마련이잖아.
남 이제 알겠어.

●●
garbage 쓰레기 **ensure** 확실히 하다
make sense 이해가 되다

10

대화를 듣고, 여자가 전화를 건 목적으로 가장 적절한 것을 고르시오.

① 길을 물어보기 위해서
② 택시를 부르기 위해서
③ 화재를 신고하기 위해서
④ 구급차를 부르기 위해서
⑤ 납치 사건을 신고하기 위해서

M 911. Do you need the fire department, the police, or an ambulance?
W The police, I'm calling to <u>report a kidnapping</u>. Please! Hurry! There's a <u>girl screaming</u> in the street.
M Where are you? Give me the <u>address</u>.
W 135 Maple Avenue. I'm in front of KNG Bank.
M Can you see her?
W Yes. A man is pushing her into a car. She's trying to <u>get away from</u> him.
M An officer will be there soon. <u>Stay on the line</u>. Number 2, Number 2, go to 135 Maple Avenue <u>immediately</u>. Very <u>urgent</u>.

남 911입니다. 소방서, 경찰, 구급차가 필요하신가요?
여 경찰이요. 납치 사건을 신고하려고 전화했어요. 제발! 빨리요! 어떤 소녀가 거리에서 비명을 지르고 있어요.
남 어디에 계신가요? 주소를 알려 주세요.
여 Maple Avenue 135번지예요. 저는 KNG 은행 앞에 있어요.
남 그 소녀가 보이나요?
여 네. 한 남자가 그녀를 자동차 안으로 밀어 넣고 있어요. 그녀는 그에게서 도망치려 하고 있고요.
남 경찰이 곧 그곳에 도착할 겁니다. 끊지 말고 기다리세요. 상황 둘, 상황 둘, Maple Avenue 135번지로 즉각 출동하라. 긴급 상황.

●●
fire department 소방서 **ambulance** 구급차 **report** 알리다, 신고하다 **kidnapping** 납치 **urgent** 긴급한

11

대화를 듣고, 남자가 여자에게 부탁한 일로 가장 적절한 것을 고르시오.

① 편지 쓰기
② 편지 보내기
③ 우편물 찾기
④ 숙제 도와주기
⑤ 우체국까지 태워주기

M Karen, are you <u>on your way</u> to work?
W Yes, I am. Why?
M Would you <u>take this letter</u> to the post office on your way to work?
W Sure.
M It's just that I'm <u>in a hurry</u>, and the letter <u>must be mailed</u> right away.
W It's no problem at all. Just <u>return the favor</u> when I need one.

남 Karen, 출근하는 중이니?
여 응. 왜?
남 출근하는 길에 이 편지를 우체국에 가서 부쳐 줄 수 있니?
여 물론이지.
남 내가 급해서 그러는데 이 편지를 지금 바로 우편으로 부쳐야 하거든.
여 전혀 문제 없어. 내가 필요할 때 보답해 주면 돼.

●●
return the favor 보답을 하다

78

12 대화를 듣고, 두 사람이 대화 직후에 할 일로 가장 적절한 것을 고르시오.

① 상점에 가기
② 병원 예약하기
③ 따뜻한 차 마시기
④ 상점 폐점 시간 문의하기
⑤ 인터넷으로 가습기 주문하기

M Why are you coughing so much?

W It's the winter weather. It's very dry here.

M Why don't we buy a humidifier? That would solve the problem.

W I know. I've just been too busy to go to the store.

M Well, let's go now. We still have an hour before it closes.

W Okay, that sounds like a good idea.

남 왜 그렇게 기침을 많이 하니?

여 겨울 날씨잖아. 여긴 무척 건조해.

남 가습기를 사는 건 어때? 도움이 될 거야.

여 알아. 너무 바빠서 가게에 갈 수 없었을 뿐이야.

남 그럼, 지금 같이 가자. 가게 문 닫기 전까지 아직 한 시간 정도 남았어.

여 그래, 좋은 생각인 것 같다.

•• cough 기침하다 humidifier 가습기

---

13 대화를 듣고, 대화 내용과 일치하지 않는 것을 고르시오.

① 남자는 여가 시간에 개를 산책시킨다.
② 남자는 여가 시간에 TV를 본다.
③ 남자는 쇼핑하는 것을 싫어한다.
④ 남자는 현재 이혼한 상태이다.
⑤ 남자는 현재의 삶에 만족한다.

W Can I ask you some questions about your life?

M Sure. Go ahead.

W What do you like to do in your free time?

M Well, I usually walk my dog, watch TV, and read magazines.

W Okay. Now, what do you hate to do the most?

M That's difficult. Hmm, I hate to go shopping with my wife. It's too boring.

W Are you married? Oh, I thought you were single. Then is there anything that you want to change in your life?

M I'm satisfied with my life. I love my life.

여 당신의 생활에 대해 몇 가지 질문해도 될까요?

남 물론이죠. 그러세요.

여 여가 시간에는 무얼 하는 것을 좋아하세요?

남 글쎄요, 전 주로 개를 산책 시키고 TV를 보고 잡지를 읽어요.

여 좋아요. 이제 가장 싫어하는 일은 무엇인가요?

남 그건 어렵군요. 흠, 저는 아내와 쇼핑하는 것을 싫어해요. 너무 지루하거든요.

여 결혼하셨나요? 오, 전 미혼이신 줄 알았어요. 그럼 당신의 삶에서 바꾸고 싶은 것이 있나요?

남 전 제 삶에 만족해요. 제 삶을 사랑한답니다.

•• married 결혼을 한, 기혼의 single 독신인, 혼자인

---

14 대화를 듣고, 남자의 마지막 말에 이어질 여자의 말로 가장 적절한 것을 고르시오.

① I'm glad you had a good time.
② You should know how to swim.
③ I hope you have a nice vacation.
④ It must be dangerous to go surfing.
⑤ Don't worry about it. You will be fine.

W Did you make plans for this vacation?

M Yes, I'm going to Hawaii with my family. I'm going to go surfing and scuba diving there.

W Have you ever been to Hawaii?

M No, this will be my first time, so I'm looking forward to it.

W I hope you have a nice vacation.

여 이번 휴가 때 계획 있니?

남 응, 난 가족들과 하와이에 가려고 해. 거기에서 서핑과 스쿠버다이빙을 하러 갈 거야.

여 하와이에 가 본 있니?

남 아니, 이번이 처음이라 이번 여행이 몹시 기대 돼.

여 멋진 휴가가 되길 바라.

① 즐거운 시간을 가졌다니 다행이야.
② 너는 수영하는 법을 알아야 해.
④ 서핑을 하러 가는 것은 위험해.
⑤ 그건 걱정 마. 괜찮을 거야.

•• surfing 서핑, 파도타기 scuba diving 스쿠버 다이빙

15 대화를 듣고, 여자의 마지막 말에 이어질 남자의 말로 가장 적절한 것을 고르시오.

① I'm sorry to hear that.

② I want to be a professor.

③ We're going to miss you so much.

④ That's great news. Congratulations!

⑤ Long time, no see. How have you been?

W It's nice of you to <u>see me off</u>.

M Not at all. I certainly hope you had a nice time <u>during your stay</u> in Seoul.

W I did <u>indeed</u>. You and your family were so kind to me. I <u>appreciate it</u> very much.

M We hope you'll be able to come back to Seoul for a <u>longer stay</u>.

W Of course I will.

M Are you going to <u>teach English</u> again when you come back?

W Yes, I <u>was offered</u> an English teaching position at a university.

M That's great news. Congratulations!

여 배웅해 주셔서 고맙습니다.

남 별말씀을요. 서울에 계시는 동안 즐거운 시간 되셨기를 바래요.

여 정말로 그랬어요. 당신과 당신 가족들은 저에게 너무 친절하셨어요. 정말 고맙습니다.

남 우리는 당신이 서울로 돌아와서 더 오래 머물 수 있기를 바래요.

여 물론 그럴 거예요.

남 돌아 오셔서도 영어를 가르치실 건가요?

여 네, 대학에서 영어 교수직을 제안 받았거든요.

남 아주 좋은 소식이네요. 축하해요!

① 그것 참 안됐네요.

② 저는 교수가 되고 싶어요.

③ 우리는 당신이 아주 많이 그리울 거예요.

④ 아주 좋은 소식이네요. 축하해요!

⑤ 오랜만이네요. 어떻게 지내셨어요?

● ●

see off 배웅하다 **indeed** 정말로, 실제로 **offer** 제안하다

◗ REVIEW TEST p. 111

A
① married, 결혼을 한, 기혼의 ② kick, (발로) 차다 ③ float, 뜨다 ④ withdrawal, 인출

⑤ abroad, 해외, 해외로 ⑥ ashamed, 부끄러운 ⑦ garbage, 쓰레기 ⑧ kidnapping, 납치

⑨ urgent, 긴급한 ⑩ cough, 기침하다 ⑪ humidifier, 가습기 ⑫ see off, 배웅하다

B
① how to use ② three times ③ get tired of

④ in particular ⑤ wrong way ⑥ makes sense

⑦ on your way ⑧ return the favor

	문제 및 정답	받아쓰기 및 녹음내용	해석

01 대화를 듣고, 여자가 설명하는 동작으로 가장 적절한 것을 고르시오.

①  ②

③ ④

⑤

M I'm so <u>tired</u> and <u>sleepy</u>.

W Why don't you try exercising and stretching?

M Okay. Can you show me <u>how</u> to <u>do</u> it?

W Sure. First, <u>put</u> your <u>feet</u> <u>apart</u>. And put your hands on the back of your head. Now, <u>twist</u> your <u>body</u> from side to side.

M That sounds easy. I can do that.

남 나 너무 피곤하고 졸려.

여 운동하고 스트레칭을 해 보는 게 어때?

남 좋아. 어떻게 하는 건지 나에게 보여 줄 수 있어?

여 물론이지. 먼저 양발을 벌려. 그리고 양손을 머리 뒤로 대. 이제 좌우로 몸을 틀어 봐.

남 쉽네. 나도 할 수 있겠다.

●●
put one's feet apart 양발을 벌리다 twist 비틀다 from side to side 좌우로

02 대화를 듣고, Jane이 누구인지 고르시오.

W It's a great day to be out <u>at the</u> <u>beach</u>.

M Yeah, but I don't know if we can find a <u>place</u> to <u>sit</u> out here. Look at all these people.

W Well, look at that girl <u>over</u> <u>there</u>. Is that Jane?

M There are so many. <u>Which</u> <u>one</u>?

W The girl <u>with</u> <u>sunglasses</u> who's sitting under the parasol.

M There are <u>a</u> <u>few</u> like <u>that</u>.

W She is wearing a <u>floral</u> <u>swimsuit</u> and drinking juice.

M Oh, I see her. Let's go and <u>say</u> <u>hi</u>.

여 해변에 가기에 너무 좋은 날이다.

남 응, 근데 우리가 여기서 앉을 곳을 찾을 수 있을지 모르겠다. 이 사람들 좀 봐.

여 근데, 저쪽에 있는 여자아이를 봐. Jane 이니?

남 너무 많은데. 누구?

여 선글라스를 끼고 파라솔 밑에 앉아 있는 여자아이 말이야.

남 그런 사람 몇 명 있는데.

여 그녀는 꽃무늬 수영복을 입고 주스를 마시고 있어.

남 아, 보인다. 가서 인사하자.

●●
parasol 파라솔 floral 꽃무늬의 swimsuit 수영복

03 대화를 듣고, 두 사람이 대화하는 장소로 가장 적절한 곳을 고르시오.

① 학교
② 마트
③ 문구점
④ 체육관
⑤ 콘서트홀

M Excuse me. Where can I get <u>pans</u>?

W Did you say <u>pens</u>? They are <u>in</u> <u>aisle</u> 5.

M No, I said, pans. Frying pans.

W Oh, pans! <u>In</u> that <u>case</u>, you should go to aisle 7.

M Thank you.

W You're welcome. I'm happy to help you, sir. <u>Enjoy</u> your <u>shopping</u>.

남 실례합니다. 팬을 어디서 구할 수 있나요?

여 펜이라고 하셨나요? 5번 통로에 있어요.

남 아니요, 제가 말한 것은 팬이에요, 프라이 팬이요.

여 아, 팬이요! 그렇다면 7번 통로로 가세요.

남 고맙습니다.

여 천만에요. 손님을 도와드릴 수 있어서 좋네요. 즐거운 쇼핑 되세요.

●●
aisle 통로

04	대화를 듣고, 두 사람의 관계로 가장 적절한 것을 고르시오.	M Welcome aboard. Can you show me your boarding pass, please?	여 탑승하신 것을 환영합니다. 탑승권 좀 보여 주시겠습니까?

04 대화를 듣고, 두 사람의 관계로 가장 적절한 것을 고르시오.

① 웨이터 – 손님
② 경찰관 – 시민
③ 승무원 – 탑승객
④ 매표소 직원 – 손님
⑤ 관광 가이드 – 여행객

M Welcome aboard. Can you show me your boarding pass, please?

W Here it is. Where is my seat?

M 12G is on the left side.

W Thank you. Oh, I would like an extra blanket.

M Certainly, ma'am. I'll be right back. Just be seated and relax.

여 탑승하신 것을 환영합니다. 탑승권 좀 보여 주시겠습니까?

남 여기요. 좌석이 어디지요?

여 12G는 왼편에 있습니다.

남 고맙습니다. 아, 여분의 담요가 있었으면 좋겠네요.

여 알겠습니다, 손님. 곧 가져다 드리죠. 앉아서 쉬고 계세요.

●●
aboard 탑승한, 승선한   boarding pass 탑승권   blanket 담요   be seated 앉다

---

05 다음을 듣고, 남자가 소개하는 물건으로 가장 적절한 것을 고르시오.

①   ②

③   ④

⑤

Today, I'm going to introduce to you our new product. It is much stronger than the one you've been using. It can clean everywhere, even in those hard-to-reach corners. And it has a cord twice as long as the old models. During this promotional period, we will give everyone who purchases this item a belt set as a token of our appreciation.

오늘 저는 여러분께 저희 회사 신제품을 소개해드리겠습니다. 이것은 여러분이 사용해오신 것보다 훨씬 더 강력합니다. 이것은 어디든지 청소할 수 있으며, 심지어 닿기 힘든 구석까지 청소하죠. 그리고 구형 모델보다 선의 길이가 두 배나 더 길답니다. 이번 홍보 기간 동안 이 제품을 구입하시는 모든 분에게는 감사의 표시로 벨트 세트를 드리도록 하겠습니다.

●●
promotional 홍보의, 판촉의   period 기간   purchase 구입하다   as a token of one's appreciation 감사의 표시로

---

06 대화를 듣고, 여자가 받을 한달 용돈으로 가장 적절한 것을 고르시오.

① $40
② $44
③ $48
④ $80
⑤ $88

M You seem to be in a good mood today.

W Well, you would be too if your parents raised your allowance.

M Good for you! How much did you receive before?

W I was receiving 40 dollars a month. Now I got a 20% increase.

M Congratulations! I guess that means you're paying for lunch.

W I guess so.

남 너 오늘 기분 좋은 것 같다.

여 너도 부모님이 용돈을 올려 주시면 기분이 좋을 거야.

남 잘됐다! 전에는 얼마를 받았었니?

여 한 달에 40달러씩 받았었어. 지금은 20% 늘었어.

남 축하해! 점심은 네가 사야겠네.

여 그러게.

●●
in a good mood 기분이 좋은   allowance 용돈   receive 받다

---

07 대화를 듣고, 여자의 심정으로 가장 적절한 것을 고르시오.

① angry
② happy
③ proud
④ nervous
⑤ surprised

W Mark, can I talk to you for a minute, please?

M Yes, Mom. What is it?

W I asked you to clean up the living room, and you didn't do it. Why?

M I forgot. I'll do it now.

W Cleaning up from time to time is not a big thing to ask.

M I know, Mom.

여 Mark, 잠깐 얘기 좀 할 수 있니?

남 네, 엄마. 뭔데요?

여 내가 너에게 거실을 치우라고 부탁했었는데 안 했더구나. 왜지?

남 잊어버렸어요. 지금 할게요.

여 가끔 치우라는 것이 무리한 요구는 아니잖니.

남 알겠어요, 엄마.

●●
from time to time 가끔

08 다음을 듣고, 두 사람의 대화가 <u>어색한</u> 것을 고르시오.

① ② ③ ④ ⑤

① M Can you <u>do me a favor</u>?
   W Maybe. What is it?
② W What are you <u>planning to</u> <u>study</u> at university?
   M I don't know yet. There are so many choices.
③ M I'll have some ice cream, please.
   W Okay. I want <u>two plates of</u> spaghetti with cheese.
④ W It's really <u>nice of you</u> to help me.
   M Oh, it's my pleasure.
⑤ M <u>How many states</u> are there in the USA?
   W Well, let's see. There are fifty.

① 남 부탁 좀 들어줄 수 있니?
   여 아마도. 뭔데?
② 여 대학에서 뭘 공부할 계획이야?
   남 아직 모르겠어. 선택할 수 있는 게 너무 많아.
③ 남 아이스크림 주세요.
   여 알겠어요. 저는 치즈가 들어간 스파게티 두 접시를 원합니다.
④ 여 날 도와줘서 정말 고마워.
   남 오, 천만에.
⑤ 남 미국에 주가 몇 개지?
   여 글쎄, 어디 보자. 50개 있네.

plate 접시 **state** (미국) 주(州)

---

09 대화를 듣고, 여자가 집에 있고 싶은 이유로 가장 적절한 것을 고르시오.

① 감기에 걸려서
② 휴식이 필요해서
③ 집에서 해야 할 일이 있어서
④ 가족과 시간을 보내기 위해서
⑤ 보고 싶은 TV 프로그램이 있어서

W I want to <u>do something</u> tonight. I don't know what to do.
M Do you want to <u>go shopping</u>?
W No. I just want to stay home.
M <u>How about</u> watching Netflix?
W Yeah, that sounds all right. I don't want to <u>think</u> tonight. I just want to <u>relax</u>.
M I know. You've been <u>working very hard</u> lately. You need a <u>break</u>.

여 오늘 밤에 뭔가를 하고 싶긴 한데. 뭘 해야 할지 모르겠어.
남 쇼핑 갈까?
여 싫어. 그냥 집에 있고 싶어.
남 넷플릭스 보는 것은 어때?
여 그래, 괜찮을 것 같다. 오늘 밤은 아무 것도 생각하고 싶지 않아. 그냥 쉬고 싶어.
남 나도 알아. 최근에 네가 너무 열심히 일했잖아. 너에게는 휴식이 필요해.

lately 최근에, 요즈음

---

10 대화를 듣고, 남자가 전화를 건 목적으로 가장 적절한 것을 고르시오.

① 안부를 묻기 위해서
② 병문안을 가기 위해서
③ 숙제를 물어보기 위해서
④ 데이트를 신청하기 위해서
⑤ 약속 시간을 변경하기 위해서

M Hello. May I <u>speak to</u> Kelly?
W This is Kelly <u>speaking</u>.
M Oh, hi! This is Kobe. How are you doing? I <u>haven't talked to you</u> in a long time.
W Kobe! I'm great. Thank you. How are you <u>getting along</u>?
M I'm the same <u>as usual</u>. How is your sister Jane doing?
W She's doing fine, too. She <u>goes to university</u> now.
M Say hello to her for me.
W Okay, I will.

남 여보세요, Kelly와 통화할 수 있을까요?
여 제가 Kelly인데요.
남 아, 안녕! 나 Kobe야. 어떻게 지내니? 너랑 이야기한지 정말 오래 됐다.
여 Kobe! 나는 잘 지내. 고마워. 너는 어떻게 지내고 있니?
남 늘 똑같아. 네 여동생 Jane은 어떻게 지내니?
여 잘 지내. 지금 대학에 다녀.
남 나 대신 안부 전해 줘.
여 그래, 그럴게.

get along 지내다

11

대화를 듣고, 남자가 출근하는 방법으로 가장 적절한 것을 고르시오.

① 택시
② 버스
③ 도보
④ 지하철
⑤ 자전거

W Sam said you come to work on foot. Is that true?

M Yes, it is. It takes about 50 minutes to get to work on foot.

W Why do you choose such a hard way to get to work?

M It's a perfect time to exercise. Walking is very healthy.

W That takes a lot of commitment. What about on rainy days?

M Even on rainy days.

W You must be determined to do it every day.

여 Sam이 넌 걸어서 출근한다고 하더라. 그게 사실이야?

남 응. 걸어서 회사까지 가는데 50분 정도 걸려.

여 왜 그렇게 힘들게 출근하는 방법을 택한 거야?

남 운동하기에 완벽한 시간이잖아. 걷는 건강에 매우 좋고.

여 그런 엄청난 노력이 필요하잖아. 비 오는 날에는 어때?

남 비 오는 날에도 걷지.

여 매일 그렇게 하다니 넌 정말 단호하구나.

●●
commitment 헌신 **determined** 단호한, 굳게 결심한

12

대화를 듣고, 두 사람이 대화 직후에 할 일로 가장 적절한 것을 고르시오.

① 차 수리하기
② 차 열쇠 복사하기
③ 운전면허 시험 보기
④ 시내에서 시험 운전하기
⑤ 고속도로에서 시험 운전하기

W That was a nice ride. When did you get your new car?

M Last week. Would you like to take it for a drive?

W Really? Are you sure?

M Yes. You're a pretty good driver. Go ahead. Take the keys.

W Thanks. Can we go right now?

M Yes, let's drive through the city.

W I think there's heavy traffic at this hour, so I'd rather drive on the highway.

M Okay, let's drive on the highway then.

여 승차감 좋다, 이 새 차 언제 구입했니?

남 지난주에. 한 번 운전해 볼래?

여 정말? 진짜로?

남 응. 넌 운전을 아주 잘 하잖아. 어서 해봐. 열쇠 받아.

여 고마워. 지금 가 볼까?

남 응, 시내를 운전해 보자.

여 이 시간에는 교통이 혼잡할 테니까 고속도로로 운전하는 것이 낫겠어.

남 그래, 그럼 고속도로에서 운전해 보자.

●●
ride 타기, 타는 기분

13

대화를 듣고, 대화 내용과 일치하지 <u>않는</u> 것을 고르시오.

① 남자는 계단에서 넘어졌다.
② 남자는 발목을 삐었다고 생각한다.
③ 남자는 혼자 걸을 수 없다.
④ 남자는 구급차를 기다리고 있다.
⑤ 남자는 응급실에 가려고 한다.

W Is something wrong?

M I fell down the stairs.

W Are you okay?

M No. I hurt my foot, and I can't walk by myself. I think I sprained my ankle.

W Do you want me to call an ambulance?

M If you could get a taxi, I think I can go to the emergency room.

W Okay. I'll get a cab.

M Thank you. Please hurry up.

여 어디가 잘못됐나요?

남 계단에서 넘어졌어요.

여 괜찮나요?

남 아니요. 발을 다쳐서 혼자서는 걸을 수가 없네요. 발목을 삔 것 같아요.

여 구급차를 불러 드릴까요?

남 택시를 잡아 주시면 응급실로 갈 수 있을 것 같아요.

여 좋아요. 제가 택시를 잡죠.

남 고마워요. 서둘러 주세요.

●●
sprain 삐다 **ankle** 발목
emergency room 응급실

14 대화를 듣고, 남자의 마지막 말에 이어질 여자의 말로 가장 적절한 것을 고르시오.

① Just be patient. You'll pass.
② Fencing is my favorite sport, too.
③ I'm sorry. I didn't mean to upset you.
④ Good for you! I knew you could do it.
⑤ Don't give up. We can do this together.

W Hi, Paul! How have you been?
M Great! It's been a long time since I last saw you.
W I know. I've been busy. How are your fencing lessons going?
M I tried to get into the second level, but I have failed twice already.
W How long have you taken lessons for?
M Almost three months now. The students I started with are in the third level now. I don't know what's wrong.
W Just be patient. You'll pass.

여 안녕, Paul! 어떻게 지냈니?
남 잘 지냈어! 지난 번에 본 이후로 오래간만이네.
여 맞아. 그 동안 바빴어. 펜싱 강습은 어떻게 되어 가니?
남 2단계로 갈려고 노력했지만 벌써 두 번이나 떨어졌어.
여 수업을 얼마 동안 받았는데?
남 지금 거의 3개월째야. 같이 시작했던 학생들은 지금 3단계야. 뭐가 잘못됐는지 모르겠어.
여 인내심을 가져. 넌 통과할 거야.
② 펜싱은 내가 가장 좋아하는 운동이야.
③ 미안해. 너를 화나게 하려던 건 아니었어.
④ 잘됐다! 네가 해낼 줄 알았어.
⑤ 포기하지마. 우리 같이 하면 돼.

fencing 펜싱 **patient** 인내하는

15 대화를 듣고, 여자의 마지막 말에 이어질 남자의 말로 가장 적절한 것을 고르시오.

① That sounds perfect!
② That's very disappointing.
③ Then I will be back tomorrow.
④ I won't be able to make your party.
⑤ Thanks for inviting me to your party.

W Hello. Momo Restaurant.
M I'd like to make a reservation for this Saturday afternoon.
W All right. What time would you like to come?
M Can I come at five thirty?
W Five thirty. How many people are there in your party?
M There are fifteen of us.
W Fifteen! I'm sorry, but we can't take such a large party.
M That's very disappointing.

여 안녕하세요. Momo 식당 입니다.
남 이번 주 토요일 오후로 예약하고 싶습니다.
여 좋습니다. 몇 시에 오실 건가요?
남 5시 30분에 갈 수 있을까요?
여 5시 30분이요. 일행이 몇 분이시죠?
남 열 다섯 명이요.
여 열 다섯 분이요? 죄송합니다만 저희는 그렇게 많은 인원은 안 됩니다.
남 정말 아쉽군요.
① 그거 좋겠군요!
③ 그럼 내일 다시 올게요.
④ 파티에 가지 못할 것 같아요.
⑤ 파티에 초대해줘서 고마워요.

party 일행 **disappointing** 실망스러운

REVIEW TEST p. 119

A
① twist, 비틀다 ② parasol, 파라솔 ③ floral, 꽃무늬의 ④ swimsuit, 수영복
⑤ aisle, 통로 ⑥ aboard, 탑승한, 승선한 ⑦ allowance, 용돈 ⑧ receive, 받다
⑨ lately, 최근에, 요즈음 ⑩ commitment, 헌신 ⑪ sprain, 삐다 ⑫ ankle, 발목

B
① put, apart ② boarding pass ③ token, appreciation
④ what to do ⑤ must be determined ⑥ a long time
⑦ make a reservation ⑧ How many, party

문제 및 정답	받아쓰기 및 녹음내용	해석

01

대화를 듣고, 오늘의 날씨로 가장 적절한 것을 고르시오.

①   ②

③   ④

⑤

M I'm so <u>excited about</u> going on the camping trip tomorrow.

W You should <u>take an umbrella</u>.

M Why? It's a beautiful sunny day.

W I know. But the <u>weather forecast</u> said it's going to rain tomorrow morning.

M That's terrible. I've been <u>looking forward to</u> this camping trip.

W Don't <u>be disappointed</u>. Fortunately, it will stop raining in the afternoon.

M That's a <u>relief</u>.

남 내일 캠핑 여행을 가게 되어서 너무 신나.

여 우산을 가져가야 할거야.

남 왜? 아름답고 화창한 날이잖아.

여 알아. 하지만 일기예보에서 내일 아침에 비가 온다고 했어.

남 너무 싫다. 난 이번 캠핑 여행을 몹시 기다려왔어.

여 실망하지 마. 다행히 오후에는 비가 그칠 거야.

남 다행이네.

●●
relief 안도, 안심

02

대화를 듣고, 여자가 가려고 하는 장소를 고르시오.

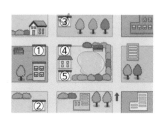

W Excuse me. <u>Do you attend</u> this school?

M Yes, I do.

W I'm <u>new here</u>. I'm looking for the student center.

M I'll show you <u>where it is</u>. Look at this campus map here.

W Okay.

M We're here. Go straight one block and turn left <u>at the corner</u>.

W And then?

M <u>Keep going</u> one block and turn right. <u>At the end of</u> the block, you'll see the student center on your right.

W Thank you very much. I think I can easily find it now.

M Welcome to the school. <u>See you around</u>.

여 실례합니다. 이 학교 다니세요?

남 네.

여 저는 신입생인데요. 학생회관을 찾고 있어요.

남 제가 어디에 있는지 알려 드릴게요. 여기 있는 캠퍼스 지도를 보세요.

여 네.

남 우리가 있는 곳이에요. 한 블록을 곧장 가서 길모퉁이에서 왼쪽으로 도세요.

여 그리고요?

남 한 블록 계속 가서 왼쪽으로 도세요. 그 블록 맨 끝 오른편에 학생회관이 보일 거예요.

여 정말 고맙습니다. 이제 쉽게 찾을 수 있을 것 같아요.

남 입학을 축하해요. 나중에 또 봐요.

03 대화를 듣고, 두 사람이 대화하는 장소로 가장 적절한 곳을 고르시오.

① 병원
② 학교
③ 체육관
④ 수영장
⑤ 스키장

M Maria, are you doing okay?
W I'm getting better. Do you know what just happened?
M What? Did you get hurt?
W I made it all the way down the slope without falling over even once.
M Really? That's pretty good for a novice. However, you need to be concerned about your form.
W All right. Would you please check my form while I am boarding?
M Okay. I'll check your form this time.

남 Maria, 잘 하고 있니?
여 나아지고 있어. 방금 무슨 일이 있었는지 알아?
남 무슨 일인데? 다쳤니?
여 내가 슬로프에서 한 번도 넘어지지 않고 끝까지 내려왔단 말이야.
남 정말이야? 초보자 치고는 제법인데. 하지만 자세에 신경을 써야 할 것 같아.
여 좋아. 내가 보드를 타는 동안 내 자세 좀 봐 줄래?
남 알겠어. 이번에는 내가 자세를 봐 줄게.

•• slope 경사지, (스키장) 슬로프 novice 초보자
be concerned about ~에 대해 걱정하대[신경 쓰다]

---

04 대화를 듣고, 남자의 직업으로 가장 적절한 것을 고르시오.

① waiter
② engineer
③ car dealer
④ hairdresser
⑤ car repairman

M How can I help you?
W Well, I'm looking for something affordable and compact.
M Perhaps I can interest you in our latest new model.
W Hmm... It looks compact, but it doesn't look very affordable.
M Don't worry. We have a special promotion right now. If you make a deal with us today, all the options are free of charge.
W All the options? That sounds like a pretty good offer.
M How about going for a test drive?
W Sure.

남 무엇을 도와드릴까요?
여 글쎄요, 적당한 가격의 소형차를 찾고 있습니다.
남 아마도 저희 최신 신모델에 관심이 있으실 것 같은데요.
여 음… 소형 같지만 가격이 적당해 보이지는 않네요.
남 걱정 마세요. 지금 특별 프로모션 중이거든요. 오늘 저희와 거래하시게 되면 모든 선택 사항들이 무료입니다.
여 모든 선택 사항이요? 아주 좋은 제안 같은데요.
남 시험 운전을 해 보시는 게 어떠세요?
여 좋아요.

•• affordable 가격이 적당한 latest 최근의, 최신의 free of charge 무료로 dealer 상인, 판매인

---

05 대화를 듣고, 여자가 설명하는 범인이 누구인지 고르시오.

①   ②

③   ④

⑤

M Out of those five men, which one do you think is the robber?
W Well... I think it's the man with the beard in the middle.
M Are you sure?
W Not really. Umm... It's him! The one with the mustache and the beard.
M Do you mean the man wearing glasses?
W No, the one on the other side. He's got his hair in a ponytail.

남 저 다섯 남자 중, 누가 강도라고 생각하시나요?
여 글쎄요… 저는 중간에 턱수염이 있는 남자라고 생각합니다.
남 확실하세요?
여 아니요. 음… 저 사람이에요! 콧수염과 턱수염이 있는 사람이요.
남 안경을 쓴 남자 말입니까?
여 아니요, 다른 편에 있는 사람이요. 그는 머리를 하나로 묶고 있어요.

•• robber 강도 beard 턱수염 mustache 콧수염 ponytail 포니테일, 말총머리

06 대화를 듣고, 여자가 지불해야 할 금액으로 가장 적절한 것을 고르시오.

① 2,000원
② 4,000원
③ 14,000원
④ 16,000원
⑤ 18,000원

W I would like to <u>send</u> <u>these</u> <u>letters</u> to the U.S., please.
M Are you sending them by <u>airmail</u> or <u>express</u> <u>mail</u>?
W <u>That</u> <u>depends</u>. How much is each?
M If you send them by airmail, they will cost <u>2,000</u> won each. Express mail will cost <u>14,000</u> won each.
W I have two letters here, and the <u>recipients</u> are different. I need this one to <u>arrive</u> <u>soon</u>, so I'll send it express.
M What about <u>the</u> <u>other</u> <u>one</u>?
W Just airmail will be fine.

여 이 편지들을 미국으로 보내고 싶어요.
남 항공 우편과 특급 우편 중 어느 것으로 보내실 건가요?
여 요금에 따라서요. 각각 얼마죠?
남 항공 우편으로 보내면 개당 2,000원입니다. 특급 우편은 개당 14,000원이고요.
여 여기 편지 두 통이 있는데 수신인이 달라요. 하나는 빨리 도착해야 하니까 특급 우편으로 보낼게요.
남 다른 하나는요?
여 항공 우편이면 돼요.

●●
airmail 항공 우편 **express mail** 특급 우편
recipient 수신인

---

07 대화를 듣고, 남자의 심정으로 가장 적절한 것을 고르시오.

① proud
② lonely
③ envious
④ regretful
⑤ ashamed

M I've finally <u>graduated</u> <u>from</u> <u>university</u>.
W Wow, congratulations! How do you feel?
M I feel a strong <u>sense</u> <u>of</u> <u>accomplishment</u>.
W Good for you. You <u>deserve</u> <u>it</u>. After all, you worked hard.
M I did, didn't I?
W A chapter of your life <u>has</u> <u>closed</u>, and a new one will <u>open</u>.

남 마침내 대학을 졸업했어.
여 와, 축하해! 기분이 어떠니?
남 강한 성취감이 들어.
여 잘됐다. 너는 그럴만한 자격이 있어. 어쨌든 열심히 노력했잖아.
남 난 정말 노력했어, 그렇지 않니?
여 네 인생의 한 장이 끝나고 새로운 장이 시작 되겠구나.

●●
graduate 졸업하다 **accomplishment** 성취 **deserve** ~할 가치가[자격이] 있다
after all 결국에는, 어쨌든 **chapter** 장, (인생의) 한 시기 **envious** 부러워하는
regretful 후회하는

---

08 대화를 듣고, 여자의 마지막 말의 의도로 가장 적절한 것을 고르시오.

① 걱정
② 비난
③ 후회
④ 조언
⑤ 격려

W Did you read today's <u>news</u> <u>article</u>?
M No, what happened?
W A doctor who was performing an operation <u>left</u> <u>something</u> inside a patient.
M That's <u>horrible</u>. What did he <u>leave</u> <u>inside</u>?
W He left some gauze inside.
M I can't believe it. The doctor <u>should</u> <u>have</u> <u>been</u> <u>more</u> <u>careful</u>.
W I hope the patient is all right now.

여 오늘 신문 기사 봤어?
남 아니, 무슨 일인데?
여 수술하던 의사가 환자의 몸 속에 뭔가를 남겨 두었대.
남 끔찍하다. 의사가 뭘 남겨 두었는데?
여 몸 안에 거즈를 남겨 두었대.
남 믿을 수가 없다. 그 의사는 더 조심했어야 했어.
여 그 환자가 지금은 무사했으면 좋겠다.

●●
article (신문) 글, 기사 **operation** 수술
gauze 거즈

09

대화를 듣고, 남자가 채소를 재배하는 이유로 가장 적절한 것을 고르시오.

① 취미가 필요해서
② 귀농을 결심하고 있어서
③ 이웃에게 자랑하기 위해서
④ 친환경적인 채소를 먹기 위해서
⑤ 필요한 채소를 자급자족하기 위해서

M This year, I'm going to <u>grow</u> <u>carrots</u> in my garden. They are so <u>tasty</u>.

W That's a good idea. <u>What</u> <u>else</u> will you grow?

M I'll grow potatoes, onions, and cucumbers.

W Oh, you <u>won't</u> <u>have</u> <u>to</u> <u>buy</u> any food at the grocery store, will you?

M My goal is to grow all the vegetables I eat <u>for</u> <u>myself</u>.

W How does it feel to grow <u>your</u> <u>own</u> <u>food</u>?

M It feels really good.

남 올해는 우리 집 정원에 당근을 재배할 거야. 당근은 참 맛있어.

여 좋은 생각이야. 그 외에 또 뭘 재배할 거니?

남 감자, 양파, 오이를 재배할 거야.

여 아, 그렇다면 식료품점에서 음식을 전혀 살 필요가 없겠네, 그렇지?

남 내 목표는 내가 먹는 채소 전부를 스스로 재배하는 거야.

여 네가 먹는 음식을 재배하는 기분이 어때?

남 정말 좋지.

● ●
cucumber 오이 **for oneself** 혼자, 스스로

10

대화를 듣고, 남자가 전화를 건 목적으로 가장 적절한 것을 고르시오.

① 카메라를 빌리기 위해서
② 숙제를 물어보기 위해서
③ 약속 일정을 정하기 위해서
④ 함께 찍은 사진을 주기 위해서
⑤ 휴대폰을 두고 왔는지 묻기 위해서

M Hi, Linda. This is Bob.

W Hi, Bob. What's <u>going</u> <u>on</u>?

M Did you <u>happen</u> <u>to</u> <u>see</u> my cellphone? I think I <u>left</u> <u>it</u> at your house.

W No, I didn't. But I'll <u>take</u> <u>a</u> <u>look</u> around the house, and then I'll ask my mom if <u>she's</u> <u>seen</u> <u>it</u>.

M Thanks, Linda. I hope that you can find it there.

W Don't worry too much. It should be here because we <u>took</u> <u>some</u> <u>pictures</u> with your phone in my room. I can <u>call</u> <u>you</u> <u>back</u> later.

M Thanks a lot. I'll <u>wait</u> <u>for</u> your phone call.

남 안녕, Linda. 나 Bob이야.

여 안녕, Bob. 무슨 일이니?

남 혹시 내 휴대폰 봤어? 너희 집에 두고 온 것 같아.

여 아니, 못 봤어. 그렇지만 집을 한번 살펴보고 나서 엄마에게 본 적이 있는지 여쭤볼게.

남 고마워, Linda. 너희 집에서 찾았으면 좋겠어.

여 너무 걱정하지마. 내 방에서 네 전화기로 사진을 찍었으니까 우리 집에 있을 거야. 내가 다시 전화할게.

남 정말 고마워. 전화 기다릴게.

11

대화를 듣고, 남자가 모임에 온 방법으로 가장 적절한 것을 고르시오.

① by car
② by bus
③ by taxi
④ on foot
⑤ by subway

M I'm sorry I'm late for the meeting. My car <u>broke</u> <u>down</u>.

W You're <u>sweating</u> so much. Please go to the washroom and clean up.

M I had <u>no</u> <u>choice</u>. It's 35 degrees outside, and I had no money to take the subway because I <u>left</u> <u>my</u> <u>wallet</u> at home.

W It really is a bad day today, isn't it?

M I <u>had</u> <u>to</u> <u>walk</u> two kilometers just to get here. I'm bushed.

W Please <u>have</u> <u>a</u> <u>seat</u> and drink some water.

남 모임에 늦어서 미안해. 내 차가 고장 났거든.

여 땀을 너무 많이 흘리고 있구나. 화장실에 가서 씻어.

남 어쩔 수가 없었어. 바깥 온도는 35도인데 지갑을 집에 두고 와서 지하철 탈 돈이 없었거든.

여 오늘은 정말 운이 나쁜 날이구나, 그렇지 않니?

남 여기 오려고 2킬로미터나 걸어야 했어. 정말 지쳤어.

여 앉아서 물 좀 마셔.

● ●
break down 고장나다 **sweat** 땀을 흘리다
washroom (공공건물의) 세면장, 화장실
bushed 몹시 지친 **have a seat** 앉다

12 대화를 듣고, 여자가 내일 저녁에 할 일로 가장 적절한 것을 고르시오.

① 수영하러 가기
② 친구에게 편지쓰기
③ 파티에 가기
④ 병원에 가기
⑤ 집에서 쉬기

M Do you have any plans for this weekend?

W Yes, I'm going to swim and write letters to my friends back in Korea.

M What about tomorrow evening?

W I don't have anything special planned.

M I was invited to a party tomorrow evening. Would you like to go with me?

W Who is having the party?

M Mike is going to have a dance party.

W Well, I'd like to go, but I'm kind of tired these days. I need some time to relax at home by myself.

M I see. In that case, you should just relax.

남 이번 주말에 무슨 계획 있니?

여 응, 난 수영하고 한국에 있는 친구들에게 편지를 쓸 거야.

남 내일 저녁에는 뭐 하는데?

여 특별한 계획은 없어.

남 난 내일 저녁에 열리는 파티에 초대 받았는데. 나와 함께 갈래?

여 누가 여는 파티인데?

남 Mike가 여는 댄스 파티야.

여 음, 나도 가고 싶지만 요즘 좀 피곤해. 집에서 혼자 쉴 시간이 좀 필요해.

남 알겠어. 그렇다면 그냥 쉬어야겠구나.

---

13 대화를 듣고, 대화 내용과 일치하지 <u>않는</u> 것을 고르시오.

① 집 주인은 일본에서 유학 중이다.
② 남자는 집 열쇠를 가지고 있다.
③ 집은 1999년에 지어졌다.
④ 남자는 시공 회사를 기억하지 못한다.
⑤ 지붕은 2년 전에 새로 얹었다.

W Well, is this the house that you mentioned?

M Right. The owner went to Japan on business, but I have the keys.

W It looks pretty nice. When was it built?

M It was built in 1999.

W What company built this house?

M I'm afraid I forgot. Is it important?

W No, not really. Is that a new roof?

M Yes. It was put on two years ago.

여 음, 이것이 당신이 말했던 집인가요?

남 맞아요. 집 주인은 사업상 일본에 갔지만 제가 열쇠를 가지고 있지요.

여 꽤 좋아 보이네요. 언제 지어진 겁니까?

남 1999년에 지어졌어요.

여 어떤 회사에서 시공했나요?

남 죄송하지만 잊어버렸어요. 그게 중요한가요?

여 아니요, 그렇지는 않아요. 지붕은 새 것인가요?

남 네. 2년 전에 얹은 거예요.

●●
on business 사업상, 업무로

14 대화를 듣고, 남자의 마지막 말에 이어질 여자의 말로 가장 적절한 것을 고르시오.

① If you like, I'll lend it to you.
② Well, the story was too boring.
③ It's a traditional American story.
④ I like this kind of story very much.
⑤ You must read it if you get the chance.

M Do you have any novels written in English?
W Yes, I have one.
M Where did you get it? I'm planning to buy one.
W I didn't buy it. My professor gave it to me.
M Have you read the whole book?
W Yes, I have. The book is so interesting that I've read it over and over again.
M What kind of story is it?
W It's a traditional American story.

남 영어로 쓰여진 소설책이 있니?
여 응, 하나 있어.
남 어디서 샀니? 나도 하나 사려고 하는데.
여 내가 산 건 아니야. 교수님이 주셨어.
남 전부 다 읽었니?
여 응, 읽었어. 책이 너무 재미있어서 읽고 또 읽었지.
남 무슨 종류의 이야기인데?
여 미국 전통 소설이야.

① 원한다면 너에게 빌려줄게.
② 음, 그 이야기는 너무 지루했어.
④ 나는 이런 종류의 이야기를 무척 좋아해.
⑤ 기회가 된다면 이 소설을 꼭 읽어봐.

novel 소설 **over and over** 계속 반복해서
traditional 전통의

---

15 대화를 듣고, 여자의 마지막 말에 이어질 남자의 말로 가장 적절한 것을 고르시오.

① It's not sour.
② Here is the receipt.
③ I'll get you a fresh one.
④ Yes. These watermelons are fresh.
⑤ We take both Visa and MasterCard.

W Are these apples ripe?
M Sure. They are very sweet and fresh.
W Give me one box. Those bananas don't look ripe.
M You're right. But these ones here are ripe and very sweet.
W How much is it for one bunch?
M Five dollars.
W Well, this one seems to be bruised.
M I'll get you a fresh one.

여 이 사과는 익은 건가요?
남 물론이죠. 맛있고 신선하답니다.
여 한 상자 주세요. 저기 바나나는 익지 않은 것 같네요.
남 맞아요. 하지만 여기 있는 것들은 맛있게 잘 익었답니다.
여 한 다발에 얼마인가요?
남 5달러입니다.
여 음, 이건 멍이 들어 보이는데요.
남 신선한 것으로 드릴게요.

① 그건 안 셔요.
② 영수증 여기 있습니다.
④ 네. 이 수박들은 신선해요.
⑤ 저희는 비자와 마스터카드 모두 받습니다.

ripe 익은 **bunch** 다발, 송이 **bruised** 멍든

▶ REVIEW TEST p. 127

A
① relief, 안도, 안심 ② novice, 초보자 ③ affordable, 가격이 적당한 ④ latest, 최근의, 최신의
⑤ robber, 강도 ⑥ beard, 턱수염 ⑦ mustache, 콧수염 ⑧ recipient, 수신인
⑨ article, (신문) 글, 기사 ⑩ operation, 수술 ⑪ ripe, 익은 ⑫ bruised, 멍든

B
① free of charge ② in a ponytail ③ by airmail
④ sense of accomplishment ⑤ deserve it ⑥ should have been
⑦ happen to see ⑧ written in English

문제 및 정답	받아쓰기 및 녹음내용	해석

01

다음을 듣고, 금요일의 날씨로 가장 적절한 것을 고르시오.

①   ②

③   ④

⑤

I'm Mina Kim with the weather for Friday, tomorrow. It's been hot for several days <u>in a row</u>. Tonight, the temperature will begin to <u>cool down</u> as clouds are expected to <u>move in</u>. There'll be a <u>high possibility</u> of rain tomorrow morning. The temperature will <u>drop to</u> 15 degrees Celsius. The clouds will <u>disappear</u> by this weekend, and you will see <u>fine weather</u>.

내일 금요일의 날씨를 알려 드릴 김민아입니다. 더운 날씨가 며칠 동안 계속되었습니다. 오늘밤은 구름이 몰려올 것으로 예상되면서 기온이 서늘해지기 시작하겠습니다. 내일 아침에는 비가 올 가능성이 크겠습니다. 기온은 섭씨 15도까지 떨어지겠습니다. 구름은 주말까지는 사라지겠으며 화창한 날씨를 보실 수 있겠습니다.

cool down 서늘해지다 **possibility** 가능성

02

다음을 듣고, 남자가 하는 말의 내용으로 가장 적절한 것을 고르시오.

① 할인 판매
② 화재 신고
③ 선거 유세
④ 소방 훈련
⑤ 체험 활동 공지

<u>Attention</u>, students! This is your <u>principal speaking</u>. Tomorrow at 11 o'clock there will be a <u>fire drill</u>. At that time, the fire alarm will ring, and you are to <u>quietly follow</u> your teacher out of the school. You must <u>stay outside</u> until the alarm rings again. This is important, so let's <u>do it right</u>.

학생 여러분, 주목하세요! 저는 교장입니다. 내일 11시에 소방 훈련이 있을 예정입니다. 그때 화재 경보가 울리면 여러분은 학교 밖으로 조용히 선생님을 따라가야 합니다. 경보가 다시 울릴 때 까지는 밖에 머물러야 합니다. 중요한 훈련이니 제대로 해 봅시다.

attention (안내 방송에서) 알려드립니다. 주목하세요 **principal** 교장 **fire drill** 소방 훈련

03

대화를 듣고, 두 사람이 대화하는 장소로 가장 적절한 곳을 고르시오.

① 은행
② 호텔
③ 환전소
④ 경찰서
⑤ 백화점

W Hi. I'd like to <u>withdraw</u> 500 dollars.

M Certainly. Please <u>fill this form out</u>. Do you want it in cash or a check?

W Cash, please. Is that all right?

M Yes. Would you please <u>press</u> your PIN number here?

W Okay.

M <u>I'm afraid</u> that your PIN number isn't right.

W Oh, sorry. I forgot it. Can I <u>reset</u> my PIN number?

M Yes. May I have your ID?

W <u>Here you go</u>.

여 안녕하세요. 500달러를 인출하고 싶은데요.

남 그럼요. 이 양식을 작성해 주세요. 현금으로 드릴까요, 수표로 드릴까요?

여 현금으로요. 이렇게 쓰는 게 맞나요?

남 네. 아, 잠깐만요. 여기에 비밀번호를 입력해 주시겠어요?

여 알겠습니다.

남 비밀번호가 맞지 않는 것 같아요.

여 오, 미안합니다. 잊어버렸어요. 제 비밀번호를 재설정할 수 있을까요?

남 네. 신분증 좀 주시겠어요?

여 여기 있습니다.

withdraw 인출하다 **check** 수표
PIN number 비밀번호 **reset** 다시 맞추다, 재설정하다

04 대화를 듣고, 두 사람의 관계로 가장 적절한 것을 고르시오.

① 교사 - 학생
② 감독 - 선수
③ 영화감독 - 배우
④ 연예인 - 매니저
⑤ 디자이너 - 모델

M Lights and camera ready? Standby. Action! Cut!
W Can we <u>take a break</u>?
M Let's just finish <u>while we're at it</u> and then take a break. Just a few more scenes…
W But I'm <u>so thirsty</u>.
M Really? Then let's <u>rest a bit</u>.
W Thank you.
M This scene is <u>taking longer</u> than I expected.
W <u>Tell me about it</u>. The weather's so hot.
M We have to hurry if we want to finish before <u>sunset</u>.

남 조명과 카메라 준비됐어요? 스탠바이. 액션! 컷!
여 잠시 쉬면 안 될까요?
남 하는 김에 마저 하고 쉬죠. 몇 장면만 더 찍고…
여 하지만 목이 너무 말라요.
남 그래요? 그럼 좀 쉽시다.
여 고마워요.
남 이번 장면 촬영은 예상했던 것보다 더 오래 걸리네요.
여 그러게 말이에요. 날씨도 덥고요.
남 해지기 전에 끝내려면 서둘러야 해요.

●●
while we are at it 하는 김에 **scene** 장면
thirsty 목마른

---

05 다음 그림의 상황에 가장 적절한 대화를 고르시오.

① ② ③ ④ ⑤

① M Can you <u>pass me the salt</u>?
　 W Here you go.
② W What would you like to order?
　 M I'd like to order <u>hot green tea</u>.
③ M I'm looking for some shorts for my brother.
　 W How about these ones <u>with leaves</u>?
④ W Is there anything you want to <u>write on the cake</u>?
　 M Could you write my mom's name on it?
⑤ M What are you doing?
　 W I'm <u>posting a photo</u> on the web.

① 남 소금 좀 건네 줄 수 있어요?
　 여 여기 있어요.
② 여 무엇을 주문하시겠습니까?
　 남 따뜻한 녹차를 주문하고 싶습니다.
③ 남 제 남동생에게 줄 반바지를 찾고 있는데요.
　 여 나뭇잎 무늬가 있는 이것은 어떠세요?
④ 여 케이크에 위에 쓰고 싶은 말이 있나요?
　 남 저희 엄마 이름을 써 주시겠어요?
⑤ 남 뭐하고 있어?
　 여 웹에 사진을 올리고 있어.

●●
pass 건네주다 **post** 올리다, 게시하다

---

06 대화를 듣고, 남자가 지불할 총 금액으로 가장 적절한 것을 고르시오.

① $27
② $30
③ $35
④ $40
⑤ $45

M I can't <u>figure out</u> this tipping system.
W What's the problem?
M Well, our bill <u>comes to</u> 30 dollars. So how much <u>should we tip</u> the waiter?
W They say we should tip <u>between</u> 10% <u>and</u> 15%.
M So will 5 dollars be okay?
W <u>I think so</u>.

남 팁 제도에 대해서 정말 모르겠어.
여 뭐가 문제니?
남 음, 우리가 계산할 금액이 30달러야. 그러면 웨이터에게 팁을 얼마나 줘야 하지?
여 10%에서 15%를 팁으로 주면 된대.
남 그러면 5달러면 되겠지?
여 그럴 것 같아.

●●
tipping system 팁 제도 **bill** 계산서, 청구서
come to (총계가) ~이 되다

07 대화를 듣고, 여자의 심정으로 가장 적절한 것을 고르시오.

① upset
② bored
③ excited
④ nervous
⑤ thankful

W Hey, you! You're so _selfish_.
M Who? Me? Are you talking to me?
W Yes, you. What _do you think_ you're doing?
M Huh? I'm just _waiting for_ a taxi. Did I do _something wrong_?
W Can't you see there's a line?
M Oh, there is? I'm sorry. I didn't mean to _cut in_. I didn't _realize_ there was a line.
W That's all right, but you should _get in line_.
M Of course, I will.

여 이봐요, 당신! 당신 참 이기적이군요.
남 누구요? 저요? 저에게 하신 말씀인가요?
여 네, 당신이요. 당신은 지금 뭘 하고 있다고 생각해요?
남 예? 저는 단지 택시를 기다리는데요. 제가 뭘 잘못했나요?
여 당신은 줄이 보이지 않습니까?
남 오, 줄이 있었나요? 죄송해요. 새치기하려던 것은 아니었어요. 줄이 있는지 몰랐어요.
여 알겠습니다만, 당신도 줄을 서야 해요.
남 물론이죠, 그럴게요.

●●
selfish 이기적인   **cut in** 끼어들다, 새치기하다

---

08 대화를 듣고, 남자가 구입할 물건으로 가장 적절한 것을 고르시오.

① 설탕, 자몽
② 설탕, 포도
③ 후추, 포도
④ 소금, 자몽
⑤ 소금, 포도

W Could you _do me a favor_, please?
M Certainly. What is it?
W Could you _run over to_ the store? We need a few things.
M Sure. What do you _want me to get_?
W Well, could you pick up _some sugar_?
M Okay. How much?
W A small bag. I guess we also need _some grapes_.
M Is that everything?
W I think so.

여 내 부탁 좀 들어 줄 수 있어요?
남 그럼요. 뭔데요?
여 가게에 잠깐 들를 수 있어요? 몇 가지가 필요해서요.
남 그럴게요. 무엇을 사다 줄까요?
여 그럼, 설탕 좀 사다 줄 수 있어요?
남 네. 얼마나요?
여 작은 봉지로요. 포도도 필요한 것 같아요.
남 그것이 다인가요?
여 그런 것 같아요.

●●
run over to ~에 잠깐 들르다

---

09 대화를 듣고, 남자가 집에서 7시 정각에 나가는 이유로 가장 적절한 것을 고르시오.

① 출근 전 운동을 하려고
② 버스에서 앉아서 가려고
③ 지하철의 혼잡을 피하려고
④ 회사 동료와 함께 출근하려고
⑤ 회사에 지각하면 벌금이 있어서

W You _leave home_ at exactly 7:00 a.m. every day, don't you?
M _Curious_, aren't you?
W Very much so. Please _tell me why_.
M If I leave home at exactly this time, I can get on the subway _before the crowds_.
W Oh, I see.
M If I am ever five minutes late leaving home, I'm caught in a tide of people _all pushing and shoving_ to get on the subway.

여 너 매일 정확히 오전 7시에 집에서 나가지?
남 궁금하구나, 그렇지?
여 너무 궁금해. 왜 그러는지 말해 줘.
남 정확히 이 시간에 집에서 출발하면 지하철이 붐비기 전에 탈 수 있거든.
여 아, 그렇구나.
남 5분이라도 집에서 늦게 출발하면 지하철을 타기 위해 밀고 잡아당기는 인파에 꼼짝없이 갇혀.

●●
curious 궁금한   **crowd** 군중   **be caught in** ~에 갇히다   **tide of people** 인파   **push and shove** 밀치락달치락하다

10 대화를 듣고, 남자가 전화를 건 목적으로 가장 적절한 것을 고르시오.

① 요금제를 변경하기 위해서
② 수리 기사를 요청하기 위해서
③ 회원 정보를 변경하기 위해서
④ 전화 요금을 납부하기 위해서
⑤ 전화 요금을 확인하기 위해서

W LS Telecom Company. May I help you?
M Yes. I think there's a <u>mistake</u> on my bill. I believe I was <u>overcharged</u>.
W I see. <u>For</u> <u>security</u> <u>reasons</u>, I have to ask you some questions. What's your name?
M My name is Peter Kim.
W What is your phone number?
M My phone number is <u>012-3377</u>-<u>0097</u>.
W All right. Please hold on, and I'll <u>check</u> <u>our</u> <u>records</u>.
M Thank you.

여 LS 통신회사 입니다. 무엇을 도와드릴까요?
남 네, 요금 청구서에 문제가 있어요. 요금이 너무 많이 나왔어요.
여 알겠습니다. 보안상의 이유로 몇 가지 질문을 하겠습니다. 성함이 어떻게 되시죠?
남 Peter Kim입니다.
여 전화번호는요?
남 제 전화번호는 012-3377-0097 입니다.
여 알겠습니다. 잠시만 기다려 주시면 기록을 확인해 보겠습니다.
남 고맙습니다.

●●
overcharge 너무 많이 청구하다 **security** 보안 **hold on** (전화상으로) 잠시 기다리다 **record** 기록

---

11 대화를 듣고, 여자가 남자에게 부탁한 일로 가장 적절한 것을 고르시오.

① 커피 사오기
② 도넛 사오기
③ 요리 도와주기
④ 병원 데려다 주기
⑤ 알레르기 치료법 알아보기

M I'm going to the donut shop. What can I <u>get</u> <u>you</u>?
W Anything. <u>Just</u> <u>make</u> <u>sure</u> there are no peanuts in it.
M Why? You don't like peanuts?
W Actually, I love them, but they don't love me. I'm <u>allergic</u> <u>to</u> peanuts.
M <u>What</u> <u>happens</u> if you eat one?
W I have to go <u>directly</u> <u>to</u> <u>the</u> <u>hospital</u>.

남 나 도넛 가게에 갈 거야. 뭘 사다 줄까?
여 아무거나. 땅콩이 들어있지만 않으면 돼.
남 왜? 땅콩을 싫어하니?
여 사실은 너무 좋아하는데, 그것들이 나를 안 좋아해. 나는 땅콩 알레르기가 있거든.
남 먹으면 어떻게 되는데?
여 곧장 병원으로 가야 해.

●●
peanut 땅콩 **be allergic to** ~에 알레르기가 있다

---

12 대화를 듣고, 여자가 내일 할 일로 가장 적절한 것을 고르시오.

① 쇼핑하기
② 전시회 가기
③ 도서관 가기
④ 집에서 책 읽기
⑤ 가족과 시간 보내기

M I'm going to go to the Korean Museum with my family tomorrow.
W That's great! Does it still have that special <u>art</u> <u>exhibit</u> there?
M Yes, that's actually <u>why</u> <u>we</u> <u>are</u> <u>going</u>.
W I went there last week. You really have to go and see it.
M Was it <u>worth</u> <u>your</u> <u>time</u>?
W Oh, yes. It was a really <u>educational</u> <u>experience</u> for me.
M Thank you for telling me. What are <u>your</u> <u>plans</u> for tomorrow?
W I was going to <u>go</u> <u>shopping</u>, but I've decided to go to the <u>library</u>.

남 내일 가족들과 함께 한국 박물관에 가려고 해.
여 좋겠다! 특별 미술 전시를 아직도 거기서 하니?
남 응, 사실은 그게 우리가 가는 이유야.
여 난 지난 주에 거기 갔었어. 너도 꼭 가서 봐야 해.
남 시간을 낼 만큼 가치가 있었니?
여 오, 그럼. 그건 나에게 정말 교육적인 경험이었어.
남 말해줘서 고마워. 내일 계획은 어떻게 되니?
여 쇼핑을 가려고 했는데 도서관에 가기로 결정했어.

●●
exhibit 전시 **worth** ~의 가치가 있는 **educational** 교육적인

13

대화를 듣고, 대화 내용과 일치하지 않는 것을 고르시오.

① 여자는 빨간색 지갑을 잃어버렸다.
② 여자의 이름은 김영미이다.
③ 여자의 지갑에는 현금이 들어 있다.
④ 여자의 지갑은 커피숍에 있다.
⑤ 여자는 1시간 30분 후에 남자를 만날 것이다.

W Hello? I left a red wallet in your coffee shop yesterday.
M Could you tell me your name?
W My name is Young-mi Kim.
M May I ask what you had in your wallet?
W I had credit cards, my driver's license, and about 30,000 won.
M Oh, yes. We have your wallet.
W I'll be there in half an hour.
M We'll be waiting for you.

여 여보세요. 어제 빨간색 지갑을 댁의 커피숍에 놓고 왔는데요.
남 성함을 말씀해 주시겠어요?
여 제 이름은 김영미입니다.
남 지갑 안에 뭐가 들어 있었는지 여쭤봐도 될까요?
여 신용카드, 운전면허증, 그리고 3만원 정도가 있었어요.
남 오, 맞아요. 우리가 당신의 지갑을 보관하고 있어요.
여 30분 후에 갈게요.
남 기다리겠습니다.

● ●
driver's license 운전면허증

14

대화를 듣고, 남자의 마지막 말에 이어질 여자의 말로 가장 적절한 것을 고르시오.

① Oh, here is a larger pair.
② Would you like a gift bag?
③ What kind of shoes do you need?
④ Here are your receipt and change.
⑤ Sure. The fitting rooms are over there.

M I want to buy a pair of black shoes.
W Do you want a pair we have in stock or one specially made?
M I'll buy a pair in stock, please.
W Okay. We have plenty of shoes. Take your pick.
M I'll try these on. Can you give me a shoehorn?
W Sure. These are the most comfortable shoes we have. How do you like them?
M I like them, but they are a little tight.
W Oh, here is a larger pair.

남 검은색 구두를 한 켤레 사려고 하는데요.
여 기성화로 드릴까요, 아니면 주문 제품으로 드릴까요?
남 기성화로 부탁합니다.
여 그러죠. 신발이 많이 있습니다. 골라 보세요.
남 이걸 신어 볼게요. 구둣주걱 좀 주시겠습니까?
여 네. 이건 저희가 가지고 있는 가장 편안한 신발 입니다. 어떻습니까?
남 마음에 들긴 하지만 조금 끼네요.
여 아, 여기 더 큰 것이 있습니다.

② 선물용 가방을 드릴까요?
③ 어떤 종류의 신발이 필요하십니까?
④ 여기 영수증과 잔돈 있습니다.
⑤ 그럼요. 피팅 룸은 저기 있습니다.

● ●
shoehorn 구둣주걱

15 대화를 듣고, 여자의 마지막 말에 이어질 남자의 말로 가장 적절한 것을 고르시오.

① I just rejected her proposal.
② It's a nice place for a vacation.
③ Have you ever been to Sokcho?
④ Okay. It's kind of you to say that.
⑤ I often took trips with her family.

W Do you have <u>anything</u> <u>planned</u> for the break?
M I'm not sure, but I <u>might</u> <u>go</u> <u>swimming</u> at the beach in Sokcho.
W Lucky you! How did that <u>come</u> <u>about</u>?
M My girlfriend rented a <u>seaside</u> <u>villa</u> in Sokcho for a week and invited me to <u>spend</u> <u>time</u> with her and her family.
W That sounds great. But why aren't you going <u>for</u> <u>sure</u>?
M Well, I'm very <u>afraid</u>. I have to spend time with her family, but I <u>have</u> <u>never</u> <u>met</u> them before.
W Come on. You will be fine. Don't be afraid of <u>her</u> <u>proposal</u>.
M <u>Okay. It's kind of you to say that.</u>

여 휴가 때 계획된 일이 있니?
남 확실하지는 않지만, 속초에 있는 바닷가에 수영하러 갈 수도 있어.
여 좋겠구나! 어떻게 그런 계획이 생겼니?
남 내 여자친구가 속초 해변에 있는 별장을 일주일간 빌렸고 그녀와 그녀의 가족들과 함께 시간을 보내도록 날 초대했어.
여 정말 멋지다. 그런데 왜 확실히 가는 게 아니야?
남 음, 난 몹시 걱정스러워. 그녀의 가족들과 함께 시간을 보내야만 하는데 전에 그들을 만나본 적이 한 번도 없거든.
여 왜 그래. 넌 잘 할거야. 그녀의 제안에 겁내지마.
남 <u>알겠어. 그렇게 말해줘서 고마워.</u>

① 나는 그녀의 제안을 거절했어.
② 그곳은 휴가 보내기에 좋은 곳이야.
③ 속초에 가본 적이 있니?
⑤ 나는 종종 그녀의 가족들과 여행을 갔어.

●●
come about 생기다, 일어나다 **seaside villa** 해변의 별장 **for sure** 확실히 **proposal** 제안

REVIEW TEST p. 135

A ① principal, 교장 ② fire drill, 소방 훈련 ③ scene, 장면 ④ thirsty, 목마른
⑤ selfish, 이기적인 ⑥ cut in, 끼어들다, 새치기하다 ⑦ crowd, 군중 ⑧ overcharge, 너무 많이 청구하다
⑨ peanut, 땅콩 ⑩ exhibit, 전시 ⑪ shoehorn, 구둣주걱 ⑫ proposal, 제안

B ① like to withdraw ② posting, on the web ③ mean to
④ security reasons ⑤ hold on ⑥ allergic to peanuts
⑦ worth, time ⑧ in stock

01 ③ 02 ④ 03 ② 04 ③ 05 ② 06 ② 07 ③ 08 ⑤
09 ① 10 ② 11 ⑤ 12 ⑤ 13 ④ 14 ③ 15 ③

문제 및 정답	받아쓰기 및 녹음내용	해석

01

대화를 듣고, 남자가 구입할 벽지로 가장 적절한 것을 고르시오.

① ②

③ ④

⑤

W Hello. What can I do for you?

M I'm looking for some <u>wallpaper</u> for my daughter's room.

W <u>How old</u> is your daughter?

M She's seven years old. Can you <u>recommend something</u> for my little girl?

W I'm pretty sure that she would like prints of <u>flowers</u> or <u>stars</u>.

M Hmm... I don't think so. Do you have any patterns of <u>animals</u>?

W How about prints of <u>rabbits</u> or <u>cats</u>?

M I think she would prefer the one <u>with</u> <u>rabbits</u>.

W Okay. I hope she likes it.

여 안녕하세요. 무엇을 도와드릴까요?

남 제 딸 방에 붙일 벽지를 찾고 있어요.

여 따님이 몇 살이에요?

남 그녀는 일곱 살이에요. 우리 딸에게 추천해줄 것이 있을까요?

여 분명히 꽃이나 별 무늬를 좋아할 거예요.

남 음… 그렇지 않을 거예요. 동물 무늬도 있나요?

여 토끼나 고양이의 무늬는 어때요?

남 제 딸은 토끼가 있는 것을 더 좋아할 것 같아요.

여 알겠습니다. 따님 마음에 들었으면 좋겠네요.

●●
wallpaper 벽지 **pattern** 무늬

02

다음을 듣고, 남자가 하는 말의 내용으로 가장 적절한 것을 고르시오.

① 도로 공사 안내
② 화재 대피 훈련
③ 가스 안전 수칙
④ 수사 협조 요청
⑤ 겨울철 화재 예방 방법

Ladies and gentlemen, your attention, please. You have to <u>step away from</u> this yellow police line right away. Someone <u>set fire</u> to this place. Your cooperation will help us <u>investigate</u> and <u>find</u> the person who set the fire. Please <u>do not touch</u> anything you find in this area. If you see <u>anyone suspicious</u>, please inform a police officer <u>immediately</u>. Thank you for <u>your cooperation</u>.

신사 숙녀 여러분, 주목해 주세요. 여러분들은 지금 즉시 이 노란 경찰 통제선으로부터 떨어지셔야 합니다. 이 곳에 누군가 불을 질렀습니다. 여러분들의 협조는 저희가 불을 지른 사람을 수사하고 찾는데 도움을 줄 것입니다. 이 지역에서 발견되는 어떤 것에도 손을 대지 마십시오. 만약 의심스러운 사람을 보시면 즉시 경찰관에게 알려주십시오. 여러분들의 협조에 감사 드립니다.

●●
step away from ~로부터 떨어지다 **set fire** 불을 지르다 **cooperation** 협조 **investigate** 수사하다, 조사하다 **suspicious** 의심스러운 **inform** 알리다

03

대화를 듣고, 두 사람이 대화하는 장소로 가장 적절한 곳을 고르시오.

① 병원
② 공항
③ 우체국
④ 경찰서
⑤ 분실물 센터

M Do you have <u>anything to declare</u>?

W No, nothing. All these are my <u>personal belongings</u>.

M Have you read the <u>customs form</u>, ma'am?

W Yes, I have.

M Okay, then could you open up your <u>suitcase</u> for me, please? You're one of the travelers <u>selected for examination</u>.

W Certainly. No problem.

남 신고해야 할 것이 있나요?

여 아니요, 없습니다. 이것들은 모두 제 개인 소지품이에요.

남 세관 양식을 읽어 보셨나요, 부인?

여 네, 읽어 봤습니다.

남 알겠습니다, 그럼 여행 가방 좀 열어 주시겠습니까? 부인은 심사 대상 여행자 중 한 분입니다.

여 물론이죠. 협조하겠습니다.

●●
declare (세관에서) 신고하다 **belongings** 소지품 **customs** 세관 **suitcase** 여행 가방 **examination** 검사, 심사

04 대화를 듣고, 두 사람의 관계로 가장 적절한 것을 고르시오.

① wife - husband
② teacher - student
③ salesclerk - customer
④ movie director - staff
⑤ hotel manager - guest

M May I help you, ma'am?
W Yes, please. I'm looking for <u>something</u> <u>for</u> <u>my</u> <u>husband</u>.
M How about <u>a pair of jeans</u>?
W Jeans for my husband? That's a great idea.
M These jeans are <u>on</u> <u>sale</u> for <u>35%</u> <u>off</u>.
W I think they'll <u>look</u> <u>good</u> <u>on</u> my husband. I'll take them.
M You've made a <u>good</u> <u>choice</u>.

남 도와드릴까요, 손님?
여 네, 도와주세요. 제 남편에게 줄 무언가를 찾고 있는 중입니다.
남 이 청바지 어떠세요?
여 남편에게 청바지요? 좋은 생각이네요.
남 이 청바지는 35% 할인 중입니다.
여 제 남편에게 잘 어울릴 것 같네요. 그걸로 할게요.
남 탁월한 선택이세요.

•• **look good on** ~에게 어울리다 **salesclerk** 점원, 판매원 **movie director** 영화감독

05 다음 그림의 상황에 가장 적절한 대화를 고르시오.

① ② ③ ④ ⑤

① W <u>How</u> <u>would</u> <u>you</u> <u>like</u> your steak?
  M I'll have mine medium.
② M I'd like to <u>check</u> <u>out</u> <u>these</u> <u>books</u>.
  W Sure. May I see your library card, please?
③ M I'd like to <u>exchange</u> <u>this</u> <u>shirt</u> for one in a bigger size.
  W What size do you need?
④ M Do you have *The Mixed-Up Chameleon* by Erick Carle?
  W I'm sorry. That book is <u>out</u> <u>of</u> <u>stock</u> now.
⑤ M Hello. I'd like to <u>check</u> <u>in</u>.
  W Sure. Do you have a reservation?

① 여 스테이크 굽기를 어떻게 해드릴까요?
  남 중간 굽기로 해주세요.
② 남 이 책들을 대출하고 싶어요
  여 네. 도서관 카드 좀 보여주시겠어요?
③ 남 이 셔츠를 큰 치수로 교환하고 싶어요.
  여 어떤 사이즈를 원하세요?
④ 남 에릭칼의 〈뒤죽박죽 카멜레온〉이라는 책 있나요?
  여 죄송합니다. 그 책은 지금 품절입니다.
⑤ 남 안녕하세요. 체크인하고 싶은데요.
  여 네. 예약은 하셨나요?

•• **check out** (책을) 대출하다 **exchange** 교환하다 **out of stock** 품절인 **check in** 체크인하다, 투숙[탑승] 수속을 하다

06 대화를 듣고, 두 사람이 만나기로 한 시각을 고르시오.

① 3:55 p.m.
② 4:55 p.m.
③ 5:00 p.m.
④ 5:05 p.m.
⑤ 5:10 p.m.

W Hey, John. What's <u>going</u> <u>on</u>?
M Not much. I just called to see if you <u>want</u> <u>a</u> <u>ride</u> <u>home</u>.
W That would be great.
M What time do you <u>get</u> <u>off</u> <u>work</u>?
W I'm off at five, but why don't you come here <u>five</u> <u>minutes</u> <u>early</u>?
M Sure, but why?
W The people in my office want to meet you.

여 이봐, John. 무슨 일이야?
남 특별한 건 없어. 그냥 너희 집까지 태워다 주길 원하는지 알아 보려고 전화했어.
여 그럼 좋지.
남 몇 시에 퇴근하니?
여 5시에, 그런데 5분 더 일찍 오는 건 어때?
남 좋아, 그런데 왜?
여 우리 사무실에 있는 사람들이 너를 만나 보고 싶어서.

•• **get off work** 퇴근하다

| 07 | 대화를 듣고, 남자가 추천하는 공부 방법으로 가장 적절한 것을 고르시오. | M We will have an exam in our next class.

W Will the English exam be difficult?

M No, it won't be difficult.

W I've read the material several times, but I can't understand all of it.

M Don't worry too much. This exam is a spelling and grammar test.

W Then how should I prepare?

M All you have to do is go over the things you've learned. | 남 우리는 다음 시간에 시험을 볼 겁니다.

여 영어 시험이 어려울까요?

남 아니요, 어렵지 않을 거예요.

여 자료를 여러 번 읽어 봤지만 전부를 이해하지는 못하겠어요.

남 너무 걱정 마세요. 이번 시험은 철자와 문법 시험이니까요.

여 그러면 어떻게 준비해야 하나요?

남 배운 것을 복습하기만 하면 됩니다. |

① 쓰면서 공부하기
② 참고 도서 활용하기
③ 배운 내용 복습하기 ✓
④ 소리 내어 읽어 보기
⑤ 매일 꾸준히 공부하기

material 자료 **spelling** 철자 **grammar** 문법 **go over** 검토하다, 복습하다

| 08 | 대화를 듣고, 여자의 마지막 말의 의도로 가장 적절한 것을 고르시오. | W I can't believe how quickly you ate the meal.

M I'm sorry if I ate like a pig. I was so hungry.

W You were finished in five minutes.

M I hadn't eaten all day, and your food was so delicious. Do you have more?

W Sure. Help yourself.

M Thank you. I think you're the best cook in the world.

W It's good to hear that. There's plenty of food, so take your time. I'm afraid you'll get a stomachache. | 여 네가 그렇게 빨리 음식을 먹다니 믿을 수가 없어.

남 내가 게걸스럽게 먹었다면 미안해. 너무 배가 고팠었거든.

여 5분 안에 해치우더라.

남 하루 종일 아무것도 못 먹었는데 네가 만든 요리가 너무 맛있었어. 조금 더 있니?

여 물론이지. 마음껏 먹어.

남 고마워. 난 네가 세계 최고의 요리사라고 생각해.

여 그런 말 들으니 좋네. 음식 많이 있으니까 천천히 먹어. 네가 배탈날까 봐 걱정돼. |

① 칭찬
② 사과
③ 비난
④ 후회
⑤ 걱정 ✓

eat like a pig 게걸스럽게 먹다
Help yourself. 마음껏 드세요.
stomachache 복통, 배탈

| 09 | 대화를 듣고, 여자의 친구가 새 아파트로 이사한 이유로 가장 적절한 것을 고르시오. | W You know Joyce, right? She moved into a new apartment.

M Why is that?

W Well, one morning, she got up to get a glass of water in the kitchen, and she saw two mice staring at her.

M How did she react? Was she afraid?

W The neighbors heard her screaming from two blocks away.

M Oh, that's too bad. Is her new place clean and free of mice?

W Oh, yes. It's a brand-new building.

M It must be expensive though.

W It is, but she feels better in the new place. | 여 너 Joyce 알지? Joyce가 새 아파트로 이사를 갔대.

남 왜?

여 글쎄, 어느 날 아침 일어나서 부엌에서 물을 마시는데, 쥐 두 마리가 자기를 쳐다보고 있는 것을 발견했대.

남 그녀의 반응은 어땠니? 무서웠대?

여 두 블록 떨어져 살고 있는 이웃들도 그녀의 비명 소리를 들었대.

남 이런, 안 됐다. 새로 이사한 곳은 깨끗하고 쥐가 없니?

여 응. 새로 지은 건물이래.

남 그렇지만 비쌀 텐데.

여 응, 하지만 새 집에서 마음이 더 편하대. |

① 집에서 쥐가 나와서 ✓
② 아파트 임대료가 비싸서
③ 이웃과 사이가 안 좋아서
④ 이웃의 시끄러운 소리 때문에
⑤ 학교까지 거리가 너무 멀어서

stare 빤히 쳐다보다, 응시하다 **react** 반응하다
neighbor 이웃 **scream** 소리를 지르다
free of ~이 없는

10 대화를 듣고, 무엇에 관한 내용인지 가장 적절한 것을 고르시오.

① 청주로 여행가기
② 어린 시절의 추억
③ 나무로 집 만드는 법
④ 자연환경의 아름다움
⑤ 주말을 즐겁게 보내는 법

M Look at that boy, Jane. I used to do that when I was a kid.

W Oh, really?

M Yeah, there was a tree house behind the house, and my brother and I used to climb the tree and hide there.

W But you don't climb trees now, do you?

M Of course not. I quit doing that when I was about 14, but I still love the woods. I'd like to live in the country someday.

W When I was very little, my family lived on a farm in Chung-ju.

M That sounds nice.

W Oh, it was. It was a nice period in my life. Every Sunday, I would go into the forest and walk for miles.

남 저 아이를 보세요, Jane. 저도 아이였을 때 저걸 했었어요.

여 오, 정말이요?

남 네, 집 뒤에 나무로 만든 집이 있었는데, 형과 제가 나무를 타고 올라가서 그곳에 숨곤 했었죠.

여 하지만 지금은 나무에 올라가지 않잖아요, 그렇죠?

남 물론 아니죠. 제가 14살 때 즈음 그만두었지만, 저는 여전히 숲을 매우 좋아해요. 언젠가는 시골에서 살고 싶어요.

여 제가 아주 어렸을 때 우리 가족은 청주에 있는 농장에서 살았어요.

남 근사하군요.

여 오, 그래요. 제 인생에서 좋은 시절이었죠. 일요일마다 저는 숲으로 가서 멀리까지 산책을 했었어요.

●●
woods[forest] 숲

---

11 다음을 듣고, 남자가 안내 방송에서 언급하지 <u>않은</u> 것을 고르시오.

① 비행기 편명
② 출발지
③ 목적지
④ 이륙 전 유의 사항
⑤ 도착 시간

Good evening, ladies and gentlemen. This is your captain speaking. I'd like to welcome you aboard Korean Airlines flight 051 from Incheon International Airport to Honolulu, Hawaii. Please put your seats in the upright position, fasten your seatbelts, and turn your cellular phones off until we take off. And no smoking is allowed in all areas of the plane. Thank you. Enjoy your flight.

안녕하십니까, 신사 숙녀 여러분. 저는 기장입니다. 인천 국제공항에서부터 하와이 호놀룰루까지 비행하는 대한항공 051편에 탑승하신 것을 환영합니다. 좌석을 바르게 세우시고, 안전벨트를 착용하신 다음 이륙할 때까지 휴대폰을 꺼 주십시오. 그리고 기내의 모든 구역에서 흡연은 허용되지 않습니다. 감사합니다. 즐거운 여행이 되시길 바랍니다.

●●
captain 기장 take off 이륙하다
be allowed 허용되다

12

대화를 듣고, 여자가 일요일에 할 일로 가장 적절한 것을 고르시오.

① 남자와 함께 점심 식사 하기
② 남자와 함께 저녁 식사 하기
③ 노트북을 고치러 수리점에 가기
④ 노트북을 구입하러 상점에 가기
⑤ 노트북을 빌리러 남자의 집에 가기

W Could you <u>do me a favor</u>?
M Yes, if it's something I can do.
W Would you <u>let me use</u> your laptop this Sunday? <u>Mine is broken</u>.
M Certainly. You <u>may use it</u> any time you want.
W Would you mind if I <u>came by</u> your house on Sunday morning to <u>pick it up</u>?
M Not at all. I'll be <u>expecting you</u>.
W Thank you. Let me take you <u>to dinner</u> tonight.
M Oh, you <u>don't have to</u> do that.

여 부탁을 좀 해도 될까요?
남 네, 제가 할 수 있는 것이라면요.
여 이번 일요일에 당신의 노트북 컴퓨터를 사용해도 될까요? 제 것이 고장 나서요.
남 물론이죠. 언제라도 원할 때 사용하셔도 돼요.
여 일요일 아침에 그것을 가지러 댁에 들러도 될까요?
남 물론이죠. 기다릴게요.
여 고마워요. 제가 오늘 저녁 식사를 대접할게요.
남 오, 그렇게까지 하지 않으셔도 돼요.

●●
come by 잠깐 들르다 **expect** 기대하다, 기다리다

13

대화를 듣고, 대화 내용과 일치하지 <u>않는</u> 것을 고르시오.

① 여자는 남자에게 전화를 했었다.
② 남자는 약속 시간보다 30분 늦게 도착했다.
③ 고속도로에서 교통사고가 났다.
④ 남자는 교통사고를 당했다.
⑤ 남자는 다치지 않았다.

W Why didn't you <u>answer my call</u>, Jason? You are 30 minutes late, and I'm <u>about to leave</u>.
M I'm sorry. There was a <u>terrible traffic accident</u> on the highway and...
W What? Are you hurt?
M What are you talking about? Hurt? I'm not hurt.
W You said you were <u>in a traffic accident</u>!
M You <u>misunderstood</u>. It wasn't my car. It was <u>another car</u>.
W What? Then why were you so late?
M I <u>was watching</u> the accident.

여 왜 내 전화 안 받았어, Jason? 네가 30분이나 늦어서 막 가려던 참이야.
남 미안해. 고속도로에서 끔찍한 교통사고가 있어서…
여 뭐? 다쳤니?
남 무슨 말 하는 거야? 다치다니? 나 안 다쳤어.
여 네가 교통사고를 당했다면서!
남 네가 오해했구나. 내 차가 아니야. 다른 차였어.
여 뭐라고? 그럼 왜 그렇게 늦었는데?
남 난 사고를 구경하고 있었지.

●●
misunderstand 오해하다

14

대화를 듣고, 남자의 마지막 말에 이어질 여자의 말로 가장 적절한 것을 고르시오.

① I need a perm today.
② I hate this color on me.
③ I like this style. Thank you.
④ Do you have a hairstyle book?
⑤ Where did you get your hair done?

W I'd like to <u>get a haircut</u>, please.
M How do you want your hair cut?
W Just a <u>trim</u>, please. Don't make it <u>too short</u>.
M How do you want <u>the back</u>?
W Please layer the back.
M <u>How do you like</u> it? If you don't want this style, please tell me now.
W I like this style. Thank you.

여 머리를 자르려고 하는데요.
남 머리를 어떻게 잘라 드릴까요?
여 그냥 다듬어 주세요. 너무 짧게는 말고요.
남 뒷머리는 어떻게 할까요?
여 뒷머리는 층이 지게 잘라주세요.
남 어떠세요? 이 모양이 맘에 안 들면 지금 말씀하세요.
여 <u>이 스타일 좋네요. 고맙습니다.</u>

① 오늘은 파마를 하려고 해요.
② 저는 이 색이 마음에 안 들어요.
④ 헤어스타일 책이 있나요?
⑤ 머리 어디서 했어요?

●●
trim 다듬기, 손질 **layer** 층이 지게 하다

15 대화를 듣고, 여자의 마지막 말에 이어질 남자의 말로 가장 적절한 것을 고르시오.

① I'd rather stay home today.
② I'll help you with the dishes.
③ Thank you for cleaning the room.
④ Okay, I will clean up my room, too.
⑤ I don't want to play with my puppy today.

W It's so messy in here. Who did this?
M Don't be angry. It was me. I did it.
W You did this to the entire room?
M Yes, it's all my fault.
W Why did you make such a mess?
M I didn't mean to. I was playing with the puppy.
W If you want to play with your puppy, please go out and play.
M Okay, I will clean up my room, too.

여 여기 너무 지저분하구나. 누가 그랬니?
남 화내지 마세요. 저예요. 제가 그랬어요.
여 네가 온 방을 이렇게 해 놓은 거니?
남 네, 모두 제 잘못이에요.
여 왜 이렇게 어질러 놓았지?
남 일부러 그런 건 아니에요. 강아지와 놀고 있었거든요.
여 강아지와 놀고 싶으면, 밖에 나가서 놀아.
남 알겠어요, 방도 치울게요.

① 오늘은 집에 있는 것이 낫겠어요.
② 제가 설거지를 도와드릴게요.
③ 방을 청소해주셔서 감사해요.
⑤ 오늘은 강아지와 놀고 싶지 않아요.

●●
messy 지저분한, 엉망인

❯ REVIEW **TEST** p. 143

A
❶ wallpaper, 벽지 ❷ investigate, 수사하다, 조사하다 ❸ belongings, 소지품 ❹ customs, 세관
❺ suitcase, 여행 가방 ❻ exchange, 교환하다 ❼ material, 자료 ❽ go over, 검토하다, 복습하다
❾ stomachache, 복통, 배탈 ❿ react, 반응하다 ⓫ take off, 이륙하다 ⓬ misunderstand, 오해하다

B
❶ suspicious, immediately ❷ on sale ❸ How would you like
❹ check out ❺ out of stock ❻ free of
❼ about to leave ❽ get, haircut

문제 및 정답	받아쓰기 및 녹음내용	해석

01

다음을 듣고, 금요일의 날씨로 가장 적절한 것을 고르시오.

①   ②

③  ④

⑤

Hello. This is Jonathan with the Toronto weather report. Let's take a look at the weather for this week. We've had freezing weather since last weekend. I'm afraid the snow will continue until Tuesday. We're expecting clear skies starting on Wednesday. As the weather continues to be clear, the atmosphere will get dry. On Thursday, there's a high chance of rain. So don't forget your umbrella when you go out. The rain will continue until Friday.

안녕하세요. 토론토 일기예보의 Jonathan입니다. 이번 주의 날씨를 살펴보겠습니다. 지난 주말부터 날씨가 몹시 추웠습니다. 안타깝게도 눈은 화요일까지 계속될 것입니다. 수요일부터는 맑은 하늘이 예상됩니다. 맑은 날씨가 계속되면서 대기가 건조해지겠습니다. 목요일에는 비가 올 가능성이 높습니다. 외출하실 때 우산을 잊지 마세요. 비는 금요일까지 계속될 것입니다.

●●
freezing 몹시 추운 **atmosphere** 대기

02

다음을 듣고, 남자가 하는 말의 내용으로 가장 적절한 것을 고르시오.

① 대학 면접
② 구직 면접
③ 직장 사직
④ 취업 성공 비결
⑤ 추천서 작성 요청

Actually, I like my present job very much, and I get along very well with my co-workers. The basic reason why I want to leave my job is that there is no room for growth. So the only chance for me to improve my career is to find a new job. I read your advertisement, and I know that your company is the right place for me. If you hire me, I will do my best.

사실, 저는 지금 하는 일을 매우 좋아하며, 제 동료들과도 매우 잘 지내고 있습니다. 제가 직장을 그만두려는 기본적인 이유는 성장의 여지가 없기 때문입니다. 그러므로 제가 경력을 향상시킬 유일한 기회는 새로운 직장을 구하는 것뿐입니다. 저는 귀사의 광고를 보았고 귀사가 저에게 적합한 곳이라는 것을 알고 있습니다. 저를 고용하신다면 최선을 다하겠습니다.

●●
present 현재의 **get along with** ~와 잘 지내다 **room** 여지 **growth** 성장 **improve** 향상시키다 **career** 경력 **advertisement** 광고 **do one's best** 최선을 다하다

03

대화를 듣고, 두 사람이 대화하는 장소로 가장 적절한 곳을 고르시오.

① hotel
② restaurant
③ dental clinic
④ car repair shop
⑤ department store

W May I help you?

M Yes, I'd like to make an appointment. My name is Steven Harper.

W Is it just for a checkup, or are you having trouble with your teeth?

M I think I want a checkup.

W Well, can you come in tomorrow morning?

M That's fine. I'll come again.

여 무엇을 도와드릴까요?

남 네, 예약하고 싶은데요. 제 이름은 Steven Harper입니다.

여 검사만 하실 건가요, 아니면 치아에 문제가 있습니까?

남 검사만 하고 싶어요.

여 그럼, 내일 아침에 오실 수 있으세요?

남 좋아요. 다시 오겠습니다.

●●
checkup 검사, 건강 검진 **dental clinic** 치과

04

대화를 듣고, 두 사람의 관계로 가장 적절한 것을 고르시오.

① 의사 - 환자
② 교사 - 학생
③ 교사 - 학부모
④ 상담원 - 고객
⑤ 은행원 - 고객

W I'm Tony's mother Nancy. Nice to meet you, Mr. Pearson.

M Nice to meet you, too. Tony <u>is the reason</u> I wanted to meet you today.

W Is there a <u>problem</u> <u>with</u> <u>him</u>?

M No, it's not really a problem. It's just that he seems a bit <u>depressed</u>, and he's <u>acting differently</u>.

W The truth is, his father and I <u>have</u> <u>recently</u> <u>divorced</u>.

M Oh, I see. That's why Tony can't <u>pay</u> attention in class.

W I'm so sorry. I <u>should</u> <u>have</u> <u>told</u> you earlier...

M No, it's a <u>relief</u> to know now. I'll be sure to pay special attention to Tony <u>from</u> <u>now</u> <u>on</u>.

여 저는 Tony의 엄마 Nancy입니다. 만나 뵙게 되어 반갑습니다, Pearson 선생님.

남 저도 만나 뵙게 되어 반갑습니다. 제가 오늘 어머님을 뵙고 싶었던 이유는 Tony 때문입니다.

여 그 아이에게 무슨 문제가 있나요?

남 아니요, 꼭 문제가 있는 건 아니고요. 단지 그 애가 좀 우울해 보이고 다르게 행동해서요.

여 사실은, 최근에 그 애 아빠와 제가 이혼을 했어요.

남 아, 그러셨군요. 그래서 요즘 Tony가 수업에 집중을 못했던 거군요.

여 정말 죄송합니다. 더 일찍 말씀을 드렸어야 했는데…

남 아닙니다, 이제라도 알게 되어 안심이네요. 이제부터 Tony에 대해 특별히 주의를 기울이도록 하겠습니다.

••
divorce 이혼하다

05

대화를 듣고, 여자가 설명하는 동작으로 가장 적절한 것을 고르시오.

① ② ③ ④ ⑤

W Do you want to <u>do</u> <u>some</u> <u>stretches</u> with me?

M What do you <u>have</u> <u>in</u> <u>mind</u>?

W Stand up and put <u>your</u> <u>feet</u> together. Raise your arms out to <u>your</u> <u>sides</u> at shoulder level parallel to the <u>ground</u>. Bend your <u>knees</u> <u>halfway</u>.

M It's not <u>easy</u> <u>to</u> <u>follow</u> you.

W Now, stand up straight again. Let's do this about <u>fifteen</u> <u>times</u>.

M I've got the idea, but can we do <u>something</u> <u>easier</u>?

W You should do this every day. Then, you'd <u>get</u> <u>used</u> <u>to</u> it.

여 나랑 같이 스트레칭 할래?

남 뭘 하려는 건데?

여 일어나서 발을 한데 모아. 팔은 어깨 높이에서 땅과 평행이 되도록 옆으로 벌려. 무릎은 반쯤 굽혀.

남 널 따라 하기가 쉽지 않아.

여 자, 다시 똑바로 서. 이걸 열다섯 번 정도 하자.

남 어떻게 하는지는 알겠는데, 좀 더 쉬운 걸 할 수는 없을까?

여 이걸 매일 해야 해. 그러면 익숙해 질 거야.

••
side 옆, 옆구리 **parallel** 평행한
bend 구부리다 **halfway** 중간에, 절반만
get used to ~에 익숙해지다

06

대화를 듣고, 현재 시각을 고르시오.

① 2:30 p.m.
② 3:30 p.m.
③ 4:00 p.m.
④ 4:30 p.m.
⑤ 5:00 p.m.

W Thanks for <u>seeing</u> <u>me</u> <u>off</u> at the train station.

M You're welcome. Please have a <u>safe</u> <u>trip</u>. When do you <u>depart</u>?

W My train leaves <u>in</u> <u>an</u> <u>hour</u>.

M Oh, so your train leaves at 3:30 p.m.?

W Yes, so we have more <u>time</u> <u>to</u> <u>talk</u>.

여 기차역까지 배웅 나와 줘서 고마워.

남 천만에. 조심해서 가. 언제 출발하지?

여 내가 탈 기차는 한 시간 후에 출발해.

남 오, 그러면 오후 3시 30분에 출발하는 거구나?

여 응, 그러니까 우리는 얘기할 시간이 더 있어.

••
depart 떠나다, 출발하다

07 대화를 듣고, 남자의 심정으로 가장 적절한 것을 고르시오.

① angry
② fearful
③ hopeful
④ surprised
⑤ indifferent

W What are those on your face?
M I have some pimples on my face.
W You should go to see a doctor.
M For some pimples? I don't really think that is necessary.
W You'd better take care of your skin.
M Don't worry. They will go away.
W I just hope you don't get pimples on your face anymore.
M Okay. I will go to see a doctor soon.

여 얼굴에 있는 것들은 뭐니?
남 얼굴에 여드름이 좀 있어.
여 병원에 가 봐야겠다.
남 여드름 때문에? 그럴 필요까지는 없을 것 같아.
여 피부에 신경을 써주는 게 좋을 것 같아.
남 걱정하지 마. 없어질 거야.
여 나는 단지 네 얼굴에 여드름이 더 생기지 않기를 바랄 뿐이야.
남 알았어. 조만간에 병원에 가 볼게.

●●
necessary 필요한 **go away** 없어지다
indifferent 무관심한

---

08 대화를 듣고, 남자가 살았던 장소가 아닌 곳을 고르시오.

① Miami
② Chicago
③ Boston
④ Los Angeles
⑤ Hawaii

M Where were you born?
W I was born in Miami.
M Really? Me, too!
W Wow, what a coincidence! What made you come from Miami to Hawaii?
M Well, first, I moved to Chicago, and then I left Chicago and went to Boston for a little while. Finally, I came to Hawaii to study.
W You've lived in a lot of places.
M Yeah, but I like Hawaii the best. I plan on staying here until I graduate.

남 어디서 태어나셨어요?
여 마이애미에서 태어났어요.
남 정말이요? 저도 그래요!
여 와, 우연의 일치네요! 왜 마이애미에서 하와이로 오셨나요?
남 음, 처음엔 시카고로 이사 갔었고, 그 다음에는 시카고를 떠나 보스턴에서 잠시 살았어요. 마지막으로 하와이에 공부하러 왔어요.
여 여러 곳에서 사셨군요.
남 네, 그래도 하와이가 제일 좋아요. 여기서 졸업할 때까지 있을 예정이에요.

●●
coincidence 우연의 일치 **plan on** ~할 예정이다

---

09 대화를 듣고, 여자가 속상해하는 이유로 가장 적절한 것을 고르시오.

① 기다리는 메시지가 오지 않아서
② 자신의 유튜브 채널이 갑자기 사라져서
③ 남자의 유튜브 채널의 구독자가 더 많아서
④ 자신의 유튜브 채널이 큰 주목을 받지 못해서
⑤ 자신의 유튜브 채널에 안 좋은 댓글이 달려서

W Can you watch the video I uploaded on my YouTube channel? Almost no one is checking it.
M Of course. I'll leave a comment after I watch it.
W Thank you. My channel has only 50 subscribers.
M Don't be too sad. I have even fewer subscribers on my channel.
W I thought I would get a lot of attention as soon as I made my channel.
M I thought so, too. Let's not be too sad.

여 내 유튜브 채널에 올린 영상 좀 봐 줄래? 거의 아무도 조회를 안 해.
남 물론이지. 보고 나서 댓글도 달아 줄게.
여 고마워. 내 채널은 구독자가 50명밖에 되지 않아.
남 너무 슬퍼하지 마. 내 채널은 구독자가 훨씬 더 적은걸.
여 난 내 채널을 만들자마자 큰 주목을 받을 줄 알았어.
남 나도 그렇게 생각했어. 우리 너무 슬퍼하지는 말자.

●●
comment 논평, 댓글 **subscriber** 구독자

10 대화를 듣고, 무엇에 관한 내용인지 가장 적절한 것을 고르시오.

① 한국의 즐길 거리
② 외국의 공중목욕탕
③ 피부를 부드럽게 하는 방법
④ 한국인들의 해외 여행 실태
⑤ 외국인들의 한국 공중목욕탕 이용

M Did you know that some tourists come to Korea just to enjoy the <u>public</u> <u>baths</u>?
W Yes, I did. But can't they go to any in their own countries?
M It is <u>easy</u> <u>to</u> <u>explain</u>. You see, Koreans make a special effort to <u>scrub</u> <u>the</u> <u>skin</u>, making it feel smooth and clean. But they don't.
W Oh, I see. I <u>had</u> <u>no</u> <u>idea</u>.

남 너 혹시 몇몇 관광객들이 공중목욕탕을 즐기기 위해 한국에 온다는 것을 알았니?
여 응, 알아. 그런데 자기 나라에 있는 목욕탕을 가면 안되는 거야?
남 그건 설명하기 쉬워. 너도 알다시피, 한국인들은 몸을 매끄럽고 깨끗하게 하느라 때를 미는데 특별한 노력을 하잖아. 하지만 그 사람들은 그렇지 않거든.
여 아, 그렇구나. 몰랐어.

●●
public bath 공중목욕탕 **scrub the skin** 때를 밀다 **smooth** 매끄러운

---

11 대화를 듣고, 남자가 여자에게 추천한 교통수단으로 가장 적절한 것을 고르시오.

① 버스
② 지하철
③ 택시
④ 승용차
⑤ 자전거

W How am I <u>going</u> <u>to</u> <u>travel</u> in this city?
M Well, the bus system is terrible. Sometimes you have to wait <u>half</u> <u>an</u> <u>hour</u> for a bus. And there aren't <u>enough</u> <u>subway</u> <u>lines</u> to go anywhere you want.
W Can I <u>take</u> <u>a</u> <u>taxi</u> here then?
M Sure, but it's <u>expensive</u> to take a taxi.
W Then what should I do?
M I think if you have a driver's license, you'd better <u>rent</u> <u>a</u> <u>car</u>.
W Isn't that expensive?
M If you rent an <u>old</u> <u>car</u>, it's not too expensive.

여 이 도시를 어떻게 여행해야 하니?
남 음, 버스 체계는 너무 엉망이야. 때로는 버스를 타려고 30분을 기다려야 해. 그리고 지하철 노선은 네가 원하는 어느 곳이든 갈만큼 충분치 않아.
여 그럼, 여기서 택시를 탈 수 있니?
남 물론이지, 하지만 택시를 타는 것은 너무 비싸.
여 그러면 어떻게 해야 하지?
남 네가 자동차 운전면허증이 있다면 차를 한 대 빌리는 것이 나을 것 같아.
여 비싸지 않니?
남 구형 차로 빌리면 아주 비싸지는 않아.

---

12 대화를 듣고, 두 사람이 대화 직후에 할 일로 가장 적절한 것을 고르시오.

① 도서관 가기
② TV 시청하기
③ 숙제 끝마치기
④ 점심 요리하기
⑤ 먹을 것 사오기

M How about going out for <u>something</u> <u>to</u> <u>eat</u>? It's two o'clock.
W I think we should <u>finish</u> <u>our</u> <u>homework</u> first.
M I don't think so. I'm so hungry, and it's so hot. We should look for a restaurant where the air conditioner <u>works</u> <u>well</u>. We can study tonight.
W Remember? There's a <u>good</u> <u>TV</u> <u>program</u> on tonight.
M That's right. I want to see *Wheel of Fortune* tonight.
W <u>Why</u> <u>don't</u> <u>we</u> get something to eat first and finish our homework before the program?
M Okay, let's go.

남 뭐 좀 먹으러 나가는 게 어때? 두 시야.
여 숙제를 먼저 끝내는 게 좋을 것 같아.
남 난 그렇게 생각하지 않아. 난 너무 배가 고프고 더워. 에어컨이 잘 되는 식당을 찾아봐야겠어. 공부는 오늘 밤에도 할 수 있잖아.
여 기억하니? 오늘 밤에 볼만한 TV프로그램이 있잖아.
남 맞아. 오늘밤에 〈Wheel of Fortune〉을 보고 싶어.
여 먹을 것 좀 사고 프로그램 시작하기 전에 숙제를 끝내는 게 어때?
남 좋아, 가자.

●●
air conditioner 에어컨

13

대화를 듣고, 대화 내용과 일치하지 <u>않는</u> 것을 고르시오.

① 두 사람은 주유소에 있다.
② 여자는 방향 지시등을 켜지 않았다.
③ 남자의 트럭이 여자의 차를 칠 뻔했다.
④ 여자는 초보 운전자이다.
⑤ 남자의 트럭에는 가스 탱크가 있다.

M Hey, lady! You <u>should</u> <u>have</u> <u>turned</u> <u>on</u> your turn signal when you changed lanes. My truck <u>almost</u> <u>hit</u> your car.

W Oh! I'm sorry. I'm an <u>inexperienced</u> driver. I forgot.

M Can't you see that I have a full tank of gas on my truck?

W You were once a <u>beginner</u> yourself, weren't you? Please <u>try</u> <u>to</u> <u>understand</u> my mistake.

M Why don't you <u>stay</u> <u>off</u> busy streets like this until you <u>get</u> <u>more</u> <u>experience</u>?

W Okay, maybe I will. Sorry.

남 여보세요, 아가씨! 차선을 변경할 때는 방향 지시등을 켰어야죠. 제 트럭이 당신 차를 거의 칠 뻔했다고요.

여 오! 죄송해요. 제가 초보 운전자라서요. 깜박했네요.

남 제 트럭에 가스가 가득 찬 탱크가 있는 것 안 보여요?

여 당신도 한 때는 초보자였잖아요, 그렇지 않나요? 부디 제 실수를 이해해 주세요.

남 좀 더 경험을 쌓을 때까지 이렇게 붐비는 도로는 피하는 게 어때요?

여 알겠어요, 그래야 겠네요. 죄송합니다.

●●
turn signal 방향 지시등 **lane** 차선
inexperienced 경험이 부족한, 미숙한
stay off 피하다, 멀리하다

14

대화를 듣고, 남자의 마지막 말에 이어질 여자의 말로 가장 적절한 것을 고르시오.

① Thank you for saying so.
② I'm planning to buy a new computer.
③ Let's play a computer game together!
④ I prefer using a laptop over a desktop.
⑤ I'm sorry. I'll be more careful from now on.

M <u>What's</u> <u>the</u> <u>matter</u> with the computer? It doesn't <u>seem</u> <u>to</u> <u>be</u> <u>working</u>.

W Really? There was no problem when I used it.

M I think the computer <u>is</u> <u>infected</u> <u>with</u> a virus. Did you open a strange link or install a program you don't know?

W Well, I <u>downloaded</u> <u>a</u> <u>file</u> while on the Internet.

M That could be the <u>cause</u> of the problem. I need to call a <u>computer</u> <u>repairman</u>.

W <u>I'm sorry. I'll be more careful</u> <u>from now on.</u>

남 컴퓨터에 무슨 문제 있니? 작동을 안 하는 것 같아.

여 정말? 내가 사용할 때는 아무 문제도 없었는데.

남 내 생각엔 컴퓨터가 바이러스에 감염된 것 같아. 이상한 링크를 열거나 모르는 프로그램을 설치했니?

여 음, 인터넷을 하다가 어떤 파일을 다운받았어.

남 그게 문제의 원인일 수도 있겠다. 컴퓨터 수리 기사를 불러야겠어.

여 <u>미안해. 이제부터는 더 조심할게.</u>

① 그렇게 말해 줘서 고마워.
② 나는 새 컴퓨터를 살 계획이야.
③ 우리 함께 컴퓨터 게임하자!
④ 나는 데스크톱 컴퓨터보다 노트북 컴퓨터 사용하는 걸 선호해.

●●
be infected with ~에 감염되다 **install** 설치하다 **repairman** 수리공, 수리 기사

15 대화를 듣고, 여자의 마지막 말에 이어질 남자의 말로 가장 적절한 것을 고르시오.

① I've never driven a car before.
② I usually go to work by subway.
③ If you want, I can give you a ride.
④ Make sure you are on time for the bus.
⑤ That's why you moved to a place closer to work.

M I heard you moved last month.
W Yeah, I did. I had a hard time commuting to work.
M Really? I thought you were using public transportation?
W Yeah, but it used to take me more than two hours by subway.
M Are you serious? Why didn't you take a bus?
W The problem was that there were only a few buses in my neighborhood.
M Well, why didn't you drive then?
W No way. It's even worse than taking the subway. The rush hour traffic was terrible.
M That's why you moved to a place closer to work.

남 지난 달에 이사했다고 들었는데.
여 그래, 이사했어. 직장까지 통근하는 데 어려움이 있었거든.
남 정말? 나는 네가 대중교통을 이용하는 줄 알았는데.
여 맞아. 하지만 지하철로 두 시간이 넘게 걸렸어.
남 정말이야? 버스를 타지 그랬니?
여 문제는 우리 동네에 버스가 단지 몇 대밖에 없다는 거야.
남 그럼, 운전하고 다니지 그랬어?
여 절대 안돼. 그건 지하철 타는 것보다 더 안 좋아. 혼잡 시간대에는 교통이 끔찍했거든.
남 그래서 회사에서 더 가까운 곳으로 이사했구나.

① 나는 전에 운전을 해본 적이 한 번도 없어.
② 나는 보통 지하철로 출근해.
③ 원한다면 내가 태워다 줄게.
④ 버스 시간에 늦지 않도록 해.

●●
public transportation 대중 교통
neighborhood 이웃, 동네 **rush hour** 러시아워, 혼잡 시간대

REVIEW TEST p. 151

A ① freezing, 몹시 추운 ② atmosphere, 대기 ③ improve, 향상시키다 ④ career, 경력
⑤ divorce, 이혼하다 ⑥ bend, 구부리다 ⑦ depart, 떠나다, 출발하다 ⑧ go away, 없어지다
⑨ comment, 논평, 댓글 ⑩ subscriber, 구독자 ⑪ lane, 차선 ⑫ neighborhood, 이웃, 동네

B ① get along, with ② hire, do my best ③ checkup, teeth
④ parallel to ⑤ coincidence ⑥ as soon as
⑦ inexperienced driver ⑧ infected with

문제 및 정답	받아쓰기 및 녹음내용	해석

01

다음을 듣고, 시애틀의 현재 날씨로 가장 적절한 것을 고르시오.

① ②

③ ④

⑤

Good morning. This is Anna Kennedy with the Seattle <u>weather</u> <u>report</u>. Right now, it's very <u>humid</u>, and the sky is covered with <u>thick</u> <u>clouds</u>. There is a chance of some rain starting tonight. It will rain <u>all</u> <u>day</u> <u>tomorrow</u>, and the temperature will drop <u>as</u> <u>low</u> <u>as</u> 5 degrees Celsius. The rain will <u>turn</u> <u>into</u> <u>snow</u> at night, and it will snow on Wednesday. Please be careful on the <u>icy</u> <u>roads</u>.

안녕하세요. 시애틀 일기예보의 Anna Kennedy입니다. 현재 상당히 습하고, 하늘이 짙은 구름으로 덮여 있습니다. 오늘 밤부터 비가 올 가능성이 있습니다. 내일은 비가 하루 종일 내리면서 기온이 5도까지 떨어지겠습니다. 밤에는 비가 눈으로 바뀌겠으며, 수요일에는 눈이 내리겠습니다. 빙판길을 조심하세요.

●●
humid 습한 **thick** 두꺼운, 짙은 **turn into** ~로 바뀌다 **icy road** 빙판길

02

다음을 듣고, 남자가 하는 말의 내용으로 가장 적절한 것을 고르시오.

① 임시 휴교 안내
② 독감 예방 방법
③ 축제 일정 소개
④ 축제 취소 공지
⑤ 학교 예산 안내

Good morning, students. I am sorry to <u>announce</u> that the faculty has <u>decided</u> <u>to</u> <u>cancel</u> this year's festival. It is due to the flu virus that <u>continues</u> <u>to</u> <u>spread</u> throughout the country. I know you've been <u>looking</u> <u>forward</u> <u>to</u> having the festival, but we have no choice. We will have more <u>funds</u> for next year's festival and will make it a good one. I hope you <u>understand</u> <u>the</u> <u>situation</u>. Thank you.

학생 여러분, 안녕하십니까. 유감스럽게도 교수진이 올해의 축제를 취소하기로 결정했습니다. 전국에 계속 퍼지고 있는 독감 바이러스 때문입니다. 여러분이 축제를 여는 것을 몹시 기다려왔다는 것을 알지만, 선택의 여지가 없습니다. 우리는 내년 축제를 위해 더 많은 자금을 가지고 좋게 만들 것입니다. 상황을 이해해 주길 바랍니다. 감사합니다.

●●
faculty 교수진 **cancel** 취소하다 **due to** ~때문에 **flu** 독감 **funds** 자금

03

대화를 듣고, 두 사람이 대화하는 장소로 가장 적절한 곳을 고르시오.

① 식당
② 문구점
③ 미술관
④ 체육관
⑤ 백화점

M Look at this <u>baby</u> <u>carriage</u>. It looks so cute!

W It's not just cute and pretty. With all these pockets and everything, it sure will <u>come</u> <u>in</u> <u>handy</u>.

M Oh, I see.

W See this button here? If you want to <u>fold</u> the carriage, all you have to do is <u>press</u> <u>this</u> <u>button</u>.

M Wow, amazing!

W Well, <u>why</u> <u>don't</u> <u>we</u> buy it?

남 이 유모차 좀 봐. 너무 귀엽다!

여 그냥 귀엽고 예쁜 것만은 아니네. 이 주머니들과 모든 것들이 아주 유용하겠어.

남 오, 그러네.

여 여기 이 버튼 보이니? 유모차를 접고 싶으면 이 버튼을 누르기만 하면 돼.

남 와, 놀라운데!

여 그럼, 이걸로 사면 어떨까?

●●
baby carriage 유모차 **come in handy** 쓸모가 있다, 유용하다 **fold** 접다

04

대화를 듣고, 두 사람의 관계로 가장 적절한 것을 고르시오.

① 의사 - 환자
② 교사 - 학생
③ 약사 - 손님 ✓
④ 수의사 - 손님
⑤ 승무원 - 탑승객

W Hello. How may I help you?
M I have a <u>headache</u>.
W Do you have a <u>fever</u>, too?
M No, just a headache. Do I need a <u>prescription</u>?
W No, you don't need one. I'll give you <u>medicine</u> for two days.
M <u>How</u> <u>often</u> should I take this?
W Take it <u>three</u> <u>times</u> <u>a</u> <u>day</u>.
M Okay. And do you have some band-aids?
W <u>Just</u> <u>a</u> <u>moment</u>, please. Here you are. It <u>comes</u> <u>to</u> 15 dollars <u>altogether</u>.
M Okay. Here is my credit card.

여 어서 오세요. 무엇을 도와드릴까요?
남 두통이 있어요.
여 열도 있나요?
남 아니요, 그냥 두통만 있어요. 처방전이 필요한가요?
여 아니요, 필요 없어요. 이틀치 약을 드릴게요.
남 이걸 얼마나 자주 복용해야 하나요?
여 하루에 세 번 복용하세요.
남 알겠습니다. 그리고 반창고도 있나요?
여 잠시만 기다려 주세요. 여기 있습니다. 다 합해서 15달러입니다.
남 네. 여기 제 신용카드 있습니다.

●●
headache 두통 **fever** 열 **prescription** 처방전 **medicine** 약

05

다음을 듣고, 여자가 시험 중 유의 사항으로 언급하지 <u>않은</u> 것을 고르시오.

① 책 덮기
② 책상 위에 펜, 지우개, 시험지만 두기
③ 시험 중 잡담하지 않기
④ 시험 중 커닝하지 않기 ✓
⑤ 시험이 끝나면 시험지 제출하기

All right, everyone. Please close your books and <u>get</u> <u>ready</u> <u>for</u> the test. Now clear your desk. Everybody <u>is</u> <u>only</u> <u>allowed</u> to have a pen or pencil, the test, and an eraser on your desk. There's <u>no</u> <u>talking</u> during the test. The test <u>will</u> <u>be</u> <u>timed</u>. When you're finished with the test, please <u>bring</u> <u>it</u> to the front. <u>Good</u> <u>luck</u> <u>on</u> your test.

자, 여러분. 책을 덮고 시험 준비를 하세요. 이제 책상을 깨끗이 하세요. 모두 펜이나 연필, 시험지, 지우개만 책상 위에 두세요. 시험 중에 잡담은 안됩니다. 시험은 시간 제한이 있습니다. 시험이 끝나면 시험지를 앞으로 가져오세요. 시험 잘 보시기 바랍니다.

●●
timed 시간이 정해진

06

대화를 듣고, 여자가 잘못 누른 전화번호로 가장 적절한 것을 고르시오.

① 356-5511
② 366-1331
③ 366-5115
④ 366-5511 ✓
⑤ 336-5115

M Hello. This is Tom speaking. May I help you?
W Hello. My name is Claire. May I speak to Mr. Smith, please?
M Sorry. There's no one here <u>by</u> <u>that</u> <u>name</u>. I think you have <u>the</u> <u>wrong</u> <u>number</u>.
W Isn't this 366-5115?
M No, this is 366-5511.
W Oh, I'm sorry to <u>bother</u> <u>you</u>.
M That's okay.

남 여보세요. 전 Tom 입니다. 무엇을 도와드릴까요?
여 여보세요, 전 Claire라고 하는데 Smith 씨와 통화할 수 있을까요?
남 죄송하지만 여기 그런 이름을 가진 사람은 없는데요. 전화를 잘못 거신 것 같습니다.
여 366-5115번 아닌가요?
남 아니요, 366-5511입니다.
여 이런, 귀찮게 해서 죄송합니다.
남 괜찮습니다.

07 대화를 듣고, 두 사람의 심정으로 가장 적절한 것을 고르시오.

① upset
② scared
③ hopeful
④ touched ✓
⑤ disappointed

W This scene always <u>makes me cry</u>.

M I agree. It's the best part of the movie.

W This is the scene where the main character <u>confesses his love</u> for the woman just before he dies.

M I usually don't like sad movies, but this is an <u>exception</u>.

W How could you <u>not like</u> this movie? It breaks my heart, but it's beautiful.

M I <u>totally agree with you</u>.

여 이 장면만 보면 항상 눈물이 나.

남 나도 그래. 이 영화의 명장면이지.

여 주인공이 죽기 직전에 여자에게 사랑을 고백하는 장면이잖아.

남 나는 보통 슬픈 영화를 좋아하지는 않지만, 이 영화만큼은 예외야.

여 어떻게 이 영화를 좋아하지 않을 수가 있겠어? 마음을 아프게 만들지만 아름다운 영화인걸.

남 네 말에 전적으로 동의해.

•• **main character** 주인공 **confess** 고백하다 **exception** 예외 **totally** 완전히, 전적으로 **touched** 감동한

---

08 다음을 듣고, 두 사람의 대화가 <u>어색한</u> 것을 고르시오.

①　②　③　④ ✓　⑤

① M May I help you?

　W I'm just <u>looking around</u>. Thank you.

② W Do you <u>have any pets</u> in your house?

　M Yes, I have a dog.

③ M Do you ever <u>go to the beach</u> in summer?

　W I go every summer, but I couldn't go this year.

④ W Will you <u>carry my bag</u>? It's too heavy.

　M I think I've left my bag in the car.

⑤ M This is my grandmother. She is <u>80 years old</u>.

　W Nice to meet you.

① 남 무엇을 도와드릴까요?

　여 그냥 둘러보는 거예요. 고마워요.

② 여 집에 애완동물이 있니?

　남 응, 개 한 마리가 있어.

③ 남 여름에 해수욕장 가니?

　여 매년 여름마다 가지만 올해는 못 갔어.

④ 여 제 가방 좀 들어 주시겠어요? 너무 무거워서요.

　남 가방을 차에 두고 내린 것 같아.

⑤ 남 이 분이 저희 할머니예요. 올해 여든이세요.

　여 만나서 반갑습니다.

•• **look around** 둘러보다, 구경하다　**pet** 애완동물 **carry** 들다

---

09 대화를 듣고, 남자가 여자에게 고마워하는 이유로 가장 적절한 것을 고르시오.

① 여자가 파티를 열어줘서
② 여자가 깜짝 선물을 줘서
③ 여자가 추천서를 잘 써줘서
④ 여자가 수학 공부를 도와줘서 ✓
⑤ 여자가 좋은 선생님을 소개해줘서

M Happy birthday!

W A surprise birthday party! I can't believe it.

M You <u>deserve it</u>. You've helped me all throughout the school year.

W Oh, it was <u>my pleasure</u>.

M <u>Without</u> your help, I <u>would have failed</u> math this year.

W You did all the work <u>yourself</u>. I just helped a little.

M You're too modest. <u>Blow out</u> your candles.

남 생일 축하해!

여 깜짝 생일 파티라니! 믿을 수가 없어.

남 넌 그럴 자격이 있어. 학기 내내 나를 도와주었잖아.

여 아, 내가 좋아서 한 거야.

남 네 도움이 없었다면 나는 올해 수학에서 낙제를 했을 거야.

여 네가 직접 다 했잖니. 난 그저 조금 도와주었을 뿐인데.

남 너무 겸손하구나. 촛불을 꺼.

•• **modest** 겸손한　**blow out** 끄다

10 대화를 듣고, 무엇에 관한 내용인지 가장 적절한 것을 고르시오.

① 세금을 내는 이유
② 수요와 공급의 법칙
③ 세금의 종류와 쓰임새
④ 가격에 영향을 주는 요인
⑤ 상품과 서비스에 부과되는 세금

M Do you know that the government is putting a 10% tax <u>on</u> <u>all</u> <u>purchases</u>?

W Oh, I didn't know. So if I buy a hundred-dollar item, then the tax will be 10 dollars?

M That's right. Taxes will be applied to the prices of services <u>as</u> <u>well</u> <u>as</u> goods.

W I see. I think it's putting a <u>burden</u> on consumers.

M Let's think <u>more</u> <u>positively</u>. Taxes are used to help the people when the economy <u>gets</u> <u>worse</u>.

W I think you're right.

남 정부가 모든 구매에 대해 10%의 세금을 부과하고 있다는 걸 아니?

여 오, 몰랐어. 그러면 100달러짜리 물건을 사면 세금이 10달러가 되는 거야?

남 맞아. 세금은 상품뿐만 아니라 서비스의 가격에도 적용돼.

여 그렇구나. 그것은 소비자들에게 부담을 주고 있는 것 같아.

남 좀 더 긍정적으로 생각하자. 세금은 경제가 나빠질 때 국민들을 돕기 위해 사용되거든.

여 네 말이 맞는 거 같아.

●●
government 정부 **tax** 세금 **apply** 적용하다 **A as well as B** A뿐만 아니라 B도 **goods** 상품, 제품 **burden** 부담 **consumer** 소비자 **economy** 경제

---

11 대화를 듣고, 여자가 남자에게 부탁한 일로 가장 적절한 것을 고르시오.

① 다시 전화하기
② 버스로 갈아타기
③ 휴대폰 수리하기
④ 약속 시간 변경하기
⑤ 지하철역으로 마중나오기

M Hello. Is Janet there?

W <u>Speaking</u>. Tony, where are you?

M I'm <u>on</u> <u>my</u> <u>way</u> to school.

W Hello. I can hardly hear you. You're <u>breaking</u> <u>up</u>.

M Really? I think the reason is that I'm <u>on the</u> <u>subway</u> now.

W Why don't you call me <u>after</u> <u>you</u> <u>get</u> <u>off</u> the subway?

M Okay. I'm getting off <u>at</u> <u>this</u> <u>station</u> anyway.

남 여보세요. Janet 좀 바꿔 주시겠어요?

여 나야. Tony, 너 어디니?

남 학교에 가는 길이야.

여 여보세요. 네 말이 거의 안 들려. 전화가 끊겨서 들리네.

남 정말? 내 생각에는 내가 지금 지하철을 타고 있어서 그런 것 같아.

여 지하철에서 내린 후에 나에게 전화하는 게 어때?

남 알겠어. 어쨌든 이번 역에서 내릴 거야.

●●
break up (전화가) 끊겨서 들리다 **get off** 내리다, 하차하다

---

12 대화를 듣고, 여자가 대화 직후에 할 일로 가장 적절한 것을 고르시오.

① 다른 디자인 보여주기
② 더 저렴한 제품 보여주기
③ 남자에게 맞는 사이즈 찾아오기
④ 인라인스케이트 착용법 설명해주기
⑤ 인라인스케이트 잘 타는 법 알려주기

W May I help you, sir?

M Well, I'd like to buy some in-line skates, but I don't know <u>which</u> <u>ones</u> to <u>choose</u>.

W Are you a <u>good</u> <u>skater</u>?

M I've only tried it five times.

W Okay. How much do you <u>want</u> <u>to</u> <u>spend</u>?

M Well, I don't have much money.

W Then I have just the pair for you. They are <u>of</u> <u>good</u> <u>quality</u>, and they're <u>on</u> <u>sale</u> now. They are made especially for <u>beginners</u>.

M Oh, I like the design and the price. Can I <u>try</u> <u>these</u> <u>on</u>? I need a size 7.

W Sure. Please wait. I will be right back <u>with</u> <u>your</u> <u>size</u>.

여 무엇을 도와드릴까요, 손님?

남 저, 인라인스케이트를 사려고 하는데, 어떤 것을 골라야 할지 모르겠어요.

여 스케이트를 잘 타세요?

남 겨우 다섯 번 타봤어요.

여 네. 어느 정도의 가격을 원하세요?

남 음, 돈이 많지는 않아요.

여 그러면 손님에게 꼭 맞는 것이 있어요. 품질이 좋고 지금 할인 중입니다. 초보자들을 위해 특별히 만들어진 거예요.

남 아, 디자인과 가격이 마음에 드네요. 신어 봐도 될까요? 사이즈 7로 주세요.

여 네. 잠시만 기다려 주세요. 손님에게 맞는 사이즈를 가지고 올게요.

●●
of good quality 질이 좋은 **especially** 특히, 특별히

13

대화를 듣고, 대화 내용과 일치하지 <u>않는</u> 것을 고르시오.

① 여자는 운동을 좋아한다.
② 여자가 가장 좋아하는 운동은 수영이다.
③ 여자는 물속에서 약 5분간 숨을 참을 수 있다.
④ 여자는 물속에서 남자보다 더 오래 숨을 참을 수 있다.
⑤ 물속에서 숨 참기 기네스 세계 기록은 약 24분이다.

M I heard that you like sports very much.
W You're right. I love sports.
M What's your favorite sport?
W I like swimming.
M Me, too. Can you stay underwater for a long time?
W I can hold my breath for about 5 minutes.
M I can do that for about 10 minutes.
W You're amazing! I heard the Guinness World Record is about 24 minutes.

남 전 당신이 운동을 좋아한다고 들었어요.
여 맞아요. 전 운동을 아주 좋아해요.
남 가장 좋아하는 운동이 뭔가요?
여 전 수영을 좋아해요.
남 저도 그래요. 물속에서 오랫동안 있을 수 있나요?
여 전 5분 정도 숨을 참을 수 있어요.
남 전 10분 정도 그럴 수 있어요.
여 대단하네요! 기네스 세계 기록은 24분 정도라고 들었거든요.

●●
underwater 물속에서   hold one's breath 숨을 참다

14

대화를 듣고, 남자의 마지막 말에 이어질 여자의 말로 가장 적절한 것을 고르시오.

① I'm glad to hear that.
② Yes, that would be great!
③ Here you go. Thanks for your help.
④ Sorry, but I don't have any right now.
⑤ The garbage truck left just a minute ago.

W Sam, can you take out the garbage for me?
M I'm sorry, Mom. I can't help you because I'm doing my homework.
W Please. The garbage truck will be here in a few minutes, and I'm busy now.
M Okay, where is it?
W It's by the front door.
M Oh, the garbage is spilling out of the bag.
W Do you want another trash bag?
M Yes. Could you give me another one, please?
W Here you go. Thanks for your help.

여 Sam, 쓰레기 좀 버리고 와 주겠니?
남 죄송해요, 엄마. 숙제를 하고 있어서 도와드릴 수가 없어요.
여 부탁한다. 쓰레기차가 몇 분 후면 이곳에 올 텐데 난 지금 바쁘구나.
남 알겠어요, 어디에 있어요?
여 현관 옆에 있단다.
남 오, 쓰레기가 봉투에서 새고 있어요.
여 다른 쓰레기 봉투 줄까?
남 네. 다른 걸로 하나 주시겠어요?
여 <u>여기 있다. 도와줘서 고마워.</u>

① 그 말을 들으니 기쁘구나.
② 그래, 그러면 좋겠구나!
④ 미안하지만, 지금은 하나도 없어.
⑤ 쓰레기차는 1분 전에 떠났어.

●●
take out the garbage 쓰레기를 내놓다
front door 현관   spill 엎지르다, 흐르다, 새다
trash bag 쓰레기 봉투

15 대화를 듣고, 여자의 마지막 말에 이어질 남자의 말로 가장 적절한 것을 고르시오.

① I've had enough. Thank you.
② Yes, I did. It was very interesting.
③ Okay. I will not forget that next time.
④ Do you think I can borrow that book?
⑤ Well, I guess I will have to read it later.

W Good morning, James. Did you read <u>today's paper</u>?
M No, I haven't seen it yet. Is there any <u>interesting news</u>?
W Yes. The front-page headline was really interesting.
M <u>What</u> was it <u>about</u>?
W It's about a robot that can read <u>emotions</u> and deliver <u>comforting words</u> through human expressions. You should read it <u>for yourself</u>.
M <u>Well, I guess I will have to read it later.</u>

여 안녕, James. 오늘 신문 읽어 봤어?
남 아니, 아직 안 봤어. 무슨 재미있는 소식이라도 있니?
여 응, 1면의 머리기사가 정말 흥미로웠어.
남 뭐에 관한 건데?
여 인간의 표정을 통해 감정을 읽고 위로의 말을 전할 수 있는 로봇에 관한 거야. 네가 직접 읽어 봐.
남 <u>음, 나중에 읽어봐야겠다.</u>

① 충분히 먹었어, 고마워.
② 응, 읽었어. 아주 흥미롭던데.
③ 알았어. 다음에는 잊지 않을게.
④ 내가 그 책 좀 빌릴 수 있을까?

●●
front-page (신문) 1면의 **headline** 표제, 머리기사 **emotion** 감정 **comforting** 위로가 되는 **expression** 표현, 표정

⊃ REVIEW TEST p. 159

A ❶ humid, 습한 ❷ thick, 두꺼운, 짙은 ❸ faculty, 교수진 ❹ cancel, 취소하다
❺ prescription, 처방전 ❻ confess, 고백하다 ❼ pet, 애완동물 ❽ modest, 겸손한
❾ consumer, 소비자 ❿ underwater, 물속에서 ⓫ spill, 엎지르다, 흐르다, 새다 ⓬ emotion, 감정

B ❶ by that name ❷ looking around ❸ Without, would have failed
❹ hardly, breaking up ❺ getting off ❻ of good quality
❼ hold my breath ❽ take out the garbage

문제 및 정답	받아쓰기 및 녹음내용	해석

01

대화를 듣고, 여자가 파티에서 입을 드레스로 가장 적절한 것을 고르시오.

 ① ②

 ③ ④

⑤

M Mina, have you decided <u>what to wear</u> for the dinner party?

W I just found the best dress.

M Oh, that's great. What does the dress <u>look like</u>?

W It's a short dress with <u>thick stripes</u>.

M What color is it?

W It's orange, and there's a piece of <u>black fabric</u> around the waist that ties in the front. It's the perfect dress for me.

M I want to <u>see you wearing</u> that dress.

남 미나야, 저녁 식사 파티에 뭘 입을지 결정했어?

여 방금 최고의 드레스를 찾았어.

남 오, 잘됐네. 드레스는 어떻게 생겼어?

여 굵은 줄무늬가 있는 짧은 원피스야.

남 무슨 색인데?

여 주황색이고, 허리에는 앞에서 묶는 검정색 천이 있어. 나에게 딱 맞는 드레스야.

남 네가 그 드레스를 입고 있는 것을 보고 싶어.

● ●

stripe 줄무늬 **fabric** 천 **tie** 묶다

02

대화를 듣고, 여자의 선생님이 누구인지 고르시오.

W Thank you for <u>driving me to school</u>, Dad.

M You're welcome. You're not late, are you?

W No, we're early. Oh, <u>look out</u> the window! There's my teacher at the bus stop!

M Who? Do you mean the man <u>holding the briefcase</u> in his left hand?

W No. I mean the man <u>next to</u> the bus stop sign.

M Oh, I see. Do you mean the man <u>in the blue suit</u>?

W That's right. He's my teacher.

여 학교까지 차로 태워다 주셔서 감사해요, 아빠.

남 천만에. 늦지는 않았지?

여 네, 일찍 도착한 걸요. 오, 창문 밖을 보세요! 버스 정류장에 저희 선생님이 계세요!

남 누구? 왼손에 서류 가방을 들고 있는 남자 말이니?

여 아니요. 제가 말하는 사람은 버스 정류장 표지판 옆에 있는 분이에요.

남 아, 알겠다. 파란색 양복을 입은 남자 말이지?

여 맞아요. 그 분이 우리 선생님이예요.

03

대화를 듣고, 두 사람이 대화하는 장소로 가장 적절한 곳을 고르시오.

① 은행
② 매표소
③ 여행사
④ 우체국
⑤ 대사관

M Can I help you?

W Yes, I'd like to <u>apply for a visa</u>. Could you tell me when I can do that?

M Certainly. You can apply <u>on any weekday</u> between nine and five.

W Thank you, Oh, and do I need anything?

M You'll need your <u>passport</u>.

W Okay, I'll <u>see you again</u> soon.

남 도와드릴까요?

여 네, 비자를 신청하고 싶은데요. 언제 할 수 있는지 알려 주시겠어요?

남 물론이죠. 주중 언제든지 9시에서 5시 사이에 신청하실 수 있어요.

여 고맙습니다. 아, 그리고 제가 필요한 것이 있나요?

남 여권이 필요할 거예요.

여 네, 그럼 곧 다시 뵙겠습니다.

● ●

weekday 평일

04

대화를 듣고, 남자의 직업으로 가장 적절한 것을 고르시오.

① pilot
② clerk
③ waiter
④ secretary
⑤ flight attendant

W Excuse me. Could I have something to drink, please?
M Sure. What would you like?
W I'd like some orange juice.
M Will that be all for you?
W Oh, and could I have some extra napkins?
M Sure. Here you go.
W And by the way, what time do we arrive in Toronto?
M Our expected arrival time is 5:30 p.m. local time.

여 실례합니다. 마실 것 좀 있나요?
남 물론이죠. 무엇을 원하세요?
여 오렌지 주스가 좋겠어요.
남 그것이 다인가요?
여 아, 그리고 냅킨 좀 더 주실래요?
남 네. 여기 있습니다.
여 그런데 토론토에는 몇 시에 도착하죠?
남 도착 예정 시간은 현지 시간으로 오후 5시 30분입니다.

●●
expected arrival time 도착 예정 시간
local time 현지 시간 **pilot** 조종사

05

다음 그림의 상황에 가장 적절한 대화를 고르시오.

① ② ③ ④ ⑤

① M How do you go to school every day?
W I usually go to school on foot.
② M I heard you had a car accident. Are you okay?
W Yes. The cars were badly damaged, but no one was hurt.
③ W I have the hiccups.
M Hold your breath for a minute.
④ M What's the matter?
W I cut my finger while I was cooking.
⑤ W Could you hand me the remote control for the TV?
M Sure. Is there anything else I can do for you?

① 남 너는 매일 어떻게 학교에 가니?
여 나는 보통 걸어서 학교에 가.
② 남 나는 네가 교통사고를 당했다고 들었어. 괜찮아?
여 응. 차는 심하게 망가졌는데, 아무도 다치지는 않았어.
③ 여 딸꾹질이 나.
남 숨을 잠시 참아봐.
④ 남 무슨 일이야?
여 요리하다가 손가락을 베었어.
⑤ 여 TV 리모컨 좀 건네줄래?
남 알겠어. 내가 더 도와줘야 할 것이 있니?

●●
damaged 손상된 **hiccup** 딸꾹질
hand 건네주다

06

대화를 듣고, 여자가 안경에 지불한 금액으로 가장 적절한 것을 고르시오.

① $20
② $40
③ $60
④ $80
⑤ $100

M Wow, you look different today. What did you do?
W I'm wearing contact lenses.
M That's it. You look good without your glasses.
W Thanks. The glasses cost twice as much as the lenses.
M I think they were a good investment.
W I do, too. The lenses only cost me 40 dollars.

남 와, 너 오늘 달라 보인다. 뭘 한 거니?
여 콘택트렌즈를 했어.
남 그거구나. 안경을 벗으니까 좋아 보인다.
여 고마워. 안경은 렌즈보다 비용이 두 배나 들어.
남 좋은 투자인 것 같구나.
여 나도 그렇게 생각해. 렌즈는 40달러 밖에 안 들거든.

●●
investment 투자

07 대화를 듣고, 여자의 심정으로 가장 적절한 것을 고르시오.

① tired
✓② angry
③ envious
④ thankful
⑤ impressed

W Do you know what?
M What?
W I lent Jim my book two months ago, but he still <u>hasn't returned it</u>.
M Really? That's very <u>inconsiderate</u>. Why don't you call him?
W I think I will. But I don't understand why I have to call him. He should have just returned it <u>on time</u>. Is he hoping to keep it?
M I don't think so. People just forget. Just <u>remind him</u> politely.
W I'm <u>in no mood for</u> politeness. This is the second time he's done this.

여 너 그거 알아?
남 뭐?
여 두 달 전에 내 책을 Jim에게 빌려 줬는데 아직도 안 돌려 줬어.
남 정말? 남을 배려할 줄 모르는구나. 그에게 전화를 해보지 그래?
여 그래야겠어. 하지만 내가 왜 그에게 전화를 해야 하는지 이해가 안 돼. 그는 그저 제때에 그걸 돌려줬어야 해. 그 책을 갖고 싶어서 그러는 건가?
남 그런 것 같지는 않아. 사람들은 그냥 잊어버리기도 하잖아. 그냥 예의를 차려서 그에게 상기시켜 줘.
여 난 예의를 차릴 기분이 아니야. 그가 이런 것이 두 번째거든.

inconsiderate 남을 배려할 줄 모르는, 사려 깊지 못한 remind 상기시키다 in no mood for ~할 기분이 아닌 politeness 예의, 공손

08 대화를 듣고, 남자가 서점에서 살 물건으로 가장 적절한 것을 고르시오.

✓① 영어 참고서
② 수학 참고서
③ 공책
④ 펜
⑤ 자

W These books are so <u>expensive</u>! I can't believe it.
M I know. This English reference book <u>costs 25,000 won</u>. I have to buy it now.
W Do you have to buy a math reference book?
M No, my brother's friend will <u>give me one</u>.
W That's great! Is there <u>anything else</u> you need?
M I need some notebooks, pens, and <u>rulers</u>, too.
W But it's a lot cheaper to buy that stuff from the <u>stationary store</u>.
M Good idea. We'll just get the <u>essential books</u> here.

여 이 책들은 너무 비싸! 믿을 수가 없어.
남 나도 알아. 이 영어 참고서는 2만 5천 원이네. 난 지금 이거 사야 해.
여 너 수학 참고서도 사야 하니?
남 아니, 우리 형 친구가 나에게 한 권 줄 거야.
여 잘됐구나! 그 밖에 또 필요한 거 있니?
남 공책, 펜, 그리고 자도 필요해.
여 하지만 그런 것은 문구점에서 사는 것이 훨씬 더 싸.
남 좋은 생각이야. 여기서는 꼭 필요한 책들만 사자.

reference book 참고 도서 ruler 자 stuff 것, 물건

09 대화를 듣고, 남자가 전화를 받지 않은 이유로 가장 적절한 것을 고르시오.

① 수업 중이어서 ✓
② 잠이 깊이 들어서
③ 점심을 먹고 있어서
④ 전화기가 고장이 나서
⑤ 전화기를 찾을 수가 없어서

M Hi, Olga.
W It's great to see you here. Where were you during lunch today?
M Were you looking for me?
W Yes. I tried to get hold of you on your cellphone, but you didn't answer.
M Oh, I turned it off.
W Why?
M Because I was in the middle of class. I couldn't answer the phone.

남 안녕, Olga.
여 여기서 널 만나다니 정말 다행이다. 오늘 점심 시간에 어디 있었니?
남 나를 찾았어?
여 응. 네 휴대폰으로 연락하려고 했는데 안 받더라.
남 아, 꺼놓고 있었어.
여 왜?
남 수업 중이었거든. 전화를 받을 수가 없었어.

●●
get hold of ~에게 연락하다
in the middle of ~의 도중에

---

10 대화를 듣고, 여자의 증상이 <u>아닌</u> 것을 고르시오.

① 콧물
② 기침
③ 인후통
④ 열 ✓
⑤ 두통

W Hello. What can I do for you?
M Good morning, Doctor. I have a runny nose and a cough. I think I've caught a cold.
W Okay. And what else?
M I have a sore throat, too.
W Let me check your temperature. Well, your temperature is normal. Did you take any medicine?
M Yes, I took a painkiller this morning because I had a headache.
W Okay. I'm going to give you a prescription. Make sure to get plenty of rest.
M Okay. Thank you, Doctor.

여 안녕하세요. 어디가 아프시죠?
남 안녕하세요, 의사 선생님. 콧물이 나고 기침이 나요. 감기에 걸린 것 같아요.
여 알겠습니다. 다른 증상은요?
남 목도 아파요.
여 체온을 재볼게요. 음, 체온은 정상이네요. 혹시 약을 복용했나요?
남 네, 두통이 있어서 오늘 아침에 진통제를 먹었어요.
여 알겠어요. 처방전을 써줄게요. 충분한 휴식을 취하도록 하세요.
남 알겠습니다. 고맙습니다, 의사 선생님

●●
runny nose 콧물 **sore throat** 인후통, 목아픔
painkiller 진통제

---

11 대화를 듣고, 남자가 여자에게 해 준 조언으로 가장 적절한 것을 고르시오.

① 낮잠 자지 않기
② 커피 마시지 않기
③ 휴식 취하기 ✓
④ 약 처방 받기
⑤ 시험공부 계획 세우기

W I'm having trouble sleeping at night these days.
M Are you under a lot of stress at school?
W Yes, I am taking midterm exams next week, and I'm really worried about them.
M Do you drink coffee?
W Yes, but I usually have coffee in the morning.
M Hmm... I think you need to relax more and try not to worry so much about your exams.
W Okay. I'll take your advice.

여 난 요즘 밤에 잠을 자는 게 힘들어.
남 학교에서 스트레스를 많이 받니?
여 응, 다음 주에 중간고사가 있는데 정말 걱정이야.
남 커피를 마시니?
여 응, 하지만 커피는 주로 아침에 마셔.
남 음… 내 생각에 너는 좀 더 긴장을 풀고 시험에 대해 너무 많이 걱정하지 않는 것이 필요해.
여 그래. 네 조언대로 할게.

12 대화를 듣고, 남자가 대화 직후에 할 일로 가장 적절한 것을 고르시오.

① 목걸이 환불해주기
② 목걸이 교환해주기
③ 영수증 재발급하기
④ 목걸이 수리 맡기기
⑤ 매니저에게 전화하기

W I bought this necklace here yesterday, but this part is broken.
M Oh, is it? May I take a look at it more closely?
W Sure. Can I exchange it?
M Yes, of course. Do you have the receipt?
W No, can I exchange it without the receipt? I lost it.
M I don't think you can. But I'll call the manager and ask.
W Thank you.

여 제가 어제 여기서 이 목걸이를 샀는데요, 이 부분이 부서졌어요.
남 오, 그래요? 제가 좀 더 자세히 봐도 될까요?
여 물론이죠. 교환할 수 있을까요?
남 네, 물론이죠. 영수증은 있으신가요?
여 아니요, 영수증 없이 교환은 가능한가요? 잃어버렸어요.
남 안될 것 같은데요. 하지만 매니저에게 전화해서 물어 볼게요.
여 고맙습니다.

---

13 대화를 듣고, 대화 내용과 일치하지 <u>않는</u> 것을 고르시오.

① 날씨에 대해 이야기 하고 있다.
② 오늘은 날씨가 매우 덥고 습하다.
③ 두 사람 모두 덥고 습한 날씨를 싫어한다.
④ 여자는 사막보다 정글 여행을 선호한다.
⑤ 두 사람은 선풍기를 틀 것이다.

W It's really hot today.
M You can say that again.
W I can't stand it when it's hot and humid.
M Me neither. The humidity makes my skin very wet.
W I like it better hot and dry.
M So if you had to travel to the desert or the jungle, would you choose the former?
W Of course.
M Let's turn on the fan and cool down.

여 오늘 정말 덥다.
남 정말 그래.
여 난 이렇게 덥고 습한 것을 견딜 수가 없어.
남 나도 마찬가지야. 습도 때문에 피부가 끈적거려.
여 난 덥고 건조한 게 더 좋아.
남 그럼, 사막이나 정글을 여행해야 한다면 전자를 택할 거니?
여 물론이지.
남 선풍기를 틀어서 시원하게 하자.

• •
You can say that again. 정말 그래., 동감이야. **former** 전자, 앞의 것 **fan** 선풍기

---

14 대화를 듣고, 남자의 마지막 말에 이어질 여자의 말로 가장 적절한 것을 고르시오.

① I can't find the remote control.
② You're sitting too close to the TV.
③ Can you turn up the volume a little?
④ How about a talk show on channel 5?
⑤ Turn off the TV if you're not watching it.

M Hey, Susan. Turn on the TV, please.
W Where is the remote control?
M It's on the table.
W What would you like to watch?
M I don't know. Let's see what's on.
W Oh, there's a cooking show on channel 12.
M Is there anything else on?
W How about a talk show on channel 5?

남 이 봐, Susan. TV 좀 켜 줘.
여 리모컨이 어디 있지?
남 탁자 위에 있어.
여 뭘 보고 싶은데?
남 모르겠어. 뭐 하는지 보자.
여 아, 12번에서는 요리 프로그램을 해.
남 또 뭘 하는데?
여 5번에서 하는 토크쇼는 어때?

① 리모컨을 못 찾겠어.
② 너는 TV에 너무 가까이 앉아 있어.
③ 소리 좀 키워줄래?
⑤ 보지 않으면 TV를 꺼.

15 대화를 듣고, 여자의 마지막 말에 이어질 남자의 말로 가장 적절한 것을 고르시오.

① No one can tell the future.
② My brother has a talent for music.
③ I guess you should quit your present job.
④ You could handle this situation by yourself.
⑤ I think you're good at writing and making stories.

M Do you know what the <u>most important quality</u> of a successful person is?
W I'm not sure, but I think <u>honesty</u> is the key to success.
M Do you know <u>what everybody says</u> nowadays?
W I don't know. What?
M <u>Creativity</u> is the key to success.
W I guess you're right. I'm afraid I'm not a very <u>creative person</u>.
M You <u>have to find</u> your hidden talents.
W What do you think my hidden talents are?
M <u>I think you're good at writing and making stories.</u>

남 성공하는 사람의 가장 중요한 자질이 뭔지 아니?
여 확실히는 모르겠지만, 나는 정직이 성공의 열쇠라고 생각해.
남 요즘에는 모두가 뭐라고 말하는지 아니?
여 몰라. 뭔데?
남 창의성이 성공의 열쇠다.
여 네 말이 맞는 것 같다. 유감스럽게도 난 별로 창의적인 사람이 아닌 것 같아.
남 너는 너의 숨겨진 재능을 찾아야 해.
여 나의 숨겨진 재능이 뭐라고 생각하니?
남 <u>너는 글을 쓰고 이야기 만드는 걸 잘하는 것 같아.</u>

① 아무도 미래를 알 수 없어.
② 내 남동생은 음악에 재능이 있어.
③ 나는 네가 지금 하는 일을 관둬야 한다고 생각해.
④ 넌 이 상황을 혼자 해결할 수 있을 거야.

●●
quality 질, 자질 **creativity** 창의성
hidden 숨겨진 **talent** 재능

◗ REVIEW TEST p. 167

A ① stripe, 줄무늬 ② tie, 묶다 ③ weekday, 평일 ④ damaged, 손상된
⑤ hiccup, 딸꾹질 ⑥ remind, 상기시키다 ⑦ ruler, 자 ⑧ sore throat, 인후통, 목아픔
⑨ painkiller, 진통제 ⑩ fan, 선풍기 ⑪ quality, 질, 자질 ⑫ talent, 재능

B ① what to wear ② see you wearing ③ apply for, visa
④ arrival time, local time ⑤ without, glasses ⑥ runny nose, cough
⑦ having trouble sleeping ⑧ key to success

MEMO

MEMO

영어듣기 모의고사
CooL
LISTENING 2

- 중학생을 위한 3단계 리스닝 프로그램
- 의사 소통에 필요한 **다양한 주제들로 구성**
- 시·도 교육청 영어듣기평가 문제 유형을 반영한 **모의고사 20회**
- 실전 TEST → **받아쓰기** → **중요 어휘·문장 복습**의 단계별 청취 훈련
- 0.8배속 / 1.0배속 / 1.2배속의 3가지 MP3 파일 제공
- 본문 QR코드 삽입으로 편리한 음원 재생

부가자료 다운로드 **www.darakwon.co.kr**
· MP3 파일 (문항별 / 3가지 배속 포함)
· 어휘 리스트 / 어휘 테스트

CooL LISTENING 시리즈